BORN

BORN

The Untold History of Childbirth

LUCY INGLIS

BLOOMSBURY CONTINUUM
LONDON · OXFORD · NEW YORK · NEW DELHI · SYDNEY

BLOOMSBURY CONTINUUM
Bloomsbury Publishing Plc
50 Bedford Square, London, WC1B 3DP, UK
Bloomsbury Publishing Ireland Limited,
29 Earlsfort Terrace, Dublin 2, D02 AY28, Ireland

BLOOMSBURY, BLOOMSBURY CONTINUUM and the Diana logo are trademarks of
Bloomsbury Publishing Plc

First published in Great Britain 2025

Copyright © Lucy Inglis, 2025

Lucy Inglis has asserted her right under the Copyright, Designs and Patents Act, 1988, to be
identified as Author of this work

For legal purposes the Acknowledgements on p. 291 constitute an extension of this
copyright page

All rights reserved. No part of this publication may be: i) reproduced or transmitted in any form, electronic or mechanical, including photocopying, recording or by means of any information storage or retrieval system without prior permission in writing from the publishers; or ii) used or reproduced in any way for the training, development or operation of artificial intelligence (AI) technologies, including generative AI technologies. The rights holders expressly reserve this publication from the text and data mining exception as per Article 4(3) of the Digital Single Market Directive (EU) 2019/790

Bloomsbury Publishing Plc does not have any control over, or responsibility for, any third-party websites referred to or in this book. All internet addresses given in this book were correct at the time of going to press. The author and publisher regret any inconvenience caused if addresses have changed or sites have ceased to exist, but can accept no responsibility for any such changes

A catalogue record for this book is available from the British Library

Library of Congress Cataloguing-in-Publication data has been applied for

ISBN: HB: 978-1-3994-1439-5; TPB: 978-1-3994-1443-2; eBook: 978-1-3994-1454-8;
ePDF: 978-1-3994-1444-9

2 4 6 8 10 9 7 5 3 1

Typeset by Deanta Global Publishing Services, Chennai, India
Printed and bound in Great Britain by CPI Group (UK) Ltd, Croydon CR0 4YY

To find out more about our authors and books visit www.bloomsbury.com and sign up for our newsletters
For product safety related questions contact productsafety@bloomsbury.com

For Irene.

For everything.

Contents

Introduction	viii
1. The Realm of Women	1
2. The Realm of Men	27
3. Darkness Falls	59
4. The Rise of the Machines	86
5. Anarcha, Betsey and Lucy	114
6. The Numbers Game	140
7. Something Wicked This Way Comes	178
8. 'A Violent and Messianic Age'	205
9. Living Memory	244
Acknowledgements	291
Image Credits	293
Notes	295
Selected Further Reading	315
Index	316

Introduction

'MAMATOTO'[1]

Mamatoto is Swahili for 'motherchild'. It is one of the few words we have to describe the physical closeness of mother and newborn in those first early months – before the two can be said to be truly separate beings. The state of mamatoto is just one part of what makes the human experience of birth unique from that of other primates and mammals: we are born before we are fully developed, and rendering us vulnerable, relying on our mothers and caregivers to feed and tend to us long after most other young animals have already left the nest. Scientists call this extended dependency, when we are no less dependent on our mother outside the womb than we were inside, 'altricial'.

This phenomenon is thought to be related to the fact that childbirth is more dangerous for us than most other animals – considering the size of newborns, our pelvises are narrow, making labour longer and more painful. This means that since the dawn of humanity, women have sought assistance and companionship during childbirth. This assistance has in turn become ritualized over the millennia, creating bonds and promoting the sharing of knowledge within communities. From ancient Minoan temples to contemporary baby showers, women have found ways to build the networks of support and advice they need to help them when the time comes to cross the transformational threshold of parenthood.

Vastly divergent traditions accompany these rituals of pregnancy and childbirth across the globe, but they often contain themes of control – from forbidden foods to prohibited sex positions, lucky colours or items of clothing. Many of these rituals persist today, reflecting the deep mysticism and psychological shift that still surrounds the physical experience of creating new life, even in cultures that have embraced science and raised our chances of survival.

In a similar way, the battle over who controls reproduction is not new. Women have always tried to control their own fertility even if, for most of history, the only truly reliable method was complete abstinence. There is evidence that even among the Palaeolithic hunter–gatherers, women limited their fertility through the means available to them. So many of the questions we are wrestling with today were faced by women thousands of years ago, and perhaps by looking back at their experiences, it can be possible to navigate the way forward.

This book contains many stories of individual women and mothers, pieced together from Ice Age bone fragments, medical scrolls and nineteenth-century pamphlets about contraception, but their voices have not been easy to find. Perhaps that is why this book took me fifteen years to research and write, and why it often felt like I was embarking on uncharted territory – searching for the stories and lived experiences that I knew existed (because for thousands of years, the majority of women gave birth) but were unrecorded. The input of women has been so often negated and overridden by the masculine voices of doctors, husbands, organized religions and theorists who have denied the needs, challenges and realities of pregnant women. But the history of childbirth includes other men too, ones who dedicated their lives to making childbirth safer and others who took on a supportive role as the women they loved and had children with went on to change the way that we think about birth and sex.

When I first set out to discover the history of childbirth, my husband and I were trying for the children we longed to have, but had eluded us. For a long time, I struggled to identify my place within the world of motherhood. Yet, as time passed, I came to realize that parenthood is far more than the quest to pass on our DNA or to build familial bonds that will shepherd us through our lives. How a society thinks about childbirth is a reflection of how it views and treats women – and so perhaps it is no surprise that this fundamental power to create and carry new life is so often used to undermine women's autonomy.

We are living in a time of fathomless change for women across the world. As my window of opportunity to have a child closed, a door opened that allowed me to learn about what birth meant for others, for society and for us as people. Ultimately, every successful birth of a healthy child is a small victory for humanity and a life-changing moment for the mother. Pregnancy and birth are attended by myriad personal, emotional, social and physical dangers, but also joy, triumph and wonder. In nine short months, from two cells, the body constructs a new life and brings it into the world in a unique moment where all is possible.

The practicalities and the power struggles of childbirth have shaped nations but also individual identities, and continue to do so. It starts in prehistory and ends today, with the reversal of *Roe* v. *Wade*, taking in the cries from the medieval birthing chair and the calls to rally of our modern age. This is how we are Born.

I

The Realm of Women

Only a few skeletons remain to tell us how our early ancestors the Neanderthals treated the death of a child over 50,000 years ago. Secreted in a niche within a deep cave near the Sea of Galilee, archaeologists discovered the bones of a ten-month-old baby, with the jawbone of a red deer laid across its pelvis.[1] The infant was carefully placed there with a ritual offering to guide its passage. Perhaps a grieving mother or father carried the dead child, clutched to their chest, into the dark of that cave, searching for somewhere safe, somewhere meaningful. While the Ice Age reigned, these warmer lands on the grassy shorelines of a large freshwater lake would have provided food and shelter for a pregnant mother-to-be and her family – even if the climate still dictated their daily lives and patterns and death remained close to life. There is much that we do not know about the Neanderthals, who for 350,000 years roamed the land mass we now divide roughly into Europe and Asia. But we know that they cared and mourned for the children they lost.

The very nature of 'prehistory' is that it lies, for the most part, beyond our reach, if not our imaginations. Only through archaeological finds, particularly graves such as that of the Neanderthal child, cave paintings and votive figurines, can we hope to glean some understanding of the people who occupied a very different planet from the one we know now. They walked lands we can only imagine, among the last of the megafauna such as the mammoth and the aurochs, remnants from times gone before.

The story of how we are born is the story of us all, and so we must go back to the start. The origins of 'modern' people, *homo sapiens*, date from between 160,000 and 145,000 years ago, as evidenced by remains discovered in 1997 of a dozen individuals in the Bouri Formation in Ethiopia. Like the Sea of Galilee, this was a verdant and temperate place where early people could thrive. Collectively, these Bouri individuals and their culture are known as Herto Man. They lived near lakes and produced stone tools, butchering bovine animals and hippopotamus. It is thought that they also de-fleshed the bodies of their deceased in some form of mortuary ritual, a practice that would persist across vastly different cultures for millennia.[2] While little remains of Herto Man, they walked upright, had larger forebrains and thinner skulls than the Neanderthals, all of which are key physical features in the history of childbirth. It is the shape of our skulls, evolving to accommodate a brain capable of forward-thinking and creativity, that has defined the human experience of birth. We have large brains but narrow pelvises, to help us walk upright – and this anatomical contradiction means it takes longer for humans to give birth than other primates, and the process is fraught with more risks. This is known as the 'Obstetrical Dilemma', and it is the reason why from our earliest days it is believed that childbirth was never something a woman chose to do alone (if she could help it). She would have needed assistance from those near to her, even if just to offer sustenance, emotional support and perhaps a cool hand on her brow.

We now know that our ancestors were more widespread during the Ice Age than previously thought: 80,000-year-old tools were found in the Dhaba's Son River Valley in India; cave paintings of warty pigs made 45,500 years ago (the oldest known paintings by anatomically modern humans) were discovered in Sulawesi, Indonesia; and other finds prove that *homo sapiens* also made use of the ancient shelter offered by the Madjedbebe cave complex in what is now the Northern Territory of Australia.[3,4] To inhabit these disparate places they must have made considerable sea journeys, although these were probably a series of very short movements completed over the course of generations rather than epic voyages. At around the same time, in Ice Age terms, as *homo sapiens* began to fan out north from Africa, the Neanderthals began their terminal decline.

No one knows for sure what events resulted in the extinction of the Neanderthals and the rise of modern humans. For each proposition there is a competing theory that claims to refute it. Their extinction was gradual, thought to have taken place over ten to fifteen thousand years, and a series of the most likely factors combine to make the most plausible theory.

The first is that there was an abrupt change brought about by the arrival of *homo sapiens*, many of whom left Africa owing to increased desertification in previously fertile areas. Many theories point towards the assimilation of Neanderthals into human societies, but there is low genetic evidence of interbreeding to the extent that it could have absorbed an entire species: modern humans of Near Eastern and European origin have only a small percentage (around 2.5 per cent) of Neanderthal DNA.[5] Another theory is that the Neanderthals were struck down by disease, that like European colonists during the Middle Ages coming into contact with First Nation peoples, the new early humans brought with them contagions against which the Neanderthals had little or no resistance.

Another possible factor is climate change. Around 42,000 years ago, a bizarre planetary event took place: the magnetic field of the Earth reversed, leading to extraordinary climatic conditions in a world still in the grip of the Ice Age. Magnetic north and south (what we now call the 'Poles') weakened so dramatically that the *Aurora borealis* could have shifted and been visible as far south as the equator. These solar conditions would have favoured cave dwelling, resulting in the sudden surge of cave art. We call this magnetic reversal the Laschamps Excursion (it was named after the preserved lava flows in Laschamps, France, which first proved that it had taken place). More pleasingly, it is also known by the teams of scientists around the world who continue to work on it as 'The Douglas Adams Event', as a nod to the supercomputer Deep Thought in the author's most celebrated work, *The HitchHiker's*

Guide to the Galaxy, which gives '42' as the answer to 'the Ultimate Question of Life, the Universe, and Everything'.

This was a time of great transition. Findings in the Bulgarian Balkans reveal to us a moment when modern humans took over a cave complex previously inhabited by Neanderthals. It provides a picture of the evolving inhabitation of the area by successive species during a defining period in the development of prehistoric societal structures. These humans slaughtered and butchered bison, horses and cave bears, occasionally using what are referred to as 'IUP toolkits' or Initial Upper Paleolithic go-bags, holding essential bone tools, and sometimes jewellery such as cave-bear teeth pendants as well as ivory beads, perhaps for barter.[6] Modern humans were beginning to shift from nomadic hunter–gatherers to what is often termed 'sedentary' peoples, although their lives were anything but sedentary in the way we use the word now.

This is when we find the first evidence for a history of childbirth. As archaeology has been for the most part a male-dominated field, research has focused largely on tools and what are perceived to be masculine activities such as hunting. In most of this research, prehistoric societies have been assigned a broadly patriarchal structure, often with little evidence to justify it. Modern research, improved archaeological scientific techniques and less paternalistic points of view are changing the way we view the deep past – indicating that it is just as possible that the dawn of humanity was not a man's world but a realm of women.

Women are shown giving birth among animals, often stags with preternaturally large antlers, bears and sometimes birds, in early hunter–gatherer cave art. It's thought that these paintings were made when caves were used for temporary shelter during hunting phases or as ritual sites. This does not, however, mean that early women simply hunkered down and gave birth during the hunt, before swiftly resuming their subordinate role in a paternalistic primitive society with minimal post-partum care (that is, during the first six weeks after labour). It is more likely that these scenes depict a symbolic part of the life cycle of a woman and represent a unity with the natural world.

THE REALM OF WOMEN

Paleolithic hunting scene from Cova Dels Cavalls, Valltorta, Spain

The baby is almost always shown emerging from the mother head first, somewhat in the manner of the queen in a pack of cards, but with the lower queen much smaller. Intriguingly, Aboriginal cave art from Australia, painted around 29,000 years ago, shows the Earth Mother giving birth to all the creatures and flora of the world in this same 'upside down' fashion.

Aboriginal rock art (Namondjok) at Nourlangie,
Kakadu National Park, Australia

These images are sometimes called 'Double Goddess Figures', although this is misleading, as they show a child being born in the safest possible way – head down – rather than a cosmic mythology we cannot hope to understand. It is not a leap to imagine that this would be something hoped for by any labouring woman, given that for much of human history a breech birth (when the baby is born the wrong way round, feet first) could spell death for both mother and child.

Women were not just represented in art; they were also makers. In eight cave complexes in France and Spain, a significant proportion of the handprints that accompanied paintings of hunts, judged by shape, size and relative finger lengths, were from hands belonging to women.[7] The handprints were made by blowing coloured powders onto a hand pressed against the rock, so the outline is printed onto the cave wall. The powder was usually red ochre, thought to signify blood as it was routinely smeared on the blades of knives, to cover the dead and also to paint images of preferred prey animals. Whether these were the 'signatures' of women who created the cave art or whether their handprints were meant to bless the hunt depicted remains unknown.

THE VENUS OF HOHLE FELS

In the densely wooded alps of Swabian Jura in Germany, known for its imposing castles and hidden limestone caves, the oldest surviving female figurine was found. She is called 'The Venus of Hohle Fels'. Only the Löwenmensch of Hohlenstein-Stadel (the Lion Man), a small sculpture depicting a man with a lion's head, also found in the Swabian Jura, is thought to be marginally older and therefore the world's oldest statue. The people who made these ancient figurines were the Cro Magnon. They descended from *homo sapiens* around 40,000 years ago, and gradually evolved into another kind of early anatomically modern humans, forming a large group that spanned from modern Spain all the way to Eastern Russia. They were around 5½ feet tall, powerfully built, with protruding chins, strong features and, intriguingly, a larger average brain capacity than humans of today, by about 10 per cent.[8]

The Cro Magnon were semi-nomadic and had begun using caves, left empty by the decline of the cave bear and sabretooth tiger, for shelter and rituals. As we know from these extraordinary figurines, they were also making three-dimensional art, as well as increasingly elaborate and skilful cave paintings, featuring mammoths, bison, horses, deer and ibex.

The Venus of Hohle Fels is unique. She is 2.4 inches tall and carved from the tusk of a woolly mammoth, with a small, figurative head, tiny in proportion to her body. There are signs that she could have been worn as a pendant or handled extensively, thus producing a polished surface – the back is flattened, which would have helped it to lie on the wearer's chest. Her hands cradle her belly, rather than her vast, engorged breasts, and the belly has been decorated with what look like stretch marks and perhaps a belt, while her arms are engraved with what may have signified either tattooing or scarification. Her back is lined with marks that look like rolls of fat. Around her distended abdomen is the first appearance of what appears to be a belt. Unlike other Venus figurines, her legs are spread wide apart to display swollen and oversized pudenda that appear more like a wound than a sexual organ. They are almost shocking in their proportions. Claims that the Venus of Hohle Fels is 'pornographic' reduce this ancient art work to the sexual, as does the rather naff but now inescapable 'Venus' terminology.[9] This is not a sculpture that invites the male gaze. The Hohle Fels woman appears far more like the strident depiction of a 'real' woman postpartum. While we can assume that the Löwenmensch was not stalking the prehistoric Swabian Jura, the Venus of Hohle Fels may well have done.

The Venus of Hohle Fels is a deeply moving work of art, and its differences from other female figurines have been partially explained by the suggestion that it was carved by a woman who had just given birth.[10] It may be that the carver was expressing how she felt within her own body: her breasts painfully swollen, her sexual organs unrecognizable to her, perhaps indicating the agonies of the perineal tearing that affects up to 90 per cent of women during labour, particularly during first births.[11] Seen as such, it is an empowering piece of self-expression.

It seems fitting and somehow unsurprising that the world's oldest known musical instrument, a flute made from a vulture bone and dating from the same period, was found less than a yard from the figurine. Later finds at Hohle Fels also include a 'realistic' and 'polished' phallus carved from stone, dating from around 28,000 years ago and measuring 7.8 inches long by 1.8 inches wide.[12] Its meaning or purpose remains a mystery, at least to those who found and catalogued it.

Subsequent Venus figurines follow a more predictable pattern. One of the most famous, the Venus of Willendorf, was found in 1908 on the green banks of the River Danube as it flows through the hills of Lower Austria. She conforms to a style of Venus figurine that dominates finds from Germany to Ukraine, from where it is possible that she originated. The figurine is worn, suggesting use or handling over a long period of time, but radiocarbon dating reveals that she was buried around 25,000 to 30,000 years ago.[13] She has no feet and, in typical Venus style, her legs are firmly together, indicating she may have been pegged into soft ground; it's possible too that she never touched the ground but was instead passed from hand to hand. She is, to put it mildly, obese, rather than obviously pregnant. Her enormous breasts and belly hang ponderously over her thighs, which in turn hang over her knees. She is thought to be a symbol of extreme fecundity over a period of time, or a votive figure for fertility rituals – or both, such is the nature of prehistoric history.

New research on almost 200 Venuses appears to indicate that they represent women as part of the overall life cycle, but that they may also represent individual women, given the details of individualistic hairstyles or caps. Some are slender, perhaps very young, and one, the Venus of Galgenberg, is dancing.[14]

Other types of votive female figures deeply associated with the natural world, such as owls and water birds, but also bears (which seem particularly associated with women) have often been discovered. Far fewer of these pieces represent male figures. When they appear, they are usually in two postures: the priapic young hunter and the seated old man. That so many of these prehistoric art works depict the experiences and life cycle of women may also be a sign that it was women who made these objects, using the time spent in early childcare or pregnancy to create images inspired by what they knew.

Academics have classified the basic needs of women giving birth in the Palaeolithic period (the earliest phase of the Stone Age) into six categories, listed in order of importance: a heat source, a safe place, emotional support, freedom to move and change position, attention to pre- and post-natal care and, finally, some kind of ritual to help negotiate the psychological effects of the birth.[15] There was no place that met all these needs better than a cave.

Heat was not only necessary for the mother's comfort: babies cannot regulate their body temperature by mechanisms such as shivering and succumb to hypothermia quickly if their core temperature is not kept at around 36 °C. A cave would not only have provided a space apart and some privacy at a supremely vulnerable moment; it would also have aided with heat regulation. Support and companionship would have been as important to a Palaeolithic birthing mother as they are to women today.

It was not until much, much later that women were expected to deliver in a supine position, compressing their respiratory systems and working against gravity. It is extremely likely that Palaeolithic women would have adopted a variety of bearing down and resting poses throughout labour, which is why having room to move would have been essential. There are also archaeological signs that, as you would expect, these women had some form of pre- and post-natal care, as indicated by evidence of possible ritual cord-cutting tools in some settlements.

An added level of security for an encampment or cave while a woman gave birth emerges in the form of domesticated wolf-type dogs, which co-existed with humans from around 32,000 years ago. It seems they were pets or companions in the sense we understand today: an extra member of the family unit. One dog was buried with a bone, thought to be that of a mammoth, placed in its mouth. The mammoth bone may be symbolic, as analysis of bone collagen at another Czech site indicates that only humans fed on mammoth – their dogs were fed on musk ox and deer. Perhaps it was rewarded for its lifelong loyalty with a prime piece of mammoth meat.

The Chauvet Cave near Vallon in the south of France holds the footprints of a child of around ten years old walking side-by-side with a large dog or wolf for 55 yards; the initial layer of soot on the footprints dates from around 26,000 years ago. The child was around 4½ feet tall and carrying a torch to light their way, leaving behind the soot that has allowed us to place them in time. The Chauvet Cave holds over 400 images of prehistoric animals, and it seems that the child and his wolf-dog were going to look at a cave where bear skulls were later found. The child slipped a few times, but child and dog were walking together.[16] Here we encounter the traces of bonds that have endured for millennia, and can feel the presence of love and companionship that speak directly to us today.

A 31,000-year-old gravesite in Krems, less than a day's walk north along the Danube from where the Venus of Willendorf was found, was recently revealed through DNA analysis to be the resting place of the first known identical twin babies.[17] Around 1 to 3 per cent of all pregnancies today are thought to be twins, with far fewer in Asia than in Africa.[18] But for most of our history these numbers would have been lower since late Ice Age Europe did not have access to modern fertility treatments which have led to the rise of multiple births in the last 50 years. Identical twins, born from the fusion of a single sperm with a single egg, are only a small percentage of all twin births and rare enough to make placing accurate figures on their frequency unreliable. A successful delivery of identical twins in Ice Age Austria would have seemed almost supernatural.

The twins did not survive long and were covered with prized red ochre and perhaps bundled in a wrapping, as a bone pin remained on one of the skeletons. The shoulder blade of a mammoth was placed over them both. However, they did not die at the same time. A study of the tooth formation (and the presence of barium) in their teeth shows that the first child made at least one attempt to breastfeed but died soon after, while his brother died at around seven weeks, when the grave was reopened to bury him alongside his twin. Beside them was the older male baby, possibly a cousin, who died at around three months. His teeth showed a complete absence of the deposits known as 'breastfeeding signals', which led the scientists involved to conclude that these children must have been born at a time of desperate food shortage. Yet these infants, who survived birth against all odds only to perish outside the womb, were not interred without care or ceremony, just like their fellow hominid the Neanderthal child.[19]

There is much that we do not know about the lives of prehistoric women, but while archaeological opinion remains divided on whether there was equality between genders, it is becoming clearer that women were not bound by a patriarchal society as many of their descendants would be. Historically, so much of the research regarding the core skills of these early peoples, such as toolmaking or butchering or tanning hides, has focused on separating hunting and domestic skills into male and female roles, but there is growing evidence that this was not the case. An *atlatl* (spear-thrower), still used by children of both genders in hunter–gatherer societies today, was found along with projectile points in the grave of a 9,000-year-old woman in southern Peru.[20] And she is not alone.

THE FERTILE CRESCENT AND THE FIRST FARMERS

When the twins died, the glaciers had already begun their slow retreat from northern Europe. The Ice Age was finally in decline, and now humans could move further north looking for animals, and for shelter. Many settled in the Fertile Crescent in the Middle East, a slice of land shaped like a crescent moon that would have been rich with biodiversity and marshland. Settlements were increasingly based around pre-existing cave complexes, with huts and shelters for various purposes added on when there was a need. Dogs roamed. Children played, although there is little or no evidence of toys at this stage, only miniature versions of the tools used by adults. People returned after a day spent farming, gathering plants or hunting not to a fire but to a hearth and the beginnings of what we now understand as home.

It is in Palestine, in a dry and rocky valley bristling with olive groves now known as Wadi Natuf, that evidence for the first farming community has been found. Early strains of rye and wheat, such as emmer and einkorn, and simple forms of barley grew there, and slowly the 'Natufians', as they became known, began to cultivate it. They also cultivated, or at the very least harvested, medicinal plants such as the opium poppy at Tell Abu Hureyra (meaning 'the village of Abu Hureyra') in what is now Syria. The opium poppy has since then played a large role in childbirth. For over a millennium these people gathered and ate a variety of wild crops such as berries and pistachios, before abandoning the settlement for 200 years. When they returned, generations later, they lived in semi-sunken structures probably covered by dome-like roofs of gazelle skin and actively farmed a broad range of cereals as well as chickpeas and lentils – all of which require skill and time to cultivate and prepare for consumption.

The remains of around 162 Natufians were found at a burial site in Abu Hureyra which was first used 11,500 years ago. Over a period of 3,000 years, '75 children and 87 adults, of whom 44 were female, 27 male and 16 of undetermined sex' were laid to rest there.[21] These skeletons, nearly all buried in the foetal position, revealed that gender-specific roles were developing among these early farmers. Most of the skeletons bore evidence of carrying heavy loads from a young age, but the female skeletons, in particular, showed 'grossly' arthritic feet associated with the use of a stone 'saddle quern' to grind grain, resulting from long hours in a squatting position.[22] It is now known that squatting, ideally without the relentless grain grinding, is beneficial for childbirth – cultures where people squat for hours every day tend to exhibit wider pelvic openings by up to an inch; in fact, Neolithic (the latter part of the Stone Age) people are often buried in a squatting position, which may signal that it was something they found comfortable.

Unlike the Cro Magnons and other groups, however, it seems unlikely from their bones that Natufian women would have had time to make votive figurines or cave paintings. This is the first sign of a cultural shift that would engulf Europe by the year 3000 BCE and profoundly impact women's experiences of childbirth and motherhood.

Hunter–gatherer populations still in existence such as the !Kung of the western Kalahari show that first pregnancies tend to occur between 16 and 18 years old, and continue at approximately four-year intervals until menstruation stops. This is accounted for by breastfeeding (which, while not foolproof, does significantly lower a woman's chances of conceiving) and an unpredictable lifestyle with relatively poor nutrition, a situation that is echoed by the remains of prehistoric women. As with much later cultures, it's probable that, given the high infant and mother mortality, it was common for women to breastfeed each other's children – forming what may have been a lifelong bond. Early agricultural societies such as the Natufians of Abu Hureyra, however, saw a sudden increase in the birth rate, perhaps because they were weaning their infants earlier. Unfortunately, we will never know what else Abu Hureyra might have revealed about Natufian motherhood or childbirth, because in 1974 it was destroyed and flooded in the creation of Lake Assad, burying its wealth of knowledge about these pioneers of early agriculture for ever.

At almost the same time as the Abu Hureyra settlers were carving out their dwellings, another prehistoric people founded a remarkable civilization at the temple site of Göbekli Tepe in Turkey. Göbekli Tepe is believed to be the oldest known temple in the world, at around 11,500 years old; this civilization, which left so much of its personality behind for us to find, is a place of great importance in our story. Its people were not only farming but creating significant amounts of beautiful art, artefacts and graffiti, much of it related to childbirth and fertility. Even the name Gobekli Tepe translates to 'the hill of the belly'.

This was the time before the invention of pottery, but the art the people of Göbekli Tepe made reflected an organized and ritualized way of life. Not only did they depict abstract human figures wearing items of clothing such as belts and loincloths, but they rendered in detail the various wild animals that surrounded them, such as snakes and ducks, and also a comical but skilful three-dimensional tusked boar and another poor unfortunate wild pig about to be leapt upon by a lion. Other graffiti and artwork suggests that particular structures within the temple complex were given over to actual childbirth or fertility rituals. One of the most famous of its many works of art is a 6 ft 3 in. stone 'totem pole' carved with successive individuals giving birth to each other: the topmost faceless figure generating a woman, who then generates the smaller figure, who is interpreted as either another woman holding the head of an even smaller individual or a man proffering his phallus.[23]

The Göbekli Tepe totem pole is extraordinary, not least because of its massive size and weight (in excess of 1100 lb.), but also because of its depiction of generations tied together by the act of giving birth. The uppermost face of the totem pole was 'obliterated in antiquity', probably when the temple was abandoned, but from the remains of its eyes and ears it is thought to represent one of the animals associated with fertility: a bear, a leopard or a lion.[24] Elsewhere on the carved pillars of the temple are many more animalistic carvings referring to an unknown mythology, but depictions of ordinary humans seem limited to graffiti, including one of a woman squatting and displaying her enlarged genitalia between two 'lion' pillars – perhaps she was scrawled by a couple trying to conceive.

Neolithic totem pole from Göbekli Tepe, 8800–8000 BCE

Other Göbekli Tepe totem poles, such as Pillar 43, depict star constellations that show an understanding of the night sky previously not thought possible at this point in history. In recent years extensive work on the material remains of Göbekli Tepe indicates that it had a role in not just mystic rituals but also social ones: highly decorated 'cups' have been found, along with large vessels of up to 42 gallons which have been analysed and contain a residue possibly from beer-brewing, rather than being simply for holding water.[25] Upon abandonment, the semi-subterranean chambers were deliberately filled with up to 16 feet of sediment consisting of 'limestone chips and fine earth', as well as smashed animal bones. Whatever the purpose of the Göbekli Tepe complex, by 8,000 BCE its time was over.

While rites surrounding birth and fertility, such as those that may have taken place at Göbekli Tepe, remain a mystery, we know more about how these ancient people dealt with death. An aspect of Neolithic life in the Fertile Crescent (and elsewhere) that can seem surprising to us today, given that they seem suddenly more recognizable than any previous prehistoric people, is that they buried the dead in their homes.[26] They quite literally lived with their dead. Cemeteries or burial sites became increasingly common as settlements grew more organized, but mostly the dead were interred either in special niches or platforms within the house or, more frequently, beneath the floor. Babies or newborns are usually found beneath the floors of rooms that include a hearth or fire, perhaps indicating a kitchen. This may be because, particularly in the case of very young children, they spent their short lives in the warm – it may have also been where they died. So it would have been a fitting place to bury them.

Across vast swathes of Eurasia, the skull became of particular importance to Neolithic peoples. Before burial, the dead often were decapitated – other times, their skulls were dug up at a later date before being either reburied or used elsewhere.[27] This curation or reuse of skulls seems odd to us, but it happened so frequently that it must have served a purpose, perhaps to allow their dead to play a ceremonial role or bear witness to an important event. One of the strangest examples was discovered in the village of Çatalhöyük, in southern Turkey, which overlooks the dry, flat lands of the Konya Plain. It is the burial of a woman who lived there 7,000 years ago whose head had been removed one year after her death, though the rest of her body was left undisturbed. She died during labour with the child still in her womb; from what we can tell from her bones there was nothing wrong with her or the unborn child, and yet both perished.[28] It is thought that the Çatalhöyük people only beheaded those who held a high status, as a sign of respect and perhaps ancestor worship. Whoever she was, it seems that she was important to her community.

When we think of these ancient peoples, we should not think their lives were lonely, or that they were wandering in the wilderness. Humans are, after all, social creatures. Archaeologists have revealed the Çatalhöyük people lived in a large and complex settlement of 5,000 people (perhaps many more) made up of fully plastered subterranean houses built so close together that people would have had to navigate the village by walking over their rooftops. There appear to have been no public buildings and no temples, although ritual artwork abounds within the houses, and one discovery included a room with a large number of horned cattle skulls embedded in the walls. The site is filled with interpretations of animal and human life, both actual and ritual.

The Çatalhöyük village is where one of the most fascinating Venus art works was uncovered: the 'seated woman with felines'. It was found in a grain bin during an excavation in 1961 and stands out as a rare discovery, as the people of Çatalhöyük made mainly animal figurines. The seated woman, a hand on each of her biddable felines, is in a commanding position. Her flaccid breasts, clearly demarcated fat rolls and authoritative posture indicate age, experience and social stature, and, like the Venus of Hohle Fels, suggest a woman who existed and played an important role in the life of the village, even if only in her clay form.

In the north of Çatalhöyük, archaeologists discovered a room with seven bodies buried in it: one was an adult male over 60 years old, one an infant around nine months old and one an adult woman who died in childbirth, her stillborn or newborn placed upon her. Under the threshold, the door that led into the space, three newborns were buried in one small grave. Until relatively recently it was common practice among some cultures to inter babies and infant children under thresholds of houses – a doorway is after all a place of entering and leaving – but Çatalhöyük is so far the first known example.

Seated woman of Çatalhöyük, Turkey, c. 6000 BCE

The three newborns buried together were not triplets. It is likely that they were not closely related at all as many of the skeletons buried under the same houses in Çatalhöyük were not biologically related to each other, indicating that in this village people lived in extended families and social circles, as seen now in the Southwest Pueblo societies of North America.[29] Analysis of the Çatalhöyük diets from their bones also tells us that it's likely that men and women occupied the same social status, as does the egalitarian fashion in which they were buried.[30] There is one unusual burial of a very young child, around seven months old, adorned in valuable anklets and bracelets, but most people who died in Çatalhöyük were laid to rest in the same way.[31] The considerable disarticulation seen in many of the skeletons (of all ages), as well as missing finger and toe bones, indicates that, like many Neolithic dead, they were either de-fleshed or left exposed to the elements for some time before being buried.

Çatalhöyük developed an artistic and egalitarian culture with complicated funereal rites we may never understand, but there were other settlements on the rise too – ones that seem to reveal a more hierarchical social structure. In 1963 the remains of Çayönü Tepesi, on the Ergani Plain of south-eastern Turkey (dated to between 8630 and 6800 BCE), were excavated. The people who lived there kept domesticated cattle and sheep, and are also thought to have been the first to have domesticated pigs.[32] However, these new sources of nutrition were not shared equally among the community. Their bones reveal one distinct difference between the people of Catalhoyuk and Çayönü Tepesi: in the latter, the men ate significantly more meat than the women, who ate more grains and vegetables.[33] Infants were also weaned earlier at Çayönü than at other Neolithic sites, and there was a higher rate of infant mortality, which perhaps accounts for the large numbers of newborns and infants discovered buried there in pits.[34]

In the early years of its settlement, the people of Çayönü buried their dead in much the same fashion as those of Çatalhöyük, but at some point they built what is known as the Skull Building. Constructed over a long period of time and holding around 70 human skulls and long bones (some of which belonged to animals), the Skull Building contains the remains of those who consumed the meat-heavy, higher-status diet – and yet DNA testing has shown that the Skull Building contained more burials of women than men.[35] Some believe that this may be proof of human sacrifice (as most women did not consume this higher-status diet), or that to be buried in the Skull Building indicated that the individual was of great worth to the community at large, regardless of sex or age. While the dietary evidence suggests it was largely men who held power, perhaps it was possible for certain women to reach an elevated status.

As it stands, we do not know. Much work remains to be done at Göbekli Tepe, Çatalhöyük and Çayönü Tepesi, but what these findings reveal is that complex societies were developing, along with rituals involving life and death – and their constant companion, childbirth. Eventually, all three settlements were abandoned for unknown reasons. Strangely, the people who left them took time to deface their sophisticated homes and art works, sometimes destroying them completely. The current theory, indicated again by skeletal evidence of malnutrition, is that a change in climate made such large settlements impossible to sustain.

THE DECLINE OF 'OLD EUROPE' AND THE ARRIVAL OF THE KURGANS

As the humid Fertile Crescent flourished, northern and western Europe was still emerging from the Ice Age. There are many theories about which tribes emerged when, but ever-advancing genome studies indicate that distinct groups formed following the success, through natural selection, of small splinter groups. It is now believed that the original population of *homo sapiens* who braved and perhaps colonized for some centuries the icebound Bering Strait, known as Beringia (the primeval land that once bridged Asia and North America), and who came to settle in the Pacific Northwest, eventually moving as far as Chile and forming the entire indigenous First Nation peoples of the Americas, were descended from an original genetic group from Lake Baikal in Siberia, the Mal'ta people. This group then split repeatedly, and was added to, creating the forerunners of America's Clovis (mammoth and mastodon hunters) and Folsom (plains bison hunters) hunter–gatherer tribes.

The people of the Mal'ta were living on a successful settlement in Siberia when, around seven thousand years ago, another mother perished while giving birth to twins in the cold mountains north-west of Lake Baikal, where the people fished, foraged and hunted game and seals.

Much can go wrong when a woman gives birth to twins – which is why most are born via C-section today. For a successful delivery the foetuses have to be 'amenable', by arranging themselves in such a way that it is possible for one to follow the other down the birth canal. The two most dangerous positions are when the first baby is breech, which can be changed by a skilled midwife, and 'interlocking twins'. Interlocking twins, when one twin's head is trapped beneath the other's chin and cannot pass through the pelvis, would – in these times – have been a threefold death sentence.

We know that this woman of the far north died because the first twin was breech, trapping both in the womb, their heads possibly interlocked but both stuck inside the pelvis. It may have been a long and difficult birth, and we can imagine that those around her would have drawn on whatever medicinal or ritual knowledge was available to them to ease her suffering. The twins were buried with her and undisturbed until their excavation – it's rare to find foetuses buried *in utero* during this period – whether because foetal bones are too fragile to survive or because they were buried separately we do not know.[36] Their mother was in her early twenties at the time of her death, and was buried with her children exactly as they had died, with the grave goods typical for both men and women at the time, and with five marmot teeth by her shoulder. The poignancy of their deaths has the ability to bridge the many thousands of years between us and them. What should have been a moment of triumph was instead a loss felt by a whole community in the harsh Siberian mountains.

Many of these archaeological discoveries, however, tell us so little about the gender roles and childbirth rites of these Palaeolithic and Neolithic people. What was the Siberian woman's role in her community? What support could she expect to receive as she prepared for motherhood? Were there rituals, prohibited behaviours or special responsibilities that defined the contours of her life, and marked her out as different from the twins' father? We do not know. One profound example of the mistakes our ignorance can lead to comes from the gentle wooded hills of Bäckaskog, in southern Sweden. Complete and well-preserved skeletons are rare in Scandinavia, owing to soil conditions and funeral rites, but these remains found in 1939 were buried in a squatting pose with a set of flint arrows used for fishing, as well as hunting tools. The skeleton was duly placed on display in the

Swedish History Museum and entitled 'The Fisherman of Barum' (inventory number 22438).

In 1970 the skeleton was removed from display for cleaning and general upkeep, and a new examination was made. Its measurements suggested an individual of 61 inches in height and of slender build. The teeth were a full set, and 'exceedingly beautiful', but with wear suggesting their owner was between 40 and 50 years old at the time of death. The pelvis proved perplexing to those examining it, as it appeared to possess both male and female traits.

The definitive answer finally came in a letter from J. L. Engel, of the Smithsonian Institute, who had seen photographs of the pelvis and formed his opinion. The *pubis* – the bone right at the front of the pelvis – becomes fused in men during adolescence, but remains linked by tough ligaments in women, so that it may stretch a little during childbirth. This gap is called the *pubic symphysis*.

No ligament at all was left on the skeleton, which is partly why it was assumed to be male, but when a woman gives birth it leaves evidence on the inside of the bone. Engel was struck by

> the degree of erosion on the inner surface of the pubic bones which indicates many births – at least 10 to 12, I would estimate. We have so far only the modern American symphysis of a lady who had eleven live births plus one or two miscarriages, dead at 33 as a murder victim, and your Mesolithic lady shows if anything a larger excavation in the bone.

Further analysis in 1996 revealed she had suffered blood poisoning in the right hand, although this was not a conclusive cause of death. From the pollen on her remains it is likely that she was buried in the spring. The Fisher of Barum, as she is now known, has been returned to her place on display in the Swedish History Museum.[37]

The Neolithic period continued on for four thousand years, depending on the location and resources available, and saw the emergence of distinctive cultures, but the world was changing.

THE REALM OF WOMEN

The Ice Age was over, leaving rivers and waterways full of fish and shellfish, so many settled by water. Others remained hunting on the plains. What was once Beringia was gone, and passage to and from the American continent was impossible for the time being. As a result, the cultural history of childbirth on the European and American continents diverges from this point for thousands of years.

The Fisher of Barum, Sweden, 7010–6540 BCE

Many of the old hunter–gatherer tribes were displaced outwards, west and north, by the arrival of the farmers from the Fertile Crescent. This in turn promoted the establishment of trade routes, based largely on pottery and copper but also foodstuffs such as seeds and medicines such as opium. This increased movement of people – looking not only to trade but for territory they could settle on – resulted in conflict, as it has tended to do throughout our history.

Such conflicts are evidenced by the *Linearbandkeramik* (a people named for their distinctive pottery decorated with lines, also known in English as the Linear Pottery Culture), who spread out along Europe's newly available waterways and lived what appeared to be peaceful lives in wattle-and-daub houses with purpose-built shelters for animals and workshops. Yet archaeologists uncovering buried *Linearbandkeramik* settlements began to realize that their villages were heavily fortified at the perimeters and, at three separate sites (Talheim and Herxheim in the Rhine Valley, Schelz-Asparn near Vienna), found evidence of harrowing massacres. Throughout *Linearbandkeramik* settlements in western Germany, human remains show signs of suffering tremendous violence: 32 per cent of the bodies examined reveal traumatic injury. If 2 per cent of their remains showed signs of injury, that would be indicative of a society engaged in war – such a high proportion points to something far darker. Skull drinking cups and signs of cannibalism were also uncovered.[38] All was not quite as pastoral or peaceful as it seemed. And alongside this extreme violence there was a move towards more defined gender roles: women tended to be buried with spinning whorls and men with axes or adzes. And further change was on the horizon.

The Kurgans occupied the Pontic steppe, a vast grassland stretching from the Black Sea to Central Asia which encompasses Ukraine, Bulgaria and Romania. They have the distinction of being the first to domesticate horses on a wide scale, probably in Ukraine. They built chariots, thereby mastering the wheel, and were keen to expand their territories in a warlike manner. It is also likely that they were the first speakers of what we call Proto-Indo-European (PIE) languages, believed to be the common ancestor of modern languages spoken across Europe and most of India today.

In 3500 BCE the Kurgans began their first wave of movement into western Europe, probably led by the Ukrainian tribe of Sredni Stog, who were the first to domesticate the horse as a mount, rather than simply a food source.[39] They obliterated the cultures they came into contact with, absorbing anything valuable and replacing the rest with their own culture by force. Their ability to mobilize at previously unthinkable speeds, in numbers, coupled with new metal weaponry, made them unstoppable.

The second Kurgan invasion, and perhaps the most important one for Europe as a whole, came from the Yamnaya tribe a few centuries later. The Yamnaya Kurgans were without doubt a patriarchal society. Great warriors were buried in a supine position, covered with red ochre and an upturned chariot, surrounded by grave goods such as weapons, horses, gold cups and jewellery. Wives of warrior chieftains sometimes ended up in the Kurgan too, along with servants in some cases.[40] It's likely that the women entered the Kurgan upon their husband's death and took poison, but we do not know. The entire grave was then covered with an enormous burial mound, also called a 'kurgan', which could be more than 50 feet high. The earthen sod excavated for the burial of one such 'king', in Chertomlyk, Ukraine, measured 185 acres.[41] It was a statement not only of grandeur but also of possession and territory.

Unremitting and devastating, the Yamnaya trampled all before them as they abandoned the barren Pontic steppe in pursuit of wealth and pasture and, perhaps most importantly, women. For those who immediately associate 'the Kurgan' with the violent, lascivious character of the same name in the 1986 fantasy-adventure movie *Highlander*, and recall his famous line 'There can be only one!', there is more truth to that than one might imagine. The arrival of the Kurgans created a population explosion across western Europe, and a dramatic study, published in 2015, showed that of 334 male DNA samples taken from 17 populations from the British Isles, across Europe and the Middle East, 64 per cent originated from three different male lineages dating from between 3,500 and 7,300 years ago.[42] There is no similar explosion in similar maternal (mitochondrial) DNA, indicating that this 'handful' of men exercised reproductive control over large numbers of women. Many of us are, distantly, their children.

With the arrival of the Kurgans, the realm of women was over. The ascent of the patriarchy had begun.

2

The Realm of Men

Over three thousand years ago an enslaved woman composed an emotional letter to her 'lord' in Old Babylonian: 'Thus says Dabitum, your slave girl. What I told you has now happened to me. For seven months, this child has been in my belly, the child is dead in my belly since one month and nobody takes care of me.'[1]

Dabitum occupied the lowest rung in society, but she was not completely without a voice and her letter about the death of her unborn child speaks to us across the centuries; it could have been written by somebody denied their rights today. Dabitum lived in the ancient city of Sippar on the banks of the River Euphrates during the height of the Babylonian empire's power, although little now remains of its ziggurat or great mud-brick walls. (Ziggurats were enormous temples believed to the dwelling places of the Babylonian gods.) Sippar was one of many cities in the Fertile Crescent. The early farmers we met in the previous chapter had turned their hands to civilization, and now literature, legal systems and much else began to rise up from the extraordinarily productive soils of Mesopotamia. It is here that we leave prehistory behind, entering the time in our human histories we call the Bronze and Iron Ages. The history of how we came to see and understand childbirth lies in these places where East meets West – in the deserts of Mesopotamia and the blue waters of the Aegean. For the first time people begin to leave written records behind, and in them we can read the words of long-dead women – like Dabitum – and men as they grapple with the anxiety, joy and mystery of birth.

THE BEGINNINGS OF UNDERSTANDING

A few years ago the British Museum began looking at a series of extraordinary photographs taken by CIA spy planes during the Cold War. When viewed from above, strange structures seemed to appear in the desert of Iraq, the outlines and indentations of something extraordinary – a city. This settlement, discovered at Girsu (modern-day Tello), was built for as many as 30,000 inhabitants by the Sumerians just over 4,000 years ago – perhaps a thousand years before Dabitum was born.

The Sumerians are, currently, the earliest known literate society. They invented their own cuneiform language (cuneiform literally means 'wedge-shaped'), which they left to us imprinted on clay tablets. They were also among the most powerful civilizations in Mesopotamia – a land 'between two rivers' (the Tigris and the Euphrates) which covered Iraq, parts of Turkey, Syria and Iran. Mesopotamia was home to many formidable empires and rich cultures, including the Assyrians, Akkadians and Babylonians, as well as the Jewish, Hittite and Elamite peoples.

The mother goddess of the Sumerians was called Ianna – she represented the fertility cycle and war. The Assyrians called their mother goddess Ishtar; like Ianna, she was associated with the star we call Venus. With the advent of the Sumerians' written records, the deep-rooted cosmic mythologies and therapeutic remedies previously passed down orally through generations were disseminated across vast tracts of the ancient world. There's no doubt that the birthing mother was hugely significant in their religious works, as the myths that have survived often tell us stories about the relationships between divine mothers and their children – but it is in documents dealing with the day-to-day medical and legal complications of life that the voices of real Mesopotamian women can be found.

Dabitum, although a slave, was part of the large community of working women who laboured in the many cities across

Mesopotamia. While some women oversaw palaces, others worked in temples or as scribes. Female administrators in Assyria were called *šakintu* and were well paid and respected. Women were also musicians, merchants, tavern keepers and, of course, midwives. Yet gender inequality persisted. Female labourers in menial jobs received only half the pay or rations of men, respectable unmarried women were expected to be affiliated with a similarly respectable household and prostitutes had already entered the margins of society.[2]

The Sumerians had a sophisticated and articulate way of expressing their hopes and fears about pregnancy and childbirth. Although it is unwise to ascribe any kind of modern sensibilities to these ancient people, we can begin to understand, through extensive modern scholarship undertaken largely in the last 50 years, how their view of fertility, reproduction and the experience of birth fitted into their societies. Writing was a new invention, but medical knowledge had long been part of these ancient cultures by the time they came to be recorded in Mesopotamian texts. There are two things that strike you straight away about these very early medical texts. The first is that the gynaecological concerns of women make up a significant proportion of their therapeutic canon of literature. From them we learn that the Sumerians were aware that conception was linked directly to sexual intercourse. An old Sumerian proverb states slyly, 'Has she become pregnant without intercourse? Has she become fat without eating?'[3] Pregnancy in this culture was often referred to as being 'fat' or 'sick', rather than pregnant. While readers today may see this as pejorative, it is equally likely to be a more straightforward, even positive, reference to the physical symptoms of pregnancy. This doesn't mean that pregnant Sumerian women didn't also struggle with some of the symptoms: another proverb translates colloquially as 'To be sick is acceptable, to be pregnant is painful; to be pregnant and sick is just too much.'[4]

For the pregnant woman, therapeutic texts offer plant-based recipes including ginseng and myrrh to stop vaginal bleeding and miscarriage. Fittingly, as the Sumerians are credited with inventing the brewing of barley, many of their herbal recipes are administered via the medium of beer. Infertility was regarded as a significant source of sadness and strain.

In most of these ancient languages, becoming pregnant meant that the woman had successfully seized or taken the male 'seed'.[5] Reflecting the imagery that would have animated daily life in these early farming societies, a woman was often said to represent ground that was to be ploughed, planted, and, with the birth of a child, produce a successful crop. Yet this does not necessarily mean that these women were viewed as passive vessels in the cycle of fertility.

These ancient texts talk elsewhere of ethical and legal issues. A Sumerian legal textbook lists the fines payable for causing a woman to miscarry through violence, in horrible detail: beating the daughter of a free man that resulted in miscarriage was graded from an 'accidental push', at 10 shekels, to 'deliberate', at 20 to 30 shekels. If a slave girl, such as Dabitum, was beaten and as a result suffered the loss of a child, the fine was 5 shekels.[6] Although these laws were enacted to dissuade people from harming pregnant women, it's impossible to overlook the fact that human life, even unborn, had taken on a monetary value. What we would call abortion was set into a legal framework too: in Mesopotamian medical texts a woman was not a mother or *ummu* until she had given birth, but there could be terrible consequences if she sought to terminate her own pregnancy.[7] In mid-Assyrian law, abortion was already outlawed and any woman found guilty would be executed by impalement, her body left to rot in public.[8]

During this period in history, it is still impossible to know with any certainty how many pregnancies led to the birth of a healthy child. In general, estimates for infant mortality in such pre-modern societies are around 25 to 30 per cent, if we take infancy to mean the age up until mobility, around one year.[9] To be pregnant was perilous in itself, and even the texts that deal with myths and ritual, rather than medicine, show the time before childbirth as one of great anxiety for everyone involved. We have records of chants and prayers that would have been sung or spoken during childbirth by those assisting the labouring women, which draw on powerful and emotive language to beg for a successful outcome for mother and child. In many of these, with the onset of labour the woman is said to be no longer simply pregnant: she is a knot to be untied, a door to be opened, a vase in danger of being broken and, perhaps less appealingly, a cow birthing a calf. A particularly touching Assyrian elegy likens a woman who died in childbirth to a ship that is lost at sea, crying out to the mother goddess *Belet-ili*: 'You are the mother of those who give birth, save my life! ... Death crept stealthily in my bed. It brought me out of my home ... set my feet toward a land from which I shall not return.'[10]

Another text, this time Akkadian, *The Cow of Sîn*, tells of the moon god Sîn who impregnates his beloved pet cow and, when he hears her cries as she goes into labour, sends two helpers down from the heavens to assist her. With their help the birth is easy, and this story underlines how important assistance during a woman's labour was, and how valued it was even many thousands of years ago. In this story it is the child's father who finds a way to make sure that the birthing mother has the help that she needs.

When children died during childbirth, or just after, other rituals were followed. Many Mesopotamian cultures buried their dead infants in jars inside the home, which may be explained by the fact that their myths and superstitions show a deep attachment to notions of home and to the idea of the body as 'home'. Jar burials of babies and children arise in various cultures throughout history, and are known to have occurred as far away as Teotihuacán in Mexico during the Mesoamerican era. No cultural contact between the two cultures is likely, so this, remarkably, seems to be something humans do organically.[11]

There is a myth from this period that tells us about the emotional significance of these home burials. It centres on the goddess-demon Lamaštu, a demon often depicted with a hairy body, lion's head and bird's talons, and her attempts to prevent a dead child from being buried inside the home of its grieving parents. Lamaštu was seen as highly dangerous for the unborn child and its mother, as she bore evil intentions towards pregnant women, who were believed to be especially at risk from sorcery. To fight this anxiety, amulets and charms made from elaborate bindings of coloured stones, sinews, threads or herbs were created to ward off evil wishes and offerings were placed at crossroads.[12]

Lamashtu amulet, Mesopotamia, 800–550 BCE

Another important figure in the Mesopotamian canon of childbirth mythology, and one that scholars continue to debate, is the Kūbu, uniformly depicted as an emaciated male figure of small stature, crouched in the foetal position, wrists to temples. The interpretation of the Kūbu varies from that of a miscarried foetus to a stillborn child who has become a demon and wanders, lost and spiteful, threatening to dry up new mothers' milk (it is also around this time that we find the earliest contracts for wet nurses, whose pay was carefully regulated). Still others interpret the Kūbu shrines as votive offerings to perhaps an individual child. To settle on one interpretation of this particular, peculiar, diminutive, wizened little figure is almost impossible in the vast swathe of history that constitutes Mesopotamia.

Finally comes the spectre of the Izbū, the deformed child. A Sumerian myth featuring the deities Enki and Ninmah shows many creative solutions for integrating disability into the community: a blind man becomes a musician, a club-footed man a silversmith and so forth. But for the Izbū there is no hope, and the Sumerians believed that the child must be cast from the household and into a river alive, from whence it will be carried to the underworld without delay, to await a chance at regeneration.[13]

All these beliefs were interwoven with superstition, religion and medicine as well as a growing legal framework to form a holistic understanding of the mechanisms and ramifications of childbirth. The peoples of ancient Mesopotamia, just like parents today, wished the best for their children, even those who did not survive. In one Sumerian epic, Gilgameš, the king of the ancient kingdom of Uruk, rescues his friend and confidant Enkidu from the netherworld, where the latter has witnessed the miserable existence of all those who exist there. Gilgameš inquires of his own children who are there, 'Did you see my stillborn little ones who did not know themselves?' Endiku replies, 'I saw them. They enjoy syrup and ghee at tables of silver and gold.'[14]

We do not know what happened to Dabitum after her letter was sent. There are records of another slave girl of the same name who was eventually freed, married and adopted a little girl but this may not have been the same person. Although she disappears from history, perhaps we can imagine that this is what she hoped for her stillborn child too – an afterlife of syrup and ghee at a table of silver and gold.

THE SUPERSTITIONS OF THE SEA

While the Mesopotamians were busy on land, the Minoans, hundreds of miles west, were building an ocean-going empire on the mountainous island of Crete. The Minoans were, alongside the Mycenaeans and Phoenicians, among the earliest civilizations to flourish along the Mediterranean. They are mysterious peoples, who developed elaborate artistry, cults and mythologies, some of which still hold sway in those regions today. While they left plentiful objects and structures which can tell us about their daily lives, in contrast to the record-keeping Mesopotamians, they left limited records. Yet such was the richness of their cultures that during the rise and fall of their respective empires they left indelible marks on the history of childbirth.

We do not even know what the Minoans called themselves: their name was given to them by English archaeologist Arthur Evans at the turn of the twentieth century, after the mythical King Minos. According to Greek myth, Minos was an adulterous king whose furious wife, Pasiphaë, bewitched him so that if he ever had sex with another woman he would ejaculate serpents, scorpions and woodlice which would then devour his mistress from the inside. To prevent this unfortunate outcome, his lover inserted a goat's bladder into her vagina to protect herself from the king's evil seed. Once he had safely discharged the serpents and woodlice, he could go home and impregnate his wife with a healthy child. This myth is the earliest known use, metaphorical or otherwise, of a prophylactic against sexual disease.[15]

The real Bronze Age Minoans based themselves around Knossos on the north coast of Crete, a huge palace complex with painted walls, airy courtyards and even bathrooms. The later Greeks used Knossos as the mythological home of the labyrinth, home of the legendary Minotaur, monstrous son of Pasiphaë, after she copulated with the Cretan Bull. Near Knossos lies an ancient site called Amnisos, known for a large cave 'temple' discovered in 1897, that appears to have been dedicated to a mother goddess since Neolithic times, and was almost certainly used as such throughout the Minoan period. The goddess, known to the Minoans as Εἰλείθυια, or Eleuthia, was said to maintain her fertility by taking a new male lover each year.

Eleuthia was also worshipped at another cave temple found at the Cretan city of Inatos (now Tsoutsouros) on the southern coast. These temples are impressive and were used by the Minoans for the usual religious prayers: everyone hopes for good harvests, favourable weather and a healthy family. Both are thought to have contained shrines replete with many votive sculptures, but they were sadly looted during the first half of the twentieth century and their artefacts scattered across the globe. However, another shrine discovered at Petsophas on a stony hilltop overlooking the ocean to the east of the island offers us a unique glimpse into the experiences of Minoan women.

The Petsophas peak sanctuary (these temples were often set high in the mountains, a phenomenon found only on Crete) is special as it contains not only goddess figurines but also crude clay figures of women depicted in various stages of childbirth, as well as clay body parts, most particularly of the belly with legs spread apart so its genitals are clearly visible. They usually have holes for suspending them from strings, or pegs so that they can be seated on small birthing stools. Many cultures throughout history have used birthing stools – usually low chairs that allow a woman to sit or squat in a position that aids her labour. The use of votive clay, metal or wax anatomical figurines representing a physical state, or a troublesome condition, is known throughout the Aegean during this period. For instance, someone with a broken arm might leave a little clay model of that arm in a healing shrine, hoping to channel the deity's attention to their limb. Women made these small sculptures of their own pregnant bodies long ago, hoping for help with their birth.

The walls of Petsophas are painted with imagery of plants used in common midwifery recipes, namely the crocus, the rose, iris, vitex and dittany (Crete was famed for its carpets of dittany), pomegranate and the opium poppy – for the pain. Also discovered were large numbers of little clay animals, called *okytokia*, and at Petsophas, uniquely, they are predominantly weasels.

The bones of these women who lived in Bronze Age Crete have revealed why they felt the need to make so many offerings and prayers. They died much younger than might be expected, with many dying at around 25 years of age (for men, it was 30 years), the peak childbearing years. Osteoporosis was found in almost all female skeletal remains from the age of 23 onwards, and women showed significantly more dental disease than men, indicating that men and women had different diets.[16] Their bones show that life on ancient Crete, despite its wealth and apparent refinement, was overpopulated and short of food, with people arriving from all directions, carrying all kinds of diseases. Health was precious, and so we can only imagine how many prayers were whispered for the birth of a healthy baby to a healthy mother.

So why the weasels? For the Neolithic peoples and the Mesopotamians, the fish and the snake had symbolized a quick and easy delivery for the expectant mother. On Crete, weasels were and often still are known as *kalogennousa*: 'she who gives birth easily'. Across the broader Aegean, weasels are still referred to as *nyfitsa*, or 'little brides', and even into the nineteenth century the symbolic *nyfitsa* was ceremonially invited to join a Greek wedding ceremony to help the new couple turn their thoughts towards bearing children.[17] The weasel brought luck, and women on this island thousands of years ago made models of them for the gods, to help their families begin, grow and prosper.

Across the sea, another rich Greek culture was forming around the Mycenaean people. If the Minoans can be characterized as an island people, the Mycenaeans were their counterparts on the mainland. They represent the last phase of Bronze Age Greece, and forged significant trading and political connections not only with Anatolia (modern-day Turkey) but also with ancient Egypt and Minoan Crete.

We know their social structure was stricter, more cohesive and hierarchical, and more warrior-like than the island-based Minoans. They had a capital city from which power radiated: Mycenae, a fortified settlement high up on a hill with clear views of its surrounding lands, located around 75 miles south-west of Athens (which at this point was smaller and less significant). Excavations of graves at the city of Pylos indicate again that women had a poor diet, and that few individuals lived past the age of 35.[18]

The Pylos Tablets refer to a hoard of over a thousand fragmented administrative texts discovered in 1939 at the Mycenaean Palace of Nestor. While they hold very little traditional historical information on the society itself, they tell us a great deal about Mycenaean workers – some of whom were pregnant women and mothers. The palatial economy at Pylos (most wealth and labour were controlled, distributed or assigned by the palace) depended on textile production, for palace consumption and to sell abroad. High-quality wool cloths were produced in bright colours using saffron for yellow and, for the highly prized bright purple cloth, many thousands of murex shells gathered from the surrounding seas, which had to be processed in a labour-intensive nine-day period.[19] In the ancient world this shell was the only way to produce purple. Lower-status women and their children worked in large numbers as wool-carders for this textile industry, usually under a work master – it's unclear whether they were slaves or not, although this seems likely, given the large numbers of foreign women and child workers recorded at the palatial site.[20]

The women were paid their wages in wheat and figs.[21] Wheat was a currency in Mycenaean Greece, so this may not just record their subsistence rations, but both were also high carbohydrate foods associated with poor dental health. The Pylos Tablets reveal that although women involved in textile production were not necessarily denied access to meat, the food they were paid in was not nutritious in comparison to the food men had ready access to. They may not have known it, but this was a disaster for pregnancy and childbirth – multiple burials of full-term yet low-birth-weight babies attest to this, as do the osteoporosis and early death rates in young girls of child-bearing age.[22] So far, the rise of civilization had not yet materially improved the lot of women and mothers.

There was, however, one route women could take to accrue wealth and wield power: religion. Cheering tales of high-status women in Mycenaean society emerge from the Pylos Tablets, including that of Eritha, priestess at the cult goddess sanctuary of Sphagianes, near Pylos, whose unresolved squabble over taxes is the oldest known legal case in Europe.[23] Sphagianes was dedicated to the Mycenaean mother goddess Potnia, meaning 'Mistress', representing life, death and rebirth. Potnia was held in high regard by the Mycenaeans, as recorded in Pylos Tablet PY cc 665, which has been translated both as '100 rams and 190 pigs' offered to the goddess 'by ship' and, more literally, as 'Fresh Penis offers the Goddess Potnia 100 rams and 190 pigs'.[24]

A gold ring forged by Mycenae's skilled metallurgists depicts a goddess seated beneath a tree, surrounded by cult Cretan images: the double axe associated with female goddesses as well as the sun and the moon. The goddess holds three poppy heads, symbols of wealth and health, and the tree is a symbol of life and fertility.[25] From the proliferation of similar figurines, both the Minoans and the Mycenaeans seem to have worshipped this female goddess through the medium of priestesses such as Eritha, who were associated with various symbols already familiar from the Neolithic Ages, such as the 'horns of consecration' (bull's horns) and the snake. The close association of the opium poppy with these fertility goddesses shows a link we may recognize today: the importance of pain relief during childbirth.

The Mycenaean and Cretan cults were reinventing Neolithic symbols to create a new religion as well as reusing older sites for new worship. Yet, as seen in Mesopotamia, as well as the Earth Mother, male gods were now fully in evidence, and the goddess herself was splitting into different and often fluid deities, such as the snake goddess and the goddess of the underworld. Over time, Eileithyia and Potnia, both single mother goddesses, became Artemis, Athena, Demeter and Persephone, each responsible for different aspects of ancient Greek mythology. The goddess Eileithyia remained, in a lesser form, recreated as the goddess of midwifery.

Alongside the Minoan and Mycenaean Greek societies were the Phoenicians of the Levant (now Lebanon), whose principal cities were Tyre in the east and Carthage in the west. The Phoenicians were seafarers, and much of their Aegean business was trading the highly prized murex shells that produced the dye for the sought-after purple cloth. They travelled widely, allegedly making it as far as the English Channel in search of Cornish tin, and perhaps even rounded the Horn of Africa – a journey that would not be attempted again for another two millennia.[26] It is through the Phoenicians that we encounter a darker thread in the history of childbirth, one that will weave itself through our story.

It is easy now to laud the Phoenicians' achievements. Their alphabet, a regularized system of writing that enabled merchants, officials and sailors to communicate across long distances, became a recognized entity in its own right and was adopted rapidly throughout large parts of the Mediterranean. It was 'phonetic', with only 22 consonants to learn, with the vowel sounds dependent on the user. It made it easy to send messages without their meaning becoming muddled on the journey; even people with rudimentary language skills could learn it and communicate with strangers. Despite this, the Phoenicians were derided by most other peoples across the ancient Mediterranean as thieves, liars, pedlars and slave traders.

They worshipped three main female deities and one principal male one. The male god was Ba'al Hamon, associated with the sun. The goddesses, on land, were Ashtart and Asherah. Ashtart was associated with sexuality and war, whereas Asherah is believed to represent the mother figure. The third of these goddesses was Tanit or, more correctly in Phoenician, Tinnīt, beloved of sailors. Tinnīt was associated with water, and closely allied to the sexual power of Ashtart.

The Phoenicians created a series of coastal sanctuaries across the Mediterranean in which they could make offerings to Tinnīt and pray for safe passage. The most famous of these is the Grotto Regina, north of Palermo in Sicily. It was discovered in 1968 by Vittorio Giustolisi and reported in the *Sicilia Archaeologica* that December, detailing the things found there: not only prehistoric drawings of a bison hunt and a portrait of a dog's head but also extensive Phoenician art. These include prayers to Tinnīt, her various symbols, such as intertwined snakes and the crescent moon, totems that already had powerful connections to female sexuality by this time, but also many drawings of individuals and individual ships. The Grotto Regina is, so far, the best-known of these Phoenician–Punic (meaning 'of Carthage') sanctuaries which exist on rocky outcrops from Ibiza to southern Lebanon. Sailors dedicated harbours to the mother, Asherah, but also the open water, where the underworld was all around them, and this part belonged to Tinnīt.[27]

The importance of both Tinnīt and Asherah to the sailors is seen not only in the artwork they made with their own hands but also in the coins minted in Phoenician cities depicting ships with Asherah or Tinnīt at the prow of the boat or standing in the stern. Tinnīt is often shown with wings, or accompanied by dolphins, which sailors even today interpret as omens. From the Phoenicians we have inherited many of our maritime superstitions, not least the attribution of the female gender to a ship and the tradition of placing a carved female figurehead at the prow.[28] Thankfully, however, some of their traditions have been consigned to the past.

The Phoenicians may have been called thieves by the Greek and Roman historians who came after them, but this was not their greatest crime. Among their offerings to Tinnīt and Ba'al it seems they made sacrifices of their own children. Ancient Hebrew and Greek traditions already told of the tradition of *mulk*, in which the firstborn son would be sacrificed by fire to grant his father's prayer, but this rite was believed to be symbolic. Yet in the third century BCE the Greek historian Kleitarchos wrote:

> Out of reverence for Kronos [Ba'al], the Phoenicians, and especially the Carthaginians, whenever they seek to obtain some great favour, vow one of their children, burning it as a sacrifice to the deity, if they are especially eager to gain success. There stands in their midst a bronze statue of Kronos, its hands extended over a bronze brazier, the flames of which engulf the child.[29]

When more than 20,000 funerary urns were uncovered at what is now called the Phoenician Tophet (meaning hell-mouth) of Carthage, or the Tophet of Tinnīt, many contained skeletal remains of infants. Opinion was initially divided on whether this discovery was proof of child sacrifice. It has only been in the last few decades that highly developed osteological research techniques, as well as additional funding, have enabled a more precise review of the urns' contents. They contained mostly the bones of infants, most of whom were only between two and five months old when they died. Their ashes were mixed with the burnt bones of immature sheep, birds and goats. The urns were buried beneath *stele* or stone slabs bearing inscriptions that gave the ancestry of the child but no name. The fact that these children died nameless is thought to indicate that they were marked for sacrifice while still inside their mothers' wombs. To leave a child nameless is one matter, but to keep a child nameless for some months, with the sacrifice approaching, must have been a colossal burden for the parents. It's hard not to imagine what it was like to prepare for birth, to feel the first contraction, knowing all the while that the child you were giving birth to was destined to die before it had even learned to walk.

Offering to Molech, Charles Foster, 1897

Throughout the twentieth century, debate has raged over whether the Phoenicians did sacrifice live children or whether tophets were in fact elite child cemeteries. Examination of other Phoenician cemeteries seemed to indicate that this practice was largely limited to this location in Carthage, but then more tophets were discovered, as far afield as Sardinia and Sicily. Other tophets also date from later than the Carthage site, indicating it was not a practice carried out under extreme and desperate circumstances during a war or famine but embedded in the Phoenician culture that Greek and Roman historians so derided.

Following the strange decline of the Mycenaeans after 1100 BCE, the palatial age of the Greek Bronze Age was viewed as entering a 500-year Dark Age until the rise of Classical Greece, the culture that would spawn war-like Sparta, democratic Athens, theatre and philosophy. Yet the Cretan cults refused to be confined to the past. In the same way that the prehistoric people before them had dug up, curated and venerated the bones of their ancestors, new peoples with new cults of their own were waiting to absorb what had gone before. They were destined to give birth to new nations and, crucially, religions.

THE IDEAL AND THE REAL IN THE ANCIENT WORLD

Animism, the idea that sacred things possess a living soul, is what inspires societies to create myths and legends. It is what impelled Minoan women to painstakingly make little clay models of their own swollen bellies in hope of a safe and easy birth. We can imagine them, some heavily pregnant, walking up the long, dusty tracks to the peak sanctuary where they could leave this small fragment of their changing bodies at the shrine of a goddess. A gift for a deity who might have the power to save them when the time came to give birth, or not. It is what led the Mycenaeans to create gold rings carved with fertility goddesses to bring good harvests. It also helps to explain why, in the darkest of times, many thousands of Phoenician mothers and fathers in Carthage promised to sacrifice their unborn children to an unknowable being.

Throughout the Bronze Age, another society further to the south had gathered around its own idea of animism, on a much larger scale than we've seen before. The ancient Egyptians were the grandest of all in terms of ascribing animism to everything, combining fertility, cosmology and polytheism to create an engine of staggering wealth and power in the Nile Valley. While the early Britons were constructing Stonehenge, Egypt's pharaohs built the Great Pyramids of Giza and the Valleys of the Kings and Queens, using a vast hierarchical social structure which they reigned over as gods on earth.

Just as the Aegean Sea states were teetering on the edge of decline, the ancient Egyptian empire's New Kingdom reached the peak of its power. The world's first nation-state, it controlled the territories from modern Egypt to the northern Sinai peninsula and the land of Canaan all the way to Lebanon. The ancient Egyptians did their best to crush all resistance to their rule, and had a voracious appetite for slaves: to fight their wars and to build their monuments, tombs and impressive national infrastructure.

For the pharaohs, birth and rebirth (or regeneration) were central tenets of their religion, which was dominated by the life cycle of the Nile. There is even a specific hieroglyph for the act of childbirth.[30] The goddess Isis, considered the divine mother of the pharaohs, is depicted giving birth in numerous friezes and murals of the New Kingdom, typically attended by two women or fellow goddesses, one before and one behind her for support. She births on a stool, rather than lying down, and the baby is then placed on a birthing brick.

Hieroglyph depicting childbirth in Kom Obo Temple, Egypt, 180–47 BCE

Birthing bricks are a source of great contention among historians. Magical or symbolic unfired clay bricks were used throughout ancient Egypt for various rituals, including bricking up tombs.[31] Birthing bricks, known as *meskhenut* after the goddess–protector of the birthing chamber Meskhenet, were known only through obscure mentions in texts until 2001, when a party from the Penn Museum uncovered one in the excavation of the mayoral residence at South Abydos in Upper Egypt.

The top of the birthing brick depicts a mother and her newborn child sitting on a throne, assisted by two women and further decorated with images of the fertility goddess Hathor, who watches over the scene. Its sides are painted with ivory wands and symbols associated with the birth of the god Re, meant to ward off evil from the child.[32] The *meskhenut* may have been placed at the four corners of the birthing chamber, or used to support the mother as she gave birth, or as a sort of warm, magical platform to lay the new arrival on while the umbilical cord was cut and the placenta (which is thought to have been considered an organ of incredible power and significance) was dealt with safely. They may have served as all three but, given the size and the fact that they don't look particularly comfortable, the last of the possibilities seems the most likely. There would be no need to create an unstable support of unfired bricks when a squatting stool, as seen in Egyptian friezes, was available. The mystery of the birthing bricks is a small part of the greater mystery of Egyptian beliefs and practices, and of the surreal nature of perfection and the 'ideal' they sought to portray to their vast empire.

The pharaohs associated themselves and their gods deeply and symbolically with the fertility cycle of the Nile. This fertility, however, was not reflected in their own lineages because they favoured marriage within the family, including father–daughter and brother–sister unions. The justification for their rapacious inbreeding was that Horus, the deity to whom all the pharaohs traced their ancestry, was the son of Osiris, the god of the earth (the Nile Valley), who married his own sister Isis, the goddess of rebirth and motherhood. There were also 'double-niece' marriages among the pharaohs, where a brother and sister married, and then the father in turn married their daughter. It did not take very long for this to cause problems.

The discovery of the tomb of the young pharaoh Tutankhamun in the Valley of the Kings in 1922 caused a worldwide sensation. Unlike so many tombs, it had not been significantly looted and contained over 5,000 items that Tutankhamun might need in the afterlife. His body was entombed in a gold sarcophagus. An autopsy conducted on his mummy showed he was only 19 years old when he died. He had a cleft hard palate but probably not a cleft lip, and he had scoliosis of the spine and bone necrosis, which meant his left foot turned in as if clubbed. He had suffered bouts of malaria, and probably died of complications following a break to his already damaged leg.[33] Tutankhamun was far from the ideal the pharaohs sought to portray.

Inside the sarcophagus with him were the mummies of two tiny foetuses. Although they show no signs of skeletal deformity, it seems that his wife and half-sister Ankhesenamun would have miscarried when she was around seven months pregnant. They are, we think, Tutankhamun's stillborn daughters.[34] The fact that he was buried with the children he had lost suggests that he wished to journey with them into the afterlife, perhaps to have the time together they never did in life.

The only known 'pregnant mummy' was discovered in 2016 during radiological research on an ancient Egyptian male's sarcophagus found in the royal tomb complex at Luxor, now residing in the National Museum of Warsaw. She was probably placed in the tomb complex by nineteenth-century looters who routinely replaced the mummies found inside grander sarcophagi with 'better' or more interesting mummies – in this instance, a woman mummified with her unborn child, found partially descended into the lower pelvis, aged between 26 and 30 weeks. It's likely that she died in labour, but the baby never left her body, even after death.[35]

What distinguishes Egyptian attitudes to pregnancy from other cultures at the time is that, as these burials suggest, importance was placed not only on a successful birth but also on the foetus. In fact, we know of the mummification of a foetus of approximately 18 weeks' gestation, in a tiny cedarwood sarcophagus measuring just 17 inches in length. It was carved and decorated in a manner indicating a high-status object, but the sarcophagus was believed to be purely decorative until the University of Cambridge Zoology Department conducted a CT scan and found that it contained a small, well-formed but probably miscarried foetus, carefully preserved with its arms crossed over its chest.[36] The body had not undergone the traditional process of organ removal and embalming; it had simply been swaddled in bandages and placed in the sarcophagus, which was then filled with molten black resin and sealed shut, never to be opened again. By preparing this child for an afterlife when it had only just developed clearly delineated fingers and toes, they showed that they believed that life did not begin with the first breath but with the mystery of the generation of life itself.

The pharaohs were figureheads: intriguing but, like the rulers of any nation-state, not representative of the rest of society. At Deir el-Medina, the Valley of the Workers (a settlement built for artisans and workers labouring on the pharaohs' tombs) lies just a short walk from the entrance to the Valley of the Kings at Luxor. Fortunately, there are many surviving accounts of the daily lives of artisans and middle classes who lived there while they built, administrated and propped up the vast wealth of ancient Egypt. Some of the more illuminating texts were written not on their tablets and papyri but on their bodies. In 2014 archaeologists discovered a female mummy with over 30 tattoos on her neck, shoulders, arms, back and hips. Tattooing in ancient Egypt was rare, although it was common in Nubia (Egypt's neighbour and sometime ally, colony and occupier) which at the time ruled over parts of what is now Ethiopia and Sudan. More importantly, until this discovery the only ancient tattoos that had been found, whether depicted on figurines or found on preserved bodies, were dots, lines or chevron patterns, whose meaning is unclear. But the Deir el-Medina mummy bears not only the patterns of snakes, lines and dots familiar from prehistory and Nubia but also Egyptian symbols including the eye of Horus (or the *wadjet* eye) and a seated baboon on either side of her neck.

The hamadryas baboon, seated, represented the moon god Thoth and symbolized the menstrual cycle. The ancient Egyptians also associated Thoth closely with the opium poppy, once again linking opium, the best analgesic available at the time, to women's reproduction.[37] All the tattoos except one, a lotus blossom in the small of her back, were designed to be seen publicly, had she worn the traditional dress of her time.

The presence of a temple to Hathor, the Egyptian cow–goddess of fertility, indicates that the Valley of the Workers was not only a quasi-dormitory for those labouring on the Valley of the Kings but also a spiritual home and community for its inhabitants. As the woman had the eye of Horus tattooed on her throat, a symbol translating as 'one that is sound' but also more widely symbolizing healing and rebirth, she may have been a healer or fertility priestess. Another woman discovered at Deir el-Medina had the dwarf god of fertility Bes tattooed on her thighs, but the density of tattoos on the woman with the eye of Horus on her throat suggests her importance to this community, where academic consensus has agreed that there was only one 'wise woman' active at any given time, accompanied by an apprentice.[38] Egyptian beliefs, like those of most Mesopotamians, were rooted in practical superstitions and the use of chants and spells, so it's possible that her throat tattoo gave her voice a special ritual power. She died young of unknown causes when she was only around 25–34, at a time when many other women in her community would have lived to over 50.

There is one female physician who lived during the building of the great pyramids, around 2500 BCE, who we know about because her name and profession were recorded on her son's tomb door in Saqqara: Peseshet, the Overseer of Female Physicians. Women like Peseshet were not the local wise women but respected professionals. Her son Akhethotep was a royal official, so his mother was firmly embedded in the literate elite classes.[39] The tomb door, however, leaves us with as many questions as it does answers. Who were the female physicians she oversaw? Who and what did they treat?

The 'professional' middle class of Peseshet and the tattooed priestess also left the world's first specific gynaecological text, the Kahun Medical Papyrus, which dates from 1825 BCE. It contains 34 paragraphs of advice that most doctors today would not recommend following, and it diagnoses almost every female complaint as being that of 'the womb'. The examination of a woman 'whose eyes are aching till she cannot see, on top of aches in her neck', which sounds like a migraine, leads to the conclusion that she must have 'discharges of the womb in her eyes'. This is treated by 'fumigating her with incense and fresh oil, fumigating her womb with it, and fumigating her eyes with goose leg fat. You should have her eat a fresh ass's liver.'[40] While fumigating her womb can't have helped, perhaps the liver at least provided some welcome nutrition. Only one examination, which sounds like a prolapse, correctly points to genuine involvement of the womb itself. It is treated by the pouring of oil, although on which part of the body is not identified. The papyrus also recommends putting a clove of garlic in your vagina before bed, and if your breath smells of garlic the next morning, it means well for the pregnancy. If not, it bodes ill.[41] The papyrus is also notable, however, for the first use of the term 'wandering womb' (Col, Lines 5-8), a term that would haunt women in various guises for another two millennia.

The immaculate record-keeping of the workers of Deir el-Medina also includes intriguing entries for absence known as *hsmn*, meaning menstruation. A set of tablets written in the reign of Ramses II cover a 280-day period in which ten prominent workmen took 'sick days' owing to *hsmn*. As men do not menstruate, this is something of a puzzle. The meaning is clarified, however, by the scribe Qenhikhopshef's fuller entry for Day 23 – he was absent due to his wife 'having her menses'.[42] That winter the foreman of the works, Neferhotep, also took time off for his daughter's period. Historians over the past century concluded that this must mean that the Egyptians thought that the menstruating body was 'unclean', but this is just speculation. There are ancient Nubian customs still found in modern Ethiopia and Sudan which warn that menstruating or pregnant women should not enter cemeteries. Perhaps it was not the women who were unclean but the workers. Rather than fearing that the husband of a menstruating woman might bring pollution to the sacred Valley of the Kings, the male workers may have been asserting their right not to 'take their work home with them'. To do so might have brought death into their homes at a time when the women in their family were vulnerable.

The elites of any society leave monuments, art and literature behind for us to find that aim to portray their patrons as somewhat superhuman, but the poor rarely leave any trace of their existence at all. It is only relatively recently that their lives began to be recorded for statistical purposes. So it is no surprise that it is from the written records of the middle classes of ancient Egypt that we learn about the first known pregnancy test, written around 1350 BCE, in the medical text known as the Berlin Papyrus. It states: 'Barley [and] wheat, let the woman water [them] with her urine every day with dates [and] the sand, in two bags. If they [both] grow, she will bear. If the barley grows, it means a male child. If the wheat grows, it means a female child. If both do not grow, she will not bear at all.' Remarkably, this theory was tested in 1963 and found to be accurate in 70 per cent of cases, although the success of gender determination was not recorded.[43] The tests have even been repeated subsequently at various intervals up until 2018 and have correctly identified 70–85 per cent of pregnant participants.[44]

WHEN IN DOUBT, ASK THE RABBI

During the reign of Ramesses VI, around 1300 BCE, something happened which tore apart these powerful civilizations. The Egyptians, Minoans and Mycenaeans – from whom we learn so much about what it was like to conceive, carry and give birth to a child when the world's first cities were still new – mysteriously collapsed or grew dangerously unstable. Although there are conflicting theories about the causes of this widespread crisis, it was undeniably a period of great change. Egypt was weakened but survived, while the Minoans and Mycenaeans abandoned their settlements and palaces – only the Phoenicians found a way to thrive amid the chaos. As this 'Dark Age' descended on the Mediterranean, new religions appeared on the scene to provide, if not hope, then at least routine and community.

It was at this time that the Semitic religions were either coalescing steadily into Judaism and the belief in one absolute god or falling by the wayside. Another monotheistic belief, system and perhaps the oldest of them all, Zoroastrianism, was flourishing in what is now Iran and northern India, where the ultimate god was represented on earth by the Persian kings. Hinduism and Jainism were also thriving, as were Confucianism, Buddhism and Shintoism. For the most part, these religions were led by men, both mortal and immortal. From now on, female deities would be relegated to secondary and often ambiguous figures.

Religion offers stability. It offers a framework, rules to be obeyed, communities to be a part of. There is safety in numbers, and protection from harm. There is also the temptation of eternal life, a better life and perhaps a perfect afterlife. Almost all established religions across the world share the same basic characteristics: a male founding deity, a creation myth, a flawed humanity which enrages said deity, a Great Flood and a hero who saves the day (and the animals) and repropagates the earth with his progeny after earning forgiveness. Shintoism is the only established religion in the world without a flood myth, which in the nineteenth century the Japanese administration took as definitive proof of their superiority – they never made their gods angry enough to deserve such a myth.

The peoples of the ancient world were becoming increasingly mobile in response to the climatic changes and wars that characterized this tumultuous period, forming new settlements and societies. The Elamites of Iran, relatively unaffected by the upheavals that rocked other regional powers, traded with Africa and Asia and were absorbed into what was becoming Persia. Elamite urban settlements in Susa (now the modern town of Shush), a large city in the foothills of the Zagros Mountains, have yielded thousands of broken female figurines piled up in the streets against the walls of houses. The figures, naked except for a girdle, and with hands cupping their breasts, represent the female body in the three trimesters of pregnancy. Elamite tradition recommended that, to prevent miscarriage, a woman in her early pregnancy should tie red thread around her ankles. The slimmest of the naked figurines also wear red threads on both ankles.

There was also an Elamite charm that women used to judge the progress of their pregnancy. When she suspected she might be pregnant, a Susan woman would buy a ready-made talisman knotted necklace from a wise woman. After 100 days had passed since her last period, she could begin to untie the knots on the necklace, marking the time until there were no more knots to untie, indicating her body was 'unknotted' and ready to give birth.[45]

The figurines for the second stage of pregnancy are heavier and more obviously gravid, and those that represent the third and last stage of the pregnancy feature very wide hips like the prehistoric Venus figurines. They also show the first known depiction of the *linea nigra*, the line of hyperpigmentation that forms vertically on the abdomen of 90 per cent of women in the latter part of pregnancy.

All the figurines were discovered smashed and had been placed either outside homes on the street or in temples and public buildings as votive offerings. The most recent modern scholarship posits the theory that these figurines, like the talisman necklace, were purchased ready-made and that, when a woman passed each stage of pregnancy, she would shatter the figurine and keep part of it in or against the wall of her house as an offering of both gratitude and supplication. Elamite tradition regarded the body, and the female body in particular, as a house or household, so to keep this record of a pregnancy close to their walls would be holding onto their beliefs.[46]

The Hittites were another distinct Anatolian people soon to be absorbed into the wider population of what is now modern Turkey and the Levant. They were perhaps the oldest tribe of the region, with a language that was still rooted in the earliest Indo-European language family. Inclined to war with their neighbours, replenishing the population was central to their social codes so they observed strong traditions regarding fertility, conception and birth. Popular curses included wishing sterility on an enemy or a betrayer. Their recipe for successful childbirth was simple but effective: a birthing stool for the mother with 'pegs' for her to hang on to during labour, cushions, blankets and a midwife. For some cultures, as we shall see, the father plays a hugely important supportive role during childbirth, but not for the Hittites: the father was not to be present at the birth.[47]

Of all the ancient religions of the Bronze Age, Judaism emerged as one of the most stable. Jewish religious texts, composed of the Torah as dictated by God to Moses on Mount Sinai, and the accompanying texts (collectively known as the Talmud) written later by rabbis (or teachers), who alone could help with their interpretation, set out a pattern for establishing religions that has been perpetuated ever since. Judaism, as one of the oldest faiths in existence, gives valuable insights not only into what people believed but into how they and others lived in the ancient world.

It is in these additional interpretations by rabbis, rather than the Torah itself, that we find the most important teachings of early Judaism concerning pregnancy and childbirth. The Talmud is the result of almost a millennium of study and experience by rabbinical scholars, who observed the formation of the Jewish faith in their communities and responded to various crises. Large trichinosis outbreaks among the swine population of the Near East, for instance, may explain some of the prohibitions of *kashrut,* or a kosher diet and lifestyle. Broad swathes of the rabbinical teachings deem things 'clean' or 'unclean'. Clean is the ideal, unclean is the reality. It has been proven by analysing zooarchaeological remains of fish from 30 Judaean sites in the southern Levant from 1550–540 BCE that eating scaleless fish such as catfish was not uncommon, despite the rabbinical writers legislating against it.[48]

Alongside strict rules regarding diet, there are strict rules about when observant married Jews should and should not have sex. Menstruation makes a woman unclean or *niddah*, and so she cannot be touched until she takes a ritual baptism bath known as the *mikveh*, which will render her cleansed and ready for intercourse. The correct time for the *mikveh* bath is deemed to be seven 'clean' days after her period finishes, which at approximately

12 days into the menstrual cycle is when a healthy woman in a regular cycle will be ovulating and at her most fertile. The rules laid out by men deeming when women are sexually clean or unclean do, in fact, facilitate a strict cycle of abstinence and intercourse that optimizes the chances of conception. This is just one example of how rabbinical rules, while having conservative ideas about sexuality, can be remarkably specific regarding subjects such as the acceptable use of contraception, abortion and even embryology.

The rabbis were not dealing in absolute truths – they were dealing with people existing in cosmopolitan societies with complex social and cultural situations, particularly when urban settlements were concerned. The rules aided disease prevention practically through frequent washing, suppression of prostitution to quell venereal disease, precautionary isolation to protect either an individual or the wider community and procedures for disinfecting or cleansing a diseased home or person. Gonorrhoea, for example, was dealt with in a straightforward manner in the Book of Leviticus: 'Speak to the Israelite people and say to them: When any man has a discharge issuing from his member, he is impure' (Lev. 15.2–13).

Healthcare was central to this framework, both of the individual and of the communal body, but, uniquely, the term 'doctor' or 'physician' was never adopted by the rabbis of this period, as God was deemed the only true healer.[49] This did not stop the writers of the rabbinical teachings absorbing knowledge from the foreign communities among which they found themselves. The Talmud even features an Akkadian vade mecum, or handbook, with treatments and recipes for blindness, nosebleeds and migraines.[50]

The Talmud does, however, appoint the titles of *rofe*, which was similar to the role of a general practitioner now, and *rofe umman*, meaning a surgeon. There are no mentions of female Jewish healers, and the only Hebrew midwives specifically named are Shifra and Puah, who were said to have attended labouring women during the time of Moses and to have defied the Pharaoh's orders to kill the newborn males.[51] As the Cradle of Civilization emerged from its 500-year Dark Age, the Jewish *rofes* became sought after, skilled not only in general healing but also in diagnosis and pharmacology.

Rabbinical teachings on embryology, in particular, are far more advanced than those of the ancient Egyptians. Passages debating the length of time necessary for a woman to be 'clean' after a miscarriage indicate that the rabbis debating this particular subject were familiar with stages of the development of the embryo and with the steps necessary for preparing a miscarried embryo or foetus for examination to further their knowledge. Jewish physicians worked on the aborted offspring of animals in their quest for knowledge, but some of their findings are incorrect: they believed, for example, that it is possible to identify the gender of a human embryo at 40 days' growth, which is not the case. Their accurate description of the nascent forming of eyes and limbs is, however, remarkable.

The rabbinical teachings also note that a foetus was formed of seed from the mother and father equally. They thought the eighth month was the most dangerous for a baby, and the tenth month the safest to deliver. Now, we accept that human gestation is nine months, but the rabbis were working according to their strict rules for marital copulation, and thus the ideal moment for pregnancy was ten lunar months or 295 days from the first day of the last menstruation, which would mean a slightly overdue and heavier baby. Unlike in ancient Egypt, the child was not considered a living entity until it had drawn its first independent breath, before which it was a part of the mother's body.

Untethered in an uncertain world, the Judaeans found strength in numbers, community and their faith, and they remain unique in introducing the first debates about the science of embryology. Their story in the history of childbirth is far from over. But now Greece was finally emerging from half a millennium of war and chaos and entering its golden age. A new era of communication and innovation, of medicine and science, was on the horizon.

THE CONCEPTION OF THE CLASSICAL: GREECE IS REBORN

The revival of Greece is marked by the writings of the poet known as Homer in the eighth century BCE. Homer's epics, the *Iliad* and the *Odyssey*, portray a courageous masculine society obsessed by war, whose women have to rely on guile and cunning to mask their weakness. This obsession with machismo grew from the five hundred years of chaos Greece endured after the collapse of the Minoans and Mycenaeans. As they regrouped, the Greeks kept the best of all the myths, legends and traditions that had survived from their history alive and incorporated some new gods and rites from the surrounding nations too. They regained their strong trade routes, love of luxury goods and natural air of superiority. The society they fashioned functioned on the civic understanding that the gods represented one 'ideal' aspect of Greek life, but the reality was childbirth, sores, venereal disease and communal lavatories, as well as haemorrhoids and the strong possibility of early death.

This contradiction is summed up neatly by Delos, a tiny island in the Cyclades archipelago thought to be the birthplace of Apollo. From the fifth century BCE, it was forbidden to die on Delos, to prevent death from befouling such a sacred site. It was also forbidden to have sex in a temple, unless it was a temple sanctified for such use, or to void the bladder or bowels. All these rules were rendered unworkable by the fact that Delos was also one of the main trading hubs of the resurgent Greek empire, importing the strange and ignorant, as well as the diseased and incurable with every tide. It's unlikely that no one was dying or defecating there.

The 'new' Greeks were relaxed when it came to sexual inhibitions, and same-sex relationships were common for both men and women. Superiority in the sexual dynamic was established by the dominant partner, who penetrated the submissive partner and was therefore thought to be more powerful than them. The upper classes rarely chose their own spouses, but the permissive attitudes to extramarital relationships made this of less consequence than it was in more illiberal societies. Husband and wife joined together for the sake of bearing legitimate children within the bonds of marriage, and to form an *oikos* (household), which according to Aristotle, the Greek philosopher and polymath, was the basic social, economic and political building block of Classical-era Greece.[52]

While Athens must have been a majestic sight, there can be no question that it was stifling for women, who were discouraged from being seen on the streets unaccompanied by a man. When marrying for dynastic purposes, women usually wed between the ages of 18 and 20, and men on average were a decade older. Outside the cities and towns, it seems likely that Greek procreation and marital traditions continued as they had in the earlier ages – the young couple would have had more of a choice in who and when they married. The one place where women had more rights than in the rest of Greece was Sparta, but not much is known of the customs and rituals surrounding Spartan childbirth. We are told that one of the founding statesmen of Sparta, a possibly mythical figure called Lycurgus, encouraged women to run, wrestle and throw javelins because he believed that it would make childbirth easier for them.

Hippocrates of Kos is often referred to as the 'Father of Medicine'. The Hippocratic Corpus, consisting of approximately 60 texts attributed to him, is now accepted to have been the work of multiple writers of the Hippocratic school of thought. Of these, ten treatises are concerned with women and reproduction, including *Diseases of Women I* and *II*, *Barren Women*, *Nature of Women*, *Generation* and *The Nature of the Child*. They contain a lot of holistic healthcare we would regard as common sense today, but they also include the first introduction of humourism, which posited that the human system was made up of the four humours: black bile, yellow bile, blood and phlegm. Hippocrates believed that illness occurred when the humours were unbalanced. This idea persisted in the West for centuries, perhaps because balance and moderation are essential to good health – although obviously humourism itself would eventually be proved incorrect.

Moreover, Hippocrates promoted the Egyptian theory of the 'wandering womb', depicting the uterus as an untethered organ that could migrate around the body, causing hysteria and other diseases such as prolapse and uterine cancer. The Hippocratic writers also distinguished between two types of women: the woman of experience and the 'shy and modest woman who lacks experience'.[53] A doctor of the Hippocratic school would attend a pregnant patient and ask her to inform him of what was wrong with her (whether she was shy or experienced), so he could then consult the appropriate recipe and instruct a root digger or *rhizotomoi* to collect the necessary ingredients, which would be dispensed to the woman in charge of her household so she could prepare the medicine. These recipes could include ingredients such as a 'putrid woman's urine' and 'titurate of beaver testes'.[54] Opium is prescribed as a medicine 21 times in the gynaecological tracts of the Hippocratic corpus, indicating the drug's importance to the female reproductive cycle.

Aristotle had some reasonably sound ideas regarding pregnancy. He prioritized the healthy environment offered by a healthy womb for creating the ideal offspring, although he did believe that said ideal offspring was male and would resemble its father. Aristotle also thought that semen acted on menstrual blood to assemble a foetus in the manner of a somewhat gory, cellular Lego kit.[55] He was continually preoccupied with the best way to have a male child and tailored his theories accordingly. He wrote: 'As a general rule women who are pregnant of a male child escape comparatively easily and retain a comparatively healthy look, but it is otherwise with those whose infant is female; for these latter look as a rule paler and suffer more pain.'[56] His high status as one of the great Classical philosophers meant that his theories, however strange, carried weight and persisted into the Renaissance.

Herophilus of Chalcedon was one of the earliest anatomists, along with his assistant Erasistratus of Ceos. Herophilus spent most of his life in Alexandria, which was more progressive than Athens. It was there that he began to dissect human corpses, laying the foundations of what would become the study of anatomy and physiology. The Ptolemaic rulers of Alexandria were determined to transform the city into a crucible of learning, encouraging the finest minds from across Europe, such as the mathematician Euclid, to come and study in the legendary Museum and Library they established there.

Later Roman historians asserted that Herophilus and Erasistratus dissected the corpses of executed criminals handed over to them by the authoritarian Ptolemaic state, and even conducted vivisections on living felons in order to establish the nature of the circulatory system. Whether his subjects were alive at the time or not, Erasistratus did identify the heart not as the seat of thoughts and feelings but as a pump that serviced the movement of blood around the body. He distinguished the differences between veins and arteries, determined that the nervous system was what gave us 'animism' and was against bloodletting, at a time when, thanks to Hippocrates and Aristotle, bloodletting was the answer to almost every medical problem.[57]

Herophilus, meanwhile, was busy identifying the ventricles of the brain, the difference between motor and sensory nerves, the membranes of the human eye and the function of heart valves. Crucially, he also documented the functional anatomy of male and female reproductive organs, discovering the ovaries and the ligaments and tubes which ensure that the womb does not, in fact, 'wander' at all.[58]

The destruction of the Library of Alexandria and the rule of Julius Caesar marked a turning point in Classical history. The primary texts of both Herophilus and Erasistratus were lost, and we rely on the writings of later Greek and Roman scholars to record their achievements. While the Greeks were far from done, the Roman empire was on the rise and soon to rule vast tracts of Europe, North Africa and the Near East through masculine military might and brutal taxation. Moreover, a new religion was coming, one that promised women one thing but ended up delivering an entirely new reality for them: Christianity.

3

Darkness Falls

In the first century BCE, Alis discovered she was pregnant. She wrote a letter to her husband Hilarion, a Roman citizen who had travelled to Alexandria for work, to tell him the news. Although her words have not survived the long journey into the modern world, we do have Hilarion's brisk, affectionate yet shocking reply:

> I send you warmest greetings. I want you to know that we are still in Alexandria. And please don't worry ... I beg you and entreat you to take care of the child and if I receive my pay soon, I will send it to you. If you have a baby before I return, if it is a boy, let it live; if it is a girl, expose it.[1]

The instructions Alis received from her husband are hard for us to fathom. She would have to wait out her pregnancy, feeling her body grow and change, not knowing whether – at the end of it all – she would have to take the baby out to some secluded spot and abandon her to almost certain death.

The ancient Greeks were preoccupied with fears of overpopulation and its resultant strain on scarce resources, an anxiety that we can read in the great Greek philosopher and naturalist Aristotle, whose dark views on the exposure of newborns can easily shock readers today. He also seemed to believe that some foreign women could easily bear five children in one pregnancy. He wrote, 'such an occurrence has been witnessed on several occasions. There was once upon a time a woman who had twenty children at four births, each time she had five, and most of them grew up.'[2] Like many outlandish ideas about women's bodies, this fantasy tells us more about the culture that produced it than about any biological reality.

The Romans, however, intent on building a civilization founded on slavery, taxation and military might, had no such qualms about their booming population. In fact, they required constant human toil to secure expansion. While their views on exposure were somewhat different from those of the Greeks, there is no doubt they practised the custom, as evidenced by Hilarion's instructions. The Romans were happy to have an excess of healthy male children who could one day labour under the empire, but they had less use for girls or any boys born with birth defects. The Romans were not the first civilization to express a preference for sons over daughters: many ancient societies had special diets, prayers or gymnastic sexual positions meant to ensure the birth of a boy, but the Romans took to it in the same way they did many other things: with brutal efficiency.

THE POWER OF THE *DOMUS*

The patrician voices of the Roman empire's senators, philosophers, poets and generals still dominate our perceptions of Rome. This can make it difficult to imagine what life was like for all the ordinary women like the woman who opened this chapter, Alis, who would have gone about their days with autonomy, respected by their families and their communities.

Roman society was, after all, obsessed with the concept of the family. The household unit was called the *domus*. Every domus was controlled by the *paterfamilias* (the most senior man in the household) and operated on the basis of a strict hierarchy. The *domus* referred to all those under the control and protection of the *paterfamilias*, which included his staff and slaves, as well as blood relations. The *domus* was more than just a family. It was a miniature, self-contained enterprise, striving for solidity and success, in which women played a vital part.

All the rights and obligations of Roman citizens were inscribed in the Twelve Tables of Rome, which placed particular importance on the seemingly endless responsibilities of the *paterfamilias*. The origins of the Twelve Tables remain disputed, but they formed the framework for what it meant to be, or to become, Roman, beyond the barriers of ethnicity or geography.

There is another way of seeing this document, however. The Twelve Tables also represent the moment when legal and societal power passed completely into the hands of men and their male offspring. We can see this even in the families of the emperors themselves – intricate adoption laws within the Tables encouraged the adoption of a male heir in case of a barren marriage in order to keep the *domus*, if not the bloodline, intact, particularly among the patrician elite. Augustus adopted Tiberius; Claudius adopted Nero; and Caesar adopted his great-nephew Octavian as his heir before his assassination.

For women the situation was very different. From the moment a girl was born, adopted or purchased, she passed into the care of the *paterfamilias* until she was of marriageable age, when she could be placed into the custody of her husband, who would be chosen for her by the *paterfamilias*. There were two kinds of marriage for Roman women: *cum manu* (by which she became the legal responsibility of her husband) and *sine manu* (by which, even after marriage, she remained the legal responsibility of her *paterfamilias*). Other lives were possible for a very few. Today in Rome you can walk through a ruin that represents a very different life for some women – the House of the Vestal Virgins. Selected from a few elite families each year, only the Vestal Virgins were legally independent from the direct control of a male relative. The girls were chosen before puberty and served only the constantly burning, purifying flame of the virgin goddess Vesta, which sat in a brazier in the temple. According to the Roman historian Livy, the Vestal Virgins were held sacred because Romulus and Remus, the legendary founders of Rome, had been born to one of the sisterhood. This was an extraordinary position of power and status, yet it came with a cost. In the rare event that a Vestal Virgin was found to have broken her vow of chastity she was entombed alive as punishment. This was ostensibly to allow her a 'clean' and bloodless death, although the reality must have felt very different.

Elite Roman women might not have been entombed alive, but their roles in public life were severely limited. Outside the *domus*, they functioned principally as heiresses and, upon marriage, benefactors. Ordinary women held more practical roles, such as shop owners, prostitutes and, of course, midwives – but their lives in the empire go virtually unrecorded. Outside of urban centres, Marcus Cato records in his *De agri cultura* the duties he felt a woman must perform to create the Roman pastoral idyll:

> she must be neat herself and keep the farmstead neat and clean. She must clean and tidy the hearth every night before she goes to bed ... pray to the household gods as opportunity occurs ... She must keep a supply of cooked food on hand for you and the servants. She must keep many hens and have plenty of eggs.

Cato also believed that excess 'wine-bibbing' by a wife was grounds for divorce.[3]

Above all, the Roman wife was responsible for the health of the *domus*. This broad term encompassed the physical health and well-being of all its members as well as the management of the household economy. In a large household it would have been quite the burden, represented by the wearing of the female equivalent of the patrician *toga*, the *stola*: a long, sleeveless dress of plain wool expected of the elite wife, symbolizing her simplicity and modesty despite the wealth and prosperity of her *domus*. The role of the Roman wife is clearly defined in law, but also in the *mos maiorum* (the accepted customs or standards, from which we take the word 'mores'). These included fidelity, piety, virtue and discipline in daily dealings.

Roman villas contained common areas such as the *atrium*, but also the *andron*, or male chamber, and the *gynaeceum*, the female chamber. The *gynaeceum* was a place for women's activities and occupations, such as weaving but also childbirth. Many Greek and Roman writers advised against pregnant women weaving, returning to old superstitions of 'knots' causing a difficult birth, yet it was a valuable economic activity that heavily pregnant women could still be engaged in and would have provided space and time for women to discuss their pregnancies and health together. So it's likely that women ignored the advice of male scholars and carried on weaving throughout their pregnancy. Unfortunately, textiles are as fragile as papyrus and much less likely to be copied, recorded and preserved by historians, so there are very few examples of the kind of tapestries and cloths these women would have spun. What little has survived, usually from the final centuries of Roman domination, is vivid, with bright colours and intricate geometric patterns.

Greek vases from the sixth century BCE, before the rise of Rome, show suggestive scenes of nubile young women with a heron or crane, harking back to the prehistoric imagery of the slim white bird figurines as a symbol of fertility.[4] Some believe that these erotic vases would have decorated the *gynaeceum*, along with other fertility motifs, such as acanthus leaves and scenes of women and children talking and playing together. This all suggests a complex and animated dynamic overseen by women, taking place within the privacy of the home.

The cornerstones of health were diet, regime, medicine and surgery. Of these four, only surgery was theoretically outside the remit of women – diet and regime were well within their control. Tending to the health of the *domus* would have involved running errands both within and outside the home. Women would need the advice of a physician and a pharmacist to mix the medicines he prescribed, since Roman physicians rarely deigned to do it themselves. If the physician prescribed a blend of local plants and roots, the pharmacist himself would often rely on a root-digger. The role of these *rhizotomoi* remained cloaked in superstition and secrecy. They were associated with the gathering of hemlock, henbane, belladonna and mandrake, which could be pain-killing soporifics but (like opium) could also be, in sufficient quantity, used as poisons.[5] The root-diggers guarded their profession with the germination of such legends as the mandrake (a psychotropic easily recognizable by its forked root and human-like torso), which killed anyone who uprooted it – the task of digging it up was therefore given to an unfortunate dog. After the handler had made three circles around the mandrake root with a sword and then dug around it facing west, and recited some aphrodisiac chants, he would retreat and summon the dog. The dog would pull up the root and fall down dead, after which the mandragora could be touched without danger. This lengthy performance no doubt added handsomely to the cost of the medication by the time it reached the domus.[6]

All the plants above contain compounds which ease pain, but we don't know which ones women would have used to relieve the pain of labour. Opium was such a common panacea for all pain that it is likely that women took it during childbirth. Medicines were used not only to alleviate the pain of birth but also to prevent it happening in the first place. It is during this period that intriguing evidence for the first oral anti-fertility drugs emerges. This would certainly have fallen under the remit of the matriarch of the *domus*, both for herself and for those in her care. There were, of course, circumstances where a pregnancy would not be welcome – if they undermined the established hierarchy of the household or a girl's marriage potential, for instance.

Childbirth scene, Ostia Antica, Roman, 400 BCE–300 CE

We call these drugs 'anti-fertility' because the ancient Romans would not have been able to discriminate accurately between a contraceptive and a very early-term abortifacient (a drug that induces abortion). The earliest and most famous of these drugs is *silphion*, a product of the North African Greek city-state of Cyrene. It was so prized that its image took pride of place on Cyrene's coinage, but it was over-harvested and became extinct by the second century BCE. The closest surviving relative of *silphion* is thought to be giant wild fennel. When *silphion* disappeared, other herbal anti-fertility drugs came to take its place. Some of these are still in use today and are effective (though not foolproof) in preventing conception or continuation of a pregnancy. They include *Artemisia* or wormwood, myrrh (also used as a traditional oral contraceptive in Indian rural medicine), pennyroyal and rue, which remained commonplace in Europe into the Middle Ages, and the wild carrot, which is still used as a 'morning-after' safeguard by women as far apart as the Appalachian Mountains of North America and Rajasthan in northern India.[7]

The Romans had absorbed much of Greek learning about health and medicine. Many favoured the Hippocratic school and the theory of the four humours, but others preferred an empirical approach. Galen was a Greek polymath who came to Rome to practise as a physician in 162 CE and thus had a foothold in both Greek tradition and the emergent Roman medical school of thought. He practised animal vivisection to understand the circulatory system better, which is why he did not endorse the notion of the 'wandering womb', having discovered it to be firmly tethered by tendons. He also drew on recipes for medicines from women such as Spendousa, Aquilia and Antiochis – all we know about them are their names – although none is for uniquely female complaints, which implies that these women were not midwives but practising physicians accustomed to treating a range of illnesses.[8] Galen was also inspired by the work of a male physician who had died about 30 years before Galen arrived in Rome – the unfortunately named author of the first book on gynaecology, Soranus of Ephesus.

THE *GYNAIKEIA:* THE ORIGINAL OBSTETRICS MANUAL

Soranus was said to have written the *Gynaikeia* based on his mother's teachings. Whether this is true or not, it is clearly the work of a physician sympathetic to the physical realities of pregnancy and birth. While debates still raged over whether men and women were even the same animal, Soranus was something of an outlier. He believed that women were not significantly different from men, aside from their capacity for childbirth and menstruation.[9] The *Gynaikeia* is packed with practical, useful information and quickly became hugely popular across the Graeco-Roman world, assisted by the fame of its great supporter Galen and the diligent work of other medical writers who copied it out.

In one of the more intriguing passages in the *Gynaikeia*, of which there are many, Soranus provides us with a list for what makes a good professional midwife. He insists that she must be 'free of superstition' and, most importantly, literate.[10] Not only must she be literate, but she must 'have her wits about her, possessed of a good memory, loving work, respectable and generally not unduly handicapped as regards her senses, sound of limb, robust, and, according to some people, endowed with long slim fingers and short nails at her fingertips'. He goes on to say that a midwife must also be trained in all branches of 'therapy (for some cases must be treated by diet, others by surgery, whilst still others must be cured by drugs)'.[11] It sounds like a demanding and respected profession.

The *Gynaikeia* is packed with snippets that reveal Soranus' extensive knowledge of the female body. He put the menarche at around 14 years old, was not entirely convinced about the validity of the hymen and was conscious that menstruation differed between women. He knew about gynaecological cancers (frequently only discovered during childbirth) and observed that women who had been raped were prone to 'heaviness in the abdomen'.[12] There is also advice on how to prevent stretch marks by applying olive oil and myrtle. The *Gynaikeia* contains the first recorded mention of *pica*:

the act of eating compulsively something not usually identified as food, or with no nutritional value, such as 'earth, charcoal, tendrils of the vine, unripe and acidic fruit'.[13] Towards the end of the first book of the *Gynaikeia* there is also a matter-of-fact discussion of unwanted pregnancy ('it is safer to prevent conception from taking place than to destroy the foetus'), and abortion is explained practically and dispassionately.[14]

Soranus explains how to destroy a full-term foetus stuck inside the womb or birth canal and endangering the life of the woman giving birth. In such cases, before C-sections were possible, the only hope of removing the obstructed foetus would have been to be to cut it up. He writes, 'It is better to have the abdomen [of the foetus] towards the orifice of the uterus; for after we have opened the abdomen and removed its contents, the body collapses and it becomes easy to change the position.' This gory and tragic description would, it is worth noting, have saved the lives of many women. Only three pages later he notes that sometimes there may be mental or emotional reasons for difficult labours, and that women struggling in such circumstances could be helped with an enema and by being encouraged to change birthing position. He offers terse advice on how to deliver the placenta ('Do not drag it') and, should the worst happen, details how to deal with a uterine prolapse.[15]

Soranus was, however, a proponent of supine delivery.[16] Supine delivery is a term used to describe giving birth lying down, on your back. It is a Graeco-Roman invention which still persists today, despite the fact that many women prefer to shift into a squat, or on all fours or even to remain constantly mobile, thus allowing gravity and contractions to work together rather than in opposition. Upon a successful birth, Soranus was inclined to leave the mother be, eschewing the smoke cleanses popular at the time.

The *Gynaikeia* is the first genuine obstetrics manual that combines acute observations of menstruating and pregnant women with a holistic approach to the problems women faced, both physical and mental. In that, it is remarkable. The survival of translations into Latin, including two originating in North Africa, indicates that during the Roman period it was the Soranic method that dominated.[17]

It is during the Roman period that more evidence for women practising medicine outside the home emerges. For a Graeco-Roman elite man like Soranus, who aspired towards general knowledge, the title of physician was something to be added to their repertoire in their quest to become polymaths, but for female medical practitioners it was a lofty, almost ludicrous, ambition. Yet some Roman women did achieve recognition as physicians, not only to other women but to all citizens. Gemina, a North African Roman woman who lived during the third century BCE, is commemorated in a memorial stone at Attiva Bibba that reads 'Saviour of all, through her medical art', and another memorial in Asia Minor paid homage to a woman, possibly called Domnina, as 'saviour of her fatherland'.[18] There is another tablet, now in the possession of the Vatican, dedicated to 'Valeria Berecunda, aged 34 years, 28 days, *iatromeia* [female doctor], of Rome, erected by her husband and daughter, for she was the best doctor in her quarter of Rome'. These dedications to extraordinary 'ordinary' women come from as far as the Appian Way, such as that of Empiria, aged 49, whose memorial was commissioned by her husband 'because of her medical skill' and that of Metilla Donata, *medica*, who demurs to memorialize her age, only saying that she *de sua pecuniadedit* (paid for it herself).[19] By the time of Julius Caesar, female physicians were held in such high regard that he decreed they become citizens and be exempt from taxes.

Most women who practised medicine, however, were like Valeria Berecunda and assumed the title *iatromaeae*, which meant a combination of physician and midwife. This indicates that they specialized in the treatment of women in general, not only the expectant or labouring. An *obstetrix* (*maia* in Greek), on the other hand, was a professional midwife who quite possibly acted as a helpmeet throughout the entirety of their patient's pregnancy rather than assisting only at the birth.[20]

Stele for a Roman medica (female physician) from the c. 200 CE.

In examining the world of the Roman *domus*, we look inwards, just as a pregnant woman often finds herself looking inwards and contemplating the inner workings of her body or reflecting on her own childhood, and the life to come. Meanwhile, the masculine focus of the Roman empire was forever gazing outwards towards the distant horizon in all directions. Rome's war machine was legendary. By the time of Julius Caesar, the empire stretched from western Europe to Asia and had begun trading with China through the silk roads of Han China, which were extending westward. Through these trade routes came medicines, spices, exotic foodstuffs and animals, precious metals, printed paper and, of course, silk.

Rome could not get enough of the pistachios and dates of Persia or African cloths and oils, but when silk arrived it created a sensation akin to a social upheaval. The commander and naturalist Pliny the Elder exclaimed: 'So manifold is the labour employed and so distant is the region of the globe drawn upon, to enable the Roman maiden to flaunt transparent clothing in public.'[21] These flimsy silk dresses were very different from the modest woollen stola of the *gynaeceum*.

Imperial Rome was a magnificent and perhaps unparalleled moment in history, if you were at the top of the heap. Unfortunately, as ever, for the elites to live in silk and eat spiced sweetmeats, whole populations had to live in servitude and slavery. General Pompey the Great captured Jerusalem for the Roman empire in 63 BCE, after a period of Jewish revolts. Rome, ever rapacious for yet more territory and taxation, turned Judah into a colony, and installed a client king, Herod, to keep things in order. It was into this disordered world that Jesus of Nazareth was born, probably somewhere between 6 BCE and 4 BCE.

AN IMMACULATE BIRTH

Few religions have been as fascinated with childbirth as Christianity. The exact date and year of Jesus' birth are unknown, but the Gospels of John and Luke (both written around a hundred years after his death) point towards late autumn, when shepherds were still living outside and watching their flocks, which they did traditionally from the Jewish festival of Passover until November, when the weather closed in.[22]

At this point, we are told that Mary had already survived a rocky start to motherhood. She had travelled to Bethlehem for the census after a somewhat curtailed *erusin* to Joseph (understood by later European translators as 'betrothal', although it was a legally binding arrangement that functioned as a preliminary before the start of cohabitation, the *missuin*), owing to an unexpected pregnancy. This meant a 90-mile walk from Nazareth to Bethlehem while heavily pregnant, after which she is thought to have given birth in a rock shelter in the overcrowded village. Despite all that, she managed to raise a healthy, if precocious, young man. The Gospels of both Matthew and Mark mention four 'brothers' of Jesus: James, Joses (a diminutive of Joseph), Simon and Jude, known as the *adelphoi*. The same gospels also mention an unknown and unnamed number of sisters.[23] However, the question of whether Mary had more children (in other words, if she ever had sex) would spark one of Christianity's earliest controversies.

The gospels and the apocrypha (accounts of Jesus' life not included in the New Testament) were composed and codified years after the death of Jesus, when Christianity was still establishing itself as a new religion. Without these texts the existence of Jesus is reduced to passing references in the works of the Romano-Jewish historian Flavius Josephus (*c.* 37–*c.* 100 CE), writing 40 years after the Crucifixion. He records Jesus as 'a wise man, if it be lawful to call him a man; for he was a doer of wonderful works', and confirms that 'Pilate, at the suggestion of the principal men amongst us, had condemned him to the cross'.[24]

The most important text concerning the construction of the myth of Mary is the Infancy Gospel of James. The writer of the Infancy Gospel claims to be James the Just, one of Jesus' four *adelphoi*, who was appointed the first leader of the Church of Jerusalem by the disciple Peter himself. It is, however, unlikely that James did write it because he was martyred sometime around 62 CE, and the Infancy Gospel, also known as the *Protoevangelium*, is thought to have been written some decades after his death. But this unsettled authorship is not out of the ordinary for an ancient text, and it offers us a unique window into how the early Christians thought about birth.

The *Protoevangelium* constructs an elaborate backstory both for Mary and for the birth of Jesus. In doing so, it somewhat gilds the lily in terms of Mary's spotlessness. It tells us that she was born to wealthy parents who were in high standing with the temple, Joachim and Anna, who were childless for a long time. Joachim fasted in the desert for 40 days and 40 nights so that Anna might conceive. Distraught, Anna wandered in their garden, tortured by her sterility and her husband's absence and possible death in the desert, when an angel appeared to her, saying, 'Anna, Anna, the Lord God has heard your prayer. You will conceive and give birth and your child will be spoken of everywhere people live.'[25]

Likewise, an angel visited Joachim and told him, 'Joachim, Joachim, the Lord God has heard your prayer. Go down from here. Look, your wife Anna has conceived in her womb.'[26] Joachim returned, and Anna ran to him and exclaimed, 'See, the widow is no longer a widow and the childless woman has conceived in her womb.'[27] In the *Protoevangelium*, Mary herself was also the product of a miraculous conception, for Anna had already conceived before the return of Joachim.

Anna sequestered Mary in a 'bedroom–sanctuary' until her third birthday, and allowed only Jewish virgins into her presence. When she was three, they gave her to the temple to be raised, 'and every house in Israel loved her'.[28] So, far from being a simple virgin betrothed to a carpenter, Mary was famous throughout Israel by the time she was a toddler. So revered was she that she was not even to eat ordinary food, but was 'fed like a dove and received food from the hand of an angel'.[29]

When Mary was 12 years old, the priests grew worried that her first period would defile the temple, so they decided to marry her off. They gathered all the widowers of Nazareth together and asked God for a sign to indicate the future husband of Mary and 'Suddenly, a dove came out of the rod and stood on Joseph's head. And the high priest said, "Joseph! Joseph! You have been chosen by lot to take the virgin into your own keeping." And Joseph replied, saying, "I have sons and am old, while she is young. I will not be ridiculed among the children of Israel."'[30] The high priest threatened Joseph with the wrath of God, so Joseph took Mary home and left her there while he went out to build houses.

The priests of the temple decided they wanted a new curtain or *parochet* to separate the main temple from the inner sanctum, and that it should be spun only by virgins. The high priest remembered Mary, and that she remained 'pure before God', and so she was summoned with other virgins to 'cast lots to see who will spin the gold and the pure and the linen and the silk and the violet and the scarlet and the true purple threads'. All of these colours and materials are symbolic: the gold of God, the purity of linen and the scarlet and the 'true' purple are now familiar as the colour of motherhood (scarlet or red) and the most highly prized of all colours: the purple of the Aegean murex shellfish. Unsurprisingly, 'Mary was appointed by lot to the true purple and scarlet threads'.[31]

It was these threads that Mary was spinning when the angel Gabriel appeared to her to tell her that she would bear a son, whose name would be Jesus. While the gospels of Luke and Matthew make it clear that Mary was a virgin up until the time of the birth of Jesus, the *Protoevangelium* hammers home her absolute purity. Mary asks, 'If I conceive from the Lord God who lives, will I also conceive as all women conceive?' And the Angel of the Lord replies, 'Not like that, Mary. For the power of God will come over you. Thus, the holy one who is born will be called son of the most high. And you will call his name Jesus, for he will save his people from their sins.'[32]

When she is six months pregnant, Joseph returns from his 'house-building' only 'to find her swelling'.[33] He promptly throws himself onto a pile of sackcloth and weeps, believing Mary an adulteress. She protests that she has never known a man, but Joseph does not believe her, asking her if she is a virgin, then where did 'this thing' in her womb come from?[34] Mary still protests that she is a virgin, and eventually both have to undergo a trial in the temple to prove that they have not fornicated. Both pass the trial, and the priests agree that Mary is indeed a virgin, carrying a miraculous child.

When the time comes for them to attend the census in Bethlehem, it is from James that we receive the legend of Mary on the donkey, which she is riding when she goes into labour: 'Joseph, take me off the donkey, the child pushing from within me to let him come out.'[35] Joseph finds a cave and leaves her there, guarded by his sons, while 'he went to find a Hebrew midwife in the land of Bethlehem'.[36]

He returns with a midwife (or *chakhamah* in Hebrew) to the cave, where Mary delivers Jesus in a wave of light too bright to bear, and when the light withdraws, baby Jesus is already at Mary's breast. Mary's birthing of Jesus, according to James, was entirely painless and silent. She escapes 'the anguish of her that bringeth forth her first child' (Jer. 4.31). According to the Bible, women experienced pain during labour as punishment for Eve's original sin (eating fruit from the Tree of Knowledge) – as Mary was born free of sin, immaculately pure, she suffered no pain. There is no mention of the midwife assisting Mary, or Mary using a traditional Jewish birthing stool of the time or of the midwife cutting the cord and dealing with the placenta. At this time, the placenta would have been carefully preserved, and the Talmud states that 'the rich women hide it in oil, the poor ones hide it in straw and sand. Both hide it in the earth, to give a pledge to the Earth.'[37] The burial of the placenta persists in many cultures: in sub-Saharan Africa some tribes will bury the placenta of a girl under the house, and that of the boys is often buried near livestock.

The midwife who, thanks to Mary's magical labour, had done nothing more than bear witness to the birth, 'departed from the cave and met Salome and said to her, "Salome, Salome, I have to describe this new miracle for you. A virgin has given birth, although her body does not allow it." And Salome said, "As the Lord my God lives, unless I insert my finger and investigate her, I will not believe that a virgin has given birth."'[38] Salome attends Mary and insists on testing that her hymen remains intact. Soon after, Salome's hand bursts into flame until it is so burnt that it 'falls' from her. She pleads with God, repenting of her sin and lack of faith, and an angel appears. He tells her that she need only to touch the child to be healed, which she promptly was.[39]

The *Protoevangelium* is valuable mainly because of its rich depth of narrative detail and descriptions of social customs, but also because it expounds the essential nature of Mary's sexual purity, which would come to be a central doctrine for Roman Catholicism, as well as many other Christian denominations.

While history looks back now on this early Christian age as one of competing theologies, many of which had only a short window of viability in a volatile geographic area, the immediate and resilient cult of Jesus refused to disappear. This was partly owing to a clever combination of old and new in the Christian doctrine.

Christianity needed to bolster its ranks as much as possible, and so it adopted the anti-infanticide stance of Judaism from its very beginning. Jesus himself never mentions infanticide in any surviving gospel, but his fondness for children is evident throughout the New Testament (Mk 10.14–16). Jewish writers of the time were also specifically against the practice. Josephus cites a Jewish 'law' which 'enjoins us to bring up all our offspring, and forbids women to cause abortion of what is begotten, or to destroy it afterward; and if any woman appears to have so done, she will be a murderer of her child, by destroying a living creature, and diminishing human kind'.[40] It is worth noting that Josephus associates infanticide specifically with women. Hilarion may have sent the order from Alexandria, but it was Alis who would have had to pick up her child and physically abandon it somewhere. The fact that it may have been a woman's responsibility to expose an unwanted baby does not necessarily mean that it was her decision.

Humility and simplicity, which had been a mainstay of Jesus' life and faith, also had a strong appeal for converts to the new faith, and were useful aspirations for a church trying to establish itself on limited means. The rich silks and ornaments of the pagans were not necessary for a good Christian, and this emphasis on modesty and restraint soon spawned an early form of religious extremism in the guise of the ascetic movement. The early ascetics believed in living as Jesus had, wearing plain clothes, not over-indulging in sensual pleasures and adhering to a simple, faithful life.

Over the next two hundred years, Christianity became dominated by new personalities and ideas, rather than the teachings of people who had purported to have 'known' Jesus. Eventually, the Romans began to persecute and legislate against Christians, but none of it slowed down its growth. In this early church, there was no rule against women becoming ministers or even deacons, such as Phoebe of Cenchrea (Rom. 16.1–1). Other independently wealthy women, such as Priscilla of Macedonia, became patrons and opened their houses to congregations.[41] Women were so prominent in the Christian church that Roman philosopher Celsus sneered that they 'show they want and are able to convince only the foolish, dishonourable, and stupid, only slaves, women, and little children'.[42]

It did not take long, however, for dissent to begin brewing in the Christian ranks against women rising to positions of authority. Tertullian of Carthage, who was born around 60 years after the first gospels were written, was an early father of the Christian church. He wrote to his wife that, should she outlive him, she must not enter the ministry as, 'Who would be willing to let his wife go through one street after another to other men's houses, and indeed the poorer cottages, to visit the brethren? Who will unsuspiciously let her go to the Lord's Supper, that feast upon which they heap such calumnies?'[43]

Rome responded to this rapid surge in converts to Christianity with ever more violent persecution until Emperor Constantine I drew up the Edict of Milan and proclaimed that all persons were free to worship the deity of their choice.[44] They granted Christians legal rights, allowed them to build churches and established religious toleration of minority faiths. Christianity was then ready to organize itself into a hierarchical religion with the bases for worship to match.

In 325 CE the First Council of Nicaea (modern Iznik, in Bursa Province, Turkey) took place. It was the first ecumenical gathering of the Christian church, and one of its first decisions was effectively to ban women from joining the clergy by agreeing that female deacons would be considered laity.[45] It took just under three centuries after the death of Jesus, who himself had many female followers during his life, to exclude women from wielding authority in the Christian church – although women continued to be ordained as deaconesses in the Eastern, orthodox branch for another seven hundred years. This remarkably rapid marginalization of women in the new Christian order had far-reaching consequences.

Rome continued in its patrician tradition, but it was also undergoing sea changes. The birth rate amongst the middle classes and elite had started to decline dramatically by the end of the first century, which other religions put down to their debauchery. It seems that the Roman state eventually took these critiques to heart, as infanticide was finally outlawed in 374 CE. During the same period, a woman called Fabiola founded Rome's first hospital in the large harbour of Portus.

Fabiola appears in a eulogy delivered by St Jerome. He describes her as 'the praise of the Christians, the marvel of the gentiles'.[46] Married young and subsequently divorced from her first husband, owing to his cruelty, she remarried while her first husband was still living, which was against Christian law. After the death of her second husband, she converted to Christianity and began to minister to the poor and the sick, dressing plainly and modestly.

Jerome categorically states that she founded 'the first hospital', meaning a hospital in the sense that we understand it today, where patients come to be treated in an institution separate from their own homes. Jerome's descriptions of Fabiola's patients suggest end-of-life care, rather than childbirth – it was a place where she 'moistened the scarce breathing lips of the dying with sips of liquid'. Her story, however, establishes another important precedent for the role of women in healthcare.[47] Fabiola was canonized following her death and today is known as the patron saint of nurses, difficult marriages, divorced women and abused spouses.

While Fabiola's hospital was indeed the earliest of the western Roman empire, the idea had already taken root in Persia. The Academy of Gondishapur (modern Shahabad, Khuzestan province, south-west Iran) was founded by Shapur I of the Sassanid empire in 271 CE. It was at this point not primarily a hospital but a seat of all learning, of which medicine was an important part.

The evolution of the hospital, while not unique to Christianity, as Nalanda in India (427) and Nisibis (489) prove, was bolstered by a particular set of circumstances. The Roman empire required a huge amount of male labour to maintain itself, and so an excess of male children was something to be welcomed. But as the Roman system of patronage (where wealthy individuals 'sponsored' young men in their endeavours) declined along with the western empire, suddenly, there were too many young men to support. The

Christian church did not offer the glamour of the Roman *domus*, but its new monasteries and convents offered food, shelter and learning. Crucially, the seclusion they offered allowed time for study and reflection, for both men and women, something not easily obtained in the hard-scrabble day-to-day life in antiquity.

These new academies and hospitals were not religious houses, but they accommodated those fleeing from the turmoil and persecution that were constant after the fall of Rome in 476 CE. Gondishapur welcomed even those of so-called heretical faiths, and established its core fields of learning as astronomy, astrology, mathematics, science and medicine. Taking advantage of the intellectual diaspora created by centuries of unrest, the Persian empire established itself as a lucrative, educated and tolerant centre of exchange between the West and the East. Yet even the far-seeing Sassanids could not have predicted what came next.

A FLAME BURNS BRIGHTLY IN THE EAST AS A CANDLE FADES IN THE WEST

Islam, much like Christianity, was shored up by women both materially and spiritually in its formative years. Muhammad's wife, Khadīja, their daughter named Fatima, Mary, the mother of Jesus, and Asiya, the wife of the Pharaoh of the Exodus, are held up as the four finest women in the world. Khadīja bint Khuwaylid, thought to be at least five years his senior, was a wealthy trader in her own right through her family lineage when she met Muhammad Ibn Abdullah. He was born around 570 in Mecca, an Arab centre where pagan worship centred around the Ka'aba, at that time adorned with idols. He was a merchant too, but not a particularly good one. According to Shia theology, Khadīja was a virgin when she married Muhammad, and in Sunni belief, she had been married perhaps twice before, and had as many as three daughters.

In 595 Khadīja hired Muhammad, then in his mid-twenties, to represent her on a trading expedition, as she did not travel with her own caravan. Muhammad escorted her caravan to Syria and back with success and was praised by everyone for his fidelity and honesty.

So taken was Khadīja with him that, through an intermediary, she proposed marriage. It is possible that Khadīja and members of her family were *ḥanīfs* or believers in one God, under the Abrahamic tradition from which Judaism and Christianity are both descended. *Hanīf* does not by default mean Christian, but it is a rejection of polytheistic paganism in favour of a single deity.

When he was around 40 years old, Muhammad was visited by the angel Gabriel. He ruminated on Gabriel's message for three years and began to preach in 613. Khadīja was his first adherent. He was by no means the only prophet of the time – there were many preaching along the same trading routes, espousing not dissimilar ideas – but Muhammad emerged as the foremost. He and Khadīja had between six and eight children during their 25-year, monogamous marriage. Among the disparate desert tribes, childbirth practices were highly individual, but no records survive that can tell us about common methods and rituals. Their two sons, Qasim and Abd Allah, died in infancy, but four daughters survived: Fatima, Zainab, Ruqayyah and Umm Kultum. Khadīja died during Ramadan in 619, by which time Islam was already gaining ground. Three years later, Muhammad and his faithful fled to Yathrib (Medina) in what became known as the Hijrah, and the beginning of the Islamic calendar.

On the death of Khadīja, Muhammad married ten more times, and two wives bore him children. His third wife, Aisha, is recorded as being six or seven years old at the time of her marriage (in and of itself not unusual, particularly among families attempting to secure dynastic futures) and nine years old at the time of consummation, when Muhammad was approximately 53.

The description of this marriage and consummation comes from the hadiths of the scholar al-Bukhari, written well over a hundred years after Aisha's death, which are considered the foremost of all hadith collections of the Sunni faith. According to al-Bukhari, Aisha said:

> The Prophet (blessings and peace of Allah be upon him) married me when I was six years old. We came to Madinah [Medina] and stayed among Banu'l-Harith ibn Khazraj. I fell sick and lost my

hair, (then I recovered) and my hair grew down to my earlobes. My mother Umm Ruman came to me when I was on a swing and some of my friends were with me. She called me loudly and I went to her, and I did not know what she wanted of me. She took me by the hand and made me stand at the door of the house, as I was gasping for breath, until I had calmed down. Then she took some water and wiped my face and head with it, then she took me into the house. There were some women of the Ansar in the house, who said: With good wishes and blessings and good luck. She handed me over to them and they adorned me, and suddenly I saw the Messenger of Allah (blessings and peace of Allah be upon him) at mid-morning, and they handed me over to him. At that time I was nine years old.[48]

Another Islamic scholar, al-Tabari, places Aisha as closer to 12 or 13 at the time of consummation, and other interpretations argue that it's far more likely she was older. For a millennium after Muhammad's death, Aisha's age was barely remarked on. While we will never know how old Aisha really was, it seems that within the text her extreme youth was seen as a symbol of her guaranteed purity – echoing Mary the Virgin's containment in the Temple until her betrothal to Joseph. Aisha herself went on to become a military leader who sang the Muslim faithful into battle from the back of her camel.

The hadiths also provide a brief but valuable insight into another practice that had already been widespread throughout Mesopotamia for hundreds of years by the time of Islam's rise: female genital mutilation (FGM). Known as female circumcision in countries where it is legal, female genital mutilation is still practised in 28 Muslim and African countries, and an unknown number of countries in Asia. UNICEF, as of 2014, estimated that 97 per cent of Egyptian girls undergo circumcision during childhood.[49] Over two thousand years ago, Herodotus the Greek historian remarked on female circumcision in his *Histories* after a visit to Egypt, and it is there and Sudan that girls today typically undergo the most extreme form of FGM. This is known as *pharaonic* or infibulation (or, more scientifically, Type III): girls have their clitoris, labia minora and labia majora removed, the remaining tissue is sewn up leaving only a small hole for urination, menses and eventually penetration by a penis.[50] The historic prevalence of this tradition around the Red Sea has led to speculation that it was associated with the ancient slave trade where it ensured purity – in transit, if not before – and therefore a higher price.[51]

The two other forms of female genital mutilation are Type II (entailing the removal of the clitoris and parts of the labia minora) and Type I, which refers to a wide range of procedures including removal of the clitoral hood and the cutting of the clitoris to remove sexual gratification. All forms of female genital mutilation are grievously harmful to women's sexual experience and pleasure, and they carry enormous risks of chronic pain, continual discomfort and infections. The more severe forms, in particular, come with a greatly elevated risk of mortality at both the time of the operation and in any subsequent childbirth.[52] Three million young women and girls undergo FGM each year as of February 2024, according to the World Health Organization.

Neither the Quran nor Islamic law, *shariah*, mentions female circumcision, but it is referenced in a hadith taken from the *sunnah*, or the collected knowledge of Muslims of Muhammad's time regarding what is right. Muhammad instructs a 'cutter of clitorises' called Umm Atiyya to be 'moderate when performing the operation of circumcision upon women' and perform what amounts to a removal of the hood of the clitoris. He implores her to 'Lightly touch and not wear out [the clitoris]. The face will become more beautiful and the husband will be delighted.'[53] While some Muslims consider all hadiths to be authentic, Islamic scholars have long recognized that hadiths vary in their reliability, with many grading this hadith as 'da'if' (weak) in terms of accuracy.

After his death Muhammad was succeeded by his disciples, the family and friends who had known him personally, known as the *caliphs* (meaning 'followers' or 'successors'). The 30-year era of the First Caliphate is seen as a pure and aspirational period in Islam, which was unfortunately followed by the Umayyads, who were heavy drinkers and hunters. One caliph had a pet cheetah that rode behind him on his horse, and his saluki dogs wore gold anklets and were looked after by their own personal slaves. It was a far cry from the ascetic desert traditions of their followers. After a further 90 years they were replaced by the stricter Abbasids, who removed the capital to what is now Baghdad, naming it Madinat as-Salam, the City of Peace.

The end of the dissolute Umayyad period heralded the beginning of the Islamic Golden Age, lasting over five centuries and spreading even more rapidly than Christianity, west as far as Spain, and east into Transoxonia (Central Asia). In Baghdad in 830 the Abbasid caliph Harun al-Rashid founded Bayt al-Hikma, the House of Wisdom, which was modelled on Gondishapur, and it too extended a welcome to scholars from all over the Islamic world to come and translate their knowledge into Arabic. The physicians and polymaths of the City of Peace brought together knowledge on anatomy, surgery, pharmacology, obstetrics and mental health.

One of the foremost polymaths was Abu Bakr Muhammad Ibn Zakariyya al-Razi (865–925), from Rey, near Tehran, known as Rhazes. His greatest achievement was the *Kitab al-Hawi*, a medical encyclopaedia that remained influential until the Renaissance in Europe, where it was known as *Liber Continens*. Although Rhazes did not include anything revelatory in his chapter on pregnancy and birth (Book III, Chapter 9), like other early Islamic physicians, his holistic approach was highly valuable as a teaching resource.

Another early Islamic physician, Abu al-Qasim al-Zahrawi (936–1013) from Spain, was a revered surgeon of his time. He was known in Europe as Abulcasis and his pioneering works, particularly on surgical instruments, are remarkable. Included are drawings of a vaginal speculum, as well as varied obstetric forceps.[54] A speculum allowed physicians to open the vagina and see inside so that they could make a more accurate diagnosis, while the forceps would be used to help deliver a baby in an awkward position or hurry along a dangerously stalled labour.

The forceps would not come into widespread use in the Western world for over five hundred years, and when we encounter them again they will be cloaked in an atmosphere of magic and pomp, rather than scientific study. To give a sense of how early European readers responded to these medical innovations, a later Latin manuscript of the fourteenth century shows an interpretation of the speculum, but upside down and with the wrong moving parts. [British Library, Add. MS36617 fol. 28v) Knowledge that may have saved many mothers was therefore lost to the West for centuries.

WHAT'S A WOMAN WORTH?

During the rise of Islam, northern Europe was still suffering from the aftershocks of a series of invasions by what were known as 'the barbarians', whose temples were 'woods and groves' alone. These warriors were the Vandals, the Goths, the Angles and Saxons, as well as others.[55] It is commonly referred to as the Great Migration and represented a proportionately huge movement of (mostly) men westward over a historically short space of time across both the Romano-Christian and Germanic European empires. For women it led to a huge step backwards.

Many pagan women had converted to Christianity and joined convents – perhaps seclusion among themselves seemed like the least miserable option available. It was the start of a tradition in northern Europe, including Britain, of 'mother-abbesses' such as Hilda of Whitby, and saints such as Bridget of Kildare, the patron saint of midwives. While the rare story of a warrior queen emerges over these intervening years, such as that of Brunhilde the queen consort of Austrasia, they tend to suffer terrible fates. In Brunhilde's case, she was torn into four pieces by horses.

There is almost no evidence of how women would have given birth during these warring centuries, beyond surviving translations of the Hippocratic corpus and assorted other works of antiquity. It's likely that women would have continued to tend to each other, to experiment with treatments and pass on that knowledge orally over generations. From the findings of Romano-British 'infant' cemeteries (sites where multiple infant burials have been found but no adult remains) and a notable lack of the expected rates of disability in adult skeletons, it is likely that British Romans continued to practise exposure – abandoning their babies to die – at selected sites.[56]

The Germanic and later the Scandinavian male population gradually took over what remained of Roman Britain. Germanic 'old laws' defined a person's worth through *wergild*: their physical value in money should harm befall them, which depended on their social standing. They are particularly specific on abortion, and 'violent abortion', caused by a beating, rather than the ingestion of abortive substances. The price varies depending on whether the foetus is 'unformed' or 'formed', meaning less or more than three months old.[57] By the time Alfred the Great, the king of the Anglo-Saxons who reigned over the final decades of the ninth century, compiled his 'dōm-bōc' (*The Doom Book*), a woman's value was simply monetary: 'If a man slay a woman with child, he shall pay full *wergild* for the woman, and half *wergild* for the dead foetus, in compensation for the husband's material loss.'[58]

Meanwhile, Alfred the Great and his successors continued to war with the Scandinavian Vikings. The Vikings had put themselves in an impossible position at home, where it is thought that infanticide left them with a population skewed dramatically towards men. In some parts of Norway, the ratio of males to females is dramatic – although it is difficult to tell whether a Viking burial contains a man or a woman from grave goods alone as women sometimes occupied traditionally male roles. Eleven Old Norse poems mention the 'carrying out' of female babies. In the Icelandic *Gunnlaugs Saga,* Thorstein, a wealthy farmer, says to his wife, Jofrid, 'So you are with child. If it is a girl, it shall be exposed, but if a boy, it shall be raised.'[59] Like Alis, Jofrid is left with the horrible task of giving birth to and then exposing her child while her husband is away. But, in a twist of fate, Jofrid refuses. Instead of killing her newborn, she smuggles her away to be raised by a neighbour – where she grows up to be the saga's beautiful heroine. So many myths and legends from cultures that practise infanticide celebrate heroes exposed at birth who survive by being raised by wild animals or rescued by kindly childless couples. Perhaps these stories comforted the parents as they returned home, alone.

4

The Rise of the Machines

A farmer on the isle of Rousay in Orkney set out to bury a dead cow near the deserted and rocky shoreline. Digging a deep hole, he noticed something unusual in the soil, a human bone – it was the skeleton of a young woman and her newborn baby. Undisturbed for over a thousand years, she had been buried with 'a pair of wool combs, a weaving batten, a bronze basin, a knife and a pair of shears' – she might, like him, have been a farmer, as a sickle was placed near her body. A Celtic brooch tucked among her belongings, dating to around 750 CE, would have already been a much-loved and cherished heirloom by the time she died. The objects that she carried into the grave with her reflect the mosaic of peoples living and dying on a remote, windblown peninsula at the very edge of civilization. The amber on her jewellery, whatever the date of its working, could have originated as far away as the Baltic Sea, while the filigree goldwork was a speciality of Anglo-Saxon metalworkers who had settled in England and southern Scotland. It is thought that she died in childbirth.

During her lifetime, the so-called Dark Ages gripped Britain and much of northern Europe. This era has been imagined as 'dark' for so long because there are fewer written records – people did not stop dreaming, innovating or producing artistic and scientific works, but what they did make is harder for us to discover. This means that there are also few written records of maternal experiences in Old

English. Two medical texts, however, have survived. They are called the *Leechbook* and the *Lacnunga*.

The *Leechbook* was owned by a man called Bald, whom we know nothing about but who was probably a physician, and it contains herbal recipes for a vast array of complaints.[1] The index tells us that there was once an entire section devoted to women's health and childbirth, but it has since been lost. The *Lacnunga,* which details many of the same remedies found in the *Leechbook*, does preserve one charm written in the female voice, for 'A Delayed Birth'. It recommends, among other things, that a woman should lie beside her husband at night and say, 'I walk up, step over you / with a living child, in no way with a killing one, / with a fully born one, in no way with a doomed one.'

It is hard to overstate how rare the female voice was in Anglo-Saxon literature, which is why it is possible that this charm was composed by (as well as for) women – and was simply recorded by a male physician. Literacy was almost non-existent, although some women involved in convents would have had a better chance of learning how to read and write. Even if women were literate, Anglo-Saxon heroic literature was largely concerned with the importance of the masculine atmosphere of the mead-hall, where men listened to, and told, great tales such as *Beowulf*. To be included in the hall's brotherhood or *comitatus* was every man's aspiration. To be exiled and cast outside was every man's greatest fear. Women, however, already lived outside of it because of the community structure; they would have been confined to outlying houses where they were occupied with domestic tasks and childrearing. Two surviving Anglo-Saxon poems in a female voice – *The Wife's Lament* and *Wulf and Eadwacer* – are both melancholy and contain moving descriptions of exclusion and loneliness. This was part of Anglo-Saxon female identity, and it is no coincidence that it is in Anglo-Saxon culture that we begin to see the evolution of the village wise woman and midwife into what would come to be called the witch.

From legal records and archaeology it's possible to glean a little more about the lives of women and their children. Law codes from this period tell us that children were considered adults at the age of ten, and were marrying very young. It is likely that there were different burial rites for those between the ages of two and ten, as there are never many children in Anglo-Saxon cemeteries. A study of over a thousand sets of remains from Anglo-Saxon burial grounds show that only 6 per cent were infants, an unthinkably low proportion given that 30 per cent of those interred in Roman and later medieval cemeteries are infants.[2] Perhaps these younger children were not given the same burial rites as adults because they weren't yet considered part of the society — furthermore, the remains would not have survived very long if the graves were shallow. These peoples were fundamentally different from us for many reasons, and many of their practices and actions appear alien now; they were forming new societies in a dark and violent time. But this was also a time that saw the emergence of something new that would radically alter the way we were born — the literary culture of the medieval age, the slow then sudden growth of science and medicine, and the invention of the machine.

MULIERES SALERITANAE

Dawn was breaking in Salerno, Italy — a thriving port town in the Lombard empire, where women enjoyed more rights, more freedom and more education than anywhere else in Europe at the time. Early medieval childbirth was a varied experience: some women gave birth in unsophisticated rural dwellings while others participated in the elaborate, well-attended rituals of the emerging aristocracies, in ornate, carefully decorated birthing chambers. In Italy these differences were even more extreme as each city-state had very different ideas about the role women should play in society.

In Salerno women were allowed to study and practise medicine alongside men. This unsurprisingly led to a flourishing of research and texts on women's health that would circulate throughout the medieval world. In the twelfth century, a physician called Trota de Salerno wrote one of the earliest treatises on childbirth, *De mulierum passionibus curandorum* ('The Diseases of Women'). It is possibly the first written by a woman. 'The Diseases of Women' is part of a compendium of texts on women's health named after the famous Trota, known as the *Trotula* – although it's likely these texts were not all authored by Trota herself but were perhaps written by women she taught or worked alongside. We know very little about Trota, but the *Trotula* deals with everything from female hygiene to pre- and post-natal care, as well as advocating for the use of opium during labour – in direct contrast to the Christian church's teaching that the pain of childbirth was a woman's punishment for Eve's sins.[3] It even contains a test for infertility which, like the ancient Egyptian pregnancy test, relies on urine and grain. Husband and wife are instructed to urinate into separate jars, each filled with bran, and if either is infertile the bran will turn foul after ten days.

The women who practised medicine in Salerno were known as the *mulieres saleritanae*. From the ninth century until the fourteenth, there were female students and even surgeons, including Constance Calenza (*fl.* 1415), who wrote a treatise on eye surgery. Bologna also emerged as a centre for gynaecological care, where women performed surgery on other women for complicated uterine surgeries and cancers. Many of these women, like Trota herself, may have been the daughters or sisters of doctors working at the medical schools and worked under their care, but they were highly respected as individuals in their own right, and literate enough to write medical manuals that stayed in print until the Renaissance. Unfortunately not everywhere was quite as enlightened as Salerno and Bologna. Trota's fame spread far and wide, though she only appears in Chaucer's *Canterbury Tales* as Dame Trot, a name that later passed into English pantomime tradition as the character of an old hag.

Another driving force behind the acceleration of medical knowledge in Italy was the Crusades. The Knights Hospitaller of Jerusalem were a military order who took women on as nurses, where no doubt they learned a great deal about field medicine. There would also have been a vast number of sex workers who must have suffered extreme hardships while pregnant, though records for this no longer exist. We know a little more about the noble women, such as Elvira of Castile, who gave birth at the Siege of Tripoli in 1096 to a child who grew to adulthood.

The Crusades acted as a powerful conduit for medical knowledge from the Islamic world, which was vastly superior to Western medicine at the time. Physicians returned to Europe with new medicines and new techniques, and Graeco-Roman medicine regained its popularity (much of it having fallen by the wayside in Europe after the fall of Rome). One unfortunate consequence was that the theory of the wandering womb made a resurgence, as did the notion that women should give birth on their backs. Yet despite these ugly old ideas rearing their heads, it was at this time that we see the women of Salerno and Bologna once more assuming the role of physician and midwife. No longer wise women or birthing companions, they were respected professionals working to a high standard.

Outside the oases of Salerno and Bologna, female physicians were still marginalized. As Italy's dominance faded slightly at the end of the Crusades, the French medical schools of Paris and Montpellier came to the forefront. Unfortunately, in 1220 France all but outlawed women acting as physicians. They now needed a diploma, or letters of recommendation and an interview, from the Paris medical school, which would have been difficult to obtain since they were not allowed to attend.

Shut out of the institutions, women would still have provided healthcare in their communities as they had always done, and there were even those who defied the status quo by taking on a broad range of clients and building a professional reputation. Around 1322 an Italian Jewish woman living in Paris called Jacqueline Felice de Almania defied the law and practised medicine with great success, to the outrage of male doctors. She was aware of the importance of testing a patient's urine for diabetes and believed that male doctors should not perform intimate examinations on women, although she had no problem treating men herself. This was too much for the authorities, and Jacqueline was brought to trial and fined 60 Parisian pounds, a huge sum at the time.[4] Various other trials of women practising medicine at the time compounded the knowledge that (outside of a couple of forward-thinking Italian city-states) women were slowly being pushed out, even more than they already were.

The Crusades themselves had thrown ideas about religion into stark relief, and increasingly the Church separated itself from the field of medicine. The clergy were initially forbidden from practising any medicine that involved shedding blood, and then from practising any medicine at all as the possibility of financial reward compromised the purity of religious faith. Understandably, the Church's ideas about the spiritual dangers of compromising the sanctity of the human body (made, as it was, in the image of God) bore less weight with physicians and soldiers who had seen the mutilations and indignities wrought by battle. Dying in a foreign land had in itself posed a vexing question for Europe's elite religious warriors, who wished to be buried in consecrated ground on the Christian lands of their forefathers. In order to transport their bodies thousands of miles home, their hearts were removed for embalming and their bones were boiled. While this broke many religious taboos (in the name of religion itself), it would have afforded a unique opportunity for the physicians involved to explore human anatomy. Autopsies were not necessarily banned everywhere, but they were rare and taboo.

Surgery was the prime beneficiary of the new knowledge that came from the Crusades. As in ancient times, it was still seen as a last resort when diet, lifestyle and medicine had failed. Fraught with risk, people often died from shock during surgery or from infection. Medical schools in Montpellier and Bologna were making progress with the use of 'soporific sponges' soaked in macerated opium gum to deal with pain during procedures, but knowledge of infection remained primitive and wounds were often packed with festering poultices made with ingredients such as eggs and mud.

Despite this, a new breed of surgeons, distinct from physicians for the first time, emerged in the thirteenth century, marking a new era of professional specialization previously only seen in dentistry, such as it existed, barber–surgery (boils and small skin lesions) and midwifery. The emergence of the surgeons was of particular importance to one deeply undignified, painful and common affliction affecting all strata of society: abscesses in and around the anus. For a Western world that spent a great deal of time in the saddle, with very different ideas regarding what constituted good personal hygiene, the risk of haemorrhoids was a constant irk of medieval, and especially male, life. If coupled with fistula (an abnormal passageway between different organs or, in the case of anal fistula, between the anus and the outer skin) this would have amounted to an agonizing near-disability known as 'Knight's Arse'. John of Arderne, who studied at the Montpellier medical school, was an English surgeon who specialized in fistula repair for the wealthy. He was a skilled anaesthetist who designed his own surgical tools and devised methods for haemorrhoid removal and gradual fistula repair that formed the basis of techniques still in use today. Crucially, these procedures were elective. Many lived in agony with these afflictions, but those who could afford Arderne's attention could at last have the possibility for relief.

'THE EXTRACTION OF THE CHILD THROUGH A LATERAL INCISION OF THE ABDOMEN ...'

The C-section, a truly vital part of the story of birth, was not a matter of choice. For many years it was almost certainly a death sentence for both mother and child – and yet, in the most extreme cases, it was the only chance they had. A C-section is a serious abdominal wound, and before anaesthesia and clean environments, opening up the abdominal cavity almost guaranteed the death of the patient. There are early mentions, such as those in the Mishnah and the Niddah (two works of rabbinic literature), that make fleeting references to C-sections, but only the Niddah gives any hope for the mother's survival.

It states that it was not necessary for a woman to observe any post-partum purification rituals if she had an abdominal birth: 'What is delivered through the belly-wall: for this they do not keep the days of cleanness and uncleanness.' These rituals involved different lengths of 'unclean' time, depending on the gender of the child – seven days for a son and 14 for a daughter. This would be followed by the ritual bath, followed by 33 days of 'purity' for a boy and 66 for a girl, during which the mother could resume her normal activities so long as she didn't touch anything sacred.[5]

The Western church remained firmly in favour of only operating on a woman in labour if she was already deceased, as recorded by Odon de Sully (1196–1208), archbishop of Paris: 'Those who have died in childbirth could be cut open when the child is believed to be still alive; however it has to be well established that they are dead.'[6] For the church, the C-section was not so much about saving the life of the newborn, who would probably die, as about the brief window it afforded to baptize the child and therefore secure its soul. For this purpose, midwives were permitted by the Church to use surgical instruments and perform emergency C-sections.

While illustrations of C-sections begin to appear in French manuscripts around 1300, and the Montpellier physician Bernard of Gordon mentions the procedure in a medical text in in 1305, death for the mother was treated as unavoidable. Then, a century later, we can see early signs that change was on the way. Pietro d'Argellata, a Bologna surgeon wrote a treatise, *Chirurgia,* in the 1420s in which he described performing at least two C-sections, one with the incision on the left of the abdomen to avoid the liver and one straight up the mid-section to the breastbone.[7] He wrote: 'I have sometimes made the incision from the breastbone to the pubic bone, carefully, so as not to touch the intestines or the child. And in this way I have extracted the child. But in truth, the first method [left-side incision] pleases me more.'[8]

While there is no proof that the women he treated survived, Argellata was operating with care and thought, rather than performing a careless post-mortem emptying of the womb – if she was already dead, he would not need to avoid the liver. It's possible that he was developing a method that would reduce shock and increase her chances for survival.

While dissection was still forbidden by the major religions, surgeons found ways to secure bodies for their private research, as they had done since the time of Galen. Strangely, it was the developing infrastructure of the settled world that presented these anatomists with a new steady source of corpses. Increasing levels of legislation and criminal prosecution resulted in a need for the dead to be examined for signs of wrongdoing; these early 'autopsies' started in central Europe, and by the time Argellata was writing they were a fact of life in Germany and northern Italy.

In Germany there are signs that the procedure was no longer the absolute death sentence that it had once been. Around 1480 a German statute describes the procedure of a C-section in rare detail, and of particular interest is the account of the incision:

> She shall start cutting in the lower part of the belly around the pubic bone, about the width of one hand. With her oiled hand she must carefully move aside the entrails ... The wound should be closed with three or four ligatures by means of a needle and a silk or other thread ... Should she survive and regain consciousness, give her a drink made of the roots of salsify and of mountain albanum sauteed in wine. And the woman will recover with God's help.[9]

This set of instructions seems to address a midwife, so, although women were largely barred from the medical profession, they were entrusted with performing one of the most complex and pioneering surgeries.

Some people were forced to take things into their own hands. In 1500 Jakob Nufer, a sow-gelder living near Lake Constance in Turgovia, Switzerland, performed a C-section on his wife, Elisabeth Alespachin, who had been in labour for several days with her first child, and been failed by 13 midwives and physicians. Her desperate husband applied to what was termed 'the authorities' of the Old Swiss Confederacy, probably the closest local council members who could be convened at short notice, for permission to operate on his wife. He did so successfully, through one long incision (as perhaps he had done before on his livestock). He did not close the uterus and used only five stitches on his wife's exterior wound, but both mother and child survived. Elizabeth is recorded as having four subsequent natural births, and a set of twins. The C-section child lived to the age of 77. Despite having more detail than almost any other early account, such as Elisabeth's maiden name and an exact location, the story of the Nufers was only recorded 80 years after it was said to have happened, by the physician Gaspar Bauhin (1560–1624), and its veracity has been repeatedly called into question. But whether or not it really happened, the fact that this story was circulated so widely shows that there was hope that one day medical innovation could save the life of both mother and child from the dangers of the childbed.

There are other stories of C-sections occurring outside Europe too, the most famous being the reports of early explorers in the nineteenth century who witnessed them being successfully performed in Rwanda and Uganda. The peoples of Uganda and Rwanda are recorded as washing their hands and the patient in banana wine before they began, and also giving some to the mother for sedation.[10] If true, it would have served as an antiseptic as well as for pain relief.

About ten years after Nufer the sow-gelder allegedly delivered his wife, Eucharius Rösslin, a German apothecary–physician from Freiburg im Breisgau, wrote *Der Rosengarten* (1513), as an instruction manual for midwives. It was a huge success, and was published in England in 1540 as *The Birth of Mankind*, as well as being translated into numerous other European languages, including Czech, Danish, Dutch, French, Italian and Spanish. It was an important landmark for the publication of medical texts in 'layman's language' rather than Latin, which the average midwife could not hope to engage with, and with useful diagrams in which the baby is shown dancing around a jar-like womb with no umbilical cord and a full head of hair.

In the Classical world, a C-section was seen as a fortuitous omen. The infant had miraculously been recovered from the body of its deceased mother. For hundreds of years, those born by C-section in Germany had been given names such as Nonnatus ('not born') and Ingenito ('unborn').[11] In the 1500s, however, a disturbing new trend emerged in which the Antichrist was depicted as a C-section birth – it was beginning to take on a demonic mantle. It was also around this time that wet-nursing (the practice of paying another woman to breastfeed your child) became more controversial. Owing to the frequency of mothers who had lost a baby and children who had lost a mother, the practice had always been viewed as a necessary fact of life, but in the medieval period it took on a more divisive aspect, regarding what was 'natural' or 'unnatural'. This idea that there was a natural way to approach childbirth and mother (and that, crucially, the natural way was always the right way) would continue to develop over the next five hundred years.

Birth of Antichrist, Germany, 1475

The Renaissance was now in full swing. What had begun with a renewed interest in the literature and learning of the Greeks and Romans – the seeds of which we saw in great places of learning like Salerno – had grown into an artistic and scientific cultural movement that redefined what it meant to be human. The emergence of the true Renaissance polymaths outside Italy, including the Flemish anatomist–physician Andreas Vesalius, elevated the art of illustrating human anatomy from the crude woodcuts of the fifteenth century to a new kind of art form in the manner of Albrecht Dürer (1471–1528). It is unknown who the artist or artists were who illustrated the works of Vesalius, but they are of extraordinary beauty, despite their subject matter. Vesalius unflinchingly depicted the reproductive systems of both men and women in vast and accurate detail for the first time. His work *The Human Body in Seven Books* was published in Basle in 1543 to universal acclaim and represents, in a broader sense, medicine's leap from the medieval to the Renaissance world.

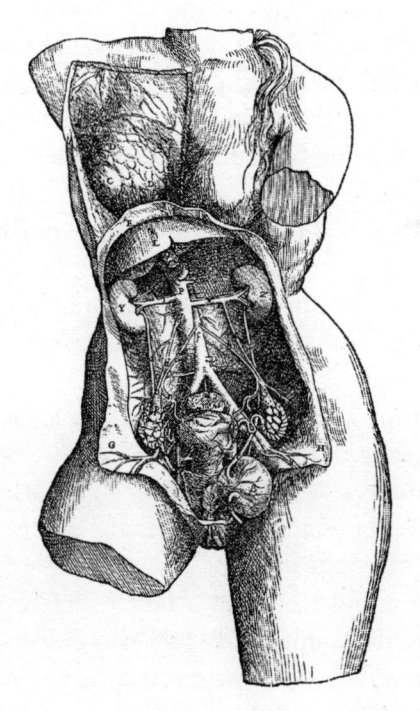

Torso and uterus, *De Humani Corporis* Fabrica, Andreas Vesalius, 1543

In 1545 a post-mortem C-section was carried out in the Duchy of Savoy, north-west of modern-day Italy. Isabella della Volpe married the local physician Marcantonio de Cusano in 1544 and a year later was heavily pregnant with their first child. Tragically, Isabella lost consciousness as she approached full term, and experienced what her doctor and family friend Battista de Crollis of Cossato called a brain *opulatione* or obstruction, which rendered her non-vocal and then unconscious. It's likely that she had suffered a stroke. Isabella never went into labour, and died four days later.

Isabella's female attendants had already summoned a midwife called Elena, who determined that the foetus was still alive. They asked de Crollis to remove it from Isabella's womb but he refused and so they sent for a barber–surgeon, Stefano de Fango. Stefano performed the C-section, and Elena received the infant, whom they named Camilla – perhaps a name that Isabella had chosen. During the operation Isabella's mouth, vagina and cervix were kept open mechanically in order to help the foetus 'breathe', a popular theory at the time. Sadly, Camilla died shortly after she was born. Isabella, though already dead, had produced a living heir and even though the child did not long outlive her mother, this meant that Isabella's absent widower retained his wife's considerable inheritance.

The tragic tale of Isabella and Camilla della Volpe offers a rare glimpse into the world of childbirth, medical practice and inheritance in sixteenth-century Europe. Amid the horror and death, the women who surrounded Isabella in her final days acted with autonomy and empathy in trying to save her daughter. They determined there was still a chance of delivering the baby alive, and they fought for a C-section, even when it meant sending for a surgeon. But they did so against vast odds. The physician, de Crollis, arrived around 40 minutes after the death of Isabella, well after the four-minute window now deemed acceptable for delivery following the death of the mother. Had de Crollis chosen to operate himself, Camilla could have had a better chance of surviving. In this unusually well-documented case, the only people who were any use were those with the lowest status in the medical hierarchy – the female attendants and the lowly barber–surgeon.[12]

THE FIVE-YEAR PREGNANCY

Ambroise Paré was a French surgeon and veteran and an outstanding example of a Renaissance genius who knew how certain things functioned as they did, even if he did not know why. Thanks to his empirical approach and extensive publications, he rose to be one of Europe's pre-eminent surgeons during the second half of the sixteenth century. Paré devised radical treatments such as ligation of arteries to prevent haemorrhage post-amputation, rather than dousing stumps in boiling oil, which more often than not resulted in the patient dying of pain. Instead he used perfumed concoctions of turpentine, which had an antiseptic effect. He was also the first to document phantom limb syndrome, and correctly identified it as emanating from somewhere in the brain, rather than from the remaining stump. There was good reason for Paré to focus on amputations. The use of firearms in Europe's various ongoing land wars meant that, increasingly, it was not abdominal puncture wounds that occupied the field surgeon but exploded limbs.

Paré's interests were not limited to battle injuries. He was also committed to aiding women in childbirth. He revived the practice of podalic version for correcting presentation, when the baby is in a breech or awkward position. This can be done by gently turning the foetus, but it had fallen out of favour with physicians since Classical times. Remarkably, he was not, hugely successful with the C-section, but he produced a generation of students in Paris who were eager to develop their own ideas.

During Paré's tenure as a leading surgeon, new levels of literacy and the increasingly rapid circulation of print pamphlets and books meant that medical cases were being recorded at a previously unknown level, revealing some of the rarer diseases and complications that can strike a pregnant woman that have always occurred but previously not been noted.

One such event was the 'Five-Year Pregnancy'. In 1545 Marguerite, the wife of George Walezer, who lived in Vienna, was pregnant with their first child. The pregnancy proceeded normally, as far as Marguerite was concerned, but when she went into labour, nothing happened. She sent for her mother and midwives, who could not deliver the child, despite contractions and all outward signs of full-term pregnancy. Then there was a loud cracking sound, and the infant ceased moving. There was no baby, and no placenta. Some days later, Marguerite thought she was going into labour again, and this time summoned physicians, who gave her expulsive drugs. Again, nothing happened. Thus, Marguerite 'resolved to let nature take its course and bore with exceeding pain for the space of four years this dead corpse in her stomach'. Finally, on 12 November 1550, she persuaded a doctor to open her abdomen, where he found the remains of a foetus, 'half rotted away'. The foetus removed, Marguerite made a steady recovery and in 1559 was well enough to conceive and bear a healthy child.

The account of Marguerite's five-year trial was featured in Pierre Boaistuau's book, published in 1560, *Histoires prodigieuses*, alongside outlandish stories such as that of a man who had the eyes of a cat blinking above his navel. For a long time this meant that it was dismissed as yet another 'monstrous tale', but it could have been a rare incidence of a woman surviving a long-term extrauterine pregnancy (when the foetus develops outside the womb).

Most extrauterine pregnancies are ectopic, which means the fertilized egg lodges in one of the fallopian tubes. During this period, such pregnancies would have proved fatal to both foetus and mother by the third month. However, in very rare cases, the fertilized egg escapes into the abdominal cavity and develops with the placenta attached to the internal organs. There is, obviously, no way to 'see' this pregnancy through the vagina since it is completely outside the womb. The foetus is essentially walled off from the outside world. So, although Marguerite's child died in labour which had been triggered by all the normal gestational hormones, it was never exposed to external bacteria. Marguerite would not have contracted deadly sepsis, but it is likely that she was in intense pain owing to constant low-level infection.

It is also possible that Marguerite was carrying a 'stone baby', known as a *lithopaedion*, which occurs when the mother's body coats the foetus in calcified deposits to shield herself from infection. Stone babies have been documented throughout history (and also discovered in livestock and hares), including an incredibly rare incidence of *lithopaedion* twins in Burla, India, in 2007, when a 40-year-old woman was admitted with abdominal pain. She had carried the stone twins for eight years. A subsequent study revealed that one in 11,000 pregnancies is extrauterine and that, of those pregnancies, 1.5–1.8 per cent result in a stone baby.[13] Astonishingly, the lengths of 'gestation' for these stone babies varied from five years, as with Marguerite, to over 60 years.[14]

From stories like that of Marguerite, Isabella and Elizabeth, it's clear that by the Renaissance abdominal delivery was not unknown, though it remained fraught with complication – and much like the battlefield, those complications arose from pain-induced shock and infection. C-section remained the last resort, but a group of new doctors who had studied under Paré in Paris were beginning to change their way of thinking. Key to this group was François Rousset. In 1581 he published his masterwork, *Traité nouveau de L'hystérotomotokie, ou enfantement césarien*. The revolutionary subtitle of this work translates as 'The extraction of the child through a lateral incision of the abdomen and uterus of a pregnant woman who cannot otherwise give birth. And that without endangering the life of the one or the other and without preventing subsequent maternal fertility.'

Rousset had argued, amiably, with Paré over whether a C-section could result in a living mother and a living child, let alone whether the mother would then be able to endure another birth. Paré remained firmly against it in all but post-mortem cases, in which he insisted on speed and decisive action in order to save the infant. This lack of enthusiasm may well be because he had observed several C-sections performed by his colleague Jacques Guillemeau, all of which had resulted in the death of both mother and child.

The *L'hystérotomotokie* was remarkable in various ways, not least because it bestowed the name 'Caesarean section' upon abdominal delivery for the first time. It also included detailed case studies of

16, what we now term C-sections, performed on living women, surgical techniques, arguments for the operation itself but also for early intervention, now known to be one of the key factors in reducing trauma to mother and infant in abdominal delivery. One woman who, owing to pelvic complications, underwent the procedure seven times – though the last would prove fatal, which Rousset attributed to the absence of her usual surgeon.

Rousset's treatise appeared at the beginning of a new wave of medical optimism that accompanied the Renaissance. But this was quickly squashed by the wars, plagues and urban disasters that rocked the seventeenth century. Yet the contemporary prominence and popularity of the *L'hystérotomotokie* proves that his ideas and accounts of those 16 women had indeed planted a seed of hope – hope that an obstructed or complicated delivery might no longer be a death sentence.

'AN ACT OF GREAT VIOLENCE'

During the Renaissance, men of letters like Paré and Rousset had tried to work out how the body, and therefore the natural world, functioned. Polymaths such as Leonardo da Vinci and Galileo invented wondrous mechanisms or 'machines', on paper and in real life, that promised to allow humanity to wield more power and knowledge than it had ever done before, even at the height of the Roman empire. They believed that it was possible for man to learn everything there was to know about the universe. When the spectre of the wandering womb was finally banished, it was through anatomization and the mapping of the reproductive organs spearheaded by the Renaissance physician Andreas Vesalius. The body was no longer a sacred mystery: it was another machine to be puzzled out.

The most significant development in reproductive history during the Renaissance, however, was an extraordinary invention promoted by a famous English family of male midwives, or *accoucheurs*, called the Chamberlens. Guillaume Chamberlen was a French Huguenot surgeon who found refuge from religious persecution in England in 1569. He went on to have two sons both named Peter (the Elder and the Younger) and then, with a remarkable lack of imagination, two more called Hugh.

The Peters followed their father into the male-midwife business with great success. They also used their father's secret invention – and devised elaborate and bizarre rituals to maintain its almost mystical reputation. If you summoned the Chamberlens to attend a birth, a special carriage would arrive outside your house. Servants would jump down and unload a large locked box covered in gilded carvings. The Chamberlens would give the impression that this gilded box contained 'some massive and highly complicated machine'.[15] The women in labour would be blindfolded, and everyone would be ordered out of the room. If you had your ear pressed up against the closed door while the Chamberlens assisted the mother-to-be, you would hear the sound of 'bells ringing and other sinister noises' as the machine went to work. This was the legend that spread across Europe.

In fact, the invention was not a machine at all. Inside the locked box was another, far smaller box that contained a carefully wrapped, extensive set of well-made, cast-iron forceps – at least five pairs. The blades were 'metal, fenestrated, and remarkably well formed'. Each had a cranial curve to fit around the baby's head. Crucially, and very cleverly, each blade was separate, but they could be fitted together through one blade possessing a metal pin and the other a hole, creating the scissor effect, after it had been fitted to the baby. If extra leverage were required, the two were lashed at the junction with cord. Peter the Younger is widely credited with the creation of the forceps, but it seems more likely that his father, Guillaume, brought them with him from France, and that they originated from an even older design. In any case, the success of the Chamberlens could not be denied, and they rose to the top of their profession.

The Chamberlens used their quasi-religious, ceremonial pageantry to dominate the London midwifery trade at a time when the persecution of witchcraft was on the rise in Britain. The Witchcraft Acts (1542–1604) saw women, and sometimes men, executed for sorcery; many of the accused women were those who tended the rural poor in childbirth, aided by plants, natural remedies and experience. As the anti-witchcraft fervour reached its peak, so too did a perverse interest in what were termed 'monstrous births'. People had always known that sometimes a healthy mother gave birth to a deformed child, but during the era of witchcraft, these were paraded both as an example of how an evil mother could deform her child through lying or bad behaviour and of how an unborn baby could be transformed at the hands of a witch masquerading as a midwife. There was a brisk trade in penny papers publicizing the latest birth in a remote village, or conjoined twins put on show for money. But the contrived, private performances of the Chamberlens managed to avoid any taint of dark magic despite all their mystery and bell-ringing.

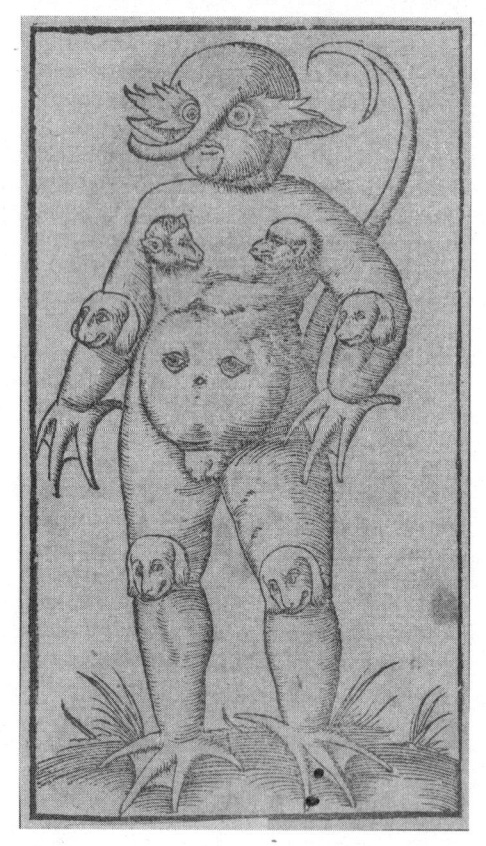

Monster supposedly born in Kraków, 'Cosmographia', Switzerland, c.1547–52

In 1668 Hugh Chamberlen the Younger was the last of the line. He wished finally to sell the family secret. He travelled to France to demonstrate the forceps to the medical community in Paris. The man he most wanted to impress was François Mauriceau, provost of the Collegium of Paris surgeons at the Saint-Côme, the best hospital in Paris at the time, who was making rapid progress in identifying and assisting at problem births.

Mauriceau took an instant dislike to Chamberlen. He was disgusted that a family of physicians could withhold a method that had the potential to save women's lives, purely for their own financial gain, for so many years. But he was interested in the secret. If Chamberlen's method was successful, Mauriceau knew it would be a pivotal development. Previously, births in which the infant's position could not be corrected ended with the 'fastening of metal hooks' into the child's head or jaw to draw it out. This way, the mother could be saved but the child would perish. Yet even the introduction of the sharp hook was full of danger for the mother. He had nothing that could save both child and mother.

Mauriceau agreed to let Chamberlen demonstrate his secret, and selected a patient. She was a 38-year-old woman with dwarfism pregnant with her first child. More dangerous still, she had rickets from a young age, which had deformed her pelvis beyond hope of a safe delivery. When she became pregnant, it was a death sentence. She had already been in labour for eight days when Chamberlen arrived, and he worked on the 'pauvre femme' for hours behind closed doors, using the forceps to try and extract the child, but in vain. After another day of agony, mother and child were dead.

Hugh Chamberlen returned to London, the secret unsold and intact. After his death, the invention of the forceps was finally published in William Giffard and Edward Hody's *Cases in Midwifry* in 1734. Their use became common almost overnight. This is a story of an invention that would change women's experience of childbirth, but also a story of extraordinary mendacity and greed. Many women reported experiencing great violence at the hands of the Chamberlens. While some did survive who would otherwise have perished with their child, the secrecy and subterfuge this family insisted on would have doubtless increased their distress for no other reason than to profit the Chamberlens' family business.

THE TWO WILLIAMS

Shortly after the secret of the forceps was revealed, the work of three men (a 'man-midwife', a surgeon and an artist) changed the lives of millions of women and their children for ever. William Smellie, William Hunter and Jan van Rymsdyk worked for decades to create textbooks focused on pregnancy and delivery that were used well into the twentieth century. In some communities such as the Amish in America, who for religious reasons cannot consult photographs, their texts are still consulted to this day.

The eighteenth century saw huge progress in medicine and the sciences, and changed Europe completely over the course of a hundred years. This was the Enlightenment. An era of coffee shops and constitutions, pamphlets and revolutions, encyclopaedias and empiricism. Enlightenment thinkers such as Isaac Newton and Descartes took the Renaissance idea that the world was a machine and ran with it. The scientific strides during this period are dizzying. In 1722 Mary Toft of Godalming in Surrey caused a national sensation when she convinced doctors that she was giving birth to rabbits (she had, in fact, packed them into her vagina). Sixty years later, in 1784, an Italian aeronaut called Vincent Lunardi took off from London's Artillery Ground in a highly decorated hot air balloon with a dog, a pigeon and an airsick cat in a wicker basket. This time the sensation that gripped the nation was a genuine marvel.

Between Mary's rabbit births and Vincent's flight, a 43-year-old-man called William Smellie arrived in London with his wife in 1740. Originally from Lanark, he set up a school in London to teach a revolutionary course in midwifery, changing the lives of poor women across the city. His interests were, however, not confined to childbirth. His journal records one of the first cosmetic labiaplasties, which he performed on a young woman worried about her wedding night. In another entry, he recalls explaining to a happily married, sexually active but childless young couple the somewhat crucial connection between penetration and conception.

William Smellie's success and reputation grew fast. Through the following decade he taught more than 280 courses on midwifery, each lasting a fortnight. He charged by ability to pay, so the many poor women who took his course paid very little, while the young men hoping to break into the lucrative industry of man-midwifery had to pay the full fee.

He also had a pregnancy 'doll', now known as a 'phantom'. It was a half-life-size anatomical model with a removable cushion fitted over the belly to hide the internal organs and uterus shown at full term inside. He would ask his students to gather round and instruct one of them to pull a string (like a tampon) from the phantom. The 'uterus' would then release a bag of small beer attached to a hidden cork, which poured out of the doll and all over the students to simulate waters breaking. Many of the young men were shocked, which was his intention. When I was at school in the 1990s, in sex education class, we had something similar: a short video of labour in which the moment the waters cascaded forth was so dramatic that a young man called Adam went bone-white, passed clean out and derailed the whole lesson.

Smellie and his phantom taught over 900 pupils of both sexes, who delivered more than 1,100 women in London's West End during their courses. Many of these women would have been poor as patients were not charged, on the condition his students could attend the birth.

At the end of the decade William's health was uncertain. He wanted his legacy to be a manual from which other men and women could learn the skills they needed to assist with difficult births. In 1752 he published the first part of his *Treatise of the Theory and Practice of Midwifery*, to huge acclaim. The book was illustrated almost entirely by Jan van Rymsdyk and immediately translated into French, German and Dutch. It catapulted its author into a fame for which, as a somewhat shy and modest man, he was ill equipped. Smellie is depicted in his portrait in his work turban rather than a wig, symbolising his dedication to his profession, a technique later used by Hogarth to denote honesty.

William Smellie had a protégé called William Hunter, who also came from Lanarkshire in the lowlands of Scotland. Born in 1718, he went to study midwifery with Smellie in 1740, staying with the family, before moving in with James Douglas, anatomist, midwife and Physician Extraordinary to Queen Caroline. Hunter was destined for great things, and had the ambition to match – Smellie's hard work among the poor was not for him. In 1746 he set up an anatomy school, where 'Gentlemen may have the opportunity of learning the Art of Dissecting during the whole winter season in the same manner as in Paris' – in other words, on corpses.

In 1748 Hunter became the midwife for the Middlesex Hospital in London, close to his anatomy school in Great Windmill Street. He wrote to a friend: 'I am busy forming a plan for being an author. In short my head is full of a thousand things.'[16] One of those things was the anatomy of pregnancy, and all that could go wrong. Jan van Rymsdyk spent over 20 years drawing women and foetuses for Hunter's book. It took until 1774 for Hunter's *Anatomy of the Gravid Uterus, Exhibited in Figures* to appear, but it was a triumph, although the books came at a terrible human cost, both for the living and for the dead.

There remain questions around how Hunter acquired some of the subjects he dissected for Van Rymsdyk to draw. Despite the rumours, it is doubtful Hunter had women murdered. He was such a gifted midwife that he had to wait until 1750 for the opportunity to dissect a woman with a full-term foetus. His brother John Hunter, however, was less scrupulous, and probably more opportunistic with regard to securing his subjects. Body-snatching was a huge preoccupation for the eighteenth-century mind.

Jan van Rymsdyk, who completes a macabre triangle with the two Williams, was an artistic genius; of that there can be no question. A 'big, raw-boned' Dutchman, it's possible he was discovered by William Hunter on a trip to Leiden in 1748. We know that he was in Covent Garden by 1750, when he began work on the first ten plates of Hunter's *Gravid Uterus*, which would keep him busy for the next two decades. He attended as the corpses were brought into Hunter's anatomy school and Smellie's more modest premises; he waited as they were opened and the veins injected with dye and preservative, the cause of death examined and established. Once he watched as an alternative baby, more suited to the illustration, was placed within the dead woman's womb – it is no surprise that the incident occurred at Hunter's. Then he took up his favourite red chalk and fine, expensive Dutch paper, and he sat with those women and children for hours, illustrating the causes of their deaths. He even engraved some of the copper plates used in the printing of the illustrations in the books.

Both doctors were desperate to leave a legacy. Smellie wanted his work to continue helping women after his death; Hunter wanted his scientific discoveries on why women miscarried, endured stillbirths and died in childbirth to ensure his fame. They both needed Van Rymsdyk. As Hunter said, the magic of Jan van Rymsdyk's work is that he 'represents what was actually seen, it carries the mark of truth, and becomes almost as infallible as the object itself'.

Measured against the camera, Van Rymsdyk was the finest artist working in London during his lifetime. He also had the strongest stomach. But the work would not leave him unscathed. He suffered two breakdowns, one of them alcoholic, during the years of his involvement with the books. The first saw him painting theatre scenery in Bristol in exchange for drink, and during the second he travelled to Jamaica to make beautiful botanical drawings for Hans Sloane, founder of the British Museum. He was not only an artist but also at times a deeply thwarted man. His life's ambition was to be a portrait painter, yet his life's work was a series of dead women and their unborn children. His images 'are amazingly powerful, not only for their subject matter but also in the confidence and beauty of their treatment'.[17]

You can visit his drawings at the Hunterian Collection in the University of Glasgow. The women's faces are never depicted, but every detail of their children is captured and there is a curious dignity, almost an adoration, in his renderings: the sitting posture of the gravid woman, with her knees covered by a blanket but her internal organs displayed by the neat flaying of the anatomist, the baby curled snugly inside her, a stray wisp of its hair escaping the womb. He summarized his own legacy accurately in one of his later letters: 'I have been very useful as a Designer, and Sacrificed my Talents to a good purpose, more so than any Painter in my Profession in this Kingdom.'[18]

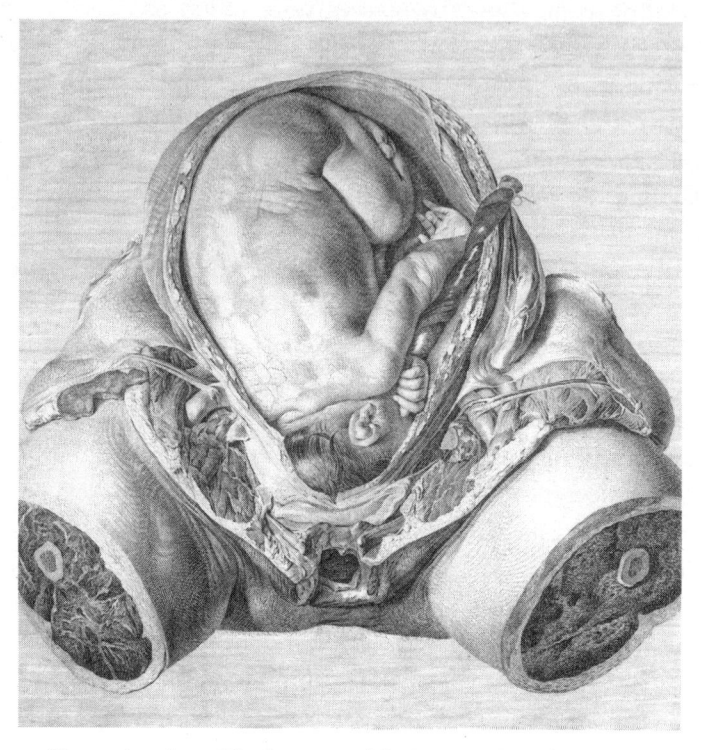

Illustration from *The Anatomy of the Human Gravid Uterus* by William Hunter, Jan van Rymsdyk, 1774

THE MIDWIVES STRIKE BACK

While Smellie, Hunter and Van Rymsdyk were working hard on their books, the charitable souls of London were busy taking donations to create five new lying-in hospitals in central London, two of which were specifically for married women. Each new hospital delivered up to 40 babies a week and they provided baby clothes, food, candles and even clocks and made up fires, as well as assisting with the births and keeping everyone clean and tidy. It must have been controlled chaos, overseen at all times by a midwife (matron) and a younger midwife (assistant matron) with a team of trainees. It offered six-month intensive training courses, and the average age of the student was 34.[19] Patients were charged £30, a significant sum, equivalent to £5,000 today.

The hospitals were ultimately overseen by a 'man-midwife', but they were only there to assist when it was a difficult birth, which was thought to be very infrequently: William Smellie estimated it as eight in a hundred births. The mortality rate in labour in the general population in London hovered around the 10 per cent mark, but in the hospitals it was 6 per cent.[20]

Overall, from the hospitals' records, they seem like small, clean and comfortable places to take a break and bond with a new baby – but not everyone was happy. The old guard of physicians and midwives were up in arms. A zealot physician called Frank Nicholls and a midwife, Elizabeth Nihell, were determined to stop this development in its tracks. Nicholls wrote a polemic in 1752 called *The Petition of the Unborn Babes*, in which he wrote the part of the unborn children whom 'Dr Pocus' and 'Dr Maulus' were going to 'distress, bruise and kill' during their births.[21] In her forceful pamphlet *Treatise on the Art of Midwifery* (1760) Nihell inveighed against 'man-midwives' putting their hands inside women. She is most amusing on the description of her nemesis William Smellie's 'doll', which she admits had an ingenious bladder full of 'small beer' and a tiny wax baby inside.[22]

Nihell accuses 'man-midwives' of being 'broken barbers, tailors, or even pork-butchers (I know myself one of this last trade, who after spending half his life stuffing sausages, who is turned intrepid physician and man-midwife)'.[23] These public houndings were turf war spats, but it is apparent how threatened Nicholls and Nihell felt about losing their trade. Despite her vehement rhetoric, however, Elizabeth Nihell seems like exactly the sort of person you'd want with you in a tight spot on the labour ward. In her pamphlet she writes that she wouldn't do 'any thing or practice tending to endanger the safety of women in childbirth', and she was very focused on the welfare of the women in her care.[24]

Giving birth at any time before the advent of antibiotics was a lottery. The chance of maternal mortality hovered at around 10–20 per cent, depending on things like a diphtheria outbreak, but anything as simple as a bad presentation and that risk could increase up to 80–100 per cent in minutes. Everyone feared the onset of puerperal (which means the first few weeks post-partum) fever in the three days after birth. It is a life-threatening illness usually caused by a bacteria that thrives in the upper genital tract, which is very vulnerable immediately post-partum. The bacteria is nearly always introduced by unsterilized equipment and dirty hands. This explains why Nichell had such strong feelings about 'man-midwives' keeping their hands away from women, especially the ones who'd previously worked as pork butchers.

Puerperal fever was first mentioned by Edward Strother in 1716 in his book *Criticon febrium*, or *Causes of Fevers*. When most women gave birth at home, people understood it as childbed fever, which was dangerous but not always fatal, though extremely nasty for weeks. Some people were lucky. With the introduction of maternity hospitals run by staff who were suddenly touching all their patients intimately, it became almost impossible to contain. When it became 'epidemic', there was little hope of survival. The abdominal pain was severe, as was the fever, and then up to ten days later the uterus would liquefy and fill the woman's body with poison. Some of the lying-in hospitals experienced 100 per cent fatalities of mothers and babies during severe outbreaks.

Part of the problem was that most physicians believed fevers to be essentially inflammatory, or an infection in one part of the body, whereas puerperal fever is septic and affects the whole system, causing organ damage. It was Alexander Gordon, another Scottish obstetrician, who realised that the same attendants were going to all the infected patients. He wrote this up in his *Treatise on the Epidemic Puerperal Fever of Aberdeen* (1795), recommending the burning of anything that had touched an infected patient and regular fumigation.

Sadly the disease remained fatal for most of the sufferers. Mary Wollstonecraft, the author of *A Vindication of the Rights of*

Woman, and, strangely, her daughter Mary Shelley – the author of *Frankenstein* – both died of puerperal fever after giving birth. Wollstonecraft's labour had gone well at first, but unfortunately the placenta had not come away completely. Her husband, William Godwin, wrote in his memoir:

> the midwife dared not proceed any further, and gave her opinion for calling in a male practitioner … On Monday, Dr. Fordyce forbad the child's having the breast, and we therefore procured puppies to draw off the milk. This occasioned some pleasantry of Mary with me and the other attendants … These were the amusements of persons in the very gulf of despair.[25]

It may be surprising for us today but, before breast pumps, puppies were sometimes recommended by doctors if a woman needed to maintain her supply or draw it off. Inversely, other animals were turned to for help supplying milk to babies. Goats and asses, in particular, were used quite widely to suckle babies in London at this period, and would make their rounds door to door for women who were experiencing difficulties lactating, or for babies who found the milk more palatable. At least the puppies gave Mary, who had written about the joy she took in breastfeeding her oldest daughter, and her husband some moments of levity in her final days.

Mary Wollstonecraft was one of the great thinkers of the Enlightenment. Passionate, fiercely intelligent, determined and at the very heart of the radical changes sweeping through Europe, she had travelled to France during the height of the Revolution to see it with her own eyes. Her books and letters would come to inform the founding principles of feminism and yet, like so many others, she did not escape the dangers of childbirth. A thousand years ago, on a windswept peninsula, a nameless woman also died in childbirth surrounded by her treasures. She lived during a time when women were excluded from the world of storytelling and left no words for us. Wollstonecraft may have died in 1797 but, as Virginia Woolf would write a hundred years later, 'we hear her voice and trace her influence even now among the living'.

5

Anarcha, Betsey and Lucy

Thousands of years ago, intrepid hunter–gatherers found their way across the icy land bridge that once connected Russia to what we now call the American continents. These settlers splintered up and down the west coast, and then moved inland. On the North American land mass they gradually separated into the coastal tribes of east and west and the Plains Nations of the interior. Just as in Europe, or any other continent, over time the tribes developed distinctive differences, both physically and culturally: the tall, muscular Crow tribe, buffalo hunters who lived on horseback, lived next to the slight, smaller Blackfoot up in Montana. The Blackfoot people are known for their unique music, unknown to any other tribe, a polyphony full of haunting loops and phrases. These people traded among a complex set of routes requiring ancient knowledge passed down as oral history. We can find some of the history of childbirth in this oral history, and in those traditions which survive today.

Of all the Native American nations, the Navajo or *Diné* ('The People') – whose reservation today covers large parts of New Mexico, Arizona and Utah – have one of the better-documented histories. Navajo traditions of childbirth show us a ritual that had barely changed for hundreds (or possibly thousands) of years until the mid-twentieth century. Some traditions are not particular to the Navajo, and are common throughout the First Nation peoples.

Knots, for example, as in the Cradle of Civilization, bear a universal significance: the pregnant woman must refrain from tying any knot for the duration of her term, or the baby will be bound inside the womb and delivery will be difficult. Taboos haunted both the mother and the father – for instance, to look upon the dead or disabled, animal or human, was thought to produce a dead or disabled child. Some said that turning a blanket the wrong way up could result in a breech birth. In direct contrast to European traditions of preparing baby clothes and wrappings, the Navajo made no preparations for the infant until it had arrived safely into the world, at which point a cradleboard and materials for swaddling the child were sourced. It was taboo to even think of names. The only ceremony a pregnant woman was allowed to attend was the Blessingway – a Navajo ceremony meant to connect the participant to the spirits of those who created mankind, including that of Changing Woman, the mother goddess of the ancient spirits.

When her contractions begin, a Navajo woman kneels on a sheepskin rug and holds onto a knotted red sash hanging from the ceiling, surrounded by her husband and female friends. We know some tribes barred the husband from the birth, but certainly for the Navajo, Comanche and the Cherokee, as well as others, he was viewed as essential. The husband kneels behind her and holds her – hands over the top of the abdomen, pressing gently and rhythmically, helping encourage contractions. The woman's hair would be ceremonially unbound, as would any knot in the dwelling (hogan). In a final gesture towards freedom, even the family livestock would be untethered and left to roam the wide open wilderness.

If there were problems with the birth, the medicine man would attend, but after a safe delivery the baby was left attached to the cord until the placenta was delivered. The cutting complete, the placenta and all fluids discharged during the birth would be safely wrapped up in the sheepskin and buried somewhere in the earth – secretly. In some tellings this was to stop the powers contained in these things being misused to harm the child. The mother, after all was done, is bathed and wrapped in the red sash which hung above her throughout the ceremony – this scarlet fabric wrapped gently around her abdomen symbolized the rebinding of her body.

When the umbilical stump, another powerful talisman, fell away it was buried with a gendered concept of the child's future life: a boy's may be buried with the livestock or by a corral, and the girl's by a hearth or under weaving equipment.[1]

These traditions demonstrate the close harmony between practical medicine and the spiritual so apparent in the prehistoric era. Likewise on the South American continent traditions persisted, most notably spreading from what is now known as the Yucatán peninsula in Mexico inland to the Aztec and Mayan peoples. Snake symbolism and the double goddess figure reappear in the form of the complex deity Tlazolteotl or 'sin/filth-eater'. She was often rendered not in paintings but in sculpture, squatting with an infant emerging between her legs. Tradition dictated that the sculpture would be placed on the chest of the labouring woman, absorbing any negative energy that might emanate from the birth. Her gurning visage, symbolic of her consumption of the corruption of the world, is probably now most recognizable as the small golden bust looted by Indiana Jones in the opening scene of the film *Raiders of the Lost Ark* (1981).

The Aztecs (*c.* 1300–1521) had a similar grinning deity, called Tlaltecuhtli, both the bringer and destroyer of life, also associated with childbirth. Like Tlazolteotl, she ate the dead and the sins of the world. For the Aztecs, women who perished in childbirth were venerated as warriors, and Tlaltecuhtli turned them into hummingbirds for their next life.[2]

In 1492 the trader and explorer Christopher Columbus arrived at what Europeans called 'the New World'. Almost a century later the colonization of North America by the British and other European nations was under way – it would alter the history of birth on both continents for ever.

The first British settlers arrived in Roanoke (now North Carolina, but then Virginia) in 1585. They were part of a forward party of men sent forth to scout opportunities, funded by Sir Walter Raleigh under the direct sponsorship of Queen Elizabeth I. Women and children followed the next year, and not long afterwards the first European child, a girl, was born on North American soil on 18 August 1587. She was named Virginia Dare. Virginia would disappear from the historical record later the same month.

When people tell the strange story of what happened to the first settlers in Roanoke, Virginia's home, they often refer to it as the 'Lost Colony'. A supply party arrived at Roanoke in 1590 to find it abandoned – approximately 80 men, 17 women and 11 children were nowhere to be found.[3] A single word, CROATAN, had been carved into the wooden palisade wall protecting the settlement. The Croatan were a small community of native people living locally, and it was thought initially that the settlers had gone to them for aid. Repeated efforts were made to find the lost colony, but there was no trace of them.

It took until 4 May 1607 for a new expedition to try again. They landed on the coast just up from what is now known as Colonial Williamsburg, Virginia. Under the aegis of the London Company (dedicated to acquiring new and lucrative territories), James Fort, named after King James I, was established in what became known as the Jamestown Colony. The new settlers did not to know that they had arrived during the worst period of drought for centuries, and that the island they chose for its lack of indigenous peoples was actually deserted because the water (when there was some to be had) was bad and the land not suitable for crops. Nevertheless in October 1608 the first women arrived with the second fleet, and in 1609 the colony's first child was born to the fort carpenter, James Laydon, and his 15-year-old wife, Anne. The baby was predictably also named Virginia. She was the first white child born in North America to survive to adulthood, and is recorded in the parish records of Elizabeth City (modern Hampton) in 1625, along with three younger sisters.[4]

The Laydons were exceptionally fortunate. In 1609–10 the winter brought horror to Jamestown on a scale few could imagine, a period referred to by later historians as the Starving Time. The settlers were unable to trade successfully with the local Powhatan tribe, who were also short of food owing to the drought (although a Powhatan chief was willing to try). The settlers recorded the time with horror and suffered not only the loss of 75 per cent of the population but also such privations that they allegedly turned to cannibalism:

> And one amongst the rest did kill his wife, powdered [salted] her, and had eaten part of her before it was known, for which he was executed, as he well deserved; now whether she was better roasted, boiled, or carbonadoed, I know not, but of such a dish as powdered wife I never heard. This was that time, which still to this day we called the starving time; it were too vile to say, and scarce to be believed, what we endured.[5]

Other accounts recorded that the wife was pregnant and the man 'murdered his wyfe Ripped the Childe outt of her woambe and threw itt into the River and after Chopped the Mother in pieces and sallted her for his foode'.[6] There were also stories of settlers digging up the dead after two to three days and eating them after all the livestock, small game and household pets had gone. Many thought these accounts were thought to be no more than an urban legend until, in 2013, an archaeological dig in the cellar of a dwelling built in 1608 revealed the partial remains of an approximately 14-year-old girl whose bones had been butchered. Her skull had been opened with a meat cleaver, and her face, tongue and neck tissue removed.[7] She was given the name Jane by the archaeologists who found her.

In November 1620 a ship called the *Mayflower* dropped anchor off what became known as Cape Cod, Massachusetts. Her cargo was 120 Puritan settlers and around 30 crew. Their journey had lasted an arduous ten weeks and had been beset by 'many fierce storms with which the ship was thoroughly shaken'. The trip was poorly planned and provisioned, and the people on board lived in extremely cramped living conditions.[8]

Of the 120 passengers on board, three were pregnant: Elizabeth Hopkins and Susanna White were both around seven months, and Mary Norris Allerton was in the early stages of pregnancy. Elizabeth Hopkins gave birth to a son, aptly named Oceanus, during the voyage, and White gave birth to her son, Peregrine, onboard the *Mayflower* while it was anchored at Cape Cod. Mary Norris Allerton's son was stillborn in Plymouth Harbour on 22 December, and she never recovered. Whether from the journey, the birth, or the harsh winter, Mary was dead by the following February. Oceanus died two winters later at Plymouth Colony, and only Peregrine, which means 'pilgrim', lived to adulthood.[9] They were all delivered by Brigit Lee Fuller, the only midwife on board.

The conditions on the *Mayflower* were physically appalling, with all the passengers crushed below decks for 66 days: the ceiling height was no more than five feet. Worse, they were sharing the space with a sailboat, ready to be used when they arrived in the New World. There were no latrine facilities besides 'the head' for the men in the forecastle and buckets for the women, and no privacy besides blankets hung from the rafters. Most passengers were not allowed on deck owing to the rough seas, and the hold was perpetually dark. Fear of fire meant that they were not allowed to cook below deck, so their rations consisted of salted meats (such as tongue and pork), fish, oatmeal biscuits and some rice, hard tack biscuits and for the early part of the journey, butter and cheese. The stench, lack of hygiene and terrible conditions, let alone the cold and constant disruption and fear occasioned by the storms, must have made for very difficult and uncomfortable pregnancies for all three women.

Once on shore, the pilgrims, as they termed themselves, arrived during a more favourable season than the Jamestown settlers. They also had maps from Captain John Smith's explorations in 1614 to give them a sound idea of the coastline, and from him they took the name New England, and New Plymouth for their harbour (now the town of Plymouth, south of Boston).

Unlike the Anglicans of Jamestown, the Plymouth settlers were Puritans who, rather than try to reform the Church of England, had decided to travel to America to create a completely new breakaway sect. Many of them had already fled once – from England, where they were forced to worship in secret, to Leiden in the Netherlands. Still unsatisfied by the lack of 'pure' worship available to them, they looked towards the New World to fulfil their spiritual needs. As Puritans, physical privations were nothing new for them, yet like their Jamestown counterparts, many of them were unaccustomed to the hard labour involved in settling a new colony. The poor weather also meant that they had landed way off course from the land they had agreed to lease from the company at the Colony of Virginia. To counteract this, and with winter upon them, the pilgrims drew up the Mayflower Compact as a set of rules they would all abide by until they had attained a stable footing in their promised land. It was signed by the men aboard ship before they disembarked, and established a self-governing colony that remained loyal to the English Crown.

The Mayflower Compact, coupled with the Pilgrims' religious beliefs, meant they established an entirely different type of English colony at Plymouth. There were more women and children in the initial fleet, and men and women enjoyed far more equality than in the Anglican or Catholic faiths. Modesty and piety were uppermost for their perceived morality, and so it was perhaps convenient for them that up to 90 per cent (or around 100,000) of the local indigenous population had been wiped out for 200 miles along the coast and around 15 miles inland by what is now thought to be either a smallpox or a leptospirosis epidemic.[10] There were no indigenous peoples for the Plymouth Pilgrims to meet, and it gave them a handy abandoned Wampanoag village to take over, called Patuxet.

It was not only English settlers who brought disease: accounts of Portuguese, Breton and British fishing boats, Basque whaling ships, French fur traders and English cod ships were established from at least 1534 up and down the coast to Newfoundland's seasonal colony.[11] These men lived largely aboard their ships, apart from salting stations for cod and herring, and day-trading with local tribes, but that did not mean they were not contagious, and brought with them the usual diseases of sailors, although it took until 1899 for the Black Death – which had decimated Europe centuries before – to reach North America.

In Europe and Asia, where measles, typhus, smallpox and influenza were endemic, almost every generation in every known country except Iceland experienced waves of constant disease more than once a generation. Iceland's relative isolation meant that smallpox, in particular, only ravaged the island every other generation, leaving the unscathed 'inbetweeners' vulnerable to new infections.

The significance of such 'virgin soil epidemics', when two entirely alien communities come into contact for the first time and diseases are able to exploit defenceless immune systems, was not only that it caused high rates of mortality. It also led to a huge rise in miscarriages and stillbirths, as well as catastrophic rates of neonatal and infant death.

During pregnancy the mother passes on protection to the foetus from her armoury of antibodies – built from the diseases she has suffered in her lifetime – and this protective transmission ramps up considerably in the third trimester. For many diseases that can harm children these antibodies provide just an adequate level of protection, but for smallpox, especially if she has had the disease and recovered, the expectant mother will transmit orthopoxvirus-specific antibodies to the foetus at such a level that the baby has her level of immunity 'if not greater' when it is born. This super-immunity is a powerful shield for the very young – it begins to wane after six months, and will return to almost no immunity by a year old.[12] The First Nation peoples had no immunity at all to smallpox, and no resources to care for children when they were sick, whereas in Europe the wealthy hired servants with smallpox scars so that they would not sicken. Worse still, pregnant mothers of any ethnicity who have no immunity through prior exposure are far more likely to develop the severest forms of smallpox. Ultimately, it is possible that smallpox wiped out around 40 per cent of the Native American population by the middle of the nineteenth century.

The Plymouth settlers are not recorded as importing smallpox, but almost half of them did die during the first winter of a disease that was probably dysentery brought with them on the *Mayflower*, coupled with the effects of malnutrition and a hard winter. The children fared better, and by the spring of 1621 almost half of Plymouth Colony – for many patriotic historians since the beginning of the story of the United States of America – was made up mostly of children and orphans.

What was it like to live as a woman on the colony? The intention was to be prosperous and multiply, but their tradition was Calvinist, so their dress and manner of living were plain and simple, even dour. They had been used to a diet of herring and hard bread in Leiden and London, so the bountiful fresh fish available around Cape Cod no doubt made a welcome change. However, one major problem was that many of them had developed scurvy during the voyage and they had arrived too late to do any planting for the winter. Squash and late berries provided them with some extra vitamins, but the diet was poor for an expectant mother, or one hoping to conceive as soon as possible. So dangerous was this combination of factors that after that first winter only four adult women still lived: Elinor Billington, Mary Brewster, Elizabeth Hopkins and Susanna White.

Constant marriage and remarriage were part of life in the colony. For younger members of the congregation, a betrothal was the first step to marriage and was a serious commitment. Fornication was considered a sin, but if you were caught the financial penalty was much lower if you were engaged; a perhaps unsurprisingly large number of babies were born before full term after the marriage ceremony.[13]

Puritan women were expected to suffer in childbirth as punishment for the sins of Eve, as dictated in Genesis 3.16 of the Reformist Puritan Geneva Bible: 'Unto the woman he said, I will greatly increase thy sorrows, and thy conceptions. In sorrow shalt thou bring forth children, and thy desire *shall be subject* to thine husband, and he shall rule over thee.' There were no painkillers available, except for alcohol, but an expectant mother would have had access to a midwife – a woman with experience of birthing her own and other children. Families in New Plymouth frequently numbered between eight and twelve children.

We're not sure whether the midwives would have consulted any books or relied more on traditional knowledge passed down to them. There is no surviving copy of any relevant medical text in any language from the Old World that we are certain was used at Plymouth. The most popular work at that time, reprinted from the original German into English, was the surprisingly informative 1545 edition of *The Birth of Mankind*, published by Thomas Raynalde and the Company of Barber Surgeons in London. This extraordinary book included various engravings of the foetus *in utero* with possible positions and complications, which might be a little rough but are all correct and clear, even to the modern eye.

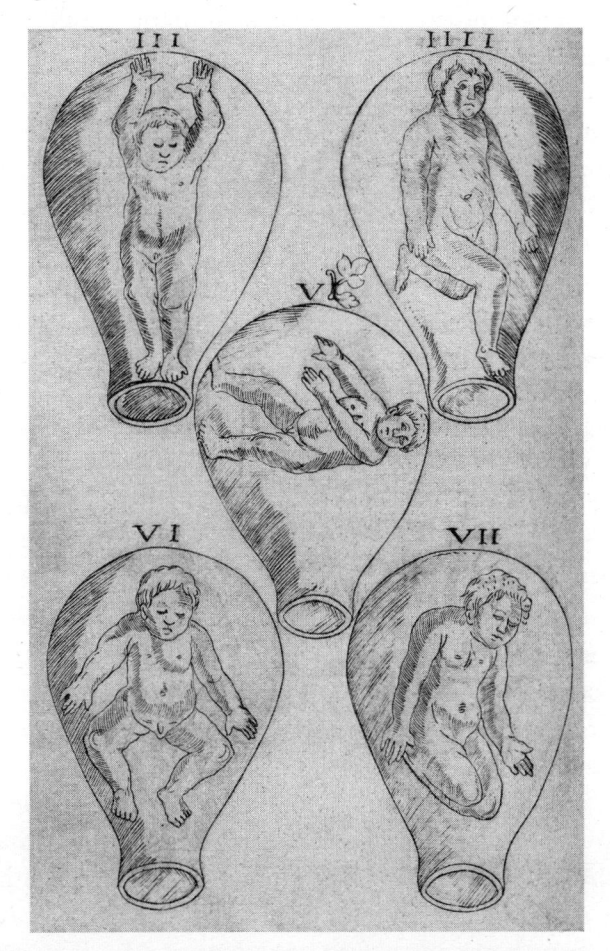

Foetus in the womb, *The Byrth of Mankynde* by Eucharius Rösslin, 1545

There were, however, myriad sermons, pamphlets and tracts by Puritan ministers on becoming conduct for an expectant mother, and the various preparations she should make for the birth. This included 'Preparation for death, the duty of those women with child, who never yet repented', or so wrote John Oliver in his book of advice for his congregant Mary Rothwell upon the occasion of her pregnancy in 1663. Oliver was convinced that wrongdoing in life caused a miscarriage of the mother's soul, which would in turn induce an actual miscarriage. He also wrote that disabled children were a stain on a family.[14]

There was a darkness in these times – one that would have a bearing on birth. A dangerous paranoia was spreading through the settlements now dotted across the east of the continent. The craze for witch trials that had begun in sixteenth-century Europe had made its way to the New World. This new fear was spread in North America through a new technology – the pamphlets and news-sheets made possible by the invention of moveable-type printing presses. In Europe almost all of the accusers and the accused were of the peasant class, and we have very little written evidence of their lives before their trials. Strangely, the accusers were usually children who had begun 'showing signs of possession' such as fitting or convulsions. Coaxed to a fever pitch by adults, they accused friends and neighbours. Zealous, usually Protestant (and increasingly, over time, Puritan) 'witchfinders' were appointed to discover these malefactors living in the midst of communities. Folk healers, with their charms and incantations meant to bring ritual to herbal remedies, were particularly vulnerable, as were midwives, whose access to the liminal moments of new life made them targets for the suspicious.

But it wasn't just peasants. James VI of Scotland (later James I of England) became so obsessed with witches that he wrote a book on the subject, called *Daemonologie*. Under his rule Scotland was the most prolific persecutor of perceived witches, and an estimated three to four thousand people were executed by burning at the stake, strangling or hanging over a 200-year period. Men as well as women were accused, usually because they stood in the way of the witchfinders. In England the Pendle witch trial (1612–34) played on the superstitions of an extremely poor rural community reliant on ancient remedies and rituals. Of the eleven people who went to trial, ten were hanged.

Across Europe the same fever was breaking out. In Torsåker, Sweden, in the winter of 1674, Minister Hornæus was charged with finding all the witches in the parish. He stationed two boys at the church door and asked them to point out any parishioner who carried the invisible mark of Satan. The boys pointed out 71 people, of whom 65 were women. They were all beheaded in one day, together nearly 20 per cent of the parishioners. This was called the 'Great Noise'.[15]

Witch trials began to wane in Europe by around 1670, just when interest in witchcraft was really taking off in the New World. Increase Mather (a Puritan minister and later president of the newly founded Harvard College) was a keen promotor of this new paranoia, publishing his essay *Remarkable Providences* in 1684 – supposedly an accurate account of the behaviour of those in league with Satan.

These outbreaks of witch-hunting couldn't have happened without febrile conditions – within a context of instability and change. The mood in the colonies was already fraught in the late seventeenth century, with the revocation of the Royal Charter of the Massachusetts Bay Colony in 1686 (the charter was revoked by Charles II because the Puritans had been ignoring English civil law, and the state was briefly absorbed by New England). The next year the Boston Revolt broke out – an uprising against church members and administrators in Boston by a highly organized militia. There were fears about the resulting possible loss of land titles, as well as local problems with infighting and strange weather, poor harvests and what felt like a general malaise. This set the scene for a season of mass hysteria. Mather and his 18-year-old son Cotton were a formidable team when it came to whipping up anti-witch sentiment.

Among the Puritans of New England, witch-finding found particularly fertile ground in the months between February 1692 and May 1693, when over 200 people were accused of witchcraft and ultimately 19 (14 women and 5 men) were executed by hanging and one man, Giles Storey, was crushed to death by stones placed on his chest. Their targets were not so different from those accused in Europe. Puritans, who had set themselves apart based on their dogmatic reading of the Bible, still relied on 'cunning folk', healers and diviners – although they regarded them as 'ungodly', and as bearing the stain of Catholic superstitions. These cunning folk were often marginalized but were sought out by those who wanted them to find lost objects, cast love or fertility charms, read futures, cure livestock or change the weather. German and Eastern European Protestants had brought with them to Jamestown and the Massachusetts Bay colonies their ancient folk tales such as Baba Yaga, the beaked, flying witch associated with long-legged birds (much like the ghoulish white bird women sculptures of prehistoric Europe), who roamed abroad at night looking for children and babies to eat.

As in Europe, the accusers were local children who had been exhibiting strange symptoms such as convulsions and delusions. During the infamous Salem witch trials the accusers, all female, were Elizabeth Hubbard (aged 17), Ann Putnam (12), Abigail Williams (12) and Betty Parris (9). Owing to a highly mobile population and tenuous land contracts in new territories, disputes were common and ongoing, and tensions were high; it had also been a wet, dank summer in Salem, and the crops, which were mainly rye grains, were poor. The final Salem trial was in May 1693 and the executions were carried out in September. Two women, Elizabeth Proctor and Abigail Faulkener, were given a stay of execution owing to pregnancy, and by the time they were due to be executed the hysteria was over and they were pardoned.

In comparison to Scotland's huge and sustained campaign of persecution, Salem is a small, provincial event. In recent years a bizarre explanation has taken root – that this outbreak was caused by mouldy rye crops. Ergotism, also called St Anthony's Fire, is caused by a fungus that grows in mouldy grain crops but particularly in rye. And it can have a wide range of symptoms that can appear as demonic possession, with twitching, convulsions and violent hallucinations. Though small, the Salem event entered the new American consciousness. It pervaded colonial literature and thought to such a level that its influence is still apparent in American art, film and writing today. It also set the scene for the continuing power struggle between American congregational religion and women who do not conform.

THE COST OF INNOVATION

In the early eighteenth century childbirth continued along settler lines, with heavy attendance from female family, friends and neighbours as well as, in usual cases, a midwife. The nature of the close-knit colonial communities meant that midwives played a more prolonged role in the process of pregnancy and post-partum care. This was in the tradition of kin-keeping, which developed out of the congregational belief of extended family through faith and proximity in strange, unfamiliar and sometimes dangerous circumstances.

Qualified doctors were in high demand, and throughout the seventeenth century we know the ratio of doctors to patients remained relatively stable at one for every thousand, or one for every eight thousand in urban Boston.[16] Harvard College, surprisingly, did not teach medicine and possessed almost no medical textbooks. This is in part because the library did not buy its own books but depended on patrons to provide them as gifts. Thus the library reflected the theological and scientific interests of the early Puritan and Protestant communities. Harvard did not establish its medical school at Cambridge until 1782, by which time it had become traditional for aspirational families to send their sons to European medical schools to gain a medical education.

The first known qualified doctor in colonial America was Dr John Clark (established 1598–1664), who performed the first trepanning – the drilling of a hole into the skull – by a European in the colonies, an act commemorated in his extraordinary portrait at Harvard. He founded a dynasty of seven generations of doctors who practised out of Boston.

Dr John Clarke trepanning a skull, 1664

Until the formalization of medical education in both Europe and America, almost a century later, 'Doctor' was an honorary term and one often given to ministers as well as men with some medical training. This was the era of the polymath, where gentlemen in Europe were educated across a broad field of scientific, medical and theological knowledge. While this is a useful skill in establishing a new society, it does mean that many specialist conditions or concerns, including those particular to pregnancy, could not be addressed. The reliance on private, imported libraries was also a significant drawback, although books, as well as lecture notes from Oxford and Cambridge, were brought in on the supply ships and circulated.[17]

Boston welcomed its first library in 1670, when 'the town, or possibly the colony, established in Boston a collection of books for public use', surprisingly late for a community so devoted to the written word. In 1677 'Henry Phillips opened a bookshop under the stairs of the Town House'.[18] The small basement bookshop became the centre for religious and general printing in Boston under a series of tenant printers on seven-year leases until it burnt down in 1747. It was known mainly for stocking the pamphlets of Increase and Cotton Mather, and the latest colonial legislation.

Oddly, it was Cotton Mather – witch persecutor extraordinaire – who also led the charge in a huge breakthrough for colonial medicine that would significantly benefit pregnant women. In 1716 he was gifted a Black African slave he named Onesimus (birth and death dates unknown), who introduced him to the variolation method of protecting against smallpox, which had been practised in his home country, which was probably Ghana. Onesimus showed Mather the scar on his arm and explained how he had been scratched with a needle or dagger carrying fresh pus from the pustules of someone infected with smallpox, 'which had given him something of the Small-Pox & would forever praeserve [sic] him from it; adding that it was often used among the Guramantese, & whoever had the Courage to use it, was forever free from the fear of Contagion'.[19] When smallpox ravaged Boston in 1721, Mather determined to put Onesimus's variolation knowledge to the test, but could only find one doctor who would try it: Zabdiel Boylston, a pioneering and risk-taking surgeon.

On 26 June 1721 Boylston inoculated his six-year-old son Thomas and his Black slave Jack (39), as well as Jack's two-year-old son Jackey. The children suffered mild symptoms for around four weeks, including fever and around 100 small pustules each, and then recovered completely. Jack barely suffered at all, with just a reaction around the site of inoculation, and Boylston surmised that this was owing to previous exposure.

The danger of smallpox for pregnant women and infants meant that the colonists feared it more than they feared plague, and because the incubation period was so unknown, quarantines proved impossible. However, Mather and Boylston struggled to convince the other settlers to try variolation. Many believed that it was an attempt by the Black slaves to poison them. Fear of insurrection from the slaves and invasion by the native population was a constant preoccupation of the colonists. So extreme was the reaction that Boylston was forced to hide in his house for a fortnight and someone threw a home-made grenade through the front window of their home.

Mather and Boylston continued their work. They wrote that they didn't 'know why 'tis more unlawful to learn of Africans, how to help against the Poison of the Small Pox, than it is to learn of our Indians, how to help against the Poison of a Rattle-Snake'.[20] Of all the patients he inoculated, there was only one miscarriage – Mrs N, who thought she was between eight and nine weeks along. At the height of her fever she experienced 'flooding', and 'an imperfect Substance' was found in the bed.[21] Of his 288 patients, there were only six deaths, compared to a loss of 844 in the rest of Boston (almost 8 per cent of the population). By sheer coincidence, Charles Maitland had begun inoculating patients in London in April of the same year under the aegis of Lady Mary Wortley Montagu, who had learned of the process in Turkey. Gradually, fear of inoculation dissipated amongst the colonists, but it took years.

In a short time-frame Boston's medical community was becoming increasingly sophisticated. Primarily this was down to one man: Silvester Gardiner, a surgeon with an apothecary shop, in which was based a medical bookshop. Born in Rhode Island and educated privately at home, he showed an aptitude for medicine and was sent to London and Paris in 1727 for eight years to become properly qualified as a surgeon. He returned to Boston not only a highly competent surgeon, particularly in dealing with problems from bladder stones, but also an apothecary, who found the state of the colony's medicine preparation in a parlous state. He opened his surgery, apothecary's shop and medical bookshop at 'the Sign of the Unicorn and Mortar' at the corner of Winter and Tremont Streets. Gardiner began to capitalize on the connections he had made in Europe, the transatlantic trade routes and the desperate need for pharmaceutical medicines in a colony that had been relying on herbal remedies. The colonies did not develop localized drug manufacturing until the nineteenth century, so drug importation was a lucrative trade. From London and Bristol he imported raw drugs, but also well-known English patent medicines, one of which was Dr John Hooper's Female Pills, imported from Hooper in Reading, Berkshire. They were a highly popular patent medicine from the 1740s until the twentieth century, and were supposed to be restorative for 'regulating' absent menstruation, which led to them being purchased as a way of terminating an unwanted pregnancy.[22]

Relying on his reputation as a surgeon and his brilliant knack for advertising, Gardiner built a hugely successful business and a chain of apothecary shops on the east coast and supplied drugs wholesale as far as Nova Scotia. At this time, the patent medicine business was exploding. The money on offer, coupled with the lack of medical regulation in the New World, unfortunately encouraged quackery, and most preparations, if they contained any medicine at all, were usually composed of opium macerated in alcohol, calomel and a laxative. These medicines were a goldmine for the apothecaries selling them to the remote interior, and the mail order business was born, eventually allowing Gardiner to build such a fortune he could buy over 100,000 acres on the Kennebec River and found the town of Gardiner, Maine.[23]

In the urban centres of Boston, Philadelphia and New York, the population burden meant that diseases endemic to overcrowding such as consumption and typhus were becoming serious problems. There were also not enough trained healthcare staff to deal with the patient load. The first American voluntary hospitals, staffed by doctors and skilled assistants for nursing, opened first in Philadelphia in 1752 and New York in 1771. The first mental hospital in America opened in Williamsburg in 1773. Payment at these hospitals was on a sliding-scale model.

For those outside the reach of these establishments, care and childbirth remained home-based. Women in rural communities were expected to look after the health of their entire family, including servants. A lot of herbal knowledge was inherited, passed from generation to generation of women, but women were now also expected to keep a reasonable home pharmacy, and many combined patent medicines ordered from news-sheets with herbal lore. Women, from what we know, continued to view birth as a social, female-only event, and skilled midwives were in high demand. We know, from her diary, that one was Martha Ballard (1735–1812), of Kennebec, Maine.

Martha was a highly accomplished rural midwife with no formal qualifications (a licence was required to practise in New York from 1716), who when she was 50 began writing a diary of her life and work that she kept until she died in 1812. Books on housewifery and care of a family had been published in the colonies since 1742, when Eliza Smith's *The Compleat Housewife* was brought over from London after it became a best-seller. Smith's book contained myriad food recipes and menus, but also declared on the title page that it included:

> a collection of nearly two hundred family receipts of medicines; viz. drinks, syrups, salves, ointments, and many other things of sovereign and approved efficacy in most distempers, pains, aches, wounds, sores, etc. never before made publick in these parts; fit either for private families, or such publick-spirited gentlewomen as would be beneficent to their poor neighbours.

Martha never mentions any reference books in her diary, so it is unknown if she possessed any, or if her knowledge was inherited orally. She bore nine children of her own before starting her diary, although judging by the amount of patients she had, she had probably been practising for some time.

Martha put in a lot of time with her patients both during their pregnancies and post-partum; she often went to lunch with the new mother after a week or so to check on her and the baby. Usually she rode on horseback to her patients, often in the dark and often in poor Maine winters. As today, this was a 24-hour calling. Frequently she stayed, or 'tarried', overnight after a birth, putting the mother to bed, clean and comfortable, with warmed napkins over her stomach.

Martha made soaps, tinctures, salves and other medicines, and tended an extensive kitchen and herb garden. Her days, when at home, were filled with visitors suffering from everything from a burnt toe to colic. She possessed remarkable energy for a woman of 50, once riding eight miles before sunrise on a borrowed horse that had been brought for her at two in the morning (25 April 1785). She arrived to find the baby delivered, returned the horse, walked home via another patient and finally got home at ten o'clock in the evening.[24] Her endless round of visits, both at home and to the homes of her patients and family, as well as household chores meant Martha had little time – we know that in 1794 she attended the Congregational meeting house in local Hallowell only 17 times for worship.

One of her additional, time-consuming duties was giving testimony in court, much like her professional counterparts in England. She testified in 20 paternity cases and at least one rape case during the period of the diary. Her life was clearly a rewarding one, despite the frequent entries in her book that simply read 'fatig'd'. Just in the diary sections we have, she delivered 814 babies, an average of 33 per year. She recorded the number of difficult births as 46. The figures for stillbirths and neonatal deaths were 14 and 20 respectively, and maternal deaths numbered only five. In contrast, a comparable diary and career from New Hampshire male midwife James Farrington, who practised nearly half a century later, from 1824 to 1859, recorded 1,233 births, an average of 35 per year, and the number of difficult births at a startling 246. Stillbirths were 36, maternal deaths were also recorded at five and no data exists for neonatal death as he did not provide it.[25]

The lying-in period was still traditional, although Ballard visited throughout. In the east coast colonies, it was customary for those who could afford it to hold what was rather wonderfully called a 'groaning party' for the female attendants at the end of the lying-in. At one such party Judge Sewell of Boston's wife Hannah served, 'Boil'd Pork, Beef, Fowls: very Good Roast Beef, Turkey Pye, Tarts' to her 17 helpers at the end of her confinement.[26]

While Ballard was an exceptional woman, and midwife, there were many more like her catering to the needs of an increasingly dispersed rural population across the centre of North America.

Demand far outstripped supply in a religious population who needed to populate their farms and new villages, towns and cities. Many of these women left scant records for historians, but they would have made a huge difference to the lives of the mothers they helped and the newborns they delivered.

The period of Martha Ballard's practice coincided with the return of many newly qualified young American doctors and male midwives from the European medical schools. They had received a fine education but had little to no practical experience. As in Europe, male physicians and midwives were sought after by those who could afford them for their social cachet. They brought with them surgical instruments of all kinds, including sets of obstetrical tools. From 1775 onwards, when specialist manufacturer Samuel Laundy of London published the first surgical instruments catalogue, designed to 'fit in a surgeon's coat pocket', a whole new industry was created. Previously, surgical instruments, including the obstetrical sets, had been made by cutlers or silversmiths.[27] London and Edinburgh were the centres for these specialist makers, and none existed in America until 1785, when John Rorer made the transition from blacksmith to cutler to instrument-maker in Philadelphia, home to America's foremost teaching hospital at that time. Rorer & Sons were also famed for their obstetrical sets, and regarded as America's finest surgical instrument-makers for the next century.[28]

Into this fervid era of innovation in all spheres of industry and science was born one of the most controversial figures in the history of obstetrics, (James) Marion Sims (1813–1883). Sims was born in Lancaster, South Carolina, to an ex-army colonel and shop owner turned sheriff. He was raised in a slave-owning family, and would have fled his boarding school frequently were it not for his dread of 'mad dogs' and runaway slaves.[29] His writings are full of such language. He attended a series of schools and colleges, and ended up taking medicine not through any particular passion but because it offered security and, he hoped, financial reward. He married his childhood sweetheart, Theresa, and they moved to Alabama to take up a partnership as a 'plantation doctor'. He became proficient at repairing club feet, cleft palates and cross-eyes, and many of his operations were on slaves. It seems this was not out of compassion: the desired outcome was that they would become better workers.

In 1840 Sims moved his family to Montgomery, Alabama, for the next 13 years. This began the most controversial period of his career. He proved a skilled surgeon and over time built a reputation that meant people travelled to come and see him for procedures. Rather than a plantation doctor, he was now a surgeon and family doctor, although treating slaves still made up a portion of his income.

In June 1845 he was called out to a 17-year-old enslaved girl at a Mr Westcott's, who had been in labour for 72 hours with no result as the child's head was 'impacted in the pelvis'. He extracted the child with forceps, although there is no mention of its fate. The mother rallied, but five days later Sims was called back as she had lost all control of her bladder and bowels. He wrote: 'Of course, aside from death, this was about the worst thing that could happen to the poor young girl ... The case was hopelessly incurable.'[30] Her name was Anarcha.

Sims had never before seen a vesicovaginal fistula (an opening between the vagina and the bladder). Like many doctors of his time, 'If there was anything [he] hated, it was investigating the organs of the female pelvis.'[31] Nevertheless, he doggedly researched the literature available to him for a possible solution. Then, a month later, a Dr Harris called on him regarding his slave, an 18-year-old married girl called Betsey, who had borne a child the previous month and could not 'hold a drop of urine since'. Sims examined Betsey and pronounced her incurable.[32]

Another month later, an old acquaintance, Tom Zimmerman, contacted Sims about 'his negro girl, Lucy, about eighteen years of age', who was in the same situation. Sims refused to see her. Zimmerman told him, 'You are putting on airs... you never objected to an investigation of their cases, and you didn't say what you would do and what not. I am going to send Lucy in. What day do you want her to come down?'[33] Sims examined Lucy the following Monday, and pronounced her, like Betsey and Anarcha, incurable. 'She was very much disappointed, for her condition was loathsome.'[34]

Sims would have given up on fistulas completely, were it not for the case of Mrs Merrill, a 46-year-old white washerwoman who had been thrown from her pony, causing a prolapse of the uterus. Upon attending her and restoring the womb to its correct position, Sims realized that there might be a way to manufacture an instrument that would open the vagina enough for him to, if not repair, at least see the extent of the damage from a fistula. Excited, he jumped into his buggy and drove back to Montgomery, stopping at the general store of Hall, Moses and Roberts at 104 Dexter Street to purchase a pewter tablespoon. Back at the hospital, he asked Betsey to kneel on a table, and he bent the tablespoon and used it to expose the fistula, seeing 'as no man had ever seen before'.[35]

He immediately set to work designing a new set of surgical instruments that would help him effect the repair, which he subsequently had made by Mr Swan the jeweller at 108 Dexter Street. In this session he invented the Sims speculum, still the primary choice for gynaecological examination today.

Sims kept Lucy back at the hospital and wrote to Westcott to inform him; he also sent for Anarcha. He wrote a chilling letter to their owners, proposing, 'If you will give me Anarcha and Betsey for experiment, I agree to perform no experiment or operation on either of them to endanger their lives, and will not charge a cent for keeping them, but you must pay their taxes and clothe them. I will keep them at my own expense.'[36] He enlarged the hospital to 12 beds, with four more beds for servants to attend to the girls.

In the three months it took for Mr Swan to make the new instruments, Sims found another half a dozen cases of enslaved girls with fistulas and had them brought to the hospital on the same terms. He operated on Lucy first, who had lost a two-inch section of the wall between her bladder and her vagina. 'That was before the days of anaesthetics, and the poor girl, on her knees, bore the operation with great heroism and bravery.' Sims also records that he had invited 12 local doctors to observe the operation. Even in the midst of a life full of indignity, this must have been almost insufferable for Lucy.[37] The operation, while not a total success (leaving two small holes which continued to leak), was promising, but Sims unthinkingly packed the space with natural sponge to absorb the urine, and Lucy developed a near-fatal sepsis that took her months to recover from.

He attempted to treat Anarcha next, and it is worth quoting Sims at length to demonstrate the desperate state many women existed in prior to such advances in obstetric and gynaecological medicine:

> She had not only an enormous fistula in the base of the bladder, but there was an extensive destruction of the posterior wall of the vagina, opening into the rectum. This woman had the very worst form of vesico-vaginal fistula. The urine was running day and night, saturating the bedding and clothing, and producing an inflammation of the external parts wherever it came in contact with the person, almost similar to confluent small-pox, with constant pain and burning. The odour from this saturation permeated everything, and every corner of the room; and, of course, her life was one of suffering and disgust. Death would have been preferable. But patients of this kind never die; they must have and suffer. Anarcha had added to the fistula an opening which extended into the rectum, by which gas – intestinal gas – escaped involuntarily, and was passing off continually, so that her person was not only loathsome and disgusting to herself, but to everyone who came near her.[38]

Like Anarcha, many women all over the world, throughout history, would have suffered with the incessant symptoms of fistula without hope.

Again, Anarcha's procedure was only a partial success; although the rectal fistula repair was effective, she still suffered from urinary incontinence. Repairs of fistulas that have healed badly are, even now, usually a series of multiple procedures, so Sims was not simply heartlessly performing experimental and unnecessary operations. He continued for another four years with Lucy, Betsey and Anarcha as his constant patients. Others he repaired well enough for them to return home, but he was still not satisfied. Other doctors lost interest, but Sims continued, training the girls themselves to assist him operating on each other, and 'notwithstanding the repeated failures, I had succeeded in inspiring my patients with confidence that they would be cured eventually. They would not have felt that confidence if I had not felt confident too; and at last I performed operations only with the assistance of the patients themselves.'[39]

One day, his brother-in-law Dr Rush Jones, arrived for a serious talk, and told Sims, 'You have no idea what it costs you to support a half-dozen niggers, now more than three years, and my advice to you is to resign the whole subject and give it up. It is better for you, and better for your family.'[40] Sims refused staunchly.

One of his major problems was that the silk stitches became too easily infected before the wound was sufficiently healed. One day, coming in from the hospital, he found a piece of very fine brass wire in the backyard and had an idea. He went to Mr Swan and asked for silver wire and small lead filaments with holes in them. Although the science of bacteriology was still three decades away, surgeons and doctors had known for centuries that silver was a safe material to use in surgical procedures.

Sims performed one more operation on Anarcha, the 30th she had endured without anaesthetic, repairing a persistent bladder fistula by clamping it between two lead filaments and poking four silver wire stitches through the holes, twisting them off and clamping them down. He then catheterized her and had her put to bed. The next day, instead of the usual cloudy urine and agony from cystitis, Anarcha's urine was 'as clear and limpid as spring water'. Sims waited impatiently for a week to examine Anarcha, and when he did, 'There was no inflammation, there was no tumefaction, nothing unnatural, and a very perfect union of the little fistula.' In the next fortnight, he repaired Lucy and Betsey with the same equipment and techniques. Both were successful. Sims concluded, 'at last, my efforts had been blessed with success, and that I had made, perhaps, one of the most important discoveries of the age for the relief of suffering humanity'.[41]

Sims remains a deeply troubling figure. Despite his repeated insistence that Lucy, Betsey and Anarcha – the only three women he refers to by name – were willing participants in their procedures, we only have his word for it. Their ability to consent was negated by their status as chattel, which meant that it would have been impossible for them to refuse – and they left no diaries of their own. He is, rightly, seen as a dedicated and ingenious problem-solving surgeon and a 'father' of modern gynaecology, as evidenced by his instruments remaining in use to this day, as are his methods of examining a woman for fistula in the most comfortable position (lying on one side, knees to chest, and facing away from the doctor). The agonies the girls suffered over a four-year period at least had a positive outcome in that they were not only cured by the time they were all in their very early twenties but were also trained medical assistants – although we know nothing of their lives after they were returned to the people who owned them.

6

The Numbers Game

By the spring of 1847 Fanny Appleton Longfellow was pregnant for the third time when she heard about a new discovery – the so-called 'fifth element'. It was called ether and it was a drug, a volatile substance, that could send you to sleep and render you completely oblivious to pain. Fanny was confident enough about the potential of this new invention to insist on using it for the upcoming birth.

It was not easy to find someone willing to give her this wonder drug, even though her husband, the poet Henry Wadsworth Longfellow, was a professor at Harvard, but Fanny was a brilliant woman, patron of the arts and a writer, and she did find someone – not a physician but a dentist. After five and a half hours of labour, the dentist began to administer ether sporadically, inhaled on a cloth, so that she remained conscious but sedated. She gave birth to a daughter half an hour later. Delighted by the whole process, Fanny declared ether 'certainly the greatest blessing of this age'. Her brother-in-law later recorded that when he had asked her whether she would have preferred a boy or a girl, she replied, 'I will take ether.'[1]

Some people glide through pregnancy, glowing, and some feel sick all the time and can smell things for miles while suffering from an overwhelming urge to eat coal or earth. When I was pregnant, I craved sauerkraut and ate it standing in the kitchen. Everyone is different, but one thing is the same for everyone: the baby (or perhaps more than one baby) is coming out. For almost all women before the 1850s, this prospect was at best worrying and at worst terrifying.

The history of childbirth cannot be separated from the history of pain. Throughout most of it, apart from using opium, which came with its own risks, there was little hope for reliable pain relief during labour until around 300 years ago. The problem with these early, sometimes very unpredictable and powerful painkillers such as opium and laudanum, was that there was no standardized method of production or delivery. People purchased them legally as proprietary preparations from local apothecaries they knew and trusted, but they were dangerous if not administered properly. This meant that during childbirth they could present a significant risk to mother and child. The new breed of professional doctors and midwives that emerged in the eighteenth century needed to protect their reputations, so the pain experienced by women during birth was regarded as secondary to the delivery of a living infant.

Although ether vapour was only first used successfully as an anaesthesic the year before Fanny gave birth, it was described as early as 760 by the Arabic physician Jabir Ibn Hayyan. Various physicians in the following centuries experimented with it, but it was not until 1735 that Wilhelm Godefroy Froden, building on the work of the polymath scientist Friederich Hoffman, synthesized ether.[2] Ether, meaning 'the substance', derives from the Greek word for 'zenith' or the moment of transcendence. The sensation it produces gives us the alternative definition of ether as 'the heavens' – and it is probably the origin of the phrase 'to get high'. As this name implies, its early usage was as much recreational as medicinal.

Ether was part of the great progress being made in the late eighteenth century in the manufacture of more reliable drugs, but it was not until the work of a group of British doctors working under the title of the Pneumatic Institution in Bristol (1799–1802) that the importance of inhaled vapours began to be understood. British and French doctors had, through vivisection on animals, reached a new understanding of the respiratory system and wished to explore the effects of gases on the human body. Ether, it was soon discovered, worked best when inhaled.

'Ether Day' (16 October) is regarded as the first successful use of inhaled ether vapour as a way of painlessly extracting a tooth, in 1846, by the dentist William Thomas Morton in front of assembled doctors at the Massachusetts General Hospital, Boston. In the words of the renowned American physician and botanist Jacob Bigelow, 'We have seen something to-day that will go around the whole world.'[3] It was the professor of anatomy at Dartmouth College, Oliver Wendell Holmes Sr, an expert on puerperal fever, who wrote to Morton that same year with his contribution to that momentous day:

> Everybody wants to have a hand in the great discovery. All I will do is give you a hint or two as to names ... The state should, I think, be called *anæsthesia*. This signifies insensibility ... the adjective will be *anæsthetic* ... I would have a name pretty soon, and consult some accomplished scholar, such as President Everett or Dr. Bigelow, senior, before fixing upon the terms, which will be repeated by the tongues of every civilised race of mankind.[4]

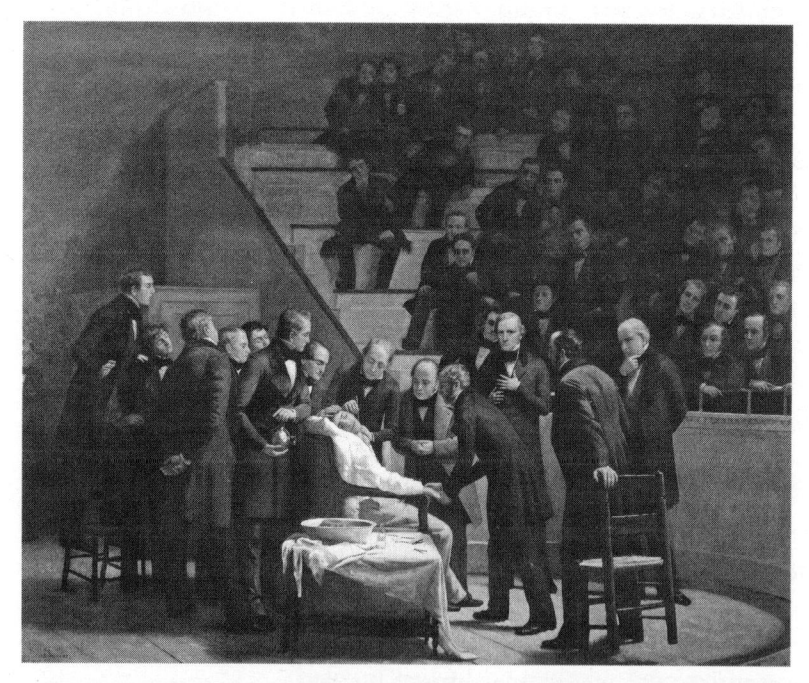

The First Operation Under Ether, Robert C. Hinkley, 1882–1893

But Morton was not the first to use ether as a surgical anaesthetic. In the tiny town of Jefferson, Georgia – population 500 souls – Dr Crawford W. Long used ether on a friend, to remove two cysts. Long next operated on an enslaved boy who had burnt his foot and needed a toe removed; unconscious with ether, the boy underwent the amputation with no reaction. So Long decided to bring him round and amputate 'a further' toe, during which the boy thrashed and fought, and had to be restrained. It is unknown whether the second toe required amputation, but it is possible that Long simply wished to further his experiments with ether by comparing the boy's surgery with and without pain relief.

Almost immediately, the religious and conservative townspeople of Jefferson became fearful of the apparently mesmeric abilities of Dr Long. As he relied on them for his living he ceased to make his experiments known but recorded that his wife, Mary, had given birth on 27 December 1845 under general anaesthetic – beating the intrepid Fanny by two years.[5] As the ability to push is reduced when unconscious, although contractions still occur, the timing of the administration of the anaesthetic and the use of forceps must work in tandem to avoid prolonging both the labour and the sedation. A lighter sedation was more desirable, but it took skill to administer the correct amount.

Long did not publish his experiences until the 1850s, and soon became famous for his work. He died of a violent brain haemorrhage in 1878, while attempting to administer ether to a woman in labour. It's unknown whether his sudden death at the age of 63 had anything to do with his frequent employment of ether. In 1992, in Atlanta, Georgia, there was a Symposium on the History of Anesthesia dedicated to Long and his work, and Coca-Cola issued what is now a highly collectable special edition bottle.[6]

Ether was followed rapidly by the development of another general anaesthetic. Chloroform was first produced in 1831, almost simultaneously, in France and America.[7] In Britain chloroform made the transition from the laboratory to surgical use quickly. The London physician John Snow and a Scottish doctor called James Young Simpson, who gassed himself unconscious in public in 1847 to prove its efficacy and safety, were key figures in the application of 'The Blessed Chloroform'. Simpson was particularly interested in childbirth. He improved on the Chamberlen forceps and invented a machine called the 'Air Tractor' for aiding difficult births using vacuum technology. He spent a whole decade experimenting with his machine before presenting it to the Edinburgh Medical Society in 1849.[8] It was imperfect yet visionary, and is the forerunner of the modern ventouse (a small vacuum still used today to assist with delivery).

Thanks to these two men, chloroform challenged ether in Britain almost immediately. Owing to the recreational popularity and market control of ether (which was often used along with nitrous oxide to hold ether or laughing gas 'parties'), chloroform took longer to gain a hold in America. Ether parties were, unsurprisingly, particularly popular among groups of medical students. However, chloroform had some distinct advantages: 'it is considered more agreeable to the taste, more rapid in its action, and takes a smaller quantity to produce the desired effect.'[9] The disadvantages were that ether was significantly safer, as it only depressed lung function to the point of unconsciousness, whereas chloroform had the real possibility of ceasing heart and lung function at the same time.[10]

Ether and chloroform introduced the possibility of an almost pain-free labour. Snow had originally won great recognition for his early work on cholera during the 1830s outbreaks, when it decimated urban populations in Britain. In 1854 he worked out that cholera travels by water and took the handle off the Broad Street pump in Soho, rapidly stemming the disease. He also recommended such radical ideas as hospital staff washing their hands between patients. Snow was deeply interested in childbirth.[11] And in 1853 he aided Queen Victoria through the birth of Prince Leopold using chloroform.

It is well known from her private correspondence that Queen Victoria liked getting pregnant with her beloved Albert, but loathed actually being pregnant and despised giving birth. The queen had not been without her reservations, especially in the face of opposition from the Church of England, who were vehemently against mothers receiving pain relief of any kind during birth. If women could give birth without pain, there was the possibility that the last vestiges of religion clinging to birth could be shaken off – as Genesis 3.16 decrees, 'in sorrow thou shalt bring forth children'. Yet, as the head of the church, Queen Victoria could do as she pleased.

Snow applied chloroform to the queen's face using a handkerchief and kept the sedation light for Prince Leopold's birth. The queen remained conscious but 'greatly relieved', and delivered Leopold 53 minutes later, as recorded in Snow's diary.[12] As Dr Long had found a decade earlier, there was strong initial opposition to the use of sedation during any surgery, but this was especially so for childbirth. There are no contemporary mentions in the main London papers of the use of anaesthetic during the queen's labour, and *The Lancet's* report of 7 May, written by Mr Wakley, the journal's 'fierce and incorruptible watchdog', just weeks after the birth vehemently denied it:

> we could not imagine that anyone had incurred the awful responsibility of advising the administration of chloroform to her Majesty during a perfectly natural labour ... we were not at all surprised to learn that in her late confinement the Queen was not rendered insensible by chloroform or by any other anaesthetic agent. We state this with feelings of the highest satisfaction. In no case could it be justifiable to administer chloroform in perfectly ordinary labour; but the responsibility of advocating such a proceeding in the case of the Sovereign of these realms would, indeed, be tremendous.[13]

Queen Victoria herself, however, while not given to revealing such personal details to her vast empire, wrote to a friend on 21 December 1859 to say she was 'very glad to hear Minnie is going on so well & had the inestimable blessing of chloroform which no one can ever be sufficiently grateful for'.[14]

The row over pain relief during childbirth was furious on both sides of the Atlantic. On the side in favour of anaesthesia, men such as Simpson brandished the Bible just as frequently as those who thought pain was God's punishment for women, quoting

Genesis 2.21 ('And the Lord God caused a deep sleep to fall upon Adam, and he slept: and he took one of his ribs, and closed up the flesh instead thereof') and asking why men should be granted unconsciousness for surgery and women not for childbirth.

Other medical men on both sides of the ocean, however, came out against pain relief. They were in favour of the 'perfect labour' and said that pain was a useful diagnostic tool during labour (and other surgeries). Much like with the debate around wet-nurses, the word 'natural' was increasingly associated with childbirth, exposing a deep and rigid set of American prejudices. Rural women, slaves and Native American women were referred to as living idealized 'natural' lives. In *Painless Childbirth or Healthy Mothers and Healthy Children,* John H. Dye describes what he calls a 'squaw' birth: 'She performs the usual drudgery up to the very hour of her labor ... gives birth, washes the young *Injun* in the cold water, straps it upon her back, and before she has scarcely been missed ... resumes her labors unconscious of having undergone any great ordeal.'[15] It is unsurprising that this book, which went through many editions well into the twentieth century, was written largely as a promotional tool to hawk Dr Dye's Mitchella Compound Tablets. They were a compound of partridge berry – called 'squaw vine' by Dye – and black cohosh, which were and are used by Native American women to aid with oestrogen regulation.

The idea that poor women, especially Black and indigenous women, could give birth painlessly validated the notion that as chattels they did not require anaesthesia or healthcare, or much time away from work should they become pregnant. Recent studies indicate that 'squatting cultures', where women are predominantly involved in manual labour in a crouch or squat, do have significantly different pelvic shapes from women who don't squat.[16] Familiarity with squatting for an extended period is also useful during childbirth, as it allows the pelvis to open up as much as 30 per cent. These studies may confirm some physical differences that could have inspired the dangerous stereotypes perpetrated by nineteenth-century American quacks and ignorant white laypeople, but they by no means indicate that people from squatting cultures give birth without pain or have any less need for healthcare and post-partum care.

THE MOVE FROM HOME TO FACTORY

The origins of these Victorian arguments and theories regarding reproductive rights and racial differences are rooted in the previous century. It's a story that will take us back to the early days of industrialization in the eighteenth century – to the time when our macabre triangle of anatomists and artist were working away in their laboratory dissecting and drawing women who died in childbirth, to the era of the first lying-in hospitals and the fevers that tore through them. While the midwives were fighting back against forceps-wielding doctors, another thread was slowly but surely weaving itself into the history of childbirth, one that would come to focus not so much on *how* women gave birth as on which women should give birth.

The Industrial Revolution had a beneficial and at the same time catastrophic effect on the way we give birth, for a wide and often unexpected array of reasons. Industrialization 'proper' in England can be dated to 1742, when shoemakers left London for Northampton, seeking larger premises and better water supplies. A growing and more affluent population meant people bought more shoes, and had money for things like hair ribbons and stylish buttons, so the ribbon- and button-makers also needed bigger premises and moved away from the increasingly cramped areas of London. More and more factories were established in towns in the comparatively impoverished but water-rich northern counties such as Lancashire and Derbyshire. Mechanized cotton-weaving is filthy, hard and dangerous work, and occupational injury was common in women and children as well as men. The patterns of life for the poor were changing dramatically.

In the medieval period, when towns were small and prosperous, poverty was more a rural phenomenon, experienced when crops failed or murrains killed off the livestock. The system of poor relief which emerged in the mid-sixteenth century concentrated on taking care of the sick or those who were old and infirm with no one else to care for them. But as towns grew up around insatiable new factories, urban poverty – unrelated to seasonal highs and lows – became part of the landscape. The burden fell mainly on women who were often left alone with children and who, without a man in the household, were the only source of income.

This led to a rise in infanticide. But unlike in ancient Rome and Sumeria, in Georgian Britain it was illegal and carried the death penalty. Between 1700 and 1800, 134 cases of infanticide were brought before the court of the Old Bailey in London. Almost all of the women charged with murdering their newborns were either unmarried, abandoned by their husbands or unsupported by a husband either in the army or at sea.[17] Almost all the children who died had been immediately thrown after their birth into 'the House of Office' (toilet), or smothered. It seems the law, however, was either sympathetic or found it hard to prove that the children weren't stillborn (midwives were asked to provide expert testimonies). Out of 134 women charged, only five were found guilty and condemned to death.[18] Unlike infanticide in the ancient world, the mother did not make their decision based on the baby's gender or whether it appeared disabled. They were motivated by shame and survival. If they were unmarried, they might lose their work and be shunned if they had a child. If they were married, it's likely they were precariously close to destitution and could not afford another.

London was filled with orphaned or abandoned infants and children even before the Industrial Revolution. In 1722 Thomas Coram was 54 and had led a hard life at sea. On his return to London, he went to work in the City but chose to live in Rotherhithe, 'the common Residence of Seafaring People'. He walked to the City at dawn, and back at dusk, and was shocked to see so many 'young Children exposed, sometimes alive, sometimes dead, and sometimes dying'. Many of these children were the offspring of street prostitutes who had themselves passed away, become too sick or too drunk on the gin craze that was plaguing the city or who had simply left them in the street.

Coram, a foundling himself, decided to build a Foundling Hospital for London's abandoned infants. There were rules for admission: the children had to be less than two months old, free from venereal disease and otherwise healthy. The adult who gave up the child would have to wait while they were examined and take them away if they proved 'unsuitable', a euphemism for severely disabled. Once the baby was admitted, any possessions, birthmarks and scars were logged, with any items placed in a numbered leather bag. The corresponding lead 'tag' would be placed on a chain around the child's neck, and its removal forbidden, thus enabling the child to be reclaimed should the parents wish to take them back at a later stage. This tag must have been a totem of some significance and hope for the child as they grew up, representing all the mystery of their birth family. The children were then given to wet nurses on the borders of London. When they returned, they would be taught how to read and how to knit, spin and sew. The boys would be destined for manual labour or the sea, and the girls for domestic service. Children born blind, which was far more common then, were trained as musicians (and much in demand at orgies).

The Duke of Richmond and the artist William Hogarth supervised the first admission of children to the Foundling Hospital in March 1741. The crowd gathered outside was so large that the porter struggled to close the door on those wanting to get in. Thirty children were admitted, made up of 18 boys and 12 girls, and 'the Expressions of Grief of the Women whose Children could not be admitted were Scarcely more observable than those of some of the Women who parted with their Children, so that a more moving Scene can't well be imagined'.[19]

London was, at this time, in the grip of the Gin Craze, a 31-year period that saw a huge change in attitudes towards not only alcohol but also to the sobriety and sexual morality of women. Gin was cheap and popular on the Continent but had not caught on in Britain until a blighted grain harvest (gin can be made from poor grain as well as good) meant the government relaxed its views on strong drink for the poor. The government welcomed the increase in tax it brought, and encouraged its trade. Strong drink was suddenly available cheaply, even to London's large working-class population. The corresponding rise in casual sex, violence and visible drunkenness shocked London's emergent middle classes.

Soon the poorest consumers were pawning their clothes and furniture for drink. But the government was in a quandary. By 1730 one quarter of revenue came from taxation of alcohol, and in no small measure this was due to gin. Hogarth produced his prints *Gin Lane* and *Beer Street*, as well as his *Four Stages of Cruelty* as a response to the destruction of both the economy and the morals of the poor wrought by gin. In *Gin Lane* a baby falls out of a drunken mother's arms and down a stairwell – as it heads towards the stone slabs far below, no one in the lane notices its imminent death. In *Beer Street* everyone is bustling with wholesome industry while occasionally sipping from a tankard of frothing ale. There are no mothers with babes on their hips at all, so we can assume that in this idyllic and gin-free London they are all safely at home. London was used to drunken men in the streets, but it feared gin-sodden women. For a woman, gin was deemed even more dangerous than it was for men, as it would not only lead to the neglect of her marital duties but also put her family and her sexual health in danger. 'Moral insanity' became an acceptable euphemism for women suffering from distressing experiences associated with extreme poverty (and sometimes syphilis).[20]

Beer Street and Gin Lane, William Hogarth, 1751

There had always been prejudice against vagrancy and sexuality, but the Gin Craze marked the beginning of the moral analysis of poverty, particularly with regards to women. It was this view that ordinary women had to be protected from excess, whether sexual or drug-and-alcohol-induced, that would later feed into debates about pain relief during childbirth and the reproductive role of women. The eighteenth century saw a period of unprecedented growth in the population of England and Wales, estimated at 5.29 in 1700 and 9.16 in 1800.[21] It also saw, with the Industrial Revolution, a massive increase in demand for labour, and not only that of men and women but also that of children.

When Adam Smith published his *Inquiry into the Nature and Causes of the Wealth of Nations* in 1776, it redefined economic theory and introduced concepts such as the free market, division of labour and the measurement of productivity. One of Smith's key tenets was that 'Labour was the first price, the original purchase-money that was paid for all things. It was not by gold or by silver, but by labour, that all wealth of the world was originally purchased.'[22] In his book the contribution of women and children was neglected, yet in the new factories of the north of England, women were playing an increasingly important role, as were children, whose small size and nimble fingers made them valuable for cleaning up lint. This meant that children, instead just being another hungry mouth to feed, could instead have a monetary value.

This value, however, was largely dependent on a cohesive family unit that included a male breadwinner. In London, in 1796, Matthew Martin opened his Mendicity Enquiry Office. Mendicity meant begging without just cause. His idea was simple but effective: he produced 6,000 numbered tickets, each promising the bearer threepence (3d.) upon its presentation at the Office. To earn their 3d., all the bearer had to was submit to an interview which Martin had devised in order to shed light on both the causes and the conditions of the increase in desperate poverty in London. In under eight months he filled dozens of volumes with the stories of over 2,000 adults and their 3,000 dependent children.

What emerged was that the vast majority of London's poor were single mothers. The numbers are telling: 192 men to 1,808 women. Martin concluded that this was because men were stronger than women, with more resources – and that women were also likely to be thrown into a state of abject poverty by the burden of children for whom they received no support. Occasionally employers kept women on through illegitimate pregnancies, but we cannot estimate how many there may have been. Martin's Mendicity Studies are one of the few to make transparent how proportionately large the poor single mother population was (whether unmarried, abandoned or widowed) . His findings were stark, and also make apparent that 'origin' had a great part to play in the situation of London's poor women: of his poor single mothers, 22.2 per cent were of 'foreign' origin and 11 per cent 'unsure' of where they came from.[23]

In addition, the new theories of Thomas Malthus and Jeremy Bentham were alarming thinkers in Britain. Britain's philosophers had long been concerned with a declining agrarian population, but Malthus told them that soon there wouldn't be enough food to feed the burgeoning poor or, as he called them, 'the lower classes', for whom he, as the son of a 'gentleman', had a blatant disregard. Bentham's utilitarianism promoted the greatest good for the greatest number, and he believed in equal rights for women and the right to divorce (although he also wondered whether masturbation should be illegal).

Among this swirling eddy of new thought and social change, quasi-charitable bodies were formed, such as the Society for the Suppression of Mendicity, in 1818. The Duke of York was the patron, the duke of Northumberland the president, and the officers included four marquesses, eight earls and Matthew Martin. Its philosophy was concerned with the economics of poverty and establishing what constituted the 'deserving poor', most of whom, as Martin had established, were single mothers.

For the first three decades of the nineteenth century it was increasingly apparent that something had to change. In 1834 the Poor Law Amendment Act ushered in a new era. The old workhouses had been designed as a temporary prop to support the poor and thus the city itself – there was a humanity to them. The new workhouses were something to be feared: they were to be run on the cheapest terms; food was of poor quality and in short measure; rules were draconian. Miserable and scanty, there was little charitable about them. The gulf between the haves and have-nots widened, and poverty became a numbers game.

It took less than 50 years for these significant changes to show a detrimental effect on Britain's poor. Diets were miserable, and the fresh produce, particularly dairy, fruit and vegetables, were not as plentiful in these new towns as they had been in the earlier villages, and they were certainly not as cheap. Working conditions were dismal, wages were kept deliberately low by voracious industrialists and workers' rights were rare. Women's rights were even rarer, and there was no such thing as maternity pay until 1911, before which time it was regarded in 'the factory system' as normal and proper that a woman should put money away for her own lying-in period. Living in cramped and unsanitary conditions, women were either dependent on a man who went out to work or worked themselves well into their third trimester.

With both husband and wife working long hours, the issue of childcare became increasingly prominent among a new, radical group of British philosophers inspired by Malthus and Bentham. One of these thinkers, Francis Place, had a life that reads like a handbook of the misery that could be brought about by intemperate reproduction and lack of funds.

Place had been born in Marshalsea debtors' prison in London, where his father was a bailiff. He was illegitimate, as his father was a bigamist and had a daughter from a previous marriage, as was later proven in a lengthy court case. The family lived mainly around the slum area south of the Strand during his childhood, and he remembered how many of the area's children were 'infested with vermin' and 'used to be combed once a week with a small toothed comb onto the bellows or into a sheet of paper in the lap of the mother'. He also wrote of the children with 'scald' heads (ringworm) and bowed shin bones he called 'cheese cutters', which was caused by rickets owing to calcium and vitamin D deficiency.[24] Place married young, at 19, and his wife was under 17. They had 15 children over the course of their marriage. Their financial circumstances were not improved by Place becoming a passionate advocate for workers' rights. Moreover, he became an outspoken promoter for contraception, despite having quite plainly failed in the endeavour himself.

Contraception had become an increasingly taboo subject over the last millennium as the established churches fought to control the role women played in their respective societies. While it was no doubt something discussed in female society, and between married couples – and abortifacient recipes, albeit risky ones, would have been quietly shared – it played no part in public debate. In 1823, making little progress with the coterie of wealthy and often single philosophers, Place began to publish at his own expense a series of cheap handbills with direct information about sex. He asked the younger members of his cause to distribute them to the poverty-stricken weavers of Spitalfields in east London. The bills promoted contraception, addressed to *The Married of Both Sexes*, *The Married of Both Sexes in Genteel Life*, and *The Married of Both Sexes of the Working People*.

Place was in no position to promote, as other philosophers did, abstinence, so he recommended *coitus interruptus* and the vaginal sponge. *Coitus interruptus* (pulling out) had long been condemned by almost all religions, and the Church of England was no different, but it had not stooped to discussing the contraceptive sponge. The handbills were widely, if covertly, circulated and no doubt proved valuable to those who received them. In one fell swoop Place, a man whose family life had been marked by extreme financial hardship and social stigma through untrammelled reproduction, had brought the subject of contraception into freely available public knowledge. The reach of the handbills went further than Spitalfields. A packet was sent to Mary Fildes, of the Manchester Female Reform Society. She, however, did not distribute them, but instead wrote letters to radical newspapers, asking them to refute the rumour that she was promoting contraception.[25]

The handbills started a more open debate on contraception among the radical communities of Britain, not only about its social and financial implications but also about its practical forms. The nature of the writings on the latter reveal that some people knew far more about contraception than they had previously acknowledged. The use of the condom, known as the *cundum* or 'sheath', was no surprise to anyone living in the centre of London. In 1732 a former prostitute, Teresia Constantia Phillips, had opened what was essentially a sex shop, the Green Canister, in Covent Garden. 'Con's preservatives', or condoms, were so famous they featured in Plate Three of Hogarth's *Harlot's Progress,* which tells the story of the downfall and death of Moll Hackabout, the eponymous harlot. Moll sits in her dilapidated boudoir taking tea with a kitten nudging at her feet, while one condom soaks in a cracked bowl and a whole washing line of them dry on the wall behind her. They were made from the caecum of a sheep's intestine, and the standard length was between seven and eight inches, secured with a coloured ribbon about the base. The treatment process to make them thin and flexible was extensive, and you had to blow them up to test them for leaks. Like Moll's, they were soaked in water then squeezed out before use, to keep them elastic and comfortable. They certainly had some degree of efficacy, and they were popular. Casanova swore by them, and bought them by the box whenever he found a reliable source.

Condoms, however, didn't find much favour with male writers, and nor did *coitus interruptus*. One author debated the three main methods and pronounced that *coitus interruptus* was 'physically injurious, and ... apt to produce nervous disorder and sexual enfeeblement', while the condom 'dulls the enjoyment, and frequently produces impotence in the man and disgust in both parties'. His solution was 'the introduction of a sponge or some other substance, to guard the mouth of the womb. This could easily be done by the woman ... Any preventative means must be used by the *woman*, as it spoils the passion and impulsiveness of the venereal act, if the man have [sic] to think of them.'[26] While contraceptives have come a long way since the nineteenth century, this attitude has been harder to shake off.

One of the most popular of these tracts, however, was also one of the most enlightened. In 1832 a Massachusetts doctor called Charles Knowlton published a lengthy pamphlet, *The Fruits of Philosophy, or, The Private Companion to Young Married People*, detailing in clear, layman's terms, the philosophical debate regarding human sexual impulses, and also contraception. His view was that the consequences of sex (pregnancy, disease) could be evil, but not sex itself – and it was within our power to prevent these consequences. Initially, he only had a few copies, which he lent to patients he thought might need the knowledge. The pamphlet consists of four chapters detailing the contemporary theories regarding the necessity for population control, the practical aspects of male and female reproductive organs, methods of contraception and, finally, the importance of the reproductive instinct. It is a remarkable text that addresses the reader as an equal. The description of the female sexual organs, both internal and external, is both accurate and clear. It is particularly notable that Knowlton explains the clitoris in some detail, writing, 'The clitoris is analogous in its structure to the penis, and like it, is exquisitely sensible, being, as it is supposed, the principle seat of pleasure. It is subject to erection and distention, like the penis, and from like causes.'[27]

The pamphlet promoted douching the vagina after intercourse with a variety of chemicals, which are mainly irritants intended to change the pH of the vagina and kill the sperm so, although the science is correct, it is somewhat unkind. Such was the influence of Knowlton's *Fruits of Philosophy* that vaginal douching, virtually unknown in Britain unless for a specific medical purpose such as thrush or bacterial vaginosis, remains a common practice in America for no other reason than a notion of 'cleanliness' (as recommended by Knowlton). He concludes with a sensible argument about the importance of sexual gratification, and the importance of the role of the doctor in imparting the knowledge that will allow a young couple to achieve it without resulting in burdensome pregnancies they could not afford.

Population theory in America was entirely different to Britain in the middle of the nineteenth century. It was still expanding westwards, taking over the Great Plains and dividing them into settlements, all of which required labour to farm so (white) population growth was considered imperative. Yet rural poverty was no less crushing than the urban variety, and a failed crop could throw a large family into poverty in a matter of a season.

A radical printer and lay preacher, Abner Kneeland, discovered the text of *Fruits of Philosophy* and reprinted it the same year, and was promptly charged by Massachusetts for blasphemy, a charge rarely used in the state and for which he served 60 days in prison. Kneeland was unrepentant, and continued to promote his views on the rights of women and contraception, though he refused to speak out on the controversial subject of interracial marriage. *Fruits of Philosophy* was soon being printed in London and widely disseminated throughout north-west Europe, where doubtless it was of great use to many struggling in the new industrial cities whose looms and forges were never still.

Manchester was the largest and most industrial of all the new cities in Britain. It had long benefited from a robust cotton economy, which allowed women to earn a wage from home, spinning and weaving. Then the invention of ever more efficient spinning machines increased potential production many times over, and women moved from the home to the new factories to work on these new machines alongside their husbands. Over 30 per cent of workers in Burnley, Lancashire, were employed in the textile industry according to the 1861 census, so fluctuations in that industry had a huge effect on the local workforce and their standard of living.[28] With too much time on their hands, and cheap, often subsidized alcohol available, the men of the households were prone to falling into bad habits, making the lot of women harder.

Alloparenting (sharing the burden of childcare communally) among women, as with the ancient hunter–gatherers, was the norm.

The 'ragged schools' such as Charter Street in Angel Meadow – something of a misnomer as it was one of Manchester's worst slums – were established to provide food, clothing and basic education for the poorest children. The Charter Street school would stamp tiny leather clogs with 'CSRS loaned, not to be pawned', indicating how desperate the situation was for these families.

Along with the ragged schools, hospitals were established. Of particular note was the Manchester Lying-In Hospital (1790), which later became St Mary's Hospital. Many of the patients had rickets, owing to poor diets and lack of sunshine, as well as many other diseases connected to malnourishment, lack of immunity and knowledge of hygiene, which contributed to significant childbed mortality. Much like the woman with dwarfism whom Chamberlen failed to save with his forceps, they often had pelvises so deformed by rickets that giving birth meant certain death for them and their child. As few had the means to consult a midwife during their pregnancy, this would only have been discovered after they arrived at the hospital in labour. Such women, desperate as they were, were the new testing ground for doctors with theories, and a new generation of gifted obstetricians emerged under the aegis of Dr Thomas Radford.

Radford's work in Manchester was among some of the poorest women who attended St Mary's. Many suffered with rickets, and what he termed *mollities ossium*, now known as *osteomalacia*. There are two main symptoms of rickets and *mollities ossium* that are pertinent to childbirth: deformation of the pelvis and softening of the bones. In his work of 1865, *Observations on the Caesarean Section and Other Obstetric Observations*, Radford puts forward the argument for the operation, and gives a detailed account of many instances in which he either assisted or performed it. When the British Medical Association was formed in the wake of the 1858 Medical Act (stating that 'it is expedient that Persons requiring Medical Aid should be enabled to distinguish qualified from unqualified Practitioners'), Radford gave the first obstetric address on the subject of the C-section. By the time of the publication of

Observations, he was probably the most qualified practitioner of the procedure in the world.

It was still a new and risky operation. The first recorded successful C-section in which both mother and child survived was performed in 1826 – when Radford was already well into his medical career. The surgeon who performed this remarkable feat was James Barry, an army surgeon from Ireland. He was, despite his small, slim stature, known for being brash and confrontational – frequently getting into fights and hurling medicine bottles around if he thought his wards weren't clean enough. He performed the successful C-section in Cape Town, South Africa, and the grateful mother named her son Barry after him. James Barry eventually died in his mid-seventies, coincidentally in 1865 the same year that Radford published his seminal work on C-sections. Upon his death, it was discovered that James Barry had in fact been born female; he was christened Margaret Anne Bulkley and may even have given birth as a teenager. He was, however, afforded respect by his friends regarding his choice of gender: his death certificate was marked 'male', and he is interred in Kensal Green cemetery under the name James Barry.

Radford's task was made infinitely more difficult because he was not operating on otherwise healthy women with nourished bodies and strong immune systems. The accounts he relates of his patients and the operations he performed are distressing in the extreme, but it is obvious from his explanations and care for his patients that he was a rational and humane man. The women he was dealing with were usually suffering the worst kind of malformations of the pelvis, brought on by disease, cancers, malnutrition or other bone deformities. In one impressive case in 1842, he assisted the celebrated surgeon (and 'Father of Ovariotomy' – removal of the ovaries) Dr Charles Clay in performing a C-section on a woman to deliver her of a tumour weighing 17½ lb, from which she made an 'excellent recovery'.[29] With no child to protect, the case constituted a valuable teaching exercise.

Radford was undeniably and honestly pro-C-section, and he states from the outset of his book *Observations* that 'To my knowledge, there has been no subject connected with medicine which has created more bitterness of feeling and animosity in the minds of those who may be classed as Caesareanists and anti-Caesareanists.'[30] Those against the procedure insisted that craniotomy – the destruction of the infant's head – was the better way to save the mother's life. But Radford believed that even after a craniotomy these women's pelvises were so deformed that they were still not physically capable of giving birth – the only solution was a C-section, even though the operation remained fraught with danger. The purpose of Radford's work, in his own words, was to have the C-section viewed 'on such medical, social, and moral grounds, as to be approved by both the profession and society at large'.[31]

The figures that he quotes are dismal: 85.7 per cent of the mothers and 41.1 per cent of the infants died.[32] It's clear why, when you take into account the collection of over 40 female pelves that Radford left to St Mary's Hospital after his death. They are extreme to the point of shocking: how the women he treated must have suffered in life is almost unthinkable. Rickets could essentially cause the pelvic girdle to shrink to dimensions as small as 1½ inches, and Radford himself had one patient whose pelvis had closed up to the point where he could not touch her cervix. C-section was the only way to save them both, although it offered the mother only a slim chance for survival.

Radford anatomized the women who died in his care, preserved their bones and made observations. He also had replicas carved from blocks of wood through which he subsequently attempted to pass the 'mutilated corpses' of infants who had undergone craniotomy, to see if it would have been possible to save the mother's life. He did so without success. 'However, it is one thing to operate on an inanimate machine, a block of wood, let it be ever so accurately formed, and another to operate on the pelvis of a living woman. I deny the possibility of bringing a mutilated full-grown child through such a pelvis, whatever appliances are used.'[33] He also shows great compassion towards the women suffering from pelvic deformity, calling physicians who expected young married women to submit to repeated vaginal examinations 'mentally blind', and arguing that frequent vaginal examinations 'should not be allowed'. Once should be enough, and in the presence of no more than two others.

For Radford, early intervention was essential. Overall, he deemed speed and confidence to be of the essence in performing a C-section. Hesitation was likely to cause the uterus to contract violently, 'and entails mischief on both the mother and the infant'. On the subject of chloroform and ether, he thought it was a decision to be made in the moment. From his casual asides, it seems that laudanum and opium were used as standard painkillers during labour, and it is hard to imagine the C-section and craniotomy procedures he describes taking place without some form of sedation.

Radford's obituary, issued by the Royal College of Surgeons after his death in 1881, stated that he was 'a notable link in the chain of able and well-known Manchester gynaecologists'. Radford corresponded widely with other doctors who were engaged in delivering difficult births and gathered information from them about the C-sections they had performed or heard about. At the back of *Observations* there is an extensive set of tables recording the statistics of every known C-section performed in Britain, such as the name and age of the patient, origin, 'operator', length of labour at the time of the procedure, the cause of the difficulty and outcome for mother and child. It mostly makes for sad reading, but the first outcome Radford records is interesting. In 1738, 33-year-old Alice O'Neil had a C-section after 12 days of labour – although the baby died, the mother miraculously survived. The operator is recorded as one Mary Donnally, a local midwife.[34]

The majority of the women who sought aid at St Mary's were in a desperate physical condition, which meant they had no choice other than to seek emergency help from a qualified physician, but the shift from home to hospital delivery was wider than Manchester. With the burgeoning population outpacing the qualification of new doctors, hospitals were the easiest place to manage the most patients with the fewest staff, in a controlled environment. Yet, as with male midwives, it was another step towards removing autonomy from the labouring mother and placing it into the hands of strangers.

SOMETHING ON THE HORIZON

While doctors, midwives and pregnant women all laboured on the new wards, something else was on the horizon. A new ideology was stirring, sparked in part by the population anxieties of thinkers like Malthus. Now more than ever, literary and scientific circles began to look around their crowded cities, seeing all the poverty and disease wrought by industrialization, and began to ask themselves whether it wouldn't be better if some people didn't give birth. After Charles Darwin published his theory of evolution, these voices only grew louder. On both sides of the Atlantic, *On the Origin of Species* was launched into a maelstrom of colonialism and slavery. No sooner had North America and the British empire made the decision to end the enslavement of diverse peoples, deeming it inhumane, than Darwin's work was seized on by the thwarted racists as a framework on which to begin building a new infrastructure of social and ethnic superiority.

Darwin published *On the Origin of Species* in 1859, six years before slavery was abolished in the United States. This was followed by *The Descent of Man and Selection in Relation to Sex* (1871) and *The Expression of the Emotions in Man and Animals* (1872), changing the understanding of the biological origins of humanity. Darwin, on his extended research trip on the *Beagle* from 1831 to 1835, amassed a huge amount of knowledge that contributed to his subsequent theories on evolution, natural selection and common descent. He was a deeply committed scientist who leaned more towards atheism as his career and writings progressed, after considering a career in the church as a young man. He believed he was furthering the knowledge of mankind, for mankind.

In the *Origin of Species* Darwin put forth the foundations of evolutionary biology. Man was not created fully formed by an omnipotent deity but was rather the result of millions of years of change over thousands of generations. Darwin believed that 'natural selection' favoured individuals with observable traits (phenotypes) that suited their environment and ensured their survival. Over generations, these individuals would reproduce, replicating the favourable traits, and this eventually created what could be recognized as a new species.

Darwinism was extremely controversial. Not only did it contradict the creation myths of almost every established religion, but it went directly against the idea of an all-powerful being controlling the universe and therefore human destiny. This, understandably, was anathema to established religions across the globe, but especially so in Europe and North America. Darwin's challenge to Genesis was based not only on his own theories but also on the increasing amount of scientific fact piling up around historical beliefs: the fast-growing field of geology was already undermining the Old Testament. The bedrock of the old orders was under threat. Also under threat were the seedling churches of America, where religion and worship continued to evolve into ever more complex splinter groups, coalescing around individual communities and preachers, all of whom were financially reliant on their congregations. Furthermore, America was facing its own internal challenges regarding slavery.

In the Americas, and particularly in the American South and the Caribbean, slaves were chosen for specific purposes. Virginia's tobacco plantations and the sugar cane industry of Jamaica purchased the strongest West African workers possible cheaply as 'cargo slaves'. They were transported far below deck in the worst possible conditions, where disease was rampant. Those who did not survive were considered collateral damage. Skilled slaves, required for carpentry and barrel-making on islands such as Trinidad, Nevis and Montserrat, were purchased at a premium.

Owing to the void into which their voices fell, the role of pregnant women and children in the crossing of 'The Middle Passage' is often overlooked, but it is vital. Babies-at-breast were leverage in ensuring compliant mothers, and slavers also considered them bonus merchandise that did not consume food rations. As early as the 1440s, a Portuguese trader recorded seeing a woman resisting as she and her children were forced on board a ship. Three sailors could not subdue her, until they realized they could just 'take her son from her and carry him to the boat; and love of the child forced the mother to follow after it'.[35]

Pregnant women were also bought on a two-for-one basis with the full knowledge that their babies would be born on board during the journey in unspeakable conditions, as recorded by ship's doctor Alexander Falconbridge in 1788. Furthermore, enslaved women, at least on Falconbridge's vessel, were sitting targets for the sailors.

> On board some ships the common sailors are allowed to have intercourse with such of the black women whose consent they can procure. And some of them have been known to take the inconstancy of their paramours so much to heart as to leap overboard and drown themselves [the enslaved women, not the sailors]. The officers are permitted to indulge their passions among them at pleasure and sometimes are guilty of such excesses as disgrace human nature.[36]

The horrors of the Middle Passage still come to us largely from accounts such as that of Falconbridge, rather than those who endured the journey below deck. The conditions aboard ship were inhumane to the point of unthinkable, and to have suffered them when pregnant or birthing defies imagination.

The indignities, let alone the physical and material cruelties, of enslaved life continued long after the Middle Passage. For the female slave population of the West Indies, things did not improve after the first Abolition of the Slave Trade Act in 1807 (which banned the slave trade in the British empire but, crucially, did not emancipate those already enslaved): without the ability to import slaves to combat the high mortality rate, plantation owners turned their attention to creating self-sustaining slave populations through breeding.

Darwin had stated in *The Descent of Man* that 'man differs widely from any strictly controlled domesticated animal; for his breeding has never been long controlled, either by methodical or unconscious selection. No race or body of men has been so completely subjugated by other men, as that certain individuals should be preserved, and thus unconsciously selected, from somehow excelling in utility to their masters.'[37] This is somewhat disingenuous of Darwin, who does mention the Prussian Infantry regiment known as the Potsdam Giants as an example of selective breeding among humans. It was a pet project of King Friedrich Wilhelm I (1688–1740), who, for reasons known only to himself, had a profound fascination with extremely tall men in uniform. Through kidnap, coercion, diplomatic gifting and selective breeding with Prussia's very tall 'village' women he amassed 3,200 of these giants during his lifetime and took a special kind of pleasure in having them parade for him. The regiment never saw battle, which is probably for the best, as fighting in an 18-inch hat might have proved something of a disadvantage.

Aside from the peculiarities of spoiled European monarchs, Darwin's claim that selective breeding in humans had 'never long been controlled' was, superficially, true – but that does not mean that it had not been attempted. Whereas previously in the Caribbean it had been easy and cost-effective to replace slaves who had died with new ones, the sudden cessation of human imports in 1807 threatened to throw the plantations into crisis. The planters responded by suddenly paying a lot of attention to the working conditions and diets of enslaved women.

Over the course of the eighteenth century, sugar-cropping Jamaica imported around 575,000 African slaves but managed to maintain a slave population of only approximately 250,000.[38] Of these imported human 'livestock', as they were termed, only around 40 per cent were women. In contrast, on Barbados, where the island was more oriented towards trade and where the majority of the African slave population was female, the island saw an indisputable overall increase in the slave population through breeding after 1807.[39] Barbados was the only British Caribbean island to show anything other than an overall decline in the slave population both before and after 1807.

Back in Jamaica, interracial marriage was becoming a fact of life in the more urbanized 'villages' and an increasing concern of white planters. It was not necessarily a concern regarding mixed-race offspring, of whom there were a considerable number owing to the plantation overseers, managers and owners availing themselves of their 'rights' over their chattels, but the fact that it signified the creation of a new mixed-race class of young men and women who, while not necessarily free (many became indentured servants), were not bound to a lifetime of slavery.

Jamaica was particularly brutal as a destination for enslaved Africans. Plantation owner Edward Long displays the typical Jamaican slave owner's attitude towards the enslaved women on his estate, writing that

> their women are delivered with little or no labour; they have therefore no more occasion for midwives than the female oran-outang or any other wild animal. A woman brings forth her child in a quarter of an hour, goes the same day to the sea, and washes herself ... it is seldom they are confined above two, at most, three days.[40]

Despite this strange insistence on the 'natural' African woman needing no midwife (much like John H. Dye's fantastical description of a 'squaw' birth), the plantations did have Black African midwives, about whom Long was equally scathing, blaming the 'unskilfulness and absurd management of the Negro midwives' for many maternal deaths.[41] It is, however, entirely possible that these women acting as attendants, who probably had experience of delivering babies, may also have been sick themselves – hence having the time to attend the birth. Tetanus, which thrived in the Caribbean, was also a major killer of newborns and mothers, when rusty or infected tools were used to aid delivery or cut the umbilical cord. Again most of the details fall into the abyss of the unknown, leaving only the voices of the plantation owners or managers, many of whom saw their human charges as little more than a set of accounts.

Matthew Lewis, author of the Gothic novel *The Monk*, was one such owner. He wrote a memoir in 1817 which detailed the 'breeding list' he implemented for his plantation in Westmoreland parish, Jamaica – complaining that he found it yielded unsatisfactory results.[42] The fact that these women were vastly overworked well into pregnancy, treated with immense physical cruelty and kept on the verge of constant hunger in squalid accommodation, seems largely to have escaped the notice of their 'owners'.

Sugar cane cropping is extremely hard physical work, requiring significant calorific intake, yet most plantation owners expected slaves to subsist on dried or fresh fish or salt pork and grains and vegetables which they grew themselves in between the sugar cane rows, so that they might be tended during the working day. The gender imbalance meant that male slaves consumed the bulk of the food supplies, despite the fact that women laboured alongside men in both work teams (the cropping and planting team, and the slightly less laborious weeding and maintenance team). This diet is low in iron and vitamin B, both of which are required in far higher doses for pregnant or lactating women. The women were often observed 'dirt-eating', where they made small flat cakes out of clay, which may have been an attempt to redress a mineral imbalance. Prior to 1807, pregnant women were expected to continue on the primary team until their pregnancy made it impossible for them to continue, at around eight months. They were expected back in the fields, even if only on the secondary team, as soon as their infant had survived the first perilous couple of weeks, or not.[43]

These physical conditions, to say nothing of the normalized brutality meted out on an average plantation, resulted in low conception rates, up to 43 per cent miscarriage and stillbirth incidence and very high rates of neonatal mortality.[44] Filthy conditions for giving birth, usually in the slave 'hospital' on the plantation where sick patients of both genders were treated for the ulcers and pustulant diseases common to sugar cane cropping and the climate, meant that women often chose to give birth in their own huts, which may or may not have been an improvement.

Long was particularly assiduous about the reproductive potential of the slaves he owned, although many of his observations are little more than common sense: 'Negroes breed the best, whose labour is least, or easiest. Thus the domestic Negroes have more children, in proportion, than those on penns [sic]; and the latter, than those who are employed on sugar-plantations.'[45]

He also believed that the supposed 'sterility' was largely down to enslaved women having too much sex, despite the fact that the incidence of venereal disease in the slave population of Jamaica was very low when it was recorded, refuting any notion of widespread promiscuity.[46] Many of Long's other observations are equally racist and broadly representative of the colonial mindset of the time. After Long moved to England for a change of climate in 1769, his ideas became deeply influential on writers in Britain who believed that different races were actually different and naturally hierarchical species, occupying various rungs of the ladder upon a Great Chain of Being. It almost goes without saying that they believed that white men ranked just below the angels and above all other races on this Great Chain. As Long himself put it, mankind reached the 'utmost limit of perfection in the pure White'.[47] Coincidentally, one of the men who touted this theory was called Charles White.

Charles White was a highly accomplished surgeon and obstetrician of the Manchester Lying-In Hospital, before Radford's time. His theories on easing the mother and infant through vaginal delivery, hand-washing, post-partum care and general improvements in the hospital experience laid the foundation for Manchester becoming the institution that later played host to Radford and the Manchester obstetricians. Unfortunately, this was not all he did. White's main work was *An Account of the Regular Gradation in Man, and in Different Animals and Vegetables*, published in 1799. It drew heavily on Long's attitudes and attempted to prove the inferiority of Black people through anatomical research and observation. This later became known as 'scientific racism'. While White claimed not 'to give the smallest countenance to the pernicious practice of enslaving mankind' or to be 'desirous of assigning anyone superiority over another, except that which arises from superior bodily strength, mental powers, and industry', his book nonetheless takes great care to argue that Black people were closer 'to the ape' than to humanity.[48]

Many of White's ideas remain current in racist discourse today.[49] Owing to his interest in all matters obstetric and reproductive, White also conducted research into the menstrual patterns of Black women. The information he gathered from naturalists and those working on slave ships (not, crucially, the women themselves) was that they tended to menstruate far more heavily than white women. There are modern studies that have shown that Black women are three times more likely than white women to suffer from fibroids, which cause excessive blood loss during menstruation, extended menstruation and pain. The reasons for this disparity are unclear, but current estimates are that 8 out of 10 Black women will develop fibroids by the age of 50, almost all suffering problematic bleeding and/or pregnancy complications as a result.[50]

White does not comment on childbirth differences, but he is somewhat fascinated by penises, and admits that in this regard his hierarchy of race may not be infallible. Another significant 'gradation' that confounded White were Jewish people. He quoted the abolitionist Thomas Clarkson when he wrote that Jews

> are scattered over the face of the whole earth. They have preserved themselves distinct by their religion; and as they never marry any but of their own sect, so they have no mixture of blood in their veins, that they should differ from each other; yet nothing is more true than that the English Jew is white, the Portuguese swarthy, the American olive, the Arabian copper, and the African black: in short, there seem to be as many different species of Jews as countries in which they reside.[51]

White found Gypsy, Roma and Traveller people equally confusing: 'Constantly refusing to participate of civilized society, they keep themselves secluded from the rest of mankind. Their singular physiognomy and manners are the same in every age and country. Their swarthy complexion in the temperate climes of Europe undergoes no change when exposed to the burning sun of Africa.'[52] White chooses to take this as proof that he is correct in his assumption that these different peoples represent different species. In the book he tabulates the proportions of racial heritages required for labels such as mulatto or creole down to factors of one-sixteenth. Scientific racism had arrived.

Darwin, fiercely opposed to slavery himself, still used the language of his time regarding other races and cultures:

> Slavery, although in some ways beneficial in ancient times, is a great crime; yet it was not so regarded until quite recently, even by the most civilized nations. And this was especially the case, because the slaves belonged in general to a race different from that of their masters ... Many instances could be given of the noble fidelity of savages towards each other, but not to strangers; common experience justifies the maxim of the Spaniard, 'Never, never trust an Indian'.[53]

Darwin's abhorrence of slavery did not equate to racial equality.

It was during his journey on the *Beagle* that Darwin developed an intense fascination with lice, specifically those on the island of Chiloé, just off the coast of Chile. He examined the local (body) lice and compared them to English lice, learning that they were 'much larger and softer'. He includes in his notes that a Mr Martial, a 'surgeon of an English Whaler', had related to him that the lice infesting the Sandwich Islanders on board the ship were different from any others he had seen, and that they did not affect the 'bodies of the English', but instead died in the bed linen after '3 or 4 days'. Darwin wrote in his notebook: 'If these facts were verified their interest would be great. – Man springing from one stock according to his varieties having different parasites. – It leads one into many reflections.'[54]

The lice question was not new. Edward Long in his *History* had also observed the different character of the lice infesting his slaves.

Charles White had considered it further support for his scientific racism too. Martial, in due course, obtained some lice for Darwin, and his fascination continued well into the writing of *Descent*. Another friend procured him some

> from Africa, namely from the Negroes of the Eastern and Western coasts, from the Hottentots and Caffres; two kinds from the natives of Australia; two from North, and two from South America ... and the fact of the races of man being infested by parasites, which appear to be specifically distinct, might fairly be urged as an argument that the races themselves ought to be classed as distinct species.[55]

Darwin wrote to his friend Henry Denny that he had encountered White's work in the library on the *Beagle* and found it a 'Foolish book', apart from the titbits on lice.[56] Darwin is famed for his work on the evolution of the finch, the tortoise and plants such as the orchid, but it was the louse, that 'disgusting vermin', which informed his views on the categorization of the human races as much as any other.

The abolition movement was growing rapidly in Europe and North America. Witnesses to the conditions on the sugar and tobacco plantations of the American South were frequently shocked by the utter brutality of the existence endured by the enslaved. American slave owners were, broadly, more violent than those in the Caribbean. This may have been in some part owing to the fact that escape seemed more tangible on a continental land mass than a series of small islands. Furthermore, freed slaves were a rarity in the Caribbean but a reality in America, offering hope to those labouring on the plantations. Following the Emancipation Act of 1833 and then the Abolition of Slavery Act in Britain in 1838 and the American Civil War of 1861–5, there was some social and cultural adjustment in terms of race relations, but broadly little had changed from Edward Long's day, in terms of stigma and status.

This is embodied in the British Slavery Compensation Act of 1837, when the Bank of England borrowed £20 million to 'reimburse' over 47,000 slave owners for their impending loss of 'property' the following year. Children counted as individual slaves when attorneys put in the applications, creating yet another moment in history when mothers and children were assigned monetary value.

> 'WHAT NATURE DOES BLINDLY, SLOWLY, AND
> RUTHLESSLY, MAN MAY DO PROVIDENTLY,
> QUICKLY AND KINDLY.'

Charles Darwin's distant cousin Francis Galton was a genius who is undeniably responsible for many modern statistical methods and a considerable amount of early 'genetic' theory. He is also partly responsible for the birth of a scientific movement that would eventually provide ideological fuel for the most lethal genocide in history.

Galton was born into a family of Quaker gun manufacturers in Birmingham, and thus began a life riven with contradictions. A bright child with an astonishing memory, he was reading as a toddler and soon moved on to memorizing whole passages from books, including Shakespeare. The day before his fifth birthday, on 15 February 1827, he wrote to his sister and tutor, Adele,

> I am four years old and can read any English book. I can say all the Latin Substantives and Adjectives and active verbs besides 52 lines of Latin poetry. I can cast up any sum in addition and multiply by 2, 3, 4, 5, 6, 7, 8, 10. I can also say the pence table. I read French a little and I know the Clock.[57]

He sounds intolerable.

A descendant of Lunar Men and Fellows of the Royal Society, he was, frankly, too clever for his school and left abruptly at 16 to study medicine first at the Birmingham General Hospital and then King's College, London. He then decided to study mathematics at Trinity College, Cambridge, but an unsurprising nervous breakdown meant he graduated with a 'pass' Bachelor's degree. The death of his rich father in 1844 left him with independent means; he chose to travel eastern Europe and the Middle East, and to shoot and hunt.

He also experimented with making the perfect cup of tea: warm the pot only with boiling water, measure the tea carefully, add off-the-boil water, steep for eight minutes. As he later wrote, 'There is no mystery in the teapot.'[58] Eventually he went to Namibia for two years in association with the Royal Geographical Society. There he recruited around 40 men, and bought large numbers of oxen, and 'slaughter' cattle and sheep. He lived rough and hunted game, as well as making contact with many different tribes of the Namibian interior. His growing obsession with numbers, counting and measurements is evident throughout his book *The Narrative of an Explorer*, including the memorable passage where he records measuring a Hottentot woman's steatopygia – fat deposits on buttocks and thighs – using his sextant, so as not to cause offence by asking to use his tape measure. He describes her body shape not as a manifestation of freakery, as many Europeans before him had seen fit to do, but as a 'gift of bounteous nature to this favoured race'.[59]

After the Namibia trip, Galton became a member of the scientific 'establishment' of London. His fortune enabled him to live in a large, comfortable house in Rutland Gate, Knightsbridge, a stone's throw from the Royal Geographical Society, which had presented him with its gold medal on his return from Africa. The views he had expressed in his account of Namibia were mixed and reveal his life-long tendency to grade and compare different groups of people. He had a distinct dislike of the Damara tribe, finding them 'filthy' and stupid in the extreme, writing that his spaniel Dinah could more easily count her six puppies than one Damara man could express the number three. Of the Hottentot people he was highly complimentary, and he was particularly well disposed towards the Ovampo, 'a race of intelligent and kindly negroes ... careful agriculturists, [who] live in a land of great fertility'.[60]

As time wore on, Galton's ideas became more entrenched. In Africa he had commented on how often some of his white recruits frequented the Cape Town prison, which seemed to be a kind of 'clubhouse' for them. This introduction to criminality influenced his later works in various ways. At one point he created 'composite portraits' from mugshots sent to him by the Home Office so that policemen might be able to read the 'signs' of a criminal character from someone's face (he also created composite portraits of 'The Jewish Type').[61] Other experiments proved more useful – his work on fingerprints revolutionized, though not immediately, the detection and prosecution of crimes.

Francis Galton was 42 when his cousin Charles Darwin published *The Origin of Species*, crystallizing Galton's ideas regarding inheritance of traits and character, and from then on, his main interest focused on the inheritance of intelligence. Galton was acutely aware of his own remarkable intelligence, as aforementioned, and that of many of his family members: this became the central preoccupation of his research.

In 1865 he published a paper titled 'Hereditary Talent and Character', in which he asserted that, if man could breed animals with certain physical characteristics, then it should be entirely possible to breed on the basis of mental characteristics.[62] However, he was frank in admitting that 'In investigating the hereditary transmission of talent, we must ever bear in mind our ignorance of the laws which govern the inheritance even of physical features'.[63]

He begins initially with his thoughts on dogs, of which he was very fond in general, writing that an intelligent dog 'is often a dexterous thief and a sad hypocrite. For these reasons an over-intelligent dog is not an object of particular desire, and therefore, I suppose, no one has ever thought of encouraging a breed of wise dogs.'[64] It is not long before he moves on to 'eminent' men, their familial connections and the ideas behind breeding more intelligent people, writing that the habit German professors displayed of marrying the daughters of other professors resulted in 'the enormous intellectual digestion of German literary men, which far exceeds that of the corresponding class of our own countrymen'.[65] He imagined a utopia, called Laputam, in which young men possessed 'qualities of talent, character, and bodily vigour' and young women those 'of grace, beauty, health, good temper, accomplished housewifery, and disengaged affections, in addition to noble qualities of heart and brain'.[66]

He posited that, 'If a twentieth part of the cost and pains were spent in measures for the improvement of the human race that is spent on the improvement of the breed of horses and cattle, what a galaxy of genius might we not create … as surely as we can propagate idiots by mating *crétins*.' These views, whose origins were deeply ingrained in Galton's past and the works of Darwin, found a fertile and receptive audience in the educated readers of his publications, and encouraged him to publish an expansion of his essay as a book, *Hereditary Genius*, in 1869.

Many of these educated readers had been rendered independently rich, or at least significantly comfortable, by the rising economic tide of the eighteenth and nineteenth centuries. Many, directly or indirectly, lived lives of comfort thanks in no small way to the Atlantic slave trade and the opium trade of the East. There was, despite Galton's protests regarding the necessity of meritocracy, a powerful and abiding sense of self-satisfied superiority among the upper middle classes of Britain and Europe at the time, to which Galton's work appealed deeply. The enthusiastic reception of his work led to his views and his evidence gathering becoming more extreme.

Some of Galton's projects can be ascribed to a certain level of eccentricity, including his famed, if now missing, 'Ugly Map' of Britain, in which he visited various towns throughout the country and graded the women he saw there from 'attractive' to 'repellent' on a punch card he kept in his pocket. London scored highest, Aberdeen lowest. In the same year he and his wife, Louisa, spent time in Vichy, France, where he used the same method to grade the local women from 'thin' to 'prize fat'. It is impossible not to wonder what Louisa, let alone the women of these various cities, thought of a middle-aged man staring at them while fiddling in his pocket.

It was during this period, the most productive of his long life, that Galton devised methods for collecting data which relied on questionnaires (he did not, as is often incorrectly proposed, 'invent' the questionnaire, but he did deploy it to greater effect than ever before), as well as developing extensive frameworks for interpreting the masses of data he collected. He studied synaesthesia, and in 1875 introduced the idea of studying twins as examples of nature versus nurture – a controversial method still very much in operation now. He created the first weather map, published on 1 April 1875 in *The Times*, and still a feature of newspapers today. The same year he also invented the dog whistle. At University College, London (UCL), he established the Anthropometric Laboratory in 1884, for the study of everything that could be measured about human individuals who either presented themselves or donated data.

By the beginning of the twentieth century Francis Galton had ideas about everything, from 'pretensions of natural equality' among mankind to immigrants, citing Athens as the only real beacon for positive immigration, as the culture there was so sophisticated that it created 'a system of partly unconscious selection [which] built up a magnificent breed of human animals'.[67]

In 1883 Galton came up with the term 'eugenics'. It means 'better breeding', which would allow 'the more suitable races or strains of blood a better chance of prevailing speedily over the less suitable'.[68] He deplored the fact that 'One of the effects of civilization is to diminish the rigour of the application of the law of natural selection. It preserves weakly lives that would have perished in barbarous lands.'[69]

In 1904 the Galton Eugenic Laboratory opened at UCL (it is now the 'Galton Laboratory'). In this period of his life Galton corresponded keenly with Karl Pearson, an early geneticist and supporter of Galtonian theory. The letters reveal his growing bigotry and the inevitable conclusion of his ideas: in a letter on 6 January 1907 he wrote: 'except by sterilisation I cannot yet see any way of checking the produce of the unfit who are allowed their liberty and are below the reach of moral control.' Also to Pearson in the same year he confided his opinion that 'Jews are specialised for a parasitical existence upon other nations.'

Galton died in 1911, the same year that Winston Churchill, as Foreign Secretary, proposed compulsory sterilization for the 'feeble-minded'. In 1927 a Mr Harold and Mrs Evadne Bolce welcomed the world's first 'eugenic' baby, conceived as a result of Mr Bolce advertising extensively for a 'mate' and then gestated and raised on eugenic principles. They named their baby girl Eugenette. G. K. Chesterton, in his extended essay *Eugenics and Other Evils* (1922), scathingly wrote: 'The fact that Mr. Bolce, the creator of perfect pre-natal conditions, was afterwards sued in a law-court for keeping his own flat in conditions of filth and neglect, cast but a slight and momentary shadow upon the splendid dawn of the science.'

Galton, like Darwin, was, as one obituary recorded, 'untrammelled by traditional barriers', down to a combination of his own intelligent and curious nature, and the fact that he was nurtured by a supportive family, wife and an enormous amount of money.[70] What he set in motion was to have immeasurable consequences for subsequent generations. By the time of his death, Galtonian principles regarding who should reproduce or not had spawned eugenics movements and legislation in more than 30 nations across the world. It is to these laws that we turn next.

7

Something Wicked This Way Comes

HOME ECONOMICS

Today on the east lawn of the imposing Indiana State Library, a small bronze plaque carries a startling message:

> By late 1800s, Indiana authorities believed criminality, mental problems, and pauperism were hereditary. Various laws were enacted based on this belief. In 1907, Governor J. Frank Hanly approved first state eugenics law making sterilization mandatory for certain individuals in state custody.[1] 'Approximately 2,500 total in state custody were sterilized'.

It's even more distressing to find that this number does not take into account the many hundreds of men that Dr Harry Sharp of the Indiana State Reformatory – a prison on the Ohio River, since burned down – had already sterilized by vasectomy. He had started his project in 1899, usually by persuading his patients it was part of their treatment – and many agreed to it, whether they understood that it meant they would never be able to have children or not. Sharp's work and testimony on sterilizing 'several hundred men over a few years' was the foundation for what would become Indiana's eugenic programme.[2]

California and Washington followed Indiana in legislating sterilization in 1909, before compulsory sterilization for the 'feeble-minded' finally passed into nationwide American law in 1927 (the same year that the first 'eugenic' baby was born). By 1935 California had sterilized at least 9,997 individuals without their consent, by far the North American leader in neutering those they deemed unfit; neighbouring Arizona sterilized just 11. By that time California, with a central eugenics programme, had also formed various splinter groups, dedicated to promoting the eugenics cause, including the Eugenics Society of Northern California, the California Division of the American Eugenics Society and the Human Betterment Foundation in Pasadena.

The story of how America came to embrace eugenics and enforce sterilization is long and winding. One of its chapters begins in 1848, on 24 January, when James W. Marshall, a worker hired by a local sawmill owner, discovered gold in the Sacramento Valley of California. The gold was found on land that had been, until recently, Mexican territory – it was handed over as part of the Treaty of Guadalupe Hidalgo, which brought an end to the Mexican–American War of 1846–8. This fortunately timed discovery played straight into the American notion of Manifest Destiny – the belief it was the divine fate of white American settlers to expand westward and occupy the entire continent – and sparked what is now known as the Gold Rush.

The Gold Rush, which began 'officially' in 1849, saw a gigantic movement of people towards California. In San Francisco, known to the Native people as Yerba Buena, the population exploded, from 459 people in 1847, of which 10 individuals were Black and 34 Native American and 40 Pacific Islanders, to 78,293 in 1860, with significant Chinese, Black and 'transient' populations.[3] This vast migration west in search of gold also spawned what became known as the California Dream: hard labour in return for rapid if not immediate accumulation of money. Wealth was a philosophical concept for the average Gold Rush migrant: an unrestrained, borderline orgiastic desire for dollars in the face of unchecked ambition began to be promoted as a national character trait.

Not everyone who arrived in California was pursuing a dream, and many were not there by choice. While Black American slavery may have notionally and legally ended with the Civil War, America was still not immune to the commercial temptations of indentured servitude. American merchant ships brought large numbers of indentured Chinese workers to the West Coast to work on the long clamoured-for Transcontinental Railroad, which aimed to connect the east and the west of the US by train. Indentured servitude indicates a level of co-operation, but the reality in Canton was press-ganging and corralling men of working age in barracoons until the merchant ships were full enough to transport their human cargo profitably. On arrival in San Francisco, which the Chinese called Dai Fou, 'The Big City', they settled in what became 'Chinatown', the only area the government would permit them to reside. By the 1850s it was well established, with more than 30 shops, numerous apothecaries, restaurants, herb shops and three boarding houses.[4] The men who arrived in America from Canton and Hong Kong were not permitted to bring their wives or children, so Chinatown was a welcoming oasis for working men living alone in a fundamentally alien city and in an extraordinarily chaotic period in America's tumultuous history.

Chinatown, however, proved immediately and immensely problematic for the white population of the new San Francisco. First of all, the cultivation of the American ideal of domesticity as represented by the family, so carefully tended for a century, was disrupted by the presence of large numbers of single Chinese men who worked extremely hard and cheaply. The term 'coolie' is a corruption of *k'u-li* meaning 'hard labour'. The merchant ships had come equipped not with wives and children but with prostitutes to keep the men occupied. These women also worked extremely hard, and cheaply – and not just for the Chinese population. The workers also undertook recreational hobbies of opium-smoking and gambling. The favoured protein of their cuisine was pork, so Chinatown's pig population also became considerable and, as Chinatown's limits were strictly proscribed, the area struck many who visited it as dense and fragrant. They discovered grain alcohol, primarily whisky at that date, and the newly imported Johnnie Walker became the 'premium brand' to aspire to. For 'respectable' white Americans, the Chinese and their 'Chinatown' represented every kind of debauchery, where, as one contemporary writer put it, 'heathen Chinese and God-forsaken women and men are sprawled in miscellaneous confusion, disgusting, drowsy, there. Licentiousness, debauchery, pollution, loathsome disease, insanity from dissipation, misery, poverty, profanity, blasphemy and death are there. And Hell, yawning to receive the putrid mass, is there also.'[5]

Furthermore, the Chinese were in direct competition with America's first immigrant 'labouring' nation, the Irish. The potato famine of 1845–52 had driven innumerable Irish workers to America in hopes of quite literally not starving to death. At once required for their manual skill in engineering projects such as mining, canals and railways yet reviled for the reality of their existence – living as single working men, drinking and keeping pigs at hand – they were determined not to be supplanted by the Chinese.

The press of the time seized on these tensions with racially motivated cartoons such as 'The Great Fear of The Period: That Uncle Sam May Be Swallowed By Foreigners', depicting caricatures of an Irishman and a Chinese man eating a small American man from both ends, with the final cartoon titled 'Problem Solved' as the Chinese man eats the Irishman.

Racial hierarchy was absolutely ingrained into early San Francisco, and it became worse after 1865, when the Central Pacific Railroad Company hired its first 50 Chinese workers for the transcontinental railroad as an experiment. By 1857 they numbered in excess of 12,000.[6] Miniature Chinatowns proliferated in the settlements the railroad reached, with Chinese restaurants and laundries springing up by the sides of the new tracks. In 1858 the California legislature tried to pass a law making it illegal for anyone of Chinese or 'Mongolian' appearance to enter the state, but this was thrown

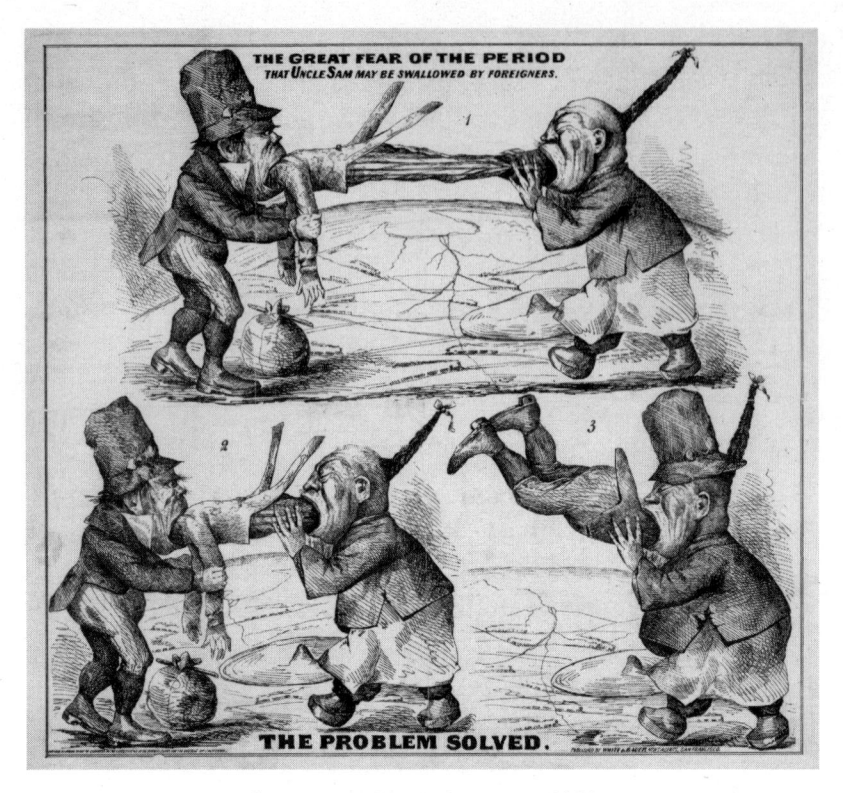

An anti-immigration cartoon, 1860

out by the Supreme Court. Racist agitation by California's white union leaders, as well as a deeply racist press, meant that in 1878 they tried again to ban Chinese people (meaning men), on whose backs their new state had largely and rapidly been built. This was finally signed into the Constitution by President Chester A. Arthur in 1882 as the Chinese Exclusion Act, which did precisely what it said: no more Chinese immigrants. Thus the Chinese American population remained largely composed of single men, living in hard circumstances, many still indentured to American merchants, racially reviled yet fundamentally necessary to the economy.

The almost inconceivable hypocrisy of the American government during this period, a migrant population themselves and many of them recent, voting in favour of banning migrants out of racial and economic prejudice, set a tone for America's 'gate-keeping' of its natural geographic borders, still prevalent today.

At the same time as immigration was restricted, the reproductive choices of ordinary, literate (white) women, America's prime breeding stock according to the press, were curtailed. In 1873 the Comstock Act was passed. Named after Anthony Comstock (1844–1913), a feverishly devout Protestant and particularly zealous postal inspector, it forbade the United States Postal Service from carrying material that was pro-abortion (including medications and instruments) or 'obscene', such as pornography.[7] Since a vast majority of women relied on the newly invented 'mail order' services for medicines to treat their families in areas with poor healthcare provision, but also for the means to control their own reproductive situation, either by prevention or 'cure', Comstock was a huge blow.

The morality police were now out in force. After the Civil War, America had demobbed a huge number of youths who had been exposed to narcotics (cheap morphine salts were supplied liberally to those on the front lines facing terrifying new artillery) and who were potentially unfit for the wholesome hard labour the nation expected in order to rebuild itself. That, and the influx of ships from China and the Far East, meant a new and vastly increased supply of opiates flooded America. Cocaine, another new import, from South America through Mexico, also invaluable in a medical setting, was used increasingly for recreation. One Confederate veteran, 'Doc' Pemberton, even came up with a special recipe for an alternative to the cheap grain alcohol and opium so many ex-soldiers relied on: cocaine and kola nuts, which he marketed as 'Coca-Cola'.[8] Addiction of all kinds became a national preoccupation, sparking a reactionary set of temperance movements concerned with prohibiting the supply and use of intoxicants.

Maine had been the first state to 'go dry' in 1851, prohibiting the sale of liquor for any other purposes than industrial. Twelve other states quickly followed. To strive for temperance itself is easy enough to understand in America, where strong grain alcohol was freely available to people who were not necessarily accustomed to it or who eked out an existence with few comforts, and where guns and domestic violence were commonplace. This made temperance particularly popular as a movement among churchgoing women, who sang rousing hymn-like songs such as 'The Lips That Touch Alcohol Shall Never Touch Mine'.[9] The wider use of female sexual leverage in the otherwise highly religious temperance movement is remarkable for its audacity.

The Gilded Age of American industry, which largely dawned with the construction and capabilities of the Transcontinental Railroad, saw the unstoppable rise of men such as Rockefeller, Carnegie and Ford, who busied themselves and their millions not only with philanthropy but also with political and social policy, which the febrile state of American politics allowed. J. D. Rockefeller was abstinent from alcohol and tobacco for his entire lifetime, in accordance with his Northern Baptist beliefs. He and his wife, Laura Spelman Rockefeller, donated large amounts of money to the Women's Christian Temperance Union (founded 1874), which agitated politically for prohibition legislation. Rockefeller and Ford collaborated regarding the Anti-Saloon League (ASL, formed 1893), now the American Council on Addiction and Alcohol Problems. 'Temperance' in the mid-nineteenth century came to stand for abstinence not only from alcohol but from all intoxicants. The ASL was focused not so much on prohibition outright as on gathering a large body of like-minded Protestant men together, with a firm eye on how they could be influenced to vote.

Rockefeller, Ford and Carnegie are now all legendary names in philanthropy, but like all humans, their characters had more than one facet. Rockefeller's father, William Avery Rockefeller, was a shyster and confidence trickster who made money out of everything from pretending to be a disabled beggar to hawking proprietary quack medicines. His obsession with cash was inherited by his rapaciously ambitious son J. D., who was subsequently exposed for suspect and predatory business practices in a series of essays by the ground-breaking investigative journalist Ida Tarbell (1857–1944), in *McClure's Magazine* in 1905. Ford was a rabid anti-Semite who purchased a publishing company, Dearborn in Indiana, in order to publish *The International Jew: The World's Problem*, his take on how Judaism was ruining everything from banking to baseball. Carnegie, a famous proponent of workers' rights and literacy for all, was involved in a series of scandals regarding the accidental flooding of a town by the exclusive hunting club of which he was he was a member, resulting in the deaths of 2,208 people, as well as various incidences of strangling unions and slashing wages. Nothing was as simple as it seemed in the story of American prosperity.

The rising anxiety about public morality was fuelled by the rapid urbanization of North America in the latter part of the nineteenth century, which brought many social issues into focus that had previously been hidden on the plains and farmsteads: prostitution rapidly became more organized and more visible, as did addiction, disease and anti-social behaviour. In England industrial cities were growing too – with all their incumbent vices. A Protestant reformer named Ellice Hopkins (1836–1904) founded the Ladies' Association for the Care of Friendless Girls in 1883 to improve 'social purity'. In the coded language of the time this meant ushering prostitutes off the street in an attempt to prevent the spread of venereal diseases and unwanted pregnancies. Hopkins also successfully appealed to Parliament to have the age of consent changed from 13 to 16 years of age in the Criminal Law Amendment Act of 1885, which also banned homosexuality outright. Although she never married, so in accordance with her religious beliefs was presumably celibate all her life, her essay 'A Plea for the Wider Action of the Church of England in the Prevention of the Degradation of Women' criticized the double standards by which women were blamed for the sexual incontinence of men. Social and moral 'purity' became accepted euphemisms, both in Britain and America, for clean living and self-restraint. It was not enough, or even particularly necessary, to be a decent human being. What was required was purity.

For all of these magnates and movements, Darwin, Galton and the field of eugenics were manna to be gobbled up and regurgitated at will to fit the context, elevating their aspirations to include racial, as well as social and moral, purity. Deeply influential to America's steadily building enthusiasm for sterilization, although now largely forgotten, was the role of one Oscar Carleton McCulloch (1843–1891), a Presbyterian preacher of the Plymouth Church in Indianapolis who studied the local poor population and was vocal about the need for their numbers to be curtailed. In his project *Tribe of Ishmael: A Study in Social Degradation* in 1881, he wrote about the Ishmaelites, a loosely related local vagrant or 'tramping' family. McCulloch thought 'Ishmael' was a pseudonym adopted by the family to aid their evasive, indigent existence, but it was in fact the real name of the core family. Perhaps he thought it was a reference to the descendants of Ishmael as described in Genesis 16.11–12: 'And he will be a wild man; his hand will be against every man, and every man's hand against him; and he shall dwell in the presence of all his brethren.' On 20 January 1878 McCulloch wrote in his diary, after seeking aid for his Ishmaelites at the relief office, that their

> Real name is not known but called so from wandering habits. They are a wandering lot of beings, marrying, inter-marrying, cohabitating, etc. They live mostly out of doors, in the river bottoms, in old houses, etc. They are largely illegitimate, subject to fits. There have been in all one hundred and thirteen who have sought aid at different times from the county – of this family and its connections. Five years ago they lived out of doors all winter. Most of the children die. They are hardly human beings. But still they can be made something of, by changed surroundings. The children ought to be taken from them and brought up separately.[10]

It's no coincidence that in his diary entry for 6 November 1877 he noted, 'Finished "The Jukes" and shall work up into sermons.'[11] *The Jukes: A Study in Crime, Pauperism, Disease and Heredity*, was a best-seller written by Richard L. Dugdale (1841–1883), a merchant and social reformer who had acted as a prison inspector for the county jails of upstate New York between 1868 and 1874. There he encountered a family he called 'Jukes', of Ulster County. Tracing the extended family, he found '1,200 living and deceased Jukeses' of whom '280 had lived in the poor house, 140 were convicted criminals, 60 more were habitual thieves, and 50 women were prostitutes'.[12] Dugdale and McCulloch between them popularized the idea of 'poverty' and 'pauperism' as two separate conditions. Poverty may befall anyone, requiring only strength of character and labour to rectify the situation, whereas pauperism was a social condition requiring active adoption or at least a passive lack of resistance from the pauper themselves.

Although many of Dugdale's facts were ultimately proved wrong, the Jukes became 'hill family' legends throughout an America reeling from the 1873 crash on Wall Street that ushered in a decade of recession and financial uncertainty. As with times of war, such crashes and recessions always herald a reactionary reversion to social and political conservatism, and so the story of a naturally criminal dynasty in upstate New York was devoured by a nation already feeling the pinch. For eugenicists, the Jukes were proof of everything they had been promoting: born criminals and deviants were a reality, no matter how they were raised.

Over the course of the ensuing years, McCulloch followed, interacted with and made detailed notes on his Ishmaelites, particularly on their physical appearance, demeanour and known activities. One, Sarah, was

> a tall, raw-boned woman, once described by a policeman as 'the Ishmael who walks like a man and talks bass'. She is one of the most persistent wanderers, and spends most of her time upon the road between Indianapolis and points in Illinois. It has often been stated that this woman has buried a number of children born to her in fence corners or on the banks of streams which thing she did while on her wanderings.[13]

The characters and dark physical appearance of the Ishmaelites are close to contemporary descriptions of gypsy or Roma people, but there is no mention by McCulloch of them as such. For McCulloch they seem more akin to Arab peoples, although the children of the Ishmael family were predominantly blond, but he was a keen student of what was then called 'the Orient', which may partly explain his fascination. He was still giving talks on the family in 1888, when he presented his findings to the Fifteenth National Conference of Charities and Correction in Buffalo, complete with a fold-out chart that covered one wall, measuring 3 feet by 12 feet, and 'containing 1720 names, showing the ramifications and interrelations of the families described'. A souvenir copy, measuring a mere 29 by 66 inches, was available for 50 cents.[14]

McCulloch died young in 1891. He never lived to see his work go on to inspire Indiana's eugenics legislation or the enforced sterilization of so many imprisoned men. His papers languished for over a decade before they were acquired and studied by the Carnegie Institution of Washington (established 1902) when it took over the Eugenics Record Office. Although the link to eugenics was shuffled off reasonably quickly, the roots of the ERO still exist in the Department of Embryology at the Carnegie Institution for Science, Baltimore, Maryland, researching 'genetics' and 'developmental biology'.

'THE ABSOLUTE MISTRESS OF HER OWN BODY': MARGARET SANGER AND THE BEGINNINGS OF PLANNED PARENTHOOD

A couple of years after the Comstock Act severely proscribed the reproductive agency of American women, Margaret Louise Higgins was born in 1879 in Corning, New York, to Irish Catholic parents. Their marriage was a particularly fertile one, with her mother, Anne Higgins, conceiving 18 times in 22 years, resulting in 11 children. She died in 1891, aged just 49.

Margaret's father was an independent thinker who embraced atheism and women's rights, including suffrage. She was supported by her sisters and received a sound education before attending nursing college, which she gave up to marry William Sanger, an architect, in 1902. They had three children, despite

Margaret suffering from tuberculosis, and lived in Westchester, New York, where Margaret converted to the Episcopalian faith. In 1911 tragedy struck when their house was razed in a fire, and they decided to move to New York City, where Margaret became involved in social and charitable works, including visiting slums in a nursing capacity. Her political leanings, and those of her husband, became increasingly socialist and she began writing for the socialist newspaper *New York Call* (active 1908–23). Between 1911 and 1913 she wrote a series of articles, published under her married name, Margaret Louise Sanger, the first of which was called 'What Every Mother Should Know', which dealt with how to explain sex and reproduction to children. It began with an explanation of the reproduction of the pea plant, based on the scientific discoveries of the Moravian monk–biologist Gregor Mendel (1822–1884).

Between 1856 and 1863 Mendel had experimented with growing sweet peas of different strains and crossing them to examine the resulting generations. He concluded that, as with the livestock he was surrounded by in Moravia, breeding certain pea stocks resulted in certain traits becoming 'dominant' and some 'recessive'. He called the mechanism behind these traits 'factors', which we now know as genes, and published his findings in the *Proceedings of the Natural History Society of Brünn* in 1866. A year later he became an abbot and discontinued his scientific work. When he died, the succeeding abbot destroyed his personal papers, thus ensuring that his work would remain in almost perfect obscurity. Even though they were contemporaries, neither Darwin nor Galton was aware of his work.

Three men were responsible for the rediscovery of Mendel's work: Erich Tschermak (1871–1962), whose maternal grandfather had taught Mendel botany when the latter was a student in Vienna; Hugo Marie de Vries (1848–1935), a Dutch botanist and early geneticist credited with the discovery of 'mutation theory', again, unaware when he did so of Mendel's work; and finally, the uniting factor of the triumvirate, Carl Erich Correns (1864–1933), a German-born, Swiss-raised botanist and later geneticist who truly understood the importance of Mendel's work and ensured the deceased monk's exposure. In the early twentieth century his work spread the idea of 'Mendelian Theory' – which attempted to explain why and how certain traits are inherited. Both De Vries and Correns built on Mendel's research to create the foundation of modern genetic science, and, much like Darwin and Galton, Mendel became a figurehead for eugenicists. From her articles it is clear that Sanger was aware of Tschermak, De Vries and Correns's work. In the 'What Every Mother Should Know' articles, Sanger moves on from the seemingly innocuous pea plants to the animal kingdom and, finally, to human reproduction and how the subject should be taught to children.

Many readers were shocked by Sanger's articles, which were provocative even for a radical publication such as *New York Call*, but her writing was also popular enough for the *Call* to publish the follow-ups, 'What Every Girl Should Know'. Such was their popularity that the pieces were collected in a book of the same name and published in 1916, the frontispiece reading, 'TO THE WORKING GIRLS OF THE WORLD THIS LITTLE BOOK IS LOVINGLY DEDICATED'.[15]

What Every Girl Should Know is a valuable and accurate discourse on the reproductive changes a woman can expect during her lifetime, coupled with advice on emotional and psychological changes. Sanger rejects the notion that female ignorance on the subject of reproduction is bliss, saying: 'I relate it only to show that the savages have recognized the importance of plain sexual talks to their young for ages, while civilization is still hiding itself under the black pall of prudery.'[16]

In all Sanger's sensible texts there are smatterings of a deeper, darker ideology. She was absolutely a keen proponent of female suffrage and female autonomy, determined that 'There will no doubt be a great change in woman's attitude on this subject in the next few years. When women gain their economic freedom they will cease being playthings and utilities for men, but will assert themselves and choose the father of their offspring.' Yet this, she qualified with a disturbing addition, would mean that 'she will hunt down her ideal in order to produce the Superman'. This was a reference to the philosopher Friedrich Nietzsche's *Übermensch* (which literally translates to 'overman' but is better understood as 'superior man' or indeed 'Superman'), first popularized in his book of 1883, *Thus Spoke Zarathustra*.

Who and what constituted the *Übermensch* was never entirely concrete, perhaps even to Nietzsche himself, but, coupled with Darwinian and Galtonian theory, it captured the public imagination and even inspired George Bernard Shaw to write a play named *Man and Superman* in 1903. (The play suggests, as Sanger does, that humanity's evolution depends on the romantic decisions of women.) It is from this that the name Superman originally passed into the collective English-speaking consciousness.

There is a lot of sensible and accurate information in Sanger's *Every Girl* – for example, in its open and useful description of the menopause: 'Among those symptoms most common are flushings or flashes, which are mostly confined to head, face and neck, are increased by heat and motion and followed by profuse sweating, giddiness, backache, headache, sleeplessness, disturbances of digestion like diarrhoea or constipation, blueness, depression of spirits, shortness of breath, palpitation and nervous irritability.'[17] However, there are regular outright racist comments too such as: 'the aboriginal Australian, the lowest known species of the human family, just a step higher than the chimpanzee in brain development, has so little sexual control that police authority alone prevents him from obtaining sexual satisfaction on the streets.'[18]

Sanger could speak openly of the sexual desires of mature women and their propensity to take a lover, a decision that could be thoughtful rather than an immature impulse earlier in life. Sanger herself, after becoming estranged from William in 1913 and fleeing to England in 1914 to avoid indictment via the Comstock Act, began an affair with the novelist and science fiction writer H. G. Wells that continued until his death in 1946.

Sanger concluded *Every Girl* with an extraordinary (for the time) statement: 'I cannot refrain from saying that women must come to recognize there is some function of womanhood other than being a child-bearing machine. Too long have they allowed themselves to become this, bowing to the yoke of motherhood from puberty to the grave ... No wonder she becomes melancholic or even insane.'[19]

Every Girl was published as a book in 1916, the same year Sanger, along with her younger sister Ethel Byrne and the Russian Jewish theatre worker and activist Fania Esiah Mindell, opened her first birth control clinic in a tall red-brick building on 46 Amboy Street, Brooklyn, New York. All three were strong characters, but Ethel in particular had had a difficult time as a wife and mother, which hardened her views. She had endured a short but deeply unhappy marriage to an alcoholic glassworker, Jack Byrne, who was violent and physically abusive to both her and their two children, Jack Jr and Olive. When Olive was a newborn, Jack threw her into a snowbank in a drunken fit and Sanger, there to intervene, had to dig the baby out. In 1906 Ethel left Byrne for good; she dropped the children off with her parents and saw them only once in the next 15 years.

The 'Brownsville Clinic' is often billed as 'America's First Birth Control Clinic', but it wasn't. That title probably goes to the clinic of Madame Restell, real name Ann Lohman (1812–1878), of Fifth Avenue, New York, at her mansion on the corner with 52nd Street. She also owned two further outposts in Philadelphia and Boston, thus pre-dating Sanger by some decades. Restell, born in the village of Painswick in Gloucestershire and entirely self-made, was both a midwife and a physical abortionist. Comstock himself hunted her down through her lucrative side business of selling mail order abortifacient medicines through the United States Post Office. He pursued her until he was sure of a conviction for distributing contraception, whereupon she committed suicide in the bath by cutting her own throat.

For New Yorkers, Restell had come to embody the dark side of birth control, even if it was based in a Park Avenue mansion: the desperation and fear that came with an unwanted pregnancy and the fear of discovery. Sanger, however, was presenting a different possibility: there appears to be no evidence that suggests Sanger ever promoted or engaged in abortion, although she was a keen proponent of avoiding unwanted pregnancy.

Nine days after the Brownsville Clinic opened, Sanger, Byrne and Mindell were arrested for 'distributing obscene material': they had been giving out birth control pamphlets in English, Italian and Yiddish and providing contraceptive pessaries and instruction on how to use them. Each was set a bail of $500, the equivalent of about $88,000 today.[20]

Margaret Sanger's first clinic in Brooklyn, 1916

Following their release, Sanger devoted herself to writing a book, *The Case for Birth Control*, published in May 1917, but Ethel became more militant in her determination to continue providing birth control advice face-to-face. This landed her back in jail. She promptly went on hunger strike, and after 185 hours of refusing food and water, became the first female prisoner in the USA to be mechanically force-fed (gavaged with a metal funnel down her throat, a brutal technique used by geese farmers).[21] When she was brought to trial, the *New York Times* led with the headline 'WOMEN NOISY IN COURT'.[22]

Margaret herself also landed before a judge again, for again distributing contraception. The case would make legal history and begin to change American attitudes towards contraception. In *The People of the State of New York* v. *Margaret H. Sanger* (*People v. Sanger*), the presiding judge, Frederick Crane, ruled that under Section 1145 of the New York Penal Code physicians could provide contraceptives to married couples for the prevention of disease. Despite this ruling Judge Crane supported the criminal conviction against Sanger herself, because she was not a physician. The Crane ruling was timely, as huge numbers of American soldiers were arriving back from the First World War, writhing with venereal disease. The new availability of vulcanized rubber condoms, supplanted by latex in 1921, would at least have allowed the afflicted time to seek treatment upon his return home.

Sanger's interest in eugenics remained throughout her life, although she began to distance herself from its more racist ideologies; instead her views concerned the fitness of the individual to birth and provide for an infant, economically, intellectually and emotionally. In 1921, the year of the finalization of her divorce from her husband, she launched the American Birth Control League (ABCL), the name taken from the title of her popular monthly magazine *The Birth Control Review*, which ran from 1917 to 1940. In the 1920s she became involved with the Black communities of New York, speaking on birth control and reproductive responsibility, and also employing Black women to advise patients at the ABCL.

In 1922 Sanger married Noah Slee, the owner of a company that manufactured Three-In-One oil for bicycles, among other things. In her flight from the law she had seen in the Netherlands a demonstration on the contraceptive diaphragm, and soon after their marriage Slee was bringing in European diaphragms to New York City through Canada, hidden in oil drums. He later became the first legal manufacturer of the contraceptive cap in America. Slee adored his wife, despite the fact that they never lived together, never had keys to each other's houses and that she was having an on-off affair with H. G. Wells. Successful in his own right, he promoted her work selflessly and tirelessly to the point that, when her least successful book, *Motherhood in Bondage* (1928), failed to sell, owing probably to the distressing nature of much of the content (it consisted of letters to Sanger from women made extremely unhappy by unwanted pregnancy), Slee bought up the remaining stock anonymously.[23]

Sanger founded the Clinical Research Bureau in 1923, staffed entirely by female clinical workers, researchers and front of house staff. John D. Rockefeller and subsequently the Rockefeller family were staunch financial supporters of the Bureau from the beginning.

From 1929 Sanger lobbied for legislation that would stop restrictions on contraceptive products, without success. So in 1932 she ordered a diaphragm by post from Japan (where the military-minded government was also beginning to crack down on contraception) to provoke the situation, which finally resulted in a court decision in 1936 overturning a portion of Comstock that prevented medical professionals from distributing or ordering contraceptives through the postal service. This prompted the American Medical Association to adopt contraception into the normal medical canon, and to begin to teach on it in medical schools.

Sanger, in her late fifties and understandably weary, decided to take this victory and move to Tucson, Arizona, where the dry climate could aid her unpredictable chest, but she found it impossible to stay away for long. The ABCL had been undergoing a series of changes related to the upper leadership, morphing into other organizations that caused friction between various factions. Sanger was no longer as powerful as she had once been, and by the time the name changed to the Planned Parenthood Federation of America in 1942 she had become a cog in what was rapidly becoming a much larger machine. She began to work on more pet projects, one of which was a collaboration with the biologist Gregory Pincus and the heiress suffragette Katherine McCormack to produce the first oral contraceptive pill, Enovid, available from 10 July 1957.

Planned Parenthood is now an international federation of organizations, in no small degree thanks to Sanger. In July 2020, Planned Parenthood severed ties with Sanger by removing her name from the New York clinic, with a statement to CNN that read: 'The removal of Margaret Sanger's name from our building is both a necessary and overdue step to reckon with our legacy and acknowledge Planned Parenthood's contributions to historical reproductive harm within communities of color ... Margaret Sanger's concerns and advocacy for reproductive health have been clearly documented, but so too has her racist legacy.'[24] Sanger died not of tuberculosis but of congestive heart failure in Arizona in 1966. She is buried next to Noah Slee in Fishkill, New York.

In a life story full of superheroes (and villains) of all kinds, Olive Byrne, the tiny niece Sanger rescued from a snowbank, deserves a final mention. Olive grew up and studied medicine, and while a student she met Elizabeth and William Hollway Marston, eventually living with them in a polyamorous 'marriage' of sorts and bearing Marston two sons. Marston, an academic psychologist by day, was also a writer, and immortalized Olive as his most famous character in 1941, for DC Comics: Wonder Woman.[25]

MARIE STOPES AND *MARRIED LOVE*

In 1913 Marie Stopes was in her early thirties and had recently filed for divorce. At a meeting at the Fabian Society, a socialist organization that helped to form the Labour Party in the UK, she was transfixed by a guest speaker from America. The speaker was Margaret Sanger, and she was there to give a talk on birth control. Afterwards Stopes approached Sanger and excitedly showed her a chapter of the book she was working on – a book about contraception.

Marie Stopes (1880–1958) was the British counterpart and almost direct contemporary of Margaret Sanger. Born in Edinburgh to an academic and open-minded family, she was raised in London in comfortable, intellectual surroundings. Her father was a palaeontologist, brewer and engineer with varied professional interests and her mother was a staunch supporter of the rights of women and female suffrage, and a Shakespeare scholar.

Stopes was raised in the south London suburb of Upper Norwood, near Crystal Palace. Energetic, with dark curly hair and a striking profile, she attended UCL from 1900 to study botany and biology and graduated early in 1902 with a first-class B.Sc. degree. That year her intellectual gadfly father died, leaving the family in a precarious financial position. The following year her former palaeobotany professor, understanding her sudden need for a job, employed her as his research assistant, inspiring in Stopes an enduring love for palaeobotany that provided a mainstay and focus throughout all the other changes in her life.

That same year she went to Munich to study sexual organs in primitive plants, earning her doctorate in little over a year. Returning to Britain as the youngest ever British doctor of science, she went to work for Manchester University until 1910, a period in which she also spent 18 months in Tokyo. Then she went to Canada to study ferns in the Bay of Fundy, and on 29 December met the Canadian researcher Reginald Ruggles Gates. They became engaged on New Year's Eve, married in March and returned to England on 1 April 1911. Stopes prospered professionally, while the transplanted Ruggles found himself struggling.

In court during their divorce, Ruggles defended himself by casting Stopes as abnormally sexually voracious, leaving him unable to keep her satisfied. Stopes sought separation on the grounds of non-consummation. In the face of two such opposing stories, the marriage was legally annulled in 1914.

Whatever the truth of the marriage, it was the genesis of a new career for Stopes. She finally found a publisher for her book, Humphrey Verdon Roe, a wealthy biplane manufacturer based in Manchester. Introduced to Stopes in 1917, he became fascinated by both her and her work, and offered to publish *Married Love*. It was an instant success, going through six reprints in the first year. In New York the Eugenics Publishing Company issued an American version in 1918. It was also an immediate hit in America. Shortly after its publication Marie Stopes and Humphrey Verdon Roe were married.

Unlike Sanger, whose no-nonsense approach to sex, married life and indeed life in general bordered on the transactional, Stopes appealed for a more holistic approach to sex and marriage. And she was no shrinking violet. She was the daughter of two 'radical' thinkers and had travelled the world as a professional in all-male environments. She wrote that in relationships the woman 'more often by the sexlife of marriage is of the two the more profoundly wounded, with a slow corrosive wound that eats into her very being and warps all her life'.[26] She advocated pleasure during sex – a radical view that scandalized many: 'The idea that woman is lowered by sex-intercourse is very deeply rooted in our present society ... mistakenly encouraging the idea that sex-life is a ... degrading necessity which a pure woman is above enjoying.'[27] Stopes was also plainly contemptuous of the notion that women only feel sexual longing when married, denouncing such ideas as 'ridiculous absurdities'.[28]

Yet in her book Stopes also promotes the risible theory of the association of the female orgasm with conception: 'From their mutual penetration into the realms of supreme joy the two lovers bring back with them a spark of that light which we call life.' She even goes so far as to follow it by paraphrasing Isaiah 9.6 with 'And unto them a child is born'.[29] Subsequently, she admits that children are also born in sexually unsatisfactory unions.

What makes the book so extraordinary is its conviction of the desperate ignorance with which many women still entered marriage, writing: 'That girls can reach a marriageable age without some knowledge of the realities of marriage would seem incredible were it not a fact.' And she states in no uncertain terms that 'When girls so brought up are married it is a *rape* for the husband to insist on his "marital rights" at once.'[30] Spousal rape, cloaked in myriad thinly veiled euphemisms, was one of the underlying preoccupations of the suffragette movement, but it is rarely expressed so baldly as in *Married Love*.

Stopes was well informed about the latest breakthroughs in biology, as her interest in hormones proves. Hormones had only been introduced into scientific thinking in June 1905, when one of her UCL colleagues, Ernest Starling, a professor of physiology, used the word in his Croonian Lecture series delivered at the Royal College of Physicians, then housed in a stately neoclassical building facing the National Gallery. Although somewhat overlooked at the time, Starling's discovery was one of the medical breakthroughs of the twentieth century, and one without knowledge of which hormonal contraception, *in vitro* fertilization (IVF) and Hormone Replacement Therapy (HRT) would be impossible.

Much of *Married Love* contains very sensible advice, but reading it today is a strange experience: great swathes of it are given over to unabashed whimsy such as 'The sensitive interrelation between a woman's breasts and the rest of her sex-life is not only a bodily thrill, but there is a world of poetic beauty in the longing of a loving woman for the unconceived child which melts in mists of tenderness toward her lover, the soft touch of whose lips can thus rouse her mingled joy.'[31]

The follow-up to *Married Love* was *Wise Parenthood: The Treatise on Birth Control for Married People*, published in November 1918. Here overtly eugenicist ideas begin to raise their head: the book is 'Dedicated to all who wish to see our race grow in strength and beauty'. The first page quotes the eugenicist Sir James Barr in the *British Medical Journal* as saying, 'There is no equality in nature among children nor among adults, and if there is to be a much-needed improvement in the race, we must breed from the physically, morally and intellectually fit.'[32]

The terminology of Sanger appears early on in the text: 'when the vicious and feeble-minded people reproduce, they do so more recklessly.'[33] Broadly though, it is aimed at married women who wish to have sex without fear of conception. To this end, Stopes recommends the rubber contraceptive cap – her favoured brand was 'ProRace' – combined with spermicides and/or douching, depending on the preference of the woman. Detailed instructions on how to insert, remove and care for the cap are meticulously recorded. How well this method would work physically or psychologically for new brides, unaccustomed to grappling intimately with the interior of their vagina, is not addressed.

Stopes acknowledges that 'women who are dissolute, harried, overworked and worried into a dull and careless apathy ... these too often will not, or cannot, take the care and trouble to adjust ordinary methods of control so as to secure themselves from undesirable conceptions'.[34] For these women Stopes recommends the precursor of the contraceptive coil, known as the 'gold pin'. It was inserted 'painlessly' by a physician, and the 'spring' opened up to ensure the mouth of the uterus, the *os*, was permanently ajar, not allowing for a fertilized ovum to embed itself in the uterine wall. Stopes admitted it was rarely used in Britain, but 'largely and successfully adopted in America by some of the leading doctors there'.[35] This was disingenuous: the gold pin was controversial in America, even when it was used, as it was unknown whether it was a contraceptive device or a permanently acting abortifacient. Nor does it look as if it would be painless to install, or hygienic and comfortable to wear, let alone during intercourse.

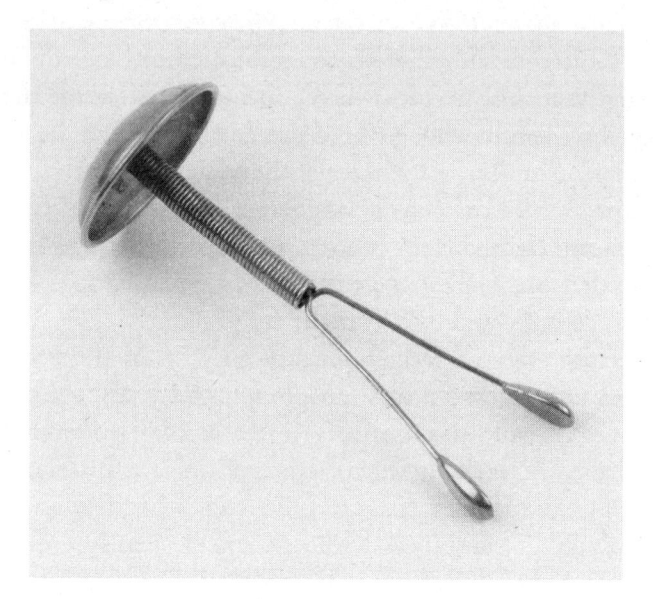

Gold contraceptive coil

Stopes, like Sanger, professes herself to be staunchly anti-abortion: 'The desolating effects of abortion and attempted abortion can only be exterminated by a sound knowledge of the control of conception. In this my message coincides with that of all the Churches in condemning utterly the taking of even an embryonic life.'[36]

Following the success, again, of *Wise Parenthood*, in 1919 Stopes condensed it into a 16-page pamphlet aimed at those with limited literacy and had it printed for free distribution in London's poorer areas, particularly the East End. The take-up was low, but the sales of *Married Love* and *Wise Parenthood* remained so strong she was unconcerned. In July of the same year, riding high on success, she entered a nursing home to give birth to her first child, at the age of 38. During the labour she was not allowed to be mobile or to assume her preferred position, which was on her knees, but instead had to lie back in the classical manner. The infant was stillborn, and Stopes remained convinced it was the fault of the attending doctor, who had not let her give birth as she wanted.

She continued what she saw as her life's mission. A subsequent edition of *Wise Parenthood* was pleased to announce that

> Realising that this, like most books, will only be of use to the educated and more thoughtful people, and that it is of great racial urgency to bring this knowledge to the poorest and least literate section of the community, my husband Mr. H. V. Roe and I opened the first Birth Control Clinic in the British Empire, in March, 1921, in a poor district in Holloway, London.[37]

Sir James Barr wrote to her, upon the clinic's opening, 'You and your husband have inaugurated a great movement which I hope will eventually get rid of our C_3 population and exterminate poverty. The only way to raise an A_1 population is to breed them.'[38]

The A, B, C and D classifications was a reference to the grading of enlisted soldiers. A_1 was fit, trained and ready to serve abroad, C-band were only fit for domestic duties and D were the wounded. The A-to-C categories, routinely used by eugenicists when classifying strata of society, are an example of the influence of an ongoing series of wars on the language of the period. During the Boer conflict of 1899–1902 Britain was shocked to find that over half of the men who joined up to serve were below 5'6" (forcing the Army to drop its height requirement to 5'), and almost half were physically unfit to serve. It sparked a political panic that played straight into the eugenicists' hands for the next 35 years.[39]

In 1920, just before the opening of the clinic, Stopes brought out *Radiant Motherhood: A Book for Those Who Are Creating the Future*, her last of the trilogy based on marital relations. It was the most overtly eugenicist tract of the three. From the first few pages she discusses 'the utter degradation which we see in the worst of the slums, and in institutions where live the feeble-minded offspring of inferior mothers who have wantonly borne children of fathers devoid of any realization of what they were doing'.[40]

Radiant Motherhood continues in a deeply apocalyptic vein: 'society allows the diseased, the racially negligent, the thriftless, the careless, the feeble-minded, the very lowest and worst members of the community, to produce innumerable tens of thousands of warped, and inferior infants.'[41] In numerous private correspondence and in speeches Stopes comes out clearly in favour of compulsory sterilization, although she remained, outwardly, firmly against abortion and no Stopes clinics performed abortions during her lifetime.

Marie Stopes's marriage to Humphrey Verdon Roe failed in 1935, after he made some poor business decisions. Ever independent, Marie refused to help him financially and he ended up in cheap lodgings, visiting their home at Norbury Park only when he was 'allowed', although he remained devoted to her for the rest of his life. Marie took lovers and, returning to the ideas of her youth, began writing poetry about young love, some of which she sent to Adolf Hitler on 12 August 1939. She had purchased the lighthouse and associated cottages on the famous fossil-hunting island of Portland Bill, off the south coast of England, to continue her palaeontological interests but subsequently let it to two naval officers. One of them, naval Lieutenant Warren Tute, wrote that he had been excited to meet his new landlady, only to find she 'had all the charm of a viper'.[42]

Marie and Humphrey's son, Harry Stopes-Roe (1924–2014), to whom Marie was devoted, decided to marry Mary Wallis, the daughter of the inventor and war hero Barnes Wallis. Mary suffered from myopia, and Marie protested vociferously against the marriage, saying that they would have children with 'defective sight and the handicap of goggles'.[43] Undeterred, Harry and Mary wed; Humphrey attended but Marie did not, and disinherited Harry on the grounds that he was marrying substandard stock. Her unshakeable, terrible beliefs had broken up their family.

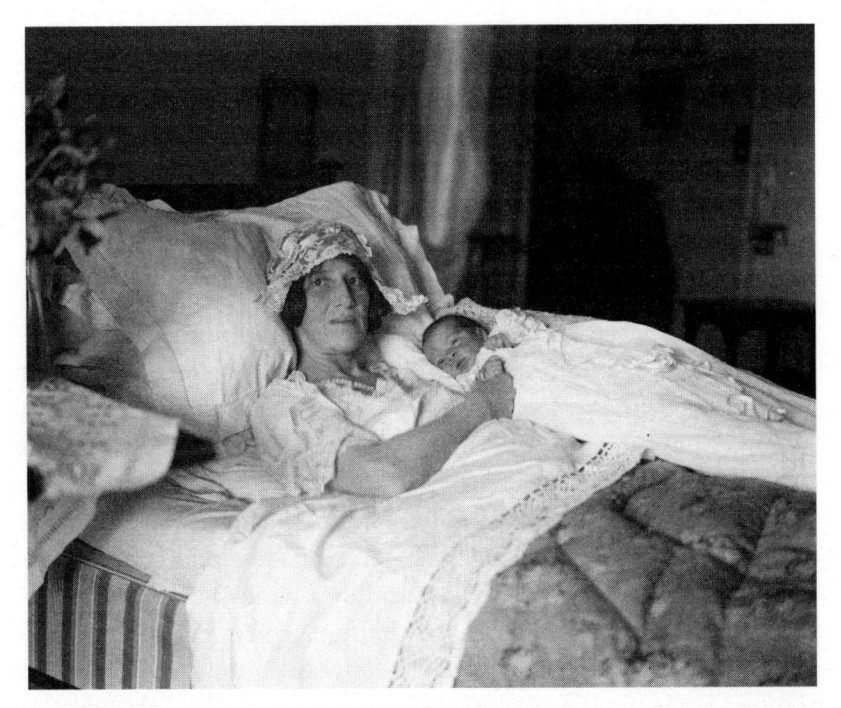

Dr Marie Stopes with her son, 1924

In the spring of 1957 she was diagnosed with breast cancer and sought treatment in Germany, but the cancer was too far advanced. Privately, Marie sought solace in reading about the occult and continued to write her poetry about young love, and a will, which included leaving all her clinics to the Eugenics Society.

Marie Stopes wrote, in the preface to *Married Love*: 'I paid such a terrible price for sex-ignorance that I feel that knowledge gained at such a cost should be placed at the service of humanity ... I hope it may save some others years of heartache and blind questioning in the dark.'[44] By the time of her lonely death in the early hours of 2 October 1958, in her bedroom at Norbury Park, it is perhaps these words that summarize Stopes's life most fittingly. Her undeniable yet controversial legacy still proves problematic for the charity she founded, rebranded MSI in 2020 in an attempt to break from the eugenicist ideals of its founder. MSI now offers abortions and contraceptive services in 37 countries across the globe. As of 2019, in excess of 32 million women, mostly in middle- or low-income countries, stay in control of their reproductive rights through the work of MSI.[45]

Stopes and Sanger, both now disassociated from the organizations they founded, did as much as for 'ordinary' women as the Suffragette Movement, if not more. 'The Vote' was of little use to a woman drowning in relentless pregnancies, poverty and domestic misery. A vote, while of substantial importance regarding long-term societal change, did not suddenly empower women sexually or financially. In addition, however, both women did much, at a key moment in world history, to redefine biological 'race' – lending their work to a eugenics movement whose cruelties would only gather a pace as the twentieth century progressed. Their characters may have been questionable; neither of them was particularly likeable, and many of their ideas are now utterly unacceptable, but their single-minded determination to put reproductive power and responsibility into the hands of women created an international movement that became undeniable.

8

'A Violent and Messianic Age'

In an innovative *Frauenklinik* in Freiburg im Breisgau at the turn of the twentieth century, two doctors were experimenting with new drugs. They wanted to create an environment in which not only would an expectant mother undergo a completely painless delivery but she would not remember it at all.

Even in the eugenics ideology, as a willing and compliant breeder of a better race, the reproductive woman was little more than a vessel incapable of deciding for herself. Her pain was secondary if not downright inconsequential compared to the needs of (a) her husband and family and (b) society. Pain, however, is not inconsequential. Some women give birth reasonably easily and find the whole procedure acceptable enough, given the positive outcome of a new baby. Some women, for physical, mental, emotional or environmental reasons, suffer huge psychological damage through the birth of a child that can and often does affect the success of subsequent births, should they even consider another pregnancy. This was particularly true at a time when tearing, fistulas and post-partum complications resulted in life-long complications for millions of women across the world.

'Twilight Sleep', or the *Dämmerschlaf*, was created by Bernhardt Krönig and his assistant Karl Gauss in 1902. Using a carefully concocted mixture of diamorphine (a painkiller) and scopolamine (also known as henbane, associated with opiate use since ancient times, also a psychotropic), they could induce a state of semi-consciousness in the mother as soon as the first labour pains were felt. They felt confident that they had found a way to bypass any potential trauma resulting from labour.

By the time of delivery a pregnant woman would have already been an outpatient at the *Frauenklinik* for a month, closely monitored by the doctors and her birth carefully planned. With the administration of the drugs, her eyes and ears would be covered to block out light and all noise. Should it be necessary, restraints could be used. During the labour she was completely unconscious. Basic locomotive reactions such as those exhibited by a dog dreaming of running were often observed, and with the perfect dose the patient remained suggestible to encouragement to push or not to push.

Strangely, if she was questioned, she often believed she was doing something entirely different such as folding linens. Gauss called these 'memory islands' and found that it was imperative that they were not traumatic or painful.[1] Should the contractions prove insufficient to deliver the baby, forceps were used to assist. As soon as the baby was delivered, it was removed from the room for the initial checks and clean-up, so that any noise would not disturb the mother, who was also tended to and left to recover. When cleaned, re-dressed and awake, the new mother was introduced to her baby, with whom she would remain in the clinic for another month to ensure the fitness of both and ensure a peaceful bonding period. After their chemically induced rest, the mothers 'woke up happy and animated, and well in body and soul; and found, with incredulous delight, their babies, all dressed, lying before them upon a pillow in the arms of a nurse'.[2]

The medical establishment was dubious, but the wealthy women of Germany were not. By 1907 Gauss was inundated with takers for the procedure, including women from the upper echelons of American society. They included 'Mrs C. Temple Emmett', aka Alida Beekman Chanler, from New York State, who opted for the *Dämmerschlaf* for all her three later pregnancies (after the death of an infant son in 1907). She promoted it enthusiastically to her New York friends. Mrs Emmett, Mrs Cecil Lewis, Mrs Mark Boyd and Mrs Francis Kermody were the next American mothers to experience Twilight Birth, all with profoundly positive experiences, and apparently without the use of forceps. In 1904 forceps were recorded used in approximately 12 per cent of deliveries in the United States. At the *Frauenklinik* the rate was 6–7 per cent.[3]

During the recovery period they were aided not by post-partum fasting, broths or gruel but by a substantial German diet of milk, beer and crackers, two or three meats and sausages, cabbage, sprouts and omelettes. This also seemed to assist milk production for the mothers, who were encouraged to get out of bed and be mobile after the first day of rest. Fasting after giving birth was a common ancient practice probably related to concepts of purification, but in most cases it is decidedly unhelpful. On the other hand, the Freiburg diet appears to have been substantial.

Markedly, none of the four women involved, in their own accounts of *Dämmerschlaf*, recorded any pervasive fear or anxiety regarding the birth or her recovery period. All travelled without their husbands. Rather than recovering from an exhausting and debilitating labour for a month in a darkened room, they were encouraged to eat, exercise and engage with the world around them. Mrs Emmett even fed a pair of carriage horses sugar lumps from her room on her first day post-delivery (presumably through a window). The mothers were also given 12 hours per day break from their babies, in which they were expected to sleep or at least rest.

Back in America, the idea of Twilight Sleep was rapidly catching on. The new, 'empowered' image of the young American women was embodied by the Gibson Girl, an advertising vehicle invented by the illustrator Charles Dana Gibson. The Gibson Girl cycled, exercised, enjoyed fresh air, sport and socializing, all while sporting an extremely restrictive swan-bill 'health' corset. Clean, stylish, robust and healthy men fell at her feet, and women wanted to be her. Until the onset of the First World War, the Gibson Girl and other models made in her image dominated American popular advertising.

In 1904 Lane (an administrative mis-spelling of Lena) Bryant opened a small clothing store on Fifth Avenue, New York, with her own handmade offerings, including maternity dresses for wearing around the house, not dissimilar in concept to modern loungewear. They proved popular immediately, not only among pregnant women but also among heavier customers. Marketing imagery of the capable American 'outdoorswoman' proliferated at the same moment as American women discovered Twilight Sleep. Lane Bryant offered the first range of purpose-made maternity clothing designed to be worn outdoors and it sold out, instantly. Pregnancy had become something to be shown off, not hidden. Almost immediately, Bryant's husband took over the 'efficient' operation of Lane Bryant and began having the maternity and 'stout' ranges mass-produced. They were immensely popular and made the Bryants very rich in a few short years.

The debates that raged around Twilight Sleep, particularly in America, were more moral than medical. Only a short time earlier the writer Thorstein Veblen, in his *The Theory of the Leisure Class: An Economic Study of Institutions* (1899), had coined the phrase 'conspicuous consumption' to encapsulate how the richer classes of America lived and demonstrated their wealth. The upper-class women who took the two months to go to Freiburg and be treated by Krönig and Gauss could well afford the excellent treatment and personal care they enjoyed there.

Less frequently mentioned are the women in the second-, third- and fourth-class wards who were also at the *Frauenklinik* for the *Dämmerschlaf*. Unlike the first-class patients, who were assured the attentions of Freiburg's best doctors and midwives (which for the Americans usually meant Krönig and Gauss themselves), the women in the more ordinary wards were administered their *Dämmerschlaf* by 'the Siegel method'. First-class patients had their drugs carefully titrated for them in the build-up to their labour and administered on demand or through the observations of the physician. Those undergoing the Siegel method were injected with a pre-mixed standardized solution of morphine and scopolamine at the beginning of their labour, then given subsequent timed doses until their birth was over.

Unsurprisingly, the Siegel method was far less effective – it simply allowed for a larger numbers of patients to be treated by fewer staff on a more efficient timetable. When asked about the Siegel method, Gauss replied: 'If you could trust to having an average woman, you could use an average dose; but the dose is easier to standardize than the woman.'[4]

Owing to the novelty of Twilight Sleep, few doctors could take the three years that Krönig and Gauss had taken themselves to perfect the process. The American doctors who attended Freiburg to learn the technique did so on the 'lower' wards over a series of days or a few weeks. These obstetricians took the Siegel method back with them to America, marketing it as *Dämmerschlaf* to an expectant (in all senses) audience. Unsurprisingly, success levels were comparatively low when measured against Freiburg, and the lack of care in administering particularly the scopolamine led to some women experiencing something akin to a bad acid trip while giving birth. Attempts to control the birthing environment included secure 'cribs' for the mother, not unlike a tiny padded cell, and nightgowns with 'a continuous sleeve' (i.e., a straitjacket) or restraints, and also a turban to prevent head-banging. It was, in many ways, a nightmarish version of Freiburg. However, some doctors such as the Midwest-based Bertha Van Hoosen, adopted Twilight Sleep carefully and with great success, to an enthusiastic reception.

The arrival of the First World War and new restrictions in America to regulate and limit the distribution of opiates and narcotics reduced the availability of Twilight Sleep. There had also been a significant backlash from the medical establishments in Berlin and America. *Dämmerschlaf* and the enormous demand for it across 'classes' 1 to 4 does, however, represent one of the first true agitations over individual reproductive rights, by women, for themselves – even if it was the right to give birth, in the railroad parlance of the time, 'as high as balls'.

FROM PERSONAL HYGIENE TO RACIAL HYGIENE

One popular sideshow of the burgeoning eugenics movement in North America was the Better Baby contest. These competitions sprang up at state fairs all over – once the arena of farmers and their show breeds, now local parents could bring their babies to be judged too. The babies who scored the highest were healthy, agreeable, without any apparent disabilities or impairments and almost always white. When Sanger and Stopes talk about 'racial improvement', they mean not 'the human race' but a specific ethnic type, be it their own or someone else's. The concept of African-American 'racial uplift', for instance, of which the influential reformer Booker T. Washington was a major proponent, refers entirely to the betterment of African-American people.

One of the key observations by Sanger and Stopes, as well as judges at the Better Baby Contests, was simply that many babies and children (and adults) were just not very clean, which in turn led to irritation, itching, infestation by pests and, eventually, disease. A century ago, without ready access to plentiful hot water, and living in a dusty or muddy agricultural situation, or a filthy industrial one, with multiple children to wash, feed and keep in clean clothes, the task of the housewife must have been a tremendous burden. Small yet common irritations that we now have simple and efficacious treatments for, such as athlete's foot, oral and vaginal thrush, heat rash or scabies, all impinged on day-to-day well-being.

One repetitive theme from the eighteenth century onwards, particularly when male midwives began to record their interactions with patients, is how very many women suffered from severe leucorrhea, or 'running of the whites'. Leucorrhea is a broad term covering vaginal discharge, which can fall into various types from completely normal to badly infected, and can be sexual or non-sexual in origin. However, again, it is a deeply uncomfortable experience both physically and psychologically, particularly if it was not possible to keep exceptionally clean both in person and in clothing. One particular type of leucorrhea is *bacterial vaginosis*, which has a strong, unpleasant smell but can also cause premature labour and be dangerous to an infant who contracts it in the birth canal.[5]

This new emphasis on hygiene, where before some doctors had resisted even the idea of washing their hands regularly, was the result of the work of Robert Koch. Koch had revolutionized medicine with his work on germ theory in the 1880s, examining blood and tissue from cows infected with anthrax. Previously, the prevailing idea was that disease travelled as a 'miasma' or bad air, but Koch's discoveries meant that people now realized that they could contract an infection or illness from another person, not just the environment. Germs could not be seen, but dirt could, so this new anxiety bred a fascination with 'cleanliness', and 'hygiene' became a catch-all euphemism that was applied to anything from body odour and epilepsy to mental health issues. Racial hygiene, and racial disease, became terms used consistently throughout the period to denote the 'improvement' or 'degeneration' of a particular ethnic subset.

From around 1890 to the end of the First World War, each nation annexed eugenics to serve its own causes. This melding of medical narrative with ideas of sexual and racial purity grew into a hydra across America and Europe. Nowhere in the world during this period was that more apparent than in the former Ottoman empire. The intellectual elite of Constantinople were widely engaged in the global social issues of the day, and regarded the temperance movement in the west with interest, particularly how it was developing in Germany.

Two of Turkey's earliest psychiatrists, Raşit Tahsin and Mazhar Usman, were particularly concerned with the effects of alcohol on the younger generation of Turkish men, which in urban areas seemed to be getting out of control: 'on the street ... drinkers ... shout at people, attack or insult them', said Usman in 1909.[6] The sharia admonishment of alcohol doesn't necessarily mean that all Muslims adhere to temperance, and Turkey's geographical position as a land bridge between east and west meant that it was dealing continually with external international influences, all of whom brought their own customs and diversions with them. The Turkey of more than a century ago was more relaxed regarding alcohol than surrounding, less well-connected Muslim countries – particularly since the Ottoman empire had accumulated if not assimilated multiple ethnicities and tribes within its borders, which covered more than 30 different modern nations.

Many of the merchant classes were ethnic Armenians and many of the 'retailers' of commodities including alcohol were Greek.

As 'middle-men', they were mistrusted and often reviled by the ethnic Turks who ruled them. With the growing alcohol issue, the Christian Armenians in particular were seen as a greedy and corrupting force. Tensions ran high between the more influential and wealthy Armenians and the Ottoman administration. Then, in 1894, under the aegis of Sultan Abdülhamid II, a series of massacres began that mark one of the first true genocides, that of the Turkish on the Armenians. It lasted two years and resulted in the death of up to 300,000 ethnic Armenians, and the displacement of approximately the same number. The only comparable event in modern history before it is the Dutch invasion of Lontor in the Banda Islands of Indonesia in 1621, where a systematic programme of extermination was put in place over a native population of approximately 15,000, of whom it is estimated fewer than 1,000 survived.[7]

One of the key elements of the Armenian massacres of 1894–7 and 1909 was the systematic use of rape and sexual enslavement of Armenian women as an instrument of the genocide. On Banda the Dutch had separated the women and children, and there had been atrocities, but their violent acts were committed in pursuit of the immense financial gain that control of the Spice Islands had to offer – just as the mindless atrocities committed in the Congo Free State by Belgium's monstrous Leopold II were a brutal economic response to the world's insatiable new desire for rubber. For the Turks, the Armenian women and children were targets for a determined barbarity fed by racial hatred.

With the onset of the First World War, the widespread theatre of war allowed the Ottoman government to act without any constraint at all. In 1915 they embarked on a campaign of extermination so abhorrent that the reports of German and American witnesses caused a moral shockwave across the west. Under the traditional fable of 'relocation' up to 1.2 million Armenians were removed from their homes and marched towards the Syrian desert. They were often marched along water courses, not for supplies, washing or rehydration, but simply because the rate of killing was such that flowing water meant the bodies could be dumped and washed away, rather than the 'Young Turks' taking the irksome responsibility of burying their victims.

The genocide's first victims were Armenian men, usually shot once the march was a safe distance from the settlement. Then the women were divided up, often according to their perceived physical appeal, and brutalized. They were 'outraged [raped] in the most cruel and disgusting manner, pregnant women ripped open, breasts cut off, delicate, refined young women compelled to travel day after day perfectly naked, innumerable cases of women being forced into Moslem harems; of children also tortured and killed in the most brutal manner'.[8] Upon arrival in a Muslim settlement, the local men were invited to rape the Armenian women while the Turks watched. The loss of any kind of inhibition or basic empathy was so abrupt that reports came out of Mush that girls as young as eight and ten were raped so forcibly that they were rendered unable to walk, and subsequently shot.[9]

Pregnant women were frequently mutilated. Soldiers cut open their womb to expose the foetus, and those who were lucky enough to avoid that fate,

> whose pains came upon them on the way[,] had to continue their journey without respite. A woman bore twins in the neighbourhood of Aintab; next morning she had to go on again. She very soon had to leave the children under a bush, and a little while after she collapsed herself. Another, whose pains came upon her during the march, was compelled to go on at once and fell down dead almost immediately. There were several more incidents of the same kind between Marash and Aleppo.[10]

The public destruction of a child *in utero* by 'opening up' is not only despicable; it is an act motivated by a desire to destroy everything about a person and their heritage. The lucky few who escaped with their lives were frequently sold into Kurdish villages to be 'Turkified', thus continuing the attempt to annihilate an ethnic minority.

The Ottoman empire's genocide of their Armenian citizens, and later their Greek citizens too, was the start of a new period in the history of 'hygiene'. It was no longer enough to breed 'purity' into one race through conscientious breeding and sterilization. The impure had to be assimilated or eliminated, so that borders could be reinforced and one homogeneous order established. This was the beginning of what became known as 'national biology'. To this day, the Turkish government flatly denies that the Armenian genocide even took place.

'A GOLDEN OPPORTUNITY'

Western Europe breathed a collective and devastated sigh of relief and took a pause to bury their dead when the First World War ended. But far from ushering in a more sympathetic age, the war functioned as a call to arms, quite literally, for the world's more extreme thinkers.

As the American economist and fervent eugenicist Irving Fisher put it in a speech to the Eugenic Research Association in 1921, 'My main thought is that there is now a golden opportunity for eugenicists to "gear in" so to speak, with the great world of events.'[11]

Fisher bemoaned the fact that 'Europe will be inhabited by the descendants of second-rate men of to-day simply because they can not be descendants of those who now sleep in Flanders Fields.'[12] Lest one think he was feeling sentimental regarding the gargantuan human loss of the First World War, Fisher was quick to point out that 'In quantity the loss of seven million men by war is not great … In a few years Europe itself will catch up.' More troubling was his view that 'small as is the number of lives lost as a fraction of population, their loss may nevertheless be the loss of most of the good male germ plasm of the nations concerned'.[13]

As with almost all American eugenicists, Fisher's emphasis was on quality, not quantity. He was firmly against post-war immigration because he thought that the surviving 'stock' of Europe was not up to scratch: 'If we allow ourselves to be a dumping ground for relieving Europe of its burden of defectives, delinquents and dependents, while such action might be said to be humane for the present generation, it would be quite contrary to the interests of humanity for the future.'[14]

The huge movements of people caused by the war also alarmed Corrado Gini, an Italian fascist and eugenicist who was deeply concerned by the potential for mixed-race marriages owing to 'increased contact with the African world'. He argued that it would be

> opportune if the various eugenic societies aimed to gain legislative orders from the governments of the various nations, where such laws do not already exist, banning marriages between Europeans and the African races, allowing only those with Mediterraneans (Berbers, Egyptians) and with non-colored Arabs. Such bans must be extended to marriages with all those population groups of mixed blood scattered throughout the African continent. The scope of the proposal is to impede the growth of a European–African mixed-blood race, which, from various points of view, is undesirable.[15]

No doubt Gini had forgotten Italy's attempt to annex Ethiopia in 1895–6, which they promptly repeated in 1935 as soon as the opportunity presented itself. The mysterious class described as 'non-colored Arabs' refers to Christian Arabs, rather than Muslim Arabs – it was an American concept introduced in 1909 by the Hutton Ruling in Los Angeles, California. The ruling further compounded the religious dimension of race among eugenicists that subsequently leached into popular American ideology.

Italian interwar eugenicist thought, allied to its fascist movement, produced a particularly rabid brand of xenophobic and severe strictures regarding who was fit to breed and who wasn't. By 1926 to be overweight was, in Italy at least, an indication of unfitness to reproduce. Catholic Italian eugenicists struggled (publicly) with the concept of birth control, and, as such, the propositions for premarital examinations so regularly apparent in the rest of European discourse on the matter were routinely suffocated in Italy as in themselves a form of birth control.

At the time, premarital medical examinations, mostly focused on testing for syphilis and gonorrhoea, were mandatory in many US states and in Scandinavia. There was an argument for these exams in post-war Europe, where many of the soldiers who did return from battle were afflicted with venereal disease. 'Syphilis' was used as a blanket term in the general media for all kinds of sexual infection before the Second World War. One of the reasons was that gonorrhoea and syphilis presented in tandem so frequently that they were not considered as two different infections, although they had been noted as such as far back as 1761 by the Padua-born doctor Giovanni Battista Morgagni.[16]

Like tuberculosis, syphilis was endemic to the global population by the First World War. Unlike TB, it bore the stigma of a sexually acquired disease and became synonymous with sexual incontinence and moral failure. It had supposedly been brought to Europe in 1493 by the Columbus expedition. By 1495 Charles VIII of France led a large army of approximately 50,000 men to Naples in an attempt to unseat its ruling monarch, Alphonso II. With the army went between 800 and 1,000 support staff and camp 'followers', as the prostitutes and/or common-law wives of the soldiers were known. That February the army was victorious and entered the city, celebrating in the customary manner of victorious soldiers the world over. Within a matter of days it was apparent that a pox was rife among the men and women, who were breaking out with nasty genital sores and fevers. In the ensuing weeks, sores broke out all over their bodies like buboes and transformed into ulcers that penetrated the bones. At night, the pain made sleep impossible. Further ulcers broke out in the cartilage of the nose and throat, eating them away. Death followed reasonably quickly. The viciousness with which the disease devastated the city has been attributed to the fact that it was an 'initial outbreak' to which those gathered in Naples had no immunity. Subsequent phases of syphilis became slightly milder, and could be classified into three stages: the initial genital sores; sleeplessness, night pain and sweats with larger bodily sores; and the final stage of the collapse of facial cartilage, bone porosity and madness.

Syphilis was quickly identified as primarily a sexually transmitted disease. Owing to its sudden and virulent appearance in Europe, as well as the lack of any known treatment, it caused significant panic in both the scientific and the religious communities. In the summer of 1495 the Holy Roman Emperor Maximilian I declared it a punishment from God for the blasphemies of mankind. This did nothing to slow the inevitable march of the disease, which reached Scandinavia and India in just over a decade, and reached Africa and Japan soon afterwards. Syphilis travelled largely in the wake of the cyclical wars that Europe underwent for centuries, although by the eighteenth century it had mutated into the less deadly form we are familiar with today, but crucially it also began to exhibit phases of 'dormancy' when it was less active. This led the sufferer to believe they might be cured.

The association of the armed forces with venereal diseases was deeply ingrained for a reason. It was expected that men on active duty would have sex with local women and prostitutes. David Starr Jordan, the founding president of Stanford University, wrote in 1915 that 'Perhaps the most shocking feature of all military service is the "barbaric drop" from all traditions of sexual purity. The ideals of womanhood which form the highest incentive to right living on the part of healthy men are lost in war.'[17]

Starr followed this up with the sentiment inevitably trotted out in such texts: 'To a virtuous woman death is incomparably less terrible than dishonor.'[18] He did, however, have the sense to quote Millicent Garrett Fawcett, the English suffragist, who said of the female survivors of the First World War: 'Let any man imagine, if he can ... what must be the mental and moral anguish of women condemned to bear children begotten in rape and hatred by a victorious enemy. Such women, in no small numbers, are facing their shattered lives today.'[19]

Not all sex in times of war, whether it resulted in pregnancy or not, was the result of coercion or force. Prostitutes had been a known and accepted element of military life since ancient times, and were even accepted on the Crusades (the ultimate campaigns for righteousness and salvation). These women also performed social services such as cooking and laundressing, and were an essential part of campaign life. Through the ages, sex work has frequently been combined with other 'casual' labour, particularly when times were hard. Part-time prostitution was a fact of life for many urban European women in the eighteenth century if their household was dependent on day labour.

The scale and monstrous mental toll of the First World War created a *carpe diem* attitude among the ranks that hastened the spread of sexually transmitted diseases, although the problem had long been evident in British society. In the late Victorian period the suffrage movement had been vocal on the health perils for wives of unfaithful husbands who visited brothels or street prostitutes, and syphilis was one of their primary concerns. In 1908 Alfred Bertheim, working in the laboratory of gifted bacteriologist Paul Ehrlich, had created an arsenic-based 'cure' of syphilis which was patented as Salvarsan. A huge instant hit, in less than a year after its release in 1910 Salvarsan – known commonly as '606', thanks to its chemical formula, or 'the magic bullet', owing to its supposed efficacy – made up one quarter of manufacturer Hoechst AG's turnover. Salvarsan, however, did nothing to stem the rising tide of infection, and its popularity only reflected the need for an antisyphilitic, whether medicinal or social.

To the latter end, in 1913 the National Council for Combating Venereal Disease was set up. The same year, suffragist and feminist agitator Christabel Pankhurst published *The Great Scourge, and How to End It*. Pankhurst was outraged by what she saw as the hypocrisy of men who 'have destroyed, and are destroying, the health and life of women in the pursuit of vice'.[20] These same men who 'would think it indelicate to utter in [women's] hearing the words syphilis and gonorrhoea, seem not to think it indelicate to infect them with the terrible diseases which bear these names'.[21] Pankhurst stated that 'A woman infected by syphilis not only suffers humiliation and illness which may eventually take the most revolting form, but is in danger of becoming the mother of deformed, diseased, or idiot children.'[22] Syphilitic children are also usually sterile, and gonorrhoea, left untreated, also bears the high risk of sterility in women, which Pankhurst also knew. She declared it emphatically 'Race suicide!'

'Race suicide' had been coined in 1900 by the American eugenicist Edward A. Ross, but it gained widespread popularity when Theodore Roosevelt used it in an impassioned speech to the National Congress of Mothers. He used it to rail against the spectre of dwindling birth rates and women who chose not to have children ('the existence of women of this type forms one of the most unpleasant and unwholesome features of modern life'). The race Ross and Roosevelt wished to multiply was, of course, the white – solidly prosperous or at the very least aspirant – race. The idea of race suicide was a particular talking point of eugenicists and scientific racists, interested in defining a hierarchy of whiteness. At the top were the 'Teutonic', 'Anglo-Saxon' or 'Nordic' – shorthand for tall and fair-haired – who were considered racially superior. This was both a precursor of Aryanism and its running mate.

Yet Pankhurst's righteous indignation over women contracting syphilis from the very men who shielded them from the world is commendable, despite her eugenicist language. She refused to be deflected from her belief that 'Sexual disease, we say again, is due to the subjection of women. It is due, in other words, to the doctrine that woman is sex and beyond that nothing.'[23]

Unfortunately, the First World War did little to dispel Pankhurst's views. Local prostitution was actively encouraged by most armed forces, and certainly by the British. Throughout Pankhurst's *Great Scourge* there are repeated references to the male 'necessity' for sexual intercourse, which she of course rejects on the grounds of the chastity expected from women. But the male urge to expend his 'germ plasm' was taken very seriously by the medical community. This did not necessarily help matters during the war, as remembered in the memoir of a private in the Guards: 'we were often told in lectures that it was natural, and all we had to do was to use the safeguards and preventatives which were at our disposal to save us from disease ... Hundreds of thousands of men who had led comparatively pure lives until they saw France learned and were even encouraged to go with impure women.'[24]

The army went so far as to establish brothels for different ranks, lit by red lamps for the common soldiers and blue lamps for the officers. The prostitutes who worked within them were monitored by the Royal Army Medical Corps for diseases, and condoms were supplied. In 1917 there were 137 approved brothels in 35 French towns and cities.[25] Sexual disease was not just a problem for the women the soldiers had sex with – at any given time, tens of thousands of British serving soldiers were invalided by venereal disease. These kinds of statistics are by no means unique to the First World War: they were repeated for America in both Korea and Vietnam, and for the British Army in the Gulf Wars, by which time effective prophylactics were both minimally inconvenient and freely available.

In 1919, just as the psychologically beleaguered, physically damaged and venereally embattled veterans made it back to America, waves of action intended on 'vice reform', partly inspired by the Rockefeller Foundation's Bureau of Social Hygiene (established 1911) and the fervent railings and copious dollars of Henry Ford, meant that brothels were closed down. Prostitution was driven onto the streets, where it became rapidly and irrevocably linked to pimping, exploitation and the trade in cheap heroin. Veterans who had become accustomed to regulated prostitution on the front lines in Europe found it a very different experience on the dimly lit backstreets of America.

A retreat into social and economic conservatism is a common reaction to any large-scale war. Emphasis is placed on the nuclear family unit, prudent household economy and the much-abused phrase 'hard-working families'. In America it was a time of mass conservatism – this was the golden opportunity that had so excited Irving Fisher. A series of legislations across America and Europe rapidly followed that aimed to control fertility, primarily the fertility of women, for myriad different political, economic, nationalist and social reasons. Not one single piece of these varied acts of law was done with the well-being of women as the primary concern.

By this stage, men and women had largely formed into two opposing camps regarding the rights of women, whether political, social or reproductive. Unquestionably, the medical process of giving birth was by this time controlled almost entirely by a raft of male doctors, from the family practitioner to the gynaecologist and obstetrician. Only the poorest women in western Europe and America, and often immigrant women isolated by language barriers, still relied solely on female assistants for advice.

Men were dominant in public and professional life, and culturally dominant in the home. Grey areas existed everywhere in the legislation regarding the rights of women. This was particularly true in America, where state and national legislation created further layers of, if not complexity, downright obfuscation, as shown to the extreme by the state age of female consent for Delaware remaining at seven years old from 1890 until 1972.

The ultimate irony of this male dominance of female reproduction is, of course, that men do not experience either pregnancy or childbirth. This is one fundamental yet often disregarded reason why male obstetricians and gynaecologists are not always best suited to understanding the requirements, be they physical, psychological or emotional, of the expectant or labouring mother.

In addition, regardless of his contribution to the mother's environment and emotional condition, the contribution of the male 'partner' to the physical reproductive experience of the human female ends with the donation of his 'germ plasm'. This does not mean that the nature and quality of the sperm itself are irrelevant, as modern scientific discoveries have revealed that small details such as the specific vigour of each sperm and even its shape can have effects on embryo development. In 1905 Nettie Stevens, an American early geneticist, had discovered through her work on mealworms that it is the male spermatozoa that decides the gender of the offspring, although at this time there was no way to 'filter' semen for gender.

The Progressive Era, however, demonstrates a fundamental inability to accept that – apart from choosing not to contribute said germ plasm – the human reproductive event is out of male control. This did not stop them from trying. Fisher was particularly incorrigible, suggesting that reproductive rights should be taken out of the hands of individuals altogether:

> If the birth-control exercised by individual parents could be controlled by a eugenic committee it could undoubtedly become the surest and most supremely important means of improving

the human race. We could breed out the unfit and breed in the fit. We could in a few generations and, to some extent even in the lifetime of us of today, conquer degeneracy, dependency and delinquency, and develop a race far surpassing not only our own but the ancient Greeks.[26]

By the time Fisher gave his speech in 1921, the First World War was over, women had the vote and America had banned narcotics and alcohol. Many states were deploying sterilization for the 'unfit', and eugenics had taken a strong hold in Europe. Theoretically, there was little to stand in the way of the march towards progress, except there was a new problem: Mexico.

California, by this stage leading the vanguard of compulsory sterilization, was placed precisely on more than one geographical fault line. While the San Andreas fault represents a constant but low-level threat of earthquake, the proximity to Mexico through Baja California, Sonora, Chihuahua, Sinaloa and Nayarit is a highly visible conduit for people, agricultural produce and the newly outlawed intoxicants. Opiates, grown in the Mexican climate since at least 1886, along with the traditional Mexican marijuana beloved of its young men and soldiers, found a ready market in San Francisco's opium dens.

In the 1,989 miles of porous border between the US and Mexico, savvy brewers who had seen the writing on the wall with Volstead, had bought land and set up their brewing operations just over into Mexico but kept legitimate business interests on American soil. They employed large numbers of young Mexican men and women, who suddenly had ostensibly legitimate reasons to move back and forth across the borders. The Mexican economy, ruined by the Mexican Revolution (1910–20) leapt on the demand for drugs and booze in America, but particularly in California, and soon the 'kingpins' were making millions of dollars. They were also sending thousands of young Mexicans across the border into America.

California, although it would no doubt have been keen to sterilize its Chinese and Japanese residents, could find little reason to do so. The Chinese were nearly all single, hard-working men, and the Japanese, usually more prosperous, brought their wives and families with them, opening tidy shops and businesses. Instead, California found a new type of undesirable – the Chicana, the young Mexican-American or indigenous girl.

After the 1909 Act, anyone committed to a Californian asylum or institution on the grounds of mental health could be sterilized before release. A common reason for admission to an institution, usually by court order, was simply that the child was a pre-adolescent orphan. These children were then tested, primarily by interview, for 'feeblemindedness' or some other character flaw, and their mental age and IQ noted. These results were published, and while the language is undeniably and offensively racist, even the 1918 *Surveys in Mental Deviation in Prisons, Public Schools and Orphanages* (Sacramento) has to admit that 'The ranges of I.Q.s obtained suggests that Mexican-Indian children are at no special disadvantage when tests are applied to them.'[27] The report also found that 'Contrary to expectations, very few children were found to have been born out of wedlock.'[28]

Despite the obviously grotesque implications and consequences of these institutional tests, there is something peculiarly single-minded and almost comical in their attempts to grade children as 'low moron', 'middle moron' or the slightly more prestigious 'high grade moron'. In one visit to a rural school of 84 pupils where 12 'suspects' were interviewed, they recorded: 'One family furnished a moron and a borderliner; another furnished a moron, a borderliner and a dull-normal. A moron girl in this school has an insane mother. The girl herself is normal looking and attractive and is already at the beginning of the reproductive period.'[29] Another girl who was interviewed had a sad but not uncommon backstory that led to her admission to the institution:

> The experience leading up to her pregnancy might easily be expected of a high-grade feeble-minded girl. 'Picked up' on the street by a man whose name she has never known, she was taken to a moving picture theater and drugged on the way home. She was found the next morning in a public park. The man has not

been seen or heard from since and his identity will probably never be revealed.[30]

These girls, often very young and disproportionately of Latina or Native American origin, were routinely sterilized before release through the fail-safe method of 'partial hysterectomy'. 'Partial' is disingenuous when it comes to the procedure these girls underwent as their uteruses were completely removed. Only the cervix and ovaries remained. Retention of the cervix permitted reasonably normal sexual experience, and leaving the ovaries meant that the girl would continue to develop secondary sexual characteristics such as breast and hip development, and the accompanying facial changes of womanhood, but there was no chance of ever conceiving a child. While the language that accompanies many of California's assessments for these young people is unsurprisingly racist and ableist, you might be tempted to think that it was more misguided than completely inhumane – until it becomes clear that the assessments were purely academic. From the moment these girls came into their care, it was already decided – they wanted to sterilize them, and they did so. The true numbers of teenage girls sterilized by the state of California during this period remains unknown.

Internationally, the 1920s and '30s were a time of an almost fervid international call for the enactment of programmes of 'race betterment'. The theories postulated by Darwin and expanded by Galton had taken hold across the West with tragic consequences for women. The same year that the United States Immigration Act was passed in 1924, Virginia passed a state law called the Sterilization Act, as 'heredity plays an important part in the transmission of sanity, idiocy, imbecility, epilepsy and crime'.[31] Perhaps feeling this an insufficient act in itself, it was followed up by a specific Supreme Court ruling in 1927, now known as *Buck v. Bell* (more correctly, *Carrie Buck v. John Hendren Bell, Superintendent of State Colony for Epileptics and Feeble Minded*). Carrie Buck was a young woman of 21 who had become pregnant at 17. This was said to be by the friend of one of her foster parents, and an act of rape. Buck was with her foster parents because her mother, Emma Bell, was under state care owing to 'feeble-mindedness'. The daughter born to Carrie was assessed and presumed 'mentally defective'. Harry Laughlin, head of the Eugenics Record Office, described them as part of the 'shiftless, ignorant, and worthless class of anti-social whites of the South'.[32] Oliver Wendell Homes Jr, jurist for the Supreme Court, passed the ruling that Carrie Buck should indeed be sterilized by the removal of her fallopian tubes with the parting comment that 'Three generations of imbeciles are enough'.

Carrie Buck was sterilized on 19 October 1927, the first of many thousands in Virginia – the true total is again unknown – until the law was repealed in 1972.

CREATING A NATIONAL BIOLOGY

In the 1840s a doctor called Miksa Hölbling studied a village in Baranya County in Transdanubia, where he observed that many peasant families had only one child – this was called *egyke*, or the 'one-child rule'. The peasantry of Hungary were largely poor. Their lands were often wet and swampy, and in parts of the country malaria was so rife that local populations had developed partial immunity to it. Many were serfs. That most families only had one child was not necessarily intentional as such (infant mortality was high), but there had been a definite drop off in the birth rate.

This declining birth rate was viewed by intellectual observers as a result of the rising vanity of young peasant women, who no longer wished to sacrifice their comforts to bear Hungary's next generations. It was instead caused by a large number of factors. Hungarian peasants had, by legal statute, to divide their land among all their children, so large families and a high death rate in general meant an ever-increasing division of plots of relatively poor land that required sheer acreage in order to support successful agriculture. In addition, these peasant villages were run on the more matriarchal *szülék* model, where the mother-in-law remained in the family home and looked after the children and the household livestock while the daughter or daughter-in-law worked on the land. The *szülék* was in control of the household, and she decided whether the family was in a viable position to add to its numbers.[33] This, coupled with the local practice of endogamy (marrying only within the community), which could be restricted to either a social or a geographical group, was not helping 'improve' the Hungarian race and became a cause for extreme concern for eugenicists and nationalists after the First World War.

Hungary, followed closely by Italy, is a prime example of where long-term concerns about what constituted a national identity went from a periodically troubling threat to a raging wildfire after the First World War. Signed on 4 June 1920 at the Paris Peace Conference, the Treaty of Trianon decimated the thousand-year-old kingdom of Hungary, redrawing it to a third of its former size, with the resulting loss of over half its population. Owing to its vast size over such a long period, the Hungarian population had naturally been made up of a large number of different ethnicities, cultures and languages. Predominantly, Hungarians saw themselves as Magyars, descendants of the original clans of Hungary who had taken over the Carpathian Basin from *c*. 896 onwards. After the ignominies of the Treaty, many thinkers were keen to reassert the power of the Hungarian man.

There was a huge proliferation of thought and publication on the subject of Hungarian identity. More liberal writers such as László Németh were of the opinion that Hungary should engage with people in Romania and Yugoslavia, while retaining what it meant to be a Finno-Ugric Hungarian, and coined the term 'hungorólogia' regarding the study of what this identity truly meant. Others, such as Kunó Klebelsberg, the Hungarian minister for Education in the 1920s and '30s, targeted non-productive women as enemies of the state and obsessed to the nation over the importance of Hungarian ethnic dominance in the Carpathian Basin.

A series of public bodies were formed to 'protect' the Hungarian race, with eugenics front and centre of their research and policies. In 1925 the Rockefeller Foundation funded the establishment of the Sanitation Reform Bureau, which targeted improving 'genetic quality', overseen by the Hungarian Secretary of State for Health, Kornél Scholtz. The Rockefeller Foundation had expanded its horizons significantly from its American base in the preceding decade, investigating family planning and eugenics on an international scale. Various other state organizations also sprang up in Hungary, such as the Social Hygiene Institute the following year. The first scientific studies of Hungarian twins began during the 1930s, and is still ongoing today.[34]

Meanwhile, the popular focus was undoubtedly on the women of Hungary and their responsibility for the future of the country and the very existence of Hungarian identity itself.[35] There was a growing fascination with the matriarchal *szülék* model, which led to the rediscovery of a book written in 1861 by Johann Jakob Bachofen called *Das Mutterrecht*, about the original power of the matriarchy in the ancient world. When it was first published, it had promptly fallen into a critical blackhole, but in the early twentieth century it found a new audience. In 1924 *Das Mutterrecht* inspired the Nobel-Prize-winning author Gerhart Hauptmann to write *Die Insel der großen Mutter* ('Island of the Great Mother').

In *Die Insel der großen Mutter* a boat sets sail to navigate the world. It sinks somewhere in the Pacific Ocean, after the brave men have loaded all of the women on board onto lifeboats along with a lone male 12-year-old child, Phaon. They reach an island and live as a group of women at peace with each other, rather pleased to have been shipwrecked. They are able to conceive with the help of a 'snake-god', but all the male children are banished to another island under the charge of Phaon, where they grow up to be industrial and prosperous. The years pass. Eventually, however, a generation of sexually available young women in the matriarchy can suddenly no longer conceive. They ask the men to come and take over, thus proving to relieved readers how self-defeating the concept of matriarchy is. The book went down very well in Hungary.

In wider society at large, this led to a growing demonization of women, particularly those associated with childbirth. This was exemplified in the sensational case of the Angel Makers of Nagyrév where, between 1911 and 1929, a group of women were said to have committed anything from 45 to 300 murders under the recommendation and assistance of the local midwife. The murders (usually the victims were their husbands, but not always) were carried out through arsenic poisoning, boiled down from the fly papers available at the time. Contemporary accounts are conflicting, but the midwife (allegedly also an illegal abortionist with an unexplained missing husband) was thought to have supplied the fly papers and to have issued words of advice and encouragement to the women.

Between 1929 and 1931 dozens of bodies were disinterred and 28 suspects (26 of whom were women) were convicted of 162 murders, resulting in six death sentences and multiple life imprisonments. The hysteria that surrounded the trials, the wildly unreliable details and the obvious 'demonic' qualities of the midwife herself illuminate how this sensational series of murders tapped into Hungarian anxieties about the role of women in family life.

Women on trial for murder in Nagyrév, Hungary, 1929

'APPLIED BIOLOGY'

Hungary, focused on convincing ethnic Hungarian women to lend their wombs to the birth of a revitalized nation, decided to stop attempting to recognize its Jewish population. They were not alone. From the late nineteenth century there had been a rising tide of overt racism and anti-Semitic media and opinion in both Europe and America. This was for a number of reasons, one of which was the displacement of the Jewish people of Russia, through pogroms and other 'social' measures. Many of these displaced Ashkenazi Jews moved to Antwerp, Amsterdam and London, but many also fled to the east coast of the United States. Industrious and inclined to build strong international and exclusive community networks, they were not always welcome in the fast mobilizing and commercial America. The 'othering' of the Jewish immigrant and its conflation with racial origin increased dramatically after the First World War with a whole new wave of German immigrants.

Germany, where the average family was materially poorer than it had been in the 1890s and economically weakened by war, grasped onto the new American ideas about industrialization and productivity, and they most certainly grasped onto both Hungary's ideology regarding racial and national biology and America's ideas on compulsory sterilization. In *Mein Kampf*, written from prison in 1924, Adolf Hitler wrote: 'There is today one state ... in which at least weak beginnings toward a better conception [of citizenship] are noticeable. Of course, it is not our model German Republic, but the United States.'

So much has been written about Adolf Hitler that there is little else to add to a vast and often spurious canon. The fundamental and outstanding fact remains that he was a man manifestly unfit for the power he craved. He took the eugenicist ideas of the time, prevalent right across Europe and America, combined them with the power of the new forms of modern media and distilled them into a machine intent on annihilation.

What remains extraordinary about Hitler is that he persuaded so many seemingly ordinary German people to adopt his ideals of racial 'purity', ideals that he so plainly did not conform to himself, either physically, intellectually or psychologically. But as a CIA report on him remarked: 'One good phrase or political catchword is worth more to him than cartloads of dry exposition and theory... A catchword gives the unthinking mob not only the material for an idea, but also furnishes them with the pleasant illusion that they are thinking themselves.'[36] The same report noted that 'The "Sieg Heil!" used in all political rallies is a direct copy of the technique used by American football cheerleaders.'[37]

This admiration of American eugenics and industrialization is evidenced by Hitler's hero-worship of Henry Ford. In late December 1931, two years before he became the German chancellor, Annetta Antona for the *Detroit News* visited Hitler in Munich, finding a large portrait of Ford in the Nazi Party headquarters there. When asked about it, Hitler responded, 'I regard Henry Ford as my inspiration' (original German unavailable; Hitler did not speak English).[38] Apocryphal stories from the same time suggest that SS officers' messes also featured pictures of Ford.

The links between the American eugenicists and the Nazi Party by no means stopped at Ford. In 1928 Ezra Seymour (E. S.) Gosney, a citrus baron of Pasadena, California, founded the Human Betterment Foundation (HBF) to support research into the results and progress of involuntary sterilization since 1909, feeling no doubt legitimized by the *Buck* v. *Bell* ruling. The front page of one of their typical pamphlets reads, in bold capital letters, 'HUMAN STERILIZATION TODAY', leaving only a few celebratory lines for 'During the last twenty-eight years, California state institutions have sterilized nearly 12,000 insane and feebleminded patients.'[39] Fellow California eugenicist C. M. Goethe, who was particularly concerned with the genetic threat apparently posed by Mexico, went on a research mission to Germany in 1934 and on his return wrote to Gosney to congratulate him on the work of the HBF:

> You will be interested to know that your work has played a powerful part in shaping the opinions of the group of intellectuals who are behind Hitler in this epoch-making

program. Everywhere I sensed that their opinions have been tremendously stimulated by American thought . . . I want you, my dear friend, to carry this thought with you for the rest of your life, that you have really jolted into action a great government of 60 million people.[40]

The time of the 'Beer Hall Putsch', as Hitler's first attempt to seize power became known, was a difficult time for Germany economically. Still bound to make reparations after the First World War, the Germans found themselves at odds with the French after welching on their new obligation to provide them with fossil fuels. The French occupied the Ruhr region between 1920 and 1925 to ensure their supply of coal and timber, sending 60,000 men initially, with the occupying troops eventually numbering around 100,000. In a calculated move the French sent colonial troops from Senegal, Indochina (now Vietnam) and Madagascar, who were stationed from the Ruhr Valley to Dortmund and numbered around 14 per cent of France's occupying soldiers at their peak.[41] This was, to put it mildly, an inflammatory tactic. They knew exactly how Germany would respond. By German newspapers it was called *Die Schwarze Schmach* ('The Black Disgrace'), and in Britain and America it was even more luridly described in the popular press as 'The Black Horror on the Rhine'. On 10 April 1920, four days after France arrived in the Ruhr, the British newspaper the *Daily Herald* ran the headline:

'BLACK SCOURGE IN EUROPE SEXUAL HORROR LET LOOSE BY FRANCE ON RHINE DISAPPEARANCE OF YOUNG GERMAN GIRLS'

Outraged politicians corresponded with each other, unable to restrain their imaginations regarding the perilous fate of the young women of the Ruhr, as 'for well-known physiological reasons, the raping of a white woman by a negro is nearly always accompanied by serious injury and not infrequently has fatal results'.[42] Further reports in the British press included asides on the supposedly uncontrollable nature of black male sexuality, syphilis and, again in the *Daily Herald*, 'dead bodies of young women discovered under manure heaps'.[43] These sensationalist headlines had their roots firmly in the American press reportage of Prohibition, beginning in 1914, when the *New York Times* began its reporting on 'Negro Cocaine "Fiends"' who they claimed were unstoppable even by .32 calibre bullets.

Germany was outraged by these stories. The Black German population was proportionately tiny before the Ruhr occupation (perhaps around 25,000 in a population of around 65 million), consisting mostly of family and extended family brought back by German missionaries. The average German individual may well have had no interaction at all with a non-white person, and the deliberate proliferation of hysterical rumours by German, British and American media of the sexually unstoppable Senegalese juggernaut that France had released into the Ruhr caused a national outcry. When mixed-race children, or *Rassenschande*, began to appear in the Ruhr, the press called them '*Rheinlandbastardes*' and the term became a byword for disgrace, although there were probably no more than around 800 children.

In 1933 Hitler became the German chancellor. His brand of furious, repetitive rhetoric was finding favour with a population that felt itself to be embattled on all sides, and whose national pride had still not recovered from the First World War. Only months after arriving in power, the Nazi Party passed the act which began compulsory sterilization for Germans who might produce 'genetically diseased offspring', or the *Gesetz zur Verhütung erbkranken Nachwuchses*. The terminology was deliberately broad and closely resembled the Virginia Act of 1924. Using this law, the Gestapo – the 'secret' political police – were able to report from the Cologne office that, finally, 'Conforming with higher directives, all descendants of occupying troops of foreign blood were sterilized in the summer of 1937.' The letter ends: 'I may point out that the matter is secret and may under no circumstances be discussed in public.'[44] Although Hitler's agenda against the Jewish people of Germany was already part of his political campaign, his first victims were the *Rheinlandbastardes*. This was the terrible conclusion of the concerted media campaign against these children and their parents.

On 15 September 1935 the Nuremberg Laws came into place, for the first time targeting Jews. The first was the Law for the Protection of German Blood and German Honour, which forbade not only marriage but also sexual intercourse between those of German gentile and Jewish descent. 'German Honour' in this context is more than antiquated phrasing: for women it was known as *Geschlechtsehre* or literally the 'gender honour' associated with *Kinder, Küche, Kirche* ('Children, Kitchen, Church'), and for men *Härte*, which equates to hardness, stoicism, physicality, loyalty and camaraderie. Notably, for women *Geschlechtsehre* was tied specifically to sexual conduct.

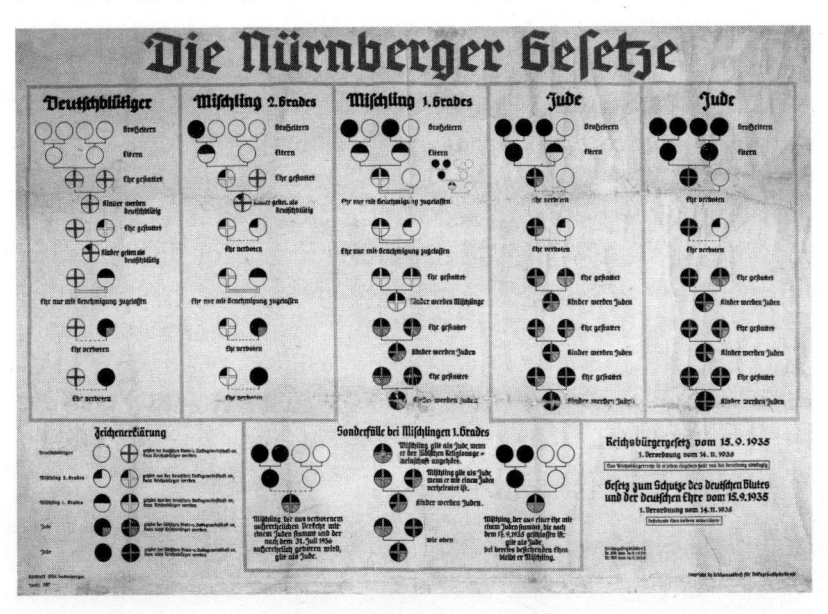

The Nuremberg Laws, 1935

The second Nuremberg Law was the Reich Citizenship Law, which further limited German citizenship to those of 'German or kindred blood'. The classification tables go to one-eighth ancestry, or great-grandparent level, and resemble closely the American tables to classify negro ancestry after the American Civil War. The Laws were expanded and amended in November 1935 to include Roma people and Black people. On 12 December the same year Heinrich Himmler instigated the *Lebensborn* ('Fount of Life') programme.

Himmler, who wanted Germany populated as quickly as possible by racially appropriate Germans, promoted extramarital sex among his 'Aryan' troops with women of sufficient Germanic quality. Far from any stigma becoming attached to these pregnancies, the women involved were taken to *Lebensborn* homes for their deliveries, after which the infants would be adopted into a suitably Germanic family to be raised as their own.

The Hitler Youth movement expanded dramatically and was made compulsory for 10- to 18-year-olds. Often away from their parents for the first time and among peers, the Hitler Youth and the League of German Girls did not always acquit themselves with the decorum their parents may have been hoping for. Expectations for the girls were particularly high as they were regarded as the guardians of the current and future *Volksgemeinschaft* or 'folk community'. *Volk*, which appears everywhere in the literature and the propaganda of the time, embodied Hitler's notion of the corps of German national and racial identity: everything was done for and in its name.

In some ways, 1938 turned out to be the year of the cross. In December the Cross of Honour of the German Mother was inaugurated, for married women of German blood who raised specific numbers of children 'in the role of a parent', thus allowing women who adopted *Lebensborn* to participate. It came in three classes: third for adopting between three and five children, second for six or seven children and first for eight children or more. A bearer of the Cross of the German Mother was considered a war hero owing to her contribution to the German nation, bringing with it echoes of the mythology that a woman in labour is a warrior.

A woman is awarded the Mother's Cross, Germany, 1943

Thus two very different sexual codes were immediately put into place between 1934 and 1935. Aryan Germans were free to copulate and reproduce at will, and indeed, the *Härte* notion embraced the idea that men not only should but must expend their sexual energy in a wholesome manner. However, for everyone else, the *Untermenschen* or subhumans, sexual desire and consequent reproduction must be repressed at all costs. This had disastrous consequences for millions of men, women and children who had been born in Germany, and who were German until Hitler came to power.

The mass extermination of a people takes work, and planning. The Holocaust did not happen overnight. A letter from a doctor, Adolf Pockorny, to Heinrich Himmler in October 1941 reads: 'The thought alone that the three million Bolsheviks, at present German prisoners, could be sterilized so that they could be used as labourers but be prevented from reproduction, opens the most far reaching perspectives.'[45]

Another doctor, Viktor Hermann Brack, also wrote to Himmler with his thoughts on how to quicken the pace of the 1934 Act:

'Sterilization, as normally performed on persons with hereditary diseases, is here out of the question because it takes too long and is too expensive. Castration by X-rays, however, is not only relatively cheap but can also be performed on many thousands in the shortest time.'[46]

Concentration camps had existed since Hitler became chancellor in 1933 and had ostensibly been built to house political prisoners. The early camps were often local structures; some were established in schools or other municipal buildings, old country houses or even farms. From the extensive manuals put together regarding prisoner treatment to the architecture of the newly constructed concentration camps there can be no doubt that they were built as monoliths to destruction and absolute domination. The things it is necessary to recount are painful, and the numbers of people involved will never be known. Jews, Roma, Black, brown and gay, political dissenters and anyone not vaguely adhering to a code were not only to be murdered, but they were murdered with distinct pleasure. All had been designated by the Nazi regime as *todeswürdig* or 'worthy of death'.

In 1939 a camp was constructed for 6,000 inmates, Germany's first camp exclusively for women: Ravensbrück. The following is taken from a 1963 testimony by Wanda Półtawska, MD PhD, born 1921, psychiatrist, professor emerita of the chair of psychiatry at the Kraków Medical Academy, formerly Director of the Institute of the Theology of the Family at the Kraków Pontifical Academy of Theology (Ravensbrück survivor no. 7709): 'The first 867 women of Ravensbrück were a mixture of dissenters, Jews, political prisoners, criminals, the 'asocial' (meaning lesbians), prostitutes and Roma women.'[47]

The *winkel*, or triangle, system meant that every woman had to wear a badge that indicated her race according to a colour and denoted her native language with a letter; odd loyalties and friendships sprang up amongst strangers. Forced labour at Ravensbrück was varied and could include adapting confiscated furs and luxury materials, knitting, making prisoner uniforms or administrative work. It could also involve road-building, quarrying and construction. The main industrial supplier was Siemens Electric Company, for whom the women laboured building V1 and V2 rockets. They did this on rations of two bowls of soup per day, and soon deaths from malnutrition began to occur. Then something else happened.

With no apparent reason, girls and women were selected for 'medical' examinations, sometimes in groups or sometimes singly. These examinations focused only on their legs, and their lower legs at that. They became known in the camp as *die Kaninchen* or 'the rabbits'. The equivalent term in English is 'guinea pigs'. The prisoners soon realized that any woman between 18 and 25 years old who arrived on a *Sondertransport* (special transport), and whose prison number was in the 7000s, would become a *Kaninchen*. The experiments began in July 1942, all on the lower legs (although an occasional abdominal incision was made), leaving the subjects in agony or dead. If they were considered worthless, they were removed and shot, but not by firing squad: they were taken behind service buildings and executed without ceremony. The majority of the *Kaninchen* were usually young Polish political prisoners; older subjects were taken only if no younger women were available.

The young *Kaninchen* of Ravensbruck organized themselves to continue some kind of education, and the older women of the camp stole food to try and keep them fed. The state of their legs became worse and worse as the operations continued. Bone surgeries were often repeated on the same patients, and the soft tissue subjects appeared to have a worse survival rate. Again, when deemed too far gone, they were removed and shot. Finally, the execution of six *Kaninchen* on the same day drove the remaining women to rebellion, leading them to be relabelled *das Piratenvolk*, or 'The Pirates', by their admiring peers.[48]

In total, in that month, 74 Polish women were operated on (alongside eight non-Polish women) and divided into 'clean' and 'dirty' groups. Many who underwent bone surgery had their bones broken repeatedly and infection introduced, so that the results might be observed. Evipan, now referred to as hexobarbitone, was used as a rapid-action sedative, followed by ether. The administering physicians were the surgeon Karl Gebhardt, Himmler's own doctor, and his assistant the physician and dermatologist Gerta Oberheuser (1911–1978). That Gebhardt was a monster is not in doubt and Ravensbrück merely served as a training ground for his 'graduation' to Auschwitz, but Gerta Oberheuser's sadism was of another class entirely: she took particular pleasure in inflicting public and humiliating pelvic examinations upon the *Kaninchen* when they arrived at the camp. When the patients asked for water after they had been incapacitated by the experiments, she ensured it was administered mixed with vinegar. She was also probably involved, as the camp doctor for 'women's diseases' or VD, in the experiments remembered by Walter Jahn (an intern in the men's camp that later sprang up at Ravensbrück) in which syphilis was injected into the spinal cords of female prisoners.[49]

The camp was also patrolled by another monster, Irma Grese, 'The Hyena'. Grese had been born into a dairying family but had wanted to be a nurse. Lacking sufficient education, she had become involved with the League of German Girls, much to the disgust of her father, who threw her out of the house. In 1942, aged 19, she became an overseer at Ravensbrück, where she would deliberately starve her dogs then let them loose among the work gangs while she rode her bicycle, watched and laughed. Emulating Hitler, she wore jackboots and carried an absurd bullwhip, with which she beat any prisoner she thought prettier than herself, and visibly enjoyed the duty of selecting new arrivals for the gas chambers that were fully in operation in the German camps by that summer.[50]

Grese became equally notorious at Auschwitz and Bergen-Belsen, again with her dogs, and a retrospective in *Die Welt* in 2014 stated that she also tied women's legs together when they arrived at the camps in labour to prevent them giving birth.[51] Dr Gisella Perl, an inmate and doctor at Auschwitz recalled: 'She was one of the most beautiful women I have ever seen. Her body was perfect in every line, her face clear and angelic, and her blue eyes the gayest, the most innocent eyes one can imagine. And yet Irma Grese was the most depraved, cruel, imaginative pervert I ever came across.'[52] Grese was unrepentant when she was captured with other members of the SS at the fall of Bergen-Belsen. She was one of only three female guards to be hanged at the end of the war. Her last word to the guards was a bored-sounding, 'Schnell'. She was 22.

Babies born to pregnant women at Ravensbruck were initially delivered in the hospital in nearby Templin. After 1942 they were delivered at the camp, where the staff 'strangled them shortly after they were born', unless there was time to get the women onto a transport for Auschwitz, so they could be gassed *in utero*.[53]

After the war Gerta Oberheuser was also tried, and was equally unrepentant regarding her involvement in these crimes. It emerged that what they had been doing to the *Kaninchen* was simulating battlefield injuries on the women; either shattered bones into which they embedded foreign bodies such as rusty nails or broken glass, or horrendous soft tissue 'shrapnel' tears which they then infected and reinfected with streptococcus, strains of 'gas gangrene' or tetanus. Many surviving *Kaninchen* never bore children, and assumed they had also been sterilized during the 'operations'.

Oberheuser was sentenced to 20 years for her part in the experiments, but released early for various administrative reasons. Instead of slinking into the shadows, she established a practice as a 'family doctor' in West Germany. In 1958 the British Medical Association discovered she was still practising and published the news. The outcry from the medical community in the July edition of the *BMJ* was palpable, drawing particular attention to her casual admission that she injected 'five or six' *Kaninchen* with petrol, knowing it would cause agonizing heart failure in minutes.[54] The motivation for the medium of petrol remained unclear. Oberheuser was barred from practising medicine, and died in a nursing home in 1978.

The planning and enactment of the Holocaust had, in almost every way, begun on *Kristallnacht* in the winter of 1938, and it was certainly well under way in October 1939, when Hitler signed off on the Aktion T4 euthanasia programme to begin the compulsory killing by lethal injection (later simply wholesale gassing) of approximately 300,000 disabled or otherwise 'lacking' individuals before 1945, a large proportion of whom were taken from religious houses and hospitals, both Protestant and Catholic. It was called *Gnadentod*, or the 'mercy death'. The killings began with children suffering from disabilities such as

Down's syndrome and cerebral palsy before graduating to adults and was overseen by one of Hitler's own doctors, Karl Brandt, and later by Philipp Bouhler. Brandt, one of Hitler's more lucid and thoughtful henchmen, was often busy with the Führer, so it was Bouhler who supervised the programme at a more practical level. After 1941 and the invasion of the Soviet Union by the Reich, T4 was scaled back as the 'war effort' was needed further east, although notable exceptions were made after the Allied bombings of Hamburg and Stettin, when Aktion T4 operatives took the opportunity to 'empty' the nursing homes there. That same year the Allied bombers arriving over Germany began to drop leaflets in German, explaining what was happening.

In the history of reproductive medicine it is often necessary to record deeds that are almost impossible to bear, but Joseph Mengele aspired to new evils. He was a man for whom the Third Reich presented myriad opportunities; empowered by a dreadful and terrifying regime, Mengele was both a product of the eugenic age and a man free to commit the most appalling acts without fear of punishment – and he was not alone.

Mengele was the product of a small cohort of men who believed that eugenic control was the way forward. Professor Ernst Rüdin, an expert on psychiatry who identified the genetic link in schizophrenia, had been one of Mengele's early teachers (and also taught researchers from the Rockefeller Foundation). He was a committed proponent of compulsory sterilization and racial hygiene. He also believed that identifying as a conscientious objector was a sign of mental illness and merited sterilization, and spearheaded the Nazi party's planning of genocide on 'psychiatric grounds' from Munich.[55] Rüdin escaped justice after the war, and claimed his knowledge of what went on in the camps was minimal.

Mengele was also taught by Professor Dr Otmar Freiherr von Verschuer, the oldest of this monstrous group, a respected eugenicist with a particular interest in twins. Verschuer was lecturing on genetics internationally as late as 8 June 1939, when he addressed the Royal Society in London. He admitted to receiving 'blood samples' that Mengele had taken at Auschwitz for his research, including human heads, eyes and tissue.[56] After the war Verschuer somehow managed to resurrect his career and is still cited in medical papers for his discoveries.

Then there was Eduard Wirths, an SS doctor based primarily at Auschwitz who oversaw the group of doctors, including Mengele, who performed experiments on the prisoners in the infamous Block 10. The majority of these prisoners were Jewish women. He was particularly interested in securing a lasting reputation for his work in gynaecology and performed many operations, often without anaesthetic, on the cervixes of women in the camp. He sent his samples back to his old teacher Hans Hinselmann, who used them to radically accelerate the development of techniques in colposcopy, still used today for cervical examination. Wirths hanged himself after his arrest in 1945.[57]

The list goes on: Carl Clauberg specialized in rendering the uterus sterile in both Auschwitz and Ravensbrück; Horst Schumann preferred to work on castration, and by the time of his trial estimated that he had sterilized 30,000 individuals and was responsible for the deaths of approximately 80,000 more; Hermann Stieve worked on the women of the Plötzensee camp from his base in Berlin, studying the effect on the menstrual cycles and reproductive organs of women sentenced to death, recording the *Schreckblutungen* or 'shock bleeds' that were often brought on by the announcement of the sentence.[58] Sigmund Rascher was the doctor who performed 'hot and cold' experiments, and also experimented with the effects of high altitude on the human body, at Dachau. These experiments were particularly hard on the Roma prisoners. Keen that he and his wife, Karoline, should be seen as good advertisements for the Nazi fertility drive, they were used in propaganda materials by Himmler, until it was proved during her fourth fake pregnancy that 'Nini' had in fact been kidnapping babies. They were both imprisoned and Sigmund Rascher was shot in his cell. Nini was later hanged at Ravensbrück.

Above all of these individuals sits Mengele – not necessarily because of the number of people he mutilated and murdered but for the sheer relish with which he undertook his tasks. He met the trains bringing in the prisoners destined for extermination, shouting

'*ZWILLINGE HERAUS! ZWILLINGE HERAUSTRETEN!*' ('Twins out! Twins step forward!').[59] The vast majority of the others were directed straight to the gas chambers, including any visibly pregnant women. Mengele's justification was as follows:

> When a Jewish child is born, or a woman comes to camp with a child already… I don't know what to do with the child. I can't set the child free because there are no longer any Jews who live in freedom … It would not be humanitarian to send a child to the ovens without permitting the mother to be there to witness the child's death … That is why I send the mother and child to the gas ovens together.[60]

The 'ovens' were where he took part in administering the deadly Zyklon B cyanide gas himself.

With his research on twins, Mengele continued the work he had begun under his tutor von Verschuer. The subjects ranged widely in age, but children were preferable because they had not yet adopted any adult lifestyles that would compromise the results. One assistant recalled in a 1945 deposition: 'In the work room next to the dissecting room, 14 gypsy twins were waiting … and crying bitterly.' The assistant went on:

> Dr. Mengele didn't say a single word to us, and prepared a 10 cc. and 5 cc. syringe. From a box he took Evipan, and from another box he took chloroform … the first twin was brought in . . . a 14-year-old girl. Dr Mengele ordered me to undress the girl and put her on the dissecting table. Then he injected the Evipan into her right arm intravenously. After the child had fallen asleep, he felt for the left ventricle of the heart and injected 10cc. of chloroform. After one little twitch the child was dead, whereupon Dr Mengele had it taken into the corpse chamber. In this manner, all 14 twins were killed during the night.[61]

Such horrors were committed not only to facilitate research into disease but also to further the Nazi dream of filling the Reich with 'true' Germans. Twins, murdered by Mengele in order to be dissected, might 'resolve the secret of the reproduction of the race. To advance one step in the search to unlock the secret of multiplying the race of superior beings destined to rule was a 'noble goal'. If only it were possible, in the future, to have each German mother bear as many twins as possible!'[62]

Mengele fled after the fall of Germany, and ended up in South America, like many of his comrades who escaped trial or execution for the rest of his natural life. He died while swimming in 1979 off the coast of Brazil, and was buried under a false name. He was exhumed in 1985, identified by DNA in 1992, and his skeleton now resides in the São Paulo Institute for Forensic Medicine, where it is used as a teaching aid.

Among the monsters who stalked the camps, there were those inmates who acted with profound and courageous humanity. Some female prisoners with medical experience aided their fellow women by providing basic care and food and comfort where they could, as well as abortions to those whose pregnancies were about to become visible. The Pirates, particularly members of the band who had been interned together for some time, stole clothing, 'excess' sheets and quilts in the stockroom and raided the soup cauldrons in the Ravensbrück officers' mess to aid the *Kaninchen*. Most ingenious was their system of swapping their triangles to hide *Kaninchen* in the ordinary inmates or among the political prisoners, closing ranks around the vulnerable when the guards were nearby.[63] One of the *Kaninchen* even managed to escape the hospital block and hid naked in a shed until she was found by a known Pirate who was walking past, and subsequently hidden among the ranks – they covered her damaged legs with stolen trousers, until the liberation of the camp.

Wanda Półtawska, the last of the Ravensbrück *Kaninchen*, died at home in Kraków on 23 October 2023, aged 101, surrounded by her family.[64]

9

Living Memory

'As my children know little of my early years, I decided to put together this album so they knew my heritage. Whilst doing so I realised that most of my life has been a series of links with portents of things to come.'[1]

This is my mother's voice. At 0728 GMT on Easter Sunday 1945, HMS *Indefatigable* was hit hard by *kamikaze* on the Okinawa front. Minutes later my mother was born on a kitchen table in the tiny village of Catwick, East Yorkshire, with the help of Dr Peterkin and Nurse Rose. Dr Peterkin had missed his morning egg and Nurse Rose only had one leg. When the news came over the wireless, things were not ideal for our grandmother Renie May either, but there is a reason Nurse Rose became known as indefatigable herself. She was a local legend. By then, she had already delivered over three thousand babies.

Nurse Rose, a woman of indomitable spirit, had been bombed out of her home in Hull during the Blitz, losing all her possessions and one leg. When discharged from hospital, she was evacuated to Leven, the village next to Catwick, where she stayed in an empty chicken shed in the garden of a feed merchant named Bill Tripp. The local people contributed some funds to make the place somewhat habitable. Nurse Rose lived there until the war was over and a house in the village became vacant. Eleven years after I was born, my aunt Jean married a merchant seaman from East Hull, who I was later to find out had also been delivered by Nurse Rose.[2]

While Nurse Rose was delivering babies and piecing her life back together, a British obstetrician was busy developing his ideas on the phenomenon that came to be known as 'natural childbirth'. Grantly Dick-Read – yet another in a long line of exceptionally unfortunate names for men involved in obstetrics – published his first book, *Natural Childbirth*, in 1933. This book would join forces with a radical medical development already underway to provide the formation of how we conceive of childbirth today.

In *Natural Childbirth* Dick-Read described childbirth as 'the perfection of womanhood' and said that most difficult labours were the result of 'the inability of obstetricians and midwives to stand by and allow the natural and uninterrupted course of labour'.[3] Whether Nurse Rose would have agreed we do not know, but Dick-Read was and remains a highly controversial figure. Like many others of his generation, he believed, without having any experience of childbirth outside the UK, that 'primitive women' did not experience pain during their 'placid' childbirth.[4] While this is plainly nonsense, it reflects the earlier beliefs advanced by many doctors and scientists, some of whom we've already met, that other races did not experience pain (and certainly pain in childbirth) in the same way as educated white women.

Interwoven with these risible views, Dick-Read did have some valuable things to say, such as his observation that a mother's birth experience is often defined by her previous birth. Dick-Read's main emphasis was on the fear of pain, an idea that he later developed for his next book, *Childbirth without Fear* (1942). A much larger and more comprehensive work than his first, it expounded on the idea that a woman could essentially experience a pain-free birth if she allowed herself to, by embracing rather than fearing labour. One of its central tenets, however, was that the mother should retain control of the process. This idea was rejected by his fellow obstetricians but welcomed by countless women.

Childbirth without Fear was immensely valuable to millions of women and medical practitioners, as the subsequent book of collected letters all written to Dick-Read from patients, doctors and nurses proved. It is also true that although definitions of 'natural' most certainly differ, childbirth is not a disease but is inherently natural. But one of the more lasting consequences of Dick-Read's work is that it did much to instil the idea that pain is a matter for the mother to deal with by strength of will, rather than modern medical care.

Pain theory has been much debated since the seventeenth century, but it became even more so with the synthesis of morphine and the invention of the hypodermic needle in the nineteenth century. The two world wars saw great strides in the advancement of pain theory owing to the vast numbers of casualties for whom even vaster amounts of pain relief were required. Further investigations into pain during the war illuminated a psychological element, now known as the Anzio Effect. At the Battle of Anzio in 1944, an anaesthetist called Henry Knowles Beecher observed that many of the men injured in the horrendous fighting claimed to experience less pain than civilians he had observed with milder injuries. He theorized that 'the intensity of the suffering is largely determined by what the pain means to the patient' and that 'the extent of the wound bears only a slight relationship (if none at all) to the pain experienced'.[5] The Anzio Effect was a valuable historical document, but it had two side effects: it linked the experience of pain to notions of bravery and bestowed an inherent moral superiority on the stoic sufferer. The idea that pain is entirely within the psychological control of the sufferer echoes the arguments made against pain relief during childbirth during the debate surrounding chloroform and ether a century earlier.

Dick-Read's work was central to the founding of one of the most important British pregnancy information and care organizations: the Natural Childbirth Association (NCA), now the National Childbirth Trust (NCT). Prunella Briance, who founded the NCA in 1956, had experienced two traumatic labours. One, a risky C-section during a power cut in 1953, had resulted in a healthy son, but the subsequent birth of a daughter had gone horribly wrong. Briance, inspired by Dick-Read's writings, had decided to take control of her second birth, but a series of seemingly medieval mishaps occurred one after the other. First the midwife dropped her while attempting to move her, and then the doctor insisted on a dose of castor oil to speed up the birth. This mysterious dose made her, understandably, violently sick, and her daughter became obstructed and died.[6]

Despite this tragedy, Briance believed wholeheartedly in Dick-Read's approach, and she founded the NCA as a means of helping expectant mothers to plan for and remain in control of their own birthing experience. Dick-Read served as its first president, and Briance remained one of his most vocal advocates, putting much emphasis on rising above the pain as well as a wide range of subjects such as breast-feeding and obstructed births. Two years after it was founded, the NCA began offering antenatal classes to women, including sessions on breathing techniques to help manage pain. Breathing techniques, known by various names now such as Lamaze or 4-7-8, have various merits. They consist primarily of breathing in through the nose, holding the breath, then exhaling slowly through the mouth. They are also recommended for patients suffering from anxiety, extreme stress or panic attacks. While not everyone finds them useful, attempting to hold your breath during a contraction or a panic attack can be as distressing as either.

Added 'performance pressure' was also being piled on top of pregnancy during the post-war period. With the extension of wartime rationing, women were increasingly urged not to gain too much weight during pregnancy and to lose it quickly after the birth. A study by Abraham Prochownik in 1901 had suggested that a 2,000-calorie-a-day diet, high in protein and low in carbohydrates, could facilitate an easier late pregnancy and labour. Many natural childbirth advocates recommended exercises (to be done inside the home) along with calorific restriction. From 1970 onwards gestational weight gains have found an overall rising trend in maternal weight gain and weight of the baby – but the approach of the 1950s and 1960s imposed yet another layer of restrictions on the pregnant mother.[7]

Coincidentally, as the natural childbirth movement began to take shape, so did the second major development set to change many women's birthing experiences – the invention of the epidural. As powerful painkillers such as morphine became increasingly widespread, many doctors began experimenting with spinal blocks for pain relief. The most advanced was Fidel Pagés, a Spanish military surgeon who fought in the Second Rif War between Spain and Berber tribes in northern Morocco. His technique for a single spinal injection spread throughout Spanish-speaking countries and into their civilian medical practice. The progress made by Pages was cut short when he died in a car accident in 1923, and the epidural fell back into obscurity.[8] In 1931 a pioneering Italian cardiac surgeon (who would later develop the heart and lung machine), Achille Mario Dogliotti, published on it and it finally received international recognition. Up until this time the epidural was regarded as something for major trauma surgery, such as amputation, but a Romanian obstetrician, Eugen Aburel, had the idea that it could be used during labour.[9] The work of these three men introduced and popularized one of the most commonly used obstetric pain-killing methods still in use today at precisely the same time as Dick-Read was holding forth on why women did not need pain relief at all. The two developments seem to reflect completely different ideas of what childbirth should be and look like, and yet together they represent something pivotal for the history and future of childbirth – choice.

HOW TO TEACH THE WORLD TO SING

From all of the disaster wreaked by the Second World War new and powerful voices arose, including those of women. Women of all classes were outside the home during the war, working directly with men and earning an independent wage, and many were not content to return to a domestic life when peacetime finally arrived. Most often thought of as labourers in munitions factories or nurses, women in fact undertook all kinds of work. The workforce of Britain's Bletchley Park, where Alan Turing and Dilly Knox famously worked on the Enigma project, had a workforce that was more than 75 per cent women, who were directly involved in working with the Colossus and Bombe machines that were so important to deciphering 'unbreakable' German code.[10] It was partly a series of scientific, social and political events that allowed women to hold onto their newfound freedoms.

On 28 September 1928 Alexander Fleming, the Scottish microbiologist, discovered what became the antibiotic penicillin in a neglected petri dish in his lab at St Mary's Hospital in London. Further experiments found it to be effective against not only tuberculosis but also gonorrhoea. There were many problems with the early development of a 'mass market' penicillin, largely owing to lack of enthusiasm from the medical community and Fleming's initial inability to produce it in stable enough forms for it to be distributed.

During the war the Surgeon General's Office for the US Army opened a pilot scheme for penicillin trials and tested groups of soldiers suffering from a variety of ailments and injuries.[11] They recorded that as well as curing gangrene, penicillin also cured four patients of syphilis. This was a giant leap forward: not only was it effective against gonorrhoea, but suddenly penicillin could also counter gonorrhoea's old stablemate, syphilis. All resources were immediately mobilized for American pharmaceutical companies to create enough stable, easily administrable penicillin for all the Allied troops in anticipation of the D-Day landings. In a feat remarkable even for America's commercial machine, this was achieved.[12] Suddenly there was a drug able to treat serving soldiers for almost every medical problem they had acquired abroad – whether sexual or combative. Fleming was knighted and received the Nobel Prize along with two key colleagues, Howard Florey and Ernst Chain, for his 'accidental' discovery.

These three men, in yet another historical coincidence in the history of human reproduction, were running almost entirely in tandem with a new set of doctors, scientists and civilians who wanted to organize a system of sexual choice and self-determination for women. The first was Katharine McCormick, an accidental heiress, fighter for suffrage, staunch supporter of birth control for women and a friend of Margaret Sanger. McCormick believed that all women should have access to birth control, and even used her lavish European shopping trips as a cover to buy all sorts of different diaphragms and smuggle them back to their waiting recipients in America. Then came Gregory Goodwin Pincus and John Rock. The three of them worked on the earliest forms of what we now call the Pill, based on progesterone control.

Katherine McCormick (then Katherine Dexter) as an undergraduate in an MIT research lab

Gregory Goodwin Pincus had been the first to achieve 'cleavage' in a fertilized rabbit egg in 1934: the moment when the cells that make us who we are first begin to divide. Ten years later Miriam Menkin (at the time John Rock's assistant) was the first to do so with humans, and she did it bearing down a microscope with her own newborn on her hip. But Pincus had been surprised to discover that his own success with test-tube rabbits had gone down poorly. It was unfortunate that his paper had appeared soon after the publication of Aldous Huxley's *Brave New World* in 1932, which is set in a dystopia where humans no longer reproduce 'naturally' but instead are conceived in test tubes in factory settings, negating familial affection. The *New York Times* was so scandalized that it published a headline that read 'LIFE IS GENERATED IN SCIENTIST'S TUBE' and referred to Pincus as Dr Frankenstein, a title he struggled to shake off.

Pincus, disappointed but determined, quietly continued with his research but was more cautious about how it might be perceived. In 1936 he published *The Eggs of Mammals*, to international acclaim, but his reputation had stuck. It was the beginning of the Great Depression and he had to find secure research work to support his family, so he ended up working on fringe zoology projects at Clark University in Worcester, Massachusetts. Luckily for Pincus, Katharine McCormick and Margaret Sanger came across his work and realized that he was the man who could help devise a new contraceptive pill for women. In 1953, after 17 years in the professional wilderness, Pincus assured them he would succeed.

Within months, Pincus proved to McCormick that he had stopped ovulation in his lab mammals using progesterone to mimic the hormonal changes that a woman's body undergoes to prevent pregnancy during non-fertile weeks. Their next challenge was to find a way to manufacture the pill commercially at a price that ordinary women could afford. Two American pharmaceutical companies, Syntex of Mexico City and G. D. Searle of Omaha, could make synthetic progesterone pills in their research laboratories. Unfortunately, neither company was keen to be seen marketing cheap oral contraceptives for women. However, they were eager to see the results when the pills were tested on women, so long as they bore none of the risk.

To this end, Pincus approached John Rock with the idea that they could collaborate on small-scale human trials in Massachusetts. Rock was a doctor from a Catholic family in Massachusetts, whose own scientific work was based mainly on how the uterus goes through stages during a hormonal cycle, which affects whether an embryo is implanted (or not). He suffered harsh professional consequences for his research but remained undeterred. He hoped that, since the Pill was essentially a medical version of the Catholic-endorsed 'rhythm method' (essentially, timing sex so it does not occur during ovulation), he might be able to convince Catholics that it was a spiritually safe contraceptive. Largely, he did not succeed. He even took on the Pope over it in 1958 and had to renounce his religion.

The trials were successful, so Pincus and Rock devised a larger-scale trial with the aid of McCormick in Puerto Rico in 1956. Birth control was legal in Puerto Rico, and it was also the location of a significant proportion of America's mass sterilizations at the time, so they knew they could test the pill on Puerto Rican women without significant backlash. The trial was a success. Soon more trials followed in, unsurprisingly, Mexico, Haiti and California.

In 1957 the Food and Drug Administration (FDA) approved Enovid, manufactured by G. D. Searle, for use in women with 'severe menstrual disorders'. It mandated that the drug must carry the warning that it would 'prevent ovulation'. Hundreds of thousands of American women promptly developed severe menstrual disorders and were prescribed Enovid by their doctors. McCormick, Sanger, Pincus and Rock had succeeded in a very short space of time.

Following the success of Enovid, in 1959 President Dwight D. Eisenhower, often known as Ike, announced in his emphatic style, 'I cannot imagine anything more emphatically a subject that is not a proper political or governmental activity of function or responsibility.' He followed it up with: 'This thing has, for very great denominations, a religious meaning ... I have no quarrel with them ... [but] ... this government will not, as long as I am here, have a positive political doctrine in its program that has to do with this problem of birth control. That's not our business.'

The conquering power of Enovid, coupled with the offer of medical treatments for once deadly (or at least extremely inconvenient) sexually transmitted diseases, ushered in what was known at the time by a new generation of students as 'free love' or the Sexual Revolution. Heterosexual sex suddenly held far fewer risks than it had done for thousands of years. The heady mix of post-war euphoria and a rising economic situation meant that the gloom and global depression of the interwar years were things of the past. Owing to technological and industrial developments during the wars, the quality and availability of condoms also improved dramatically, although they tended to be used more within marriage, particularly in the US.

Still a long way from sexual equality, there was at least the possibility at last that women might be able to take real control of their own reproductive lives. It's unlikely that either Sanger or McCormick, in their endeavours to help some of the poorest women in America manage their fertility, foresaw the free love movement, or approved of it, but their achievements, along with those of Pincus and Rock, changed the history of human reproduction for ever.

THE HARD ROAD TO ROE

The sudden availability of cheap and reliable contraceptives did not mean they were universally welcomed by authorities. The US, thanks to its long legal history of banning the distribution of contraceptives, had some hard decisions to make, and Ike's strident views were not agreed with by every state. In Connecticut, birth control of any kind remained illegal, but with the advent of Enovid individuals began to take more public and positive action.

In December 1961 Dr C. Lee Buxton (the chairman of Yale Medical School's OBGYN department) and Estelle Griswold (the director of the Connecticut branch of Planned Parenthood) opened four Planned Parenthood clinics across the state. Both were promptly arrested. However, their actions succeeded in bringing significant national attention to Connecticut's outdated anti-birth control law. *Griswold* v. *Connecticut* finally came to trial in 1965 (381, U.S. 479), when the Supreme Court agreed that the use of contraceptives by married couples was no one's issue but their own. While it was hardly a ringing endorsement, it did recognize the fact that a husband and wife had the right to limit the size of their family.

In the same year New York state legalized abortion, along with Alaska, Hawaii and Washington. The latter three required residency, so New York became the go-to destination for those who could afford it and needed a fast, legal abortion. This move towards reproductive rights was compounded in 1972 by a Supreme Court ruling that said William Baird, a campaigner for reproductive rights, was not breaking the law when he handed out condoms at a campus talk at Boston University. The ruling justice, Justice William J. Brennan Jr, invoked the 14th Amendment when he declared: 'If the right of privacy means anything, it is the right of the individual, married or single, to be free from unwarranted governmental intrusion into matters so fundamentally affecting a person as the decision whether to bear or beget a child.'[13]

Theoretically, the development of the Pill should have pleased the eugenicists still lurking in the wings. But they were unhappy that it seemed to be largely families who could afford to reproduce and raise large families who chose to have fewer children. More often it was poorer families, perhaps through lack of education or social and cultural stigma, who continued to have larger families. All these issues further complicated the ever-shifting debates around who should and who should not reproduce. For the more conservative older generations of America and western Europe, the new era of permissiveness visible in the media and on the streets subverted many of their values about the sanctity of home and family, particularly among the more religious. A woman's newly won right to control her own reproductivity became not only a personal but a social and political dilemma.

In 1969 two lawyers, Linda Coffee and Sarah Weddington, were looking for clients who wished to procure a legal abortion in Texas but were unable to do so. Middle-class women could afford to travel to states where abortion was legal, and Weddington herself had travelled to Mexico for an abortion after finding out she was pregnant by her future husband during her third year at law school. They were looking for someone who did not have the option of travelling out of state, and they found their ideal candidate when the pregnant 21-year-old Norma McCorvey was referred to them.

Norma McCorvey was born Norma Nelson in Louisiana, but her family moved to Houston, Texas, when she was very young. Her father was a television repair man and a Jehovah's Witness, and her mother was alleged to be a violent alcoholic. As Norma's mother later recalled, when installed in a Dallas nursing home, 'I beat the fuck out of her.'[14] Norma's problems became even more serious when she was ten and stole money from a gas station in order to run away to Oklahoma City with a girlfriend. They somehow managed to con their way into a cheap motel room, but were caught kissing in the same bed by a maid and the authorities were called. Norma was made a ward of the state and placed in a Catholic boarding school, but later relocated to the state girls' school in Gainsville, Texas, where she remained on and off until she was 15, by which time her father had left. Quite how she escaped compulsory sterilization in Texas at this point in her life is something of a mystery, as the bar was low and they would have considered her a prime candidate. Norma was working in a drive-through diner when Woody McCorvey, a sheet metal worker aged 21, and certainly a man possessed of a way with words, drove in and ordered a 'furburger'. Norma got in his car and drove off with him.[15] They married in 1963, when she was 16. It turned out however, that Woody was violent and after he assaulted her, she returned to her mother's home, where she gave birth to her daughter Melissa in 1965.

After Melissa's birth, things took a turn for the worse as Norma developed a severe drug and alcohol dependence. She also came out as a lesbian, and consequently her lifestyle and friendship groups changed, although events indicate that she did not exclusively have sex with women. After going away on a trip with friends, she returned home to discover that her mother had replaced Melissa with a doll, saying that the police had removed the child – and refusing to let her see her daughter. Three months later her mother allegedly deceived her into signing adoption papers for Melissa. This account was disputed by her mother, who subsequently adopted her granddaughter. Soon after the incident, Norma was pregnant again and later gave birth to another daughter, Jennifer, who was adopted.

At the age of 21 in 1969, Norma was pregnant for the third time and determined not to bear the child. As abortion was not legal in Texas unless the life of the mother was endangered, she considered fabricating a story about being gang-raped by multiple Black men, which would have facilitated securing an abortion. But after an unsuccessful attempt to secure a back street abortion, she consulted a doctor who told her to travel to one of the states where abortion was legal. Understandably, she was in no position to afford to travel to these states, let alone secure accommodation and an abortion once there. She had barely left Texas. The doctor then steered her instead to an adoption lawyer, Henry McCluskey, to whom he would 'deliver' unwanted newborns after he had actually delivered them.

Henry McCluskey was born in 1943 in Texas and raised a Baptist. He was gay, and in 1969 filed a suit that challenged the anti-sodomy laws of Texas.[16] When McCluskey learned that Norma was determined to have an abortion, he referred her to Weddington and Coffee, whom he knew. Henry Wade was the District Attorney who was assigned the case, and he proved a formidable opponent for the Coffee–Weddington team. A lifelong conservative Texan, and one of 11 children, he was deeply unsympathetic to both Norma McCorvey and the 'cause'. He was also high-profile: he supervised the prosecution of Jack Ruby for the killing of Lee Harvey Oswald after the assassination of President John F. Kennedy in 1963, and was a highly popular figure among conservative voters of the South.

While they waited for their day in court, Norma gave birth to an unnamed daughter who was adopted. When the ruling finally came in 1973, the child, now Shelley Thornton, whose identity was only revealed in 2021, was thriving in an entirely new life and family.[17]

The essential thrust of Coffee and Weddington's argument was that the abortion laws of Texas were unconstitutional. They cited the Texas Penal Code of 1961 that dealt with procurement of abortion, including those sections that prevented anyone assisting another person to have an abortion, and challenged them. Texas abortion laws had always been somewhat deliberately vague, not in terms of interpretation but rather in how you could defend yourself against them.

Finally, a judicial panel was put together to hear what by this time had become known as the 'Roe Case', as Norma McCorvey remained anonymous until after the trial. The judicial panel, remarkably, found in her favour on the grounds that the Texas abortion laws contravened the right to privacy.[18] By this time it was of course too late for McCorvey to have the abortion and the case still had to go to the Supreme Court, which it did in January 1973. The Court found in favour of upholding the judgement by seven to two. There were caveats that meant that a woman's right to an abortion was not absolute, and which allowed the state to protect its own interests in preserving foetal life. It did this by defining the rights according to the trimester of the pregnancy: women had an absolute right to an abortion in the first trimester; the government had the right to protect the life of either mother or foetus in the second trimester; and there was strict governance over the necessity for an abortion in the third trimester. This meant that a woman had complete autonomy over whether or not to have an abortion in the first 12 weeks, that states could regulate but not ban abortions in the second trimester and that in the third trimester states could protect the life of the foetus and permit abortions only in extreme circumstances. The 'third trimester rule', however, introduced new legal issues because it concerned the moment when a foetus is deemed able to live outside the womb. Scientific and medical developments mean that many newborns delivered prematurely can now be termed 'viable' when in previous ages they would have perished or indeed been exposed.

President Richard Nixon was in office when the judgement was made. One of the US's most famous and often more reviled presidents, Nixon was chest deep in the Watergate scandal during *Roe* v. *Wade* and could afford no controversy by making a public statement on the ruling, but private recordings he made which have since been archived by the Richard Nixon Presidential Library and Museum reveal his ambivalence. Speaking to his former Special Counsel Charles Colson, he said, 'I admit there are times when abortions are necessary, I know that.' He went on to make comparisons between 'a black and a white' pregnancy. 'Or rape,' Colson said. 'Or rape,' agreed the ever thoughtful and considerate Richard Nixon.[19]

None of these huge developments made much difference to Norma McCorvey. She had not achieved her aim in securing an abortion, and the wider debate did not impact her life unless she could make a living from it. Henry McCluskey, the adoption lawyer who had set all the wheels in motion, was murdered by an acquaintance, David Hovila, the year of the ruling. McCorvey went on to meet the woman who became her life partner, Connie Gonzalez, and there were no more pregnancies. She worked for the pro-choice movement and started pro-choice charitable foundations, although no one was very sure where the money ended up. In the 1980s she claimed that her daughter 'Jane Roe' had been the result of a rape, but later admitted it wasn't true, causing huge outrage among pro-lifers. Then, in the 1990s, she found religion and became as pro-life as she had been pro-choice, again founding organizations to fundraise.

After what must have seemed like a lifetime embroiled at the centre of one of the twentieth century's 'watershed' legal cases, McCorvey died of heart failure in 2017 in Katy, Texas. While the events of the court case defined reproductive choice for millions of women in America, she never led a life that was much more than 'less pro-choice or pro-life than pro-Norma'.[20]

THE POPULATION BOMB

After the Holocaust, eugenicists discovered that they could no longer reputably use their old rhetoric and arguments about 'improving' the race. However, attempts to control who could reproduce on a nationwide scale did not unfortunately end with the Second World War. Eugenicists found a new clarion call in the idea of 'overpopulation' and the rising anxieties that it would soon be impossible to produce enough food for: the world's ever-increasing inhabitants. 'The battle to feed all of humanity is over', wrote Paul Ehrlich, the creator of the syphilis drug Salvarsan, in his best-selling and hugely influential 1968 book *The Population Bomb*. Ehrlich gave them a new cause – an earnest concern for finite world resources.

Spearheading the charge, as ever, were the Rockefeller and Ford foundations. Ostensibly under the banner of providing assistance to the poorer 'overpopulated' countries of the world, the Rockefeller and Ford foundations launched new programmes in Asia at the beginning of the 1950s. The Rockefeller Foundation was the first to become involved with grants of aid to India, but it also used its influence to conduct medical research. The Ford Foundation threw its hat into the ring in 1951 with agriculture initiatives, namely to try and introduce high-yielding wheat varieties in an attempt to feed the masses.[21]

The involvement of these two foundations in India in some ways initially harked back to the missionary movements of earlier times. Christian missionaries had a hard time convincing the Hindu and Muslim populations that Jesus was the way and light simply by talking to them: they had to demonstrate their good intentions through practical assistance. This led to a large number of broadly 'Christian' white British and later Americans being in charge of philanthropic institutions in India. It was natural that the representatives of these institutions in Asia, with so many poor, sick and disabled on their hands, would turn to cash-rich foundations for philanthropic assistance. While both organizations had religious leanings and charitable leanings, however, these cloaked other motives.

Before the Partition of India and Pakistan on 15 August 1947, America's interests in India had been screened, for better or worse, by the vast, grinding machine of the British Raj. Once British control had fallen away, businesses throughout the world were far freer to involve themselves in India commercially, although in a caste-based society this did not always have the 'trickle-down' effect that was perhaps optimistically envisioned.

India was by no means naive regarding the intentions of either foundation, and the level of control that Rockefeller, in particular, sought to achieve is summarized in a meeting between Moraji

Desai, India's finance minister, and Dean Rusk, president of the Rockefeller Foundation, when Desai said, 'there is also risk of undue pride on the side of donors and loss of self-respect on the side of recipients, which damage the character of both'. He added: 'If donors are unwilling to extend their aid in due humility and through procedures which protect the self-respect of the recipients, India will gladly do without their gifts.'[22]

Rusk, though thwarted in his own great and arrogant vision for India, had no intention of lessening the Rockefeller foundation's involvement as the new government took hold of a 'new' nation. He felt a deep sense of competition with the Ford Foundation, which he rather splendidly referred to as 'the fat boy in the canoe'.[23]

From the outset, Rockefeller concerned itself mainly with setting up medical research centres to further specific scientific knowledge in India. Ford took the route of developing agriculture following its successes with cultivating high-yield dwarf wheat varieties in Mexico. To this end, they sent Douglas Ensminger, a specialist in rural sociology, to Delhi in 1951. He remained in the subcontinent for Ford until 1970, tackling agricultural and other projects in India, Pakistan, Nepal and Bhutan. But Ensminger was also involved in a programme that ended up bringing great shame to both foundations – a rural mass sterilization campaign in the name of 'birth control'.

India was not clueless when it came to birth control, and the use of contraceptives, which are dealt with in their earliest medical texts, far outstripped the West in terms of knowledge and sophistication for most of history. From 1927 until his death in 1953. Professor Raghunath Dhondo Karve from Maharashtra published a magazine titled *Samaj Swasthya,* in which he discussed all things to do with reproduction, gender equality and sexuality. He and his wife, Malati, opened the first birth control clinic in Mumbai in 1921, at a time when infanticide of female newborns was presenting serious social problems. Karve was convinced that a better quality of life for all could be achieved by sensible birth control. His staunch and highly public views were not without their detractors. Mahatma Gandhi, for one, was not a fan, yet Karve's work was popular and valuable for huge numbers of people. In 1949, directly after Partition, the

Indian government founded a family planning association. With the assistance of the Ford and Rockefeller foundations, this became a much more organized 'central family planning board', symbolized by a downward-pointing red triangle.[24]

The original campaigns saw people on the streets with megaphones handing out flyers containing advice on birth control. There was a deliberate carnival atmosphere to these events, and even a splendid decorated elephant who went around dispensing free contraceptives.

Writing in Hindi reads: 'My job is to spread happiness among the people ... A small family is a happy family. Not more than two or three children.' Ratangarh village, 20 January 1969

However, not even the wonderful red triangle was deemed effective enough at slowing India's growing population, and with Communism viewed as the threat in every corner, something more had to be done. Under the aegis of Ford's rural sociologist Douglas Ensminger, the government's family planning board began to go out into the countryside with their campaigns and set up what amounted to mobile 'field hospitals' in tents. In these small encampments, which attempted to retain their carnivalesque atmospheres, the emphasis was no longer on advice and contraceptives and instead was firmly focused on sterilizing women and men. They preferred sterilizing men via vasectomy as it was faster and less invasive than the procedure is for women, and thus it was very heavily promoted. Men were even offered small gifts, such as a clock.[25] Unfortunately, many of the new staff working on the procedures had not been adequately trained to carry out so many operations in such a short amount of time, and cross-infections and unhygienic conditions had the predictable consequences. The Ford Foundation under Ensminger also began to set 'quotas' for sterilization in each state. The numbers were in their millions. Ensminger, initially a mild-mannered sociologist from Pennsylvania, had become a sterilization statistician. More was still not enough, as he wrote in 1969 the year before he, thankfully, left India and returned to the United States.

By the time Ensminger left, Indira Gandhi was in power as the prime minister of India. She genuinely wished to eliminate India's problem with poverty. The problem was that she confused it with eliminating the poor themselves. Much the same happened as had already occurred in London when the British government attempted a mass 'improvement' of their capital in c.1904–6 and cleared out many very small, dilapidated slums in the centre of the city, rehoming them in the east. Unfortunately, they only succeeded in creating one vast slum, which persisted until the regenerations of the 1970s. The more powerful Indira Gandhi became, the more her focus turned not only to the clearing and destruction of India's urban slums but also to accelerating the sterilization programmes started by Ford and Rockefeller. Both foundations had dialled back their influence by this time, as the mood in the West had changed distinctly with the advent of second wave feminism and the civil rights movement. Nevertheless, the infrastructures they had been fundamental in putting into place were by then too established. All they could do was try to create some distance.

In 1975, worried about her political position, Indira Gandhi declared a state of national emergency, citing both internal and external threats, which lasted until 1977. During this period she increased slum demolition and introduced what was tantamount to compulsory sterilization for 'degenerates'. Compulsory sterilization had been carried out on leprosy and TB sufferers for a long time, but now that group was extended to include disabled beggars, people found asleep on the streets and, finally, passengers found travelling without a railway ticket.[26] Bihar, an infamously impoverished state in India, implemented new rules to its food rationing system – if you had three children and didn't submit to sterilization, your government food rations would cease. The national emergency did nothing to elevate Indira Gandhi's popularity or to alleviate India's poverty. She was assassinated by her own bodyguards in 1984.

A British-born woman called Joan Dunlop had gone to work in America for the Ford Foundation in communications between 1960 and 1967, the peak time of both foundations' drives to increase mass sterilization. After her time at Ford, she began as an adviser to John D. Rockefeller III on how his foundation should proceed in the light of changing times and attitudes.

After a long interview process, which amounted to her sitting in Rockefeller's office and talking to him about the day-to-day reproductive experiences of women she knew, including the illegal abortion she had had in London, as well as her ideas on the future of population control, he offered her a job. After her retirement Dunlop mused that she often wondered, later, if the admission of her own abortion – her father was Sir Maurice Alfred Lister Banks, not quite a family name one would associate with a backstreet termination – prompted Rockefeller to offer her a job. Dunlop agreed to work for Rockefeller for one year and to report back at the end with what she had learned over that time. As a sensible, intelligent woman, she knew to expect inordinate levels of sexism and racism (which she duly encountered) in the foundation's policies, but she was concerned with how shocked Rockefeller might be by the results of her findings. In an interview recorded by *The New York Times* in 1998, Dunlop said, 'The subtext was always *those* people ... Those black and brown people should not have more children.' It wasn't only black and brown people, Rockefeller himself had mooted sex determination during pregnancy so that the parents could choose to abort by gender if they wished.[27]

In 1984 Dunlop founded the International Women's Health Coalition (IWHC), which gravitated away from population control towards women's rights, and was hugely influential in securing important international consensus on various issues, perhaps most importantly the legal right for a married woman to refuse to have sex with her husband. While this is, of course, an intellectual 'right' only, agreed on at an international conference at a remove from the realities of daily life across the world, it has been of great practical importance for women seeking help or restitution, or whose husbands are infected with sexual diseases such as HIV.

Dunlop's legacy at Rockefeller, assisting with the changes that JDR, as she called him, made to the foundation's approach, are lasting. As JDR said himself publicly, after working with her and listening to her reports, it was time for more 'effective and humane action'. After retiring from the IWHC in 1998, Dunlop continued to work tirelessly for women's rights, particularly for safe and legal abortion, from her apartment in New York, accompanied by a kitten called Carrot.

JOY IN THE WINTER OF DISCONTENT: A NEW ERA OF REPRODUCTIVE RIGHTS

While *Roe* v. *Wade* centred on the right not to carry a pregnancy to term, elsewhere, for millions of other women, the wish to have a baby of their own was a fundamental part of their lives. In the mid-twentieth century many couples married relatively young, owing to a number of social and economic factors, and some tried for children for a number of years with no success. At the time there was no recourse for them other than tedious and painful pelvic examinations which usually found nothing amiss. For many, this caused huge distress and marital strain. So much time and effort, it seemed, had gone into creating new contraceptives – but what if that was precisely the opposite of what you wanted?

Patrick Steptoe was an obstetrician who worked in the district hospital of Oldham in the north-west of England. After serving in the war he became an expert in laparoscopy (keyhole surgery) and its uses in all manner of reproductive and gynaecological matters, such as ectopic pregnancy. One thing he discovered during the many procedures he performed was that a leading cause of infertility was not the mother's inability to conceive, or the quality of her eggs, but the simple fact that her fallopian tubes were obstructed or 'blocked'. This can happen for a number of reasons, but it is most commonly caused by endometriosis – an overgrowth of the womb's lining. Steptoe had an idea. He asked many of the infertile women he had operated on to donate their eggs for further study.

Robert Edwards was a gynaecologist who had also served in the war. He became a Ford Foundation Fellow at the University of Cambridge, in the Department of Physiology, and after reading Steptoe's work on laparoscopy, contacted him with a view to collaborating. Jean Purdy, a nurse and embryologist, joined their team in 1969. For ten years they struggled with failure and hostility from the medical profession: in 1971 they applied for a grant from the Medical Research Council and were turned down flat on 'ethical grounds'.[28]

The trio continued doggedly on a mixture of funds both public and private during very hard times in the north of England, commonly referred to as the coming of the Winter of Discontent. Then in 1977, Jean Purdy was examining a fertilized egg in the laboratory when she saw it cleave itself into two: she had just witnessed cell division. Lesley and John Brown, a couple who had been trying for a child for nine years and who regarded the experimental trial as their last hope of ever conceiving, faced an agonizing wait before the embryo was sufficiently stable to be implanted into Lesley's womb, which eventually happened on 10 November. The pregnancy was a tense time for the Browns and the Oldham team.

On 25 July 1978 in Oldham Hospital, obstetrician John Webster delivered the Browns' baby by a planned C-section. The child was a healthy baby girl, weighing 5 pounds and 12 ounces. She was named Louise Joy Brown. Her sister Natalie was born in 1982, also through *in vitro* fertilization, by then known simply as IVF.

In those short years the medical community at large performed an abrupt volte-face to support IVF enthusiastically. The knowledge and technology rolled out quickly first to Spain and Spanish-speaking countries, where infertile couples suffered not only personal anguish but also social and religious stigma, followed by the US, where Elizabeth Jordan Carr was born in Norfolk, Virginia, on 28 December 1981. Carr's mother, Judith, had endured three ectopic pregnancies, which had resulted in the total removal of her fallopian tubes, but using IVF she was able to carry and deliver Elizabeth safely.

Owing to the techniques used with egg implantation, early IVF procedures were reasonably likely to result in twins, although this rate has decreased now. Gender selection is possible using IVF embryos, and the overall success rate, in terms of delivering a healthy baby, varies globally but is between 20 and 38 per cent.

IVF had also had a significant by-product: surrogacy. Suddenly it was possible for a woman to achieve pregnancy and birth through an egg that was not her own, by a man she had not had sex with. The use of 'donor' sperm in the case of a fertile female partner but a sterile male partner, whether the donor sperm is introduced by coitus or by another method, has been long established. However, IVF made it possible for the first time for a woman to bear a child to which she has no biological relationship. Surrogacy remains wildly controversial on multiple levels, and for good reason. Nepal found it necessary to ban surrogacy in 2015 after disgraceful predators in the form of 'fertility agencies' descended on the country after it suffered a catastrophic earthquake, hoping to take advantage of clean-living Nepalese women.

Robert Edwards received the Nobel Prize in 2010 for his contributions to IVF. While many protested that Steptoe and Purdy had been ignored, the Nobel Prize is not awarded posthumously and both had passed away by that time. Worse, perhaps, was that Jean Purdy's name was left off the blue plaque installed at Oldham hospital in 1982 recognizing the work of Steptoe and Edwards, despite the fact that Edwards insisted they include her. In 2015 Purdy's omission was corrected when Professor Andrew Steptoe, Patrick Steptoe's son, unveiled a new plaque dedicated to all three of them.

Sister Muriel Harris also joined the team at the same time and was the world's first dedicated IVF nurse, although her contribution has largely been forgotten. She continued to work in the same role for the rest of her long career. The late lamented and famously decent singer George Michael anonymously paid for IVF treatment for two women after seeing them on the television. Jo Maidment and Lynette Gillard both gave birth thanks to his help.

To date, more than 12 million babies have been born through IVF. An unexpected yet obvious side effect of the success of IVF gave rise to yet another moral dilemma: should we clone human beings? The technology became available with IVF, and no global consensus has yet been reached on the appropriate ethical standpoint. Controversial Italian doctor Severino Antinori stated at a Dubai conference in 2001 that he had a patient eight weeks pregnant with a cloned embryo, causing consternation among the audience. Antinori has skirted the edge of the profession ever since, but remains a popular and successful fertility doctor in Rome. It is highly likely that human cloning experiments are currently being conducted around the world, out of the public eye. It is perhaps one of the greatest scientific dilemmas in the 'Just because we can, does it mean we should?' category.

A BLUE BABY

In May 1977, in a hospital not so very far from Oldham, a 'blue baby' was born to a first-time mother. A 'blue baby' is a colloquial term for a baby that is insufficiently supplied with oxygen owing to complications during labour. The mother's waters had broken unexpectedly but the delivery was proving slow. The baby was in an awkward breech position not seen before in that hospital known as 'a footling', so the mother had to endure multiple awkward examinations by various curious professionals in an experience she later likened to something akin to a 'bingo hall', with everyone's eyes looking down. Many labouring and pregnant women experience this feeling, where the pregnant body suddenly becomes the public body. When the baby was eventually delivered, she was a small baby girl, but she was blue. This too was not a usual situation in the hospital, but the baby soon 'pinked up' and had all the correct numbers of everything in the right ratios. Quite right, that baby was me – an astonishing 48 years ago. Between then and now there have been tremendous strides forward in obstetric and neonatal care. Babies that would never have survived when I was born are now healthy adults with children of their own.

During the 1970s the natural childbirth movement of Grantly Dick-Read had gained momentum under women such as Sheila Kitzinger. A staunch believer in natural childbirth and a strong advocate for breastfeeding, Kitzinger published widely on all subjects to do with childbirth and neonatal care; her work on attendant issues such as episiotomy, the deliberate cutting of the vaginal opening to prevent tearing and even fistula, were hugely informative for expectant mothers. Her vast collection of papers and research was donated to the Wellcome Collection in Euston, London, and remains an invaluable resource for mothers and healthcare professionals. She had a long association with the NCT, but her views fell out of favour with the modern feminist movement and caused a fracture. This was largely over Kitzinger's authoritarian tone, rather than her ideas.

Dick-Read also inspired the pioneering American midwife Ina May Gaskin, who embraces natural childbirth not only on the Dick-Read model but also on far older models, inspired by prehistory. Gaskin has a highly sympathetic philosophy, but our very limited knowledge of prehistoric birthing practice means her approach is more anti-interference than pro-prehistoric birthing. The South African Janet Balaskas is also a fan of little or no interference and of 'active birth', which means letting the mother move around and choose her own birthing posture, which after two thousand years of the Soranus supine position seems eminently sensible. Water births became popular in Europe and Russia in the 1960s and, although they go in and out of fashion, those who have experienced one usually wholeheartedly advocate for them. However, one mother did tell me it felt rather like 'human soup'.

While writing this book, I was talking about all these changes with our mother. I asked her if anything changed between having me and having my sister two and a half years later, and she said, 'I discovered Lycra.' I said, 'I know, I meant during childbirth', and she said, 'Oh, your sister was nothing like you. It was like shelling peas!' This is not to say Mum's journey to two healthy baby girls by her mid-thirties was plain sailing. As is the case for millions of women, her experience of birth was accompanied by loss. Miscarriage is the spectre that waits in the wings of every pregnancy, manifesting itself as a nightmare. Often it's accompanied by a strange sense of vacancy as the body registers that it is returning to the singular state. One woman described the moment she was climbing the stairs, her hands full of bundled, paired socks and, halting abruptly, as the sense of a sudden void arrested her out of the blue. As another put it, 'To lose a baby is a reckoning with absence.'[29]

For some women, the first sign is bleeding. Early miscarriages usually present as a particularly heavy period with significant clotting owing to the formation of the placenta (the blood-rich gas and nutrient exchange barrier between mother and child). The loss of amniotic fluid (which varies in volume from woman to woman) is another physical reckoning to be endured. In all the messy reality of a miscarriage, a tiny foetus can be undetectable. In more developed pregnancies, the foetus is more apparent: one woman, uncertain how to cope with the heavy bleeding, remembers sitting alone on the toilet and hearing 'a distinct plop'.[30] The loss of a recognizable yet clearly unviable foetus is another moment the mother often has to cope with entirely alone both emotionally and physically. This is how most women miscarry – at home or in the workplace; sometimes it takes days and sometimes it happens very fast.

Every spontaneous loss of a foetus is a 'miscarriage' until 24 weeks (or 28 weeks, depending on the nation or study), after which it is additionally termed a 'stillbirth'. Women with a dead foetus *in utero* are usually expected to deliver the baby vaginally and often with minimal assistance unless they are themselves in danger. Stillbirths of formed babies are relatively rare after 27 weeks of gestation, but increase significantly after 40 weeks, when the foetus continues to grow rapidly and has more chance of becoming obstructed. Figures vary, but in California they stand at 10.8 per cent per 10,000 live births.[31] In the UK in 2022, they were recorded as a total of 2,433 babies, which equates to 4 per cent.[32] The latest reliable estimates are that 77 per cent of all stillbirths each year occur in sub-Saharan Africa and South Asia, and that Finland has the lowest of all global stillbirths, with 1.9 per thousand, representing less than 0.2 per cent.[33] Finland and Iceland usually more or less tie for the top spot. In 2019 the UNICEF global estimate for stillbirths was approximately 2 million babies annually.[34]

After a stillbirth in the UK, a medical certificate is issued which allows the parents to arrange a funeral for their child. In September 2018 the UK introduced a 'Baby Loss Certificate' so that people could register a miscarriage occurring before 24 weeks' gestation. It is of great emotional, if not legal, value. No birth or death certificate can be issued after a stillbirth, nor are they included in population figures, as a baby has to be born alive in order to be declared dead.

My own experiences with miscarriage are much like anyone else's: painful, bloody and sad. And in many ways, mundane. Although it's not talked about as much, the moment-to-moment heartache is difficult for a supportive partner. In the aftermath, when it seems that recovery should have already begun, the grief – and it is grief – often finally sets in, accompanied by a hormonal upheaval as the body undoes its preparations. A woman in the middle of a miscarriage is likely to be absorbed by coping with what is happening within her body – without the promise of tears of joy or new life. It's a time that can cause confusion and conflict for the woman and those closest to her. When it happened to me, it felt like a naturally exclusive and protective state, and there was little anyone else could do to help. Laundry, maybe. Tea. I do not remember crying when it happened, but I remember thinking (and saying), 'Fuck'. In the years following, I would find myself saying it again ('Fuck it all'), and finally, 'That's that, then.' We stopped trying before the introduction of the Baby Loss Certificates. I only know the resting place of one son. It is a beautiful, peaceful and inherently happy place on which the sun always seems to shine, and it is good to know he is there.

The majority of women who experience miscarriage will give birth one day, but not all. At this point a divide emerges between the fertile and the infertile; the haves and the have-nots. No sentence should ever begin 'As a mother ...' in an attempt to negate the views of another woman, on any subject. No one truly knows anyone else's experiences, and many women are so heartbroken by a miscarriage that they never speak of it. The expectations on women to spontaneously conceive and reproduce, particularly after marriage, remain phenomenal. The sense of failure that is attached to infertility is a particularly insidious form of social shame. In one woman's words, 'I felt like a failed project, a failed woman, a failed human, and the world felt harsh and inhospitable in its judgment of me for getting this one basic thing so very, very, wrong.'[35]

DOBBS V. *JACKSON*: MAKING AMERICA GREAT AGAIN

On 19 August 2022 a 28-year-old nursing student, Amber Nicole Thurman, died 20 hours after presenting herself to Piedmont Henry Hospital in Atlanta, Georgia, with complications arising from taking medication to halt her pregnancy. While the foetus had been expelled, some tissue left behind in her womb became infected. The required procedure was simple, called a 'dilation [of the cervix] and curettage [a removal of the womb lining]'. It is known as a D&C, or in less sophisticated medical parlance, 'a scrape'. In the UK, it is common for a woman to have a D&C after a miscarriage to ensure nothing has been left behind to fester. It's also a straightforward and common gynaecological procedure carried out for many non-pregnancy-related conditions. Yet, in Georgia, D&Cs had been made illegal that year unless the woman's miscarriage was deemed 'spontaneous'. Thurman had to endure almost a day of agony as sepsis set in and her organs failed while the doctors watched. Finally reviewed in 2024, her death was ruled by ten doctors and other 'experts' to have been preventable and due to the 'delay'.[36]

On 24 June 2022 the right to legal abortion according to the will of the mother was ended in the United States of America. When *Dobbs v. Jackson Women's Health Organization* (597 US 215) devolved control of abortion to the individual state, 13 states immediately passed 'trigger bills' to put their own plans into action: Arkansas, Idaho, Kentucky, Louisiana, Mississippi, Missouri, North Dakota, Oklahoma, South Dakota, Tennessee, Texas, Utah and Wyoming. Alabama steals the crown for most restrictive law, with up to 99 years in prison for anyone performing an abortion and no exceptions for rape, human trafficking, incest or foetal abnormalities that render a living child unviable. A woman must carry to term, no matter what.

Overturning Roe was the result of a long, and sporadically violent, campaign. As soon as Roe passed, the Catholic Church formed the National Right to Life Committee (NRLC) to campaign against abortion. The NRLC quickly devolved into splinter groups, but it remains the largest anti-abortion movement in North America. In need of funds, throughout the 1970s it allied itself increasingly with the American right. The legal chipping away at Roe also began almost instantly. The Hyde Amendment, passed on 30 September 1976, during Jimmy Carter's administration, forbade the use of federal funds to pay for abortions in all but the most exceptional cases. This reduced the number of abortions by approximately 300,000 per year.

Ronald Reagan was publicly against abortion, but even he was careful not to go beyond the broad limitations set by Roe, instead using amendments to limit wholesale 'on demand' abortion. When he came into office, abortion was a cross-party issue, with Democrat and Republican voters holding broadly the same mix of opinions on the subject. By the time Reagan was voted in for his second term in 1984, public opinion had polarized and Republican voters swung pro-life and Democrat voters pro-choice.[37] Broadly, this polarization came about because of Hyde, with people who did not approve of abortion finding their resentment validated by the 'inappropriate' use of federal funds or their 'tax dollars'. Tax dollars are a highly emotive and inflammatory subject in American politics, frequently wheeled out to help sway the electorate in a particular direction. The Hyde Amendment appealed to the new, wealthy and socially conservative masses of the 1980s, who did not see why they, as responsible citizens, should pay tax to fund abortions for the feckless. The Reagan administration picked up this ball and ran with it.

In 1982 the Pennsylvania Abortion Control Act stipulated that women must give 'informed consent' and imposed a 24-hour waiting period for consideration before the procedure was performed. During this window they would be further informed of the outcome and ramifications of their decisions. The Act also specified that minors must have consent from their parents, except in cases of 'hardship' (which was left undefined), and married women should inform their husbands of their intention except in a medical emergency. Finally, all abortion clinics had to register with the state.

The 24-hour waiting period allowed various religious and political factions to bombard women with printed information about the spiritual and physical ramifications of their choice, either through the clinic itself or as they made their way to and from it. More problematic was stipulation regarding spousal knowledge of the intention to terminate. In an ideal world, within a marriage or long-term supportive partnership, a termination would be a joint decision. We do not, however, live in an ideal world, and ultimately the responsibility for bringing a child into existence resides with the mother – notwithstanding the risk of abuse and coercive control if the partners are not in agreement.

Yet Reagan's new position as the champion pro-natalist (which is different from pro-life in that pro-natalism is more focused on the notion of population growth rather than on the forced completion of a pregnancy) was hard to square with his stance in 1967, when, as Governor of California, he had signed the Therapeutic Abortion Act, which created an 'increase in conditions under which an abortion may legally be induced' and saw abortion in California skyrocket.[38] Abortions rose from 518 that year to approximately 100,000 per annum until the end of his term in 1975. This furthered California's reputation as 'liberal', but was, of course, directly in line with its long-held interests in controlling the population.

On 20 July 1970 *Peanuts* cartoonist and American social barometer Charles Schultz published his daily syndicated strip in which Linus asks Lucy: 'What would happen if there were a beautiful and highly intelligent child up in Heaven waiting to be born and his or her parents decided that the two children were enough?' To which Lucy replies, 'Your ignorance of theology and medicine is appalling!' Linus is left musing, 'I still think it's a good question.'

The strip so 'haunted' Reagan that he wrote to Schultz himself, as he did on occasion, saying:

> I cannot accept that simply on whim even a mother has the right to take the life of her unborn child simply because she thinks that child will be born less than perfect or because she just doesn't want to be bothered. Well, the bill was amended to meet my demands, and I signed it into law. Now, however, I have discovered some of our psychiatrists are particularly willing to declare an 'unwed mother-to-be' to have suicidal tendencies, and they do this on a five minute diagnosis. The result is that our medical program will finance more than fifty thousand abortions of unwed mothers in the coming year.[39]

Abortion aside, Reagan makes the egregious error of mistaking Linus for Charlie Brown, although he does sign off with typically upbeat and familiar Ronald charm, 'Well, I didn't mean to let you in on all my problems but just to give the background of why you touched a nerve with your strip the other day. Thanks very much. Nancy sends her best and please give our regards to your lovely girl.'[40]

In 1982 the underground anti-abortion terrorist group the Army of God formed. It claims to have no formal organization and minimal communication between members, for legal reasons, yet it still manages to arrange itself into 'chapters' who spend their time advocating the use of lethal violence against doctors who perform abortions and those associated with them.

In the election year of 1984 Reagan and his running mate, George H. W. Bush, were already looking strong when on 25 June an abortion clinic called the Ladies Center in Pensacola, Florida, was destroyed in a pipe bomb attack carried out in the early hours. There were no casualties and the centre quickly relocated nearby, but on Christmas Day that year the new centre was also destroyed by pipe bombs, again with no casualties. Two 21-year-old men, Matt Goldsby and Jimmy Simmons, were arrested along with their girlfriend and wife respectively, both aged 18. It transpired they were also responsible for the attack earlier that summer. The defence at their trial tried various tactics: they attempted to have the young men declared insane; they tried to cite their righteous religious fervour; they tried to have each of the three pipe bombs used on Christmas Day declared a separate and less serious incident; and finally they called upon God as 'the thirteenth juror'. The judge, the Honorable Clyde Roger Vinson, was having none of it and on 25 April 1985 the jury found the men guilty on all counts (ten years), and the women guilty of aiding and abetting (five years' probation). Throughout the trial, frothing Christian evangelist and Klan member John Burt paraded up and down in front of the courthouse, carrying with him an aborted four-month-old foetus preserved in a jar, which he wrapped in a blanket and called Baby Charlie.

John Burt claimed he was the spiritual adviser to Goldsby and Simmons, working from the halfway house called 'Our Father's

House' that and his wife had established for unmarried mothers. He bought the plot next to the Ladies Center so that a restraining order would have no validity as he could claim access rights. On 25 March 1986 Burt and five others, including his daughter, trashed the centre, injuring two women. He was charged with burglary and assault. In 1988 John Brockhoeft, another follower of Burt, left Our Father's House carrying bomb-making equipment intending to target the Ladies Center again, but he was apprehended and Burt was sentenced to two years' house arrest.

On 20 January 1985 the Reagan administration introduced the Mexico City Rule, also known as the Global Gag, preventing any non-governmental organization (NGO) in receipt of United States funding from promoting or carrying out abortion anywhere in the world. Then, a couple of years later, he introduced the President's Pro-Life Act to Congress, which banned the provision of pro-choice literature or media to any pregnant woman considering abortion. Reagan swept his audience away with numbers: 'Since the legalization of abortion on demand in 1973, there have been an estimated 21 million abortions in this country. The bill I am sending you has been named the "President's Pro-Life Act of 1988" to emphasize the urgent need to reduce the number of abortions in this country and to reaffirm life's sacred position in our Nation.'[41] He went on, 'there is no right to abortion secured by the Constitution, and ... the Supreme Court erred in its decision in *Roe* v. *Wade* in failing to recognize the humanity of the unborn child'.[42] Reagan finished his speeches on the subject with a moist eye and a hushed, imploring tone, invoking God's blessing on his nation. There is little doubt that his faith was genuine and deeply felt; it was also handy at a time when the Christian right emerged as essential to the political fate of the nation. During these televised speeches, 'Ron' was usually surrounded on the podium by glassy-eyed women who rose on cue to applaud delightedly, as if the Holy Spirit himself was looking on, benevolent. Slowly but surely, tinkering at the edges of Roe was closing down avenues of access to safe and legal abortion. Protests at abortion clinics became more violent. Reagan was succeeded by George H. W. Bush in 1989. Bush's father, Prescott Bush, had been an early supporter of Planned Parenthood, and George Bush himself had been a moderate until he ran with Reagan and saw which way the campaign dollars were flowing. His interferences were broadly minor, but in 1992 he notably vetoed a Democrat effort to pass legislation allowing stem cell research on aborted foetuses. The same year another milestone marker in the fight for reproductive rights reached the Supreme Court: *Planned Parenthood* v. *Casey*.[43] Robert Casey was the Governor of Pennsylvania and so the *de facto* defendant in the trial.

Planned Parenthood v. *Casey* addressed the 1982 Pennsylvania Abortion Control Act on five points, but was mainly concerned with what constituted informed consent, spousal notification and the need for permission from a parent or guardian for a minor to undergo the procedure. Planned Parenthood posited that all these things created an 'undue burden', placing obstacles in the path of a woman seeking an abortion. Medical advances had also raised questions about the trimester system and the threshold of viability for premature babies. The judges were not unanimous in their decision, but they agreed that *Roe* v. *Wade* should hold.

Pro-choice march in response to *Planned Parenthood* v. *Casey*, 1992

In January 1993 a change blew into the White House in the form of the Clintons. Bill and Hillary Clinton were an intellectual two-for-the-price-of-one only seen before in the Roosevelts. Like Reagan, Bill Clinton had performed an about-turn regarding abortion, but in the opposite direction. As Governor of conservative Arkansas, he had opposed abortion, although mainly on financial grounds to do with federal funds. He was described by the chairman of the National Right to Life Committee as 'pretty slippery' on the subject. In his election campaign of 1992 he coined his subsequently well-used phrase regarding abortion: 'safe, legal and rare'. In typical slippery style, he gave no details on exactly how rare it should be and under what circumstances. In the year of his election the Clintons faced many challenges, including the murder of respected rural OBGYN Dr David Gunn outside the Ladies Center in Pensacola by 31-year-old Michael Frederick Griffin, 'a fundamentalist Christian and a loner with a bad temper'.[44]

Gunn was murdered by three shots to the back from a .38 calibre handgun. The moment marked the beginning of a new era in anti-abortion protesting. People who yearned to be right about something, anything, gravitated towards ever more violent and evangelistic pro-life groups in the hope of finding something that had so far eluded them: meaning. What could, after all, be more meaningful than protecting unborn life?

Again John Burt featured in the trial. Griffin's defence argued that Burt had 'brainwashed' the defendant with anti-abortion propaganda, driving him to the point of a breakdown.[45] During Griffin's trial, a man named David Ware arrived at Burt's halfway house in Pensacola from Houston. He intended to bomb Dr David Gunn's memorial service, thereby killing as many pro-choice doctors and sympathizers as possible. In a rare attack of conscience (or self-preservation), Burt informed the authorities and Ware was arrested.

David Ware's planned massacre did not deter Burt from his holy mission, and he began to act as spiritual adviser to Paul Hill. Hill, who was approaching 40, with a wife and three small children, had had a troubled adolescence. At 17 his parents staged an intervention because he was smoking marijuana and had admitted to a friend he'd had a couple of bad trips on LSD, and he was committed to a drug programme. He emerged without any intention of giving up weed, much to the disappointment of his family. Then one day, while working in construction, he was told to clean out a filthy swimming pool with another man who preached at him all day. That night he went home and as he washed off the dirt, he spontaneously converted to Christianity. Paul Hill's drug habit ceased and he took to weightlifting. His pursuit of a fanatically healthy lifestyle was matched only by his commitment to his new Christian faith. He married an accountant, had children and became a preacher but, over time, fell out with each of his new churches. Finally he ended up in Pensacola, listening to John Burt. Soon Hill was screaming through the railings of the Ladies Center, 'Mommy, Mommy, don't kill me.' He was excommunicated by his church after he phoned into the Phil Donahue show to proclaim himself the new leader of those who sought to kill abortion providers.

At 7 a.m. on 29 July 1994 Hill was laying white crosses in the path of anyone who tried to access the Ladies Center abortion clinic. A policeman who knew him, Bruce Martin, told him to move them away, which he did. Then, just before 7.30, Dr John Britton, who had taken Dr David Gunn's position, drove into the clinic lot with his volunteer bodyguard, retired Air Force Lieutenant Colonel James Barrett, and Barrett's wife, June, a retired nurse, who also volunteered at the centre. Britton wore a bulletproof vest on his commute owing to the prior attacks on the clinic and staff. Hill approached the vehicle, raised a shotgun and shot both men in the head. He shot June in the chest and arm, but she survived. Hill waited to be arrested by Bruce, the officer who had told him to move the crosses only minutes earlier.

At his trial, Hill chose to defend himself. He claimed that he had only done the Lord's work and would receive his reward in Heaven. In his mind he was defending 'the unborn' and claimed he was involved with the underground anti-abortion terrorist group the Army of God. The jury took him at his word, and found him guilty in three hours. He was sentenced to death. Hill was not executed until 2003, when the order was finally signed by Governor Jeb Bush. His last words before the lethal injection was administered were 'May God help the unborn child.'[46]

With almost tiresome predictability, by the time Paul Hill was sent to join his saviour, John Burt had been arrested on five counts of child molestation. His victims were the teenagers and unwed mothers who sought refuge at Our Father's House. With the tawdry lack of imagination common to almost every sex offender, the charges relay how he had managed to 'fall' on one girl and had propositioned another for oral sex, which she refused. He subsequently showed her a note describing his particular requirements, pressed it to the glass of the kitchen window so she could read it, then made an obscene gesture. The girl walked up to him, took the note and called the police. The jury found him guilty on all counts, and he was sentenced to 18 years in jail, where he died in 2013 after repeated failed appeals. The Army of God wrote a eulogy for him on their website, calling him a 'prophet'. Perhaps appropriately for a man who created so much ugliness, the font is Comic Sans.

The continual erosion of Roe continued until Clinton started vetoing Republican bills that attempted to make changes to outlying restrictions on abortion. Before he left office, Clinton managed to see the FDA approve the Morning After Pill in 2000, which in 2023 accounted for 63 per cent of all US abortions.[47] It is, in fact, two pills – mifepristone to halt the pregnancy and misoprostol to cause the uterus to empty. It is used three to five days after unprotected sex and is therefore an extremely early kind of 'abortion'.

In contrast, George W. Bush concentrated firmly on the opposite end of pregnancy. 'Gee Dubya' found God in 1986 after waking up from a rowdy collective 40th birthday party feeling particularly battle-weary. Instead of embracing Alka Seltzer, he embraced the Lord, and he didn't care who knew it.[48] The 'partial-birth abortion' ban became the aim of Bush's administration. By partial-birth abortion, they meant a second trimester procedure (usually performed after 20 weeks) when the pregnancy is terminated and the foetus is extracted vaginally because of unviability, birth defects or to save the mother. What makes it different from other second-trimester procedures is that the foetus is terminated by injection and removed largely intact – it was developed to reduce recovery time for the patient and lower risks of damaging the cervix with surgical tools.

The anti-abortion groups put forward long yet simplistic and sentimental descriptions of the atrocities they claimed were committed on a foetus during this procedure, including 'decapitation' and the removal of 'babies' brains'. Destructive or late term abortions are, naturally, a horrendous experience for everyone involved, and have been so for the thousands of years for which we have accounts. From Soranus to Mauriceau to Radford, no true physician or doctor *wants* to perform these operations, and yet sometimes they are necessary. Such is the fascination with this procedure that historic destructive tools, often highly individual and designed by doctors such as Marion Sims for their own use, fetch extraordinary prices in the commercial market before they are squirrelled away into private (and predominantly American and Swiss) collections.[49]

The language of the Partial-Birth Abortion Act, which Gee Dubya signed with alacrity in 2003, declared that 'A moral, medical, and ethical consensus exists that the practice of performing a partial-birth abortion … is a gruesome and inhumane procedure that is never medically necessary and should be prohibited.'[50] In all the hubbub surrounding partial-birth abortion another player let itself in through the service entrance just a few months later: the Unborn Victims of Violence Act. It conferred 'personhood' on a foetus with associated rights as a citizen, and was therefore a Trojan Horse that quietly enabled the dismantling of *Roe* v. *Wade*.

In 2009 Barack Obama arrived in the White House. He was only the second candidate in US history to be endorsed by Planned Parenthood, under the aegis of Cecile Richards. In characteristic fashion Obama attempted to choose a middle way on the issue of abortion. Instead of involving himself with the laws surrounding when and how abortions could be performed, as previous administrations had done, he included abortion provision in the Affordable Care Act of 2010, popularly known as Obamacare. This wrong-footed the staunch pro-life groups. The issue also became mired in the controversial Contraception Mandate, which required that employers and/or health insurers cover the cost of female contraception, which of course sent religious and conservative employers up in arms. Not only was birth control against their beliefs, but it was going to cost them money.

Ultimately, Obama left the White House with millions more Americans entitled to health insurance than when he arrived – although now the birth control that it guaranteed to millions of women is under threat. When Donald Trump ran for President of the United States of America, it beggared belief that he would actually win. A man so semi-coherent he appears more like a candidate for a medical examination than for the highest public office in the land. A man who was taped talking about women in 2005 saying, 'Grab them by the pussy. You can do anything.'

Trump embraced the Republican 'War on Women'. It is one of a series of unwinnable wars the Republican Party has announced: on crime, drugs, immigration, terrorism, all of them domestic. As with previous candidates, he had changed his opinion since his first public statement regarding abortion in 1999, when he said that he was 'very pro-choice. I hate the concept of abortion ... I just believe in choice. Again, it may be a little bit of a New York background, because there is some different attitude in some different parts of the country. ... But I am strongly pro-choice.' When questioned on whether he would ban partial-birth abortion, Trump said, 'No. I am pro-choice in every respect in as far as it goes. But I just hate it.'[51]

In an interview with MSNBC's Chris Matthews in 2016, Trump was unable to articulate his views on abortion other than 'pro-life'. Matthews pressed him on the outcome for women who chose to proceed with abortion and Trump said the 'answer is that there has to be some form of punishment, yeah'.[52] He later said: 'the doctor or any other person performing this illegal act upon a woman would be held legally responsible, not the woman. The woman is a victim in this case as is the life in her womb.'[53] In a presidential debate in the same year, he burbled, 'Millions of millions of women – cervical cancer, breast cancer – are helped by Planned Parenthood ... I would defund it because I'm pro-life, but millions of women are helped by Planned Parenthood.'[54]

Still, he was elected, and many of his voters were women.

Trump was slower off the mark regarding abortion law than might have been imagined from his rhetoric, but events set in motion in one term often take place in another. It was Trump who appointed the judges to the Supreme Court who he knew would vote to dismantle Roe. Whatever his private views on abortion, Joe Biden toed the line regarding Roe when he was installed in the White House in 2021. He had aired his stance as early as 1974, when he said: 'when it comes to issues like abortion, amnesty, and acid, I'm about as liberal as your grandmother. I don't like the Supreme Court decision on abortion. I think it went too far. I don't think that a woman has the sole right to say what should happen to her body.'[55] He was, at the time, a young man who had just lost his wife and daughter in a car accident, and had been left with two very injured small boys to take care of, which he did by leaning heavily on his Catholic faith. However, it is to be hoped that time and some further life experience would have impressed on him the essential fact that a woman *should* have the sole right to say what should happen to her body.

Furthermore, in the long decades since 1974, the pro-choice movement had so firmly allied itself to the Democrats that Biden really didn't have any option, whatever his private feelings on the subject. He was reported to be deeply upset in his first year as president when conservative Catholic bishops said he should no longer be allowed to receive communion owing to his pro-choice stance. So disturbed was he by this that at the Vatican in October 2021 he met privately with Pope Francis, who assured him that his communion would not be withheld.[56]

In 2022 *Dobbs* v. *Jackson Women's Health Organization* (597 U.S. 215) came before the Supreme Court. Jackson Women's Health Organization was Mississippi's only operational abortion clinic.

The case revolved around a law passed in Mississippi in 2018, the Gestational Age Act, which banned abortion after 15 weeks unless the life of the mother was seriously in danger, regardless of whether the pregnancy was a result of rape or incest. As most incest is also rape, and largely happens to minors with limited sexual knowledge, the risk of pregnancy is relatively high. An average sexually active North American woman with an established menstrual cycle and financial, physical access to over-the-counter pregnancy tests will suspect and discover they are pregnant between five and six weeks after their last period. Statistically, women and girls living on low incomes, minors whose menstrual cycle may not have stabilized and those pregnant against their will are likely to discover their pregnancies later, and some after the first trimester.[57] This, when linked to alcohol, tobacco and recreational drug use, as well as possible consumption of various OTC medications that shouldn't be used by expectant women, can lead to faults in the development of the foetus.[58] Mississippi's Gestational Act takes none of these factors into account, and the removal of the rape and incest exceptions further erodes agency and consent from these victims in their sexual lives.

Dobbs v. *Jackson* came to the lower court in 2018 and Judge Carlton W. Reeves found in favour of the clinic, citing evidence that, despite significant medical advances, there was still little chance that a child born before 23 weeks would survive. The wrangling continued until the case reached the Supreme Court. After voting in favour of Mississippi in June 2022, the court overturned both *Roe* v. *Wade* and *Planned Parenthood* v. *Casey*. The right for a woman to choose whether to continue a pregnancy or not was swept away; that power now resides with the administration of the state in which she lives. In 2021 there were approximately 3,800 legal terminations in Mississippi. In 2023, none were recorded, and 'Abortion facilities' are recorded proudly at the top of the page as 'o'.[59] Interviewed by Fox News that month, Trump said, 'God made the decision.' He then added, 'I think, in the end, this is something that will work out for everybody.'

During his second campaign for the presidency, Trump said repeatedly that the matter of abortion should be 'left to the [individual] states'. A month before the election, extracts were published from his wife Melania's upcoming autobiography (*Melania*) in which she declared herself pro-choice: 'Why should anyone other than the woman herself have the power to determine what she does with her own body? A woman's fundamental right of individual liberty, to her own life, grants her the authority to terminate her pregnancy if she wishes.'[60] Bolder still was the video she posted on X on 3 October, confirming her stance: 'Without a doubt, there is no room for compromise when it comes to this essential right that all women possess from birth: individual freedom. What does my body, my choice really mean?'

Perhaps it is fitting that I write this on 20 January 2025, the day of Donald Trump's second inauguration as president of the United States of America. It is hard to imagine an individual less fit for public office. Yet he won. In his own words, 'I was saved by God to Make America Great Again.'

Religious faith hovers around 63 per cent for Americans, as of 2022, with 22 per cent of no faith at all, and the remainder undeclared/Wiccans/Jedis. Faith is not in itself detrimental to childbirth: in Iceland, where a similar two-thirds of the population believe in the *huldufólk*, 'hidden people' or elves, the birth success rate equals that of Finland as the best place to experience pregnancy and birth in the world.[61] But in the US the reproductive rights of millions of women are at stake, in a country whose birth success rate as a developed nation is one of the worst on the planet – all in the name of 'God'.

> 'It's hard not to imagine future generations one day asking: "When there was so much at stake for our country, what did you do?" The only acceptable answer is: 'Everything we could.'"

These are the words of Cecile Richards, the dynamic leader of Planned Parenthood, who died from brain cancer on the day of Donald Trump's inauguration, at the age of 67.

Under Richards, Planned Parenthood expanded from an organization that strove to help women protect themselves from more pregnancies than they could cope with to one that fought vigorously for women's rights. Richards's mother was Ann Richards, the great Democrat governor of Texas in the 1980s, who said that Ginger Rogers did everything Fred Astaire did, 'just backwards in high heels'. Her daughter was equally inspirational. Indeed, she inspired fellow Texan Democrat Wendy Davis to deliver a 13-hour filibuster to oppose new restrictions on women's reproductive rights in the state on 25 June 2013. While ultimately unsuccessful in halting the Texan march towards banning abortion, Davis's actions galvanized a new generation of female voters, not least because she had a catheter fitted to avoid the need to leave the floor.

After *Dobbs* v. *Jackson* there were murmurings in Britain and South Africa about the need to restrict access to the morning-after pill. In both countries, where church and state are divorced, the pro-life push was quickly shut down within government and in the popular press. It was an obvious testing of the waters, which fortunately received the response from the electorates that it deserved – total indifference.

The maternal journey in 2025 is an immeasurably different experience from my own, only a decade ago. Then, the elective C-section was still a thorny subject and the phrase 'Too Posh To Push' all too common. It's another snide rejection of the notion that a woman is free to make her own choices regarding her birthing experience, much like the Twilight Sleep debates. That is largely now a thing of the past, although anecdotal evidence suggests that women are still discouraged from choosing a C-section. Largely, and in part owing to the twin developments of the epidural and natural birth, women in the UK have more of a choice than their ancestors did in terms of what kind of birth they'd like to experience.

Support for expectant mums comes in all forms now. Books proliferate, the internet is full of wonderful and some very strange advice and most women feel much more comfortable discussing their bodies and their experiences. Let us never forget the legendary Mumsnet, established in London in 2000 by Justine Roberts as a mothers' discussion forum. While things can get pretty heated, it's full of life experience and the wonderful 'Am I The Asshole?'

(AITA) threads. It can provide hours of endless fun when you are laid up with swollen ankles and indigestion. Apps such as bumpf and Sprout enable an expectant mother to log her physical changes, envisage foetal growth and keep track of her pregnancy in general. Cecile Richards pioneered the Charley app that allows women in states where abortion is banned to identify legal providers in nearby states.

The return of the home birth continues, usually with great success. In Britain 'Changing Birth' was a 1993 parliamentary report that recommended placing autonomy back into the hands of mothers. It is still being resisted by some in the medical profession. It included valuable and practical recommendations such as a named midwife for every mother and informed choice. When you are pregnant, every day is a choice of one kind or another, and advice in making the bigger decisions is vital. Without obvious complications and adequate assistance, home birth seems to suit many people, and many First Nation peoples of North America fare far better, statistically, in their own surroundings at home than they do in a medicalized setting.[62] Black women in the UK and America experience significantly and statistically proven poorer treatment in hospitals during their labours than their white peers, which is abhorrent and must change.[63]

Compulsory sterilization remains hidden in the shadows in many countries around the world. Sweden was the last nation to stop it 'officially' in 2016. Iceland also claims to be close to 'eradicating' Down's syndrome, which is highly unlikely as Down's is a chromosomal abnormality rather than a disease. However, the subtext is that they are close to not seeing people with Down's in the living population.

Progress is being made in some quarters. In 2008 Scotland introduced blanket vaccination for 12- and 13-year-old girls against the human papillomavirus (HPV), which is sexually transmitted and is responsible for the vast majority of cervical cancers and pelvic inflammatory disease. In January 2024 Public Health Scotland was able to confirm for the first time that no new cases of cervical cancer had been reported in Scotland. This has huge implications for sub-Saharan Africa, where HPV is a leading cause of infertility, and cancer. In the same month, an all-party parliamentary group (APPG) on birth trauma was formed by the British government, to investigate the experiences of women whose labour and delivery were distinctly suboptimal. Even after researching this book, I found that the stories recounted there are deeply upsetting. Pregnant and birthing women, indeed, any woman undergoing gynaecological or obstetric procedures, are often patronized, misbelieved and disparaged by the healthcare professionals who have chosen what should be a supportive and nurturing vocation. Still, the very existence of this new APPG is valuable. As Cecile Richards wrote after being awarded the Presidential Medal of Freedom by Joe Biden, 'there are no permanent wins and no permanent losses. We have to fight for every inch of progress, and we can't take anything for granted.'

What will the next few decades bring for women and their reproductive rights? We live in an age now where women are supposed to be able to 'have everything', but at the same time the richest nation on Earth is stripping away their right to 'personhood'. At its worst, these measures reduce women, once again, to the role of vessels. Reproductive rights are a wholly female issue: men cannot generate another human inside their body, and men are rarely subject to legal restrictions on how, where and when they are allowed to reproduce. The idea that men require a sexual outlet in order to function in society is gaining ground through the social media 'manosphere', via men who proclaim themselves 'alphas' while spewing 'toxic masculinity'. These men are as ridiculous and laughable as they sound, and yet it feels too optimistic to say that they won't secure the cultural and legal shift they are after.

We are living in a time of fathomless change for women across the world. As my window of opportunity to have a child closed, a door opened that allowed me to learn about what birth meant for others, for society and for us as people. Ultimately, no matter the marital or socio-economic circumstances, every successful birth of a healthy child is a small victory for humanity and a life-changing moment for the mother. Pregnancy and birth are attended by myriad personal, emotional, social and physical dangers, but also joy, triumph and wonder. In nine short months, from two cells, the body constructs a new life and brings it into the world in a unique moment where all is possible. In the words of the magnificently named Audrey Flake Tiberius, who gave birth to naturally conceived identical triplets in March 2022 (at chances of 200 million to one), 'Motherhood is the toughest job you will ever love.'[64]

Science will continue to advance; more congenital diseases will be identified and become preventable; more premature and sick babies will survive. Mothers should experience better births, with fewer physical repercussions, less trauma and better emotional and psychological support, all of which is possible right now. If that doesn't happen, it is not science that will have failed us.

The right to give birth at the appropriate time and in the appropriate place by choice, unsullied by unnecessary interference from strangers or governments, is what we must fight to establish and to preserve. How we will achieve it is not yet known, but we must keep going. Keep pushing. Keep striving towards the light. Not just for the one, but for the many. This, is how we are born.

Acknowledgements

They say it takes a village to raise a child. *Born* has been more than that. It has taken Jason Bartholomew, Tomasz Hoskins and Octavia Stocker with their vision, clarity, patience, and firm hands on the wheel to see her to publication. Thanks also to Fahmida Ahmed, Sarah Head and Katherine MacPherson for their great efforts on *Born*'s behalf.

Thanks must go to, as ever, Team Bad (they know who they are) and Team Black Horse, as well as Romain Daude and Jean Rieux, Emy and Laeti, Karen and Kevin, Paul Clarke, Mark O'Neill, Sophie Perinot, Paul Carps, Sarah Phelps and Richard Courtney. The boots on the ground kudos goes to the Hamilton, Sedler, Rolleston, and Michie families, as well as the Taylors and the Cowboys and girls.

Special thanks go to the women who shared their personal experiences of birth and loss with me, so generously. They too know who they are.

Born has been an emotional rollercoaster from the very beginning. The last two years have seen many white-knuckle moments and the book is dedicated to our mother, Irene, without whom it never would have been written, in any sense. Thanks also to my sister Sally, for the moments of levity.

Love and endless gratitude goes to my husband, Richard, who has managed to survive the writing of this book. Wits and humour intact, at least. Just. And to our beloved rescue dachshund, Whitney Houston aka All the Crime, All the Time.

Finally, thanks to you, the reader. For your time, your patience, and your curiosity. *Born* no longer belongs to me. It belongs to us all.

Image Credits

Page 5: Cave art pattern made of ancient wild animals, horses and hunters. © jupiter55, iStock

Page 5: Aboriginal rock art (Namondjok) at Nourlangie, Kakadu National Park, Northern Territory, Australia. © NSP-RF / Alamy Stock Photo

Page 15: Neolithic totem pole from Göbekli Tepe, Layer II, 8800–8000 BCE, in Turkey, Şanlıurfa Museum. © DICK OSSEMAN / Wikimedia Commons / CC BY-SA 4.0

Page 18: Seated Woman of Çatalhöyük, Museum of Anatolian Civilizations, Ankara, Turkey. © Nevit Dilmen / Wikimedia Commons / CC BY-SA 4.0

Page 23: The Fisher of Barum, Swedish History Museum © Sven Rosborn / Wikimedia Commons / CC BY-SA 4.0

Page 32: Amulet with a figure of Lamashtu. © The Trustees of the British Museum

Page 41: Offering to Molech. © Dauster / Wikimedia Commons / Public Domain

Page 43: Ancient Egyptian Hieroglyph showing childbirth and motherhood. © Frank11 / Alamy Stock Photo

Page 64: Marble plaque showing parturition scene, Ostia, Italy, 400 BCE –300 CE. © Wellcome Collection / CC BY-SA 4.0

Page 69: Stele for a Roman medica (female physician) from the 2nd c. © Photography Laurianne Kieffer – Musée de La Cour d'Or – Eurométropole de Metz

Page 96: Birth of the Antichrist (woodcut). Illustration from Illustrierte Sittengeschichte von Mittelalter bis zur Gegenwart, by Eduard Fuchs (Albert Langen Verlag fur Litteratur und Kunst, Munich, c. 1910). © Look and Learn / Bridgeman Images

Page 97: Vesalius, Female Torso and Uterus, 1543. © Science History Images / Alamy Stock Photo

Page 104: A monster born at Kracόw in 1547; whole-length figure with webbed feet and hands, a trunk and animal faces at his joints; illustration to an unidentified Latin edition of Sebastian Münster, 'Cosmographia', probably printed by Petri in Basel, c.1547–52. Woodcut. © The Trustees of the British Museum

Page 110: Anatomy of late pregnancy. Copperplate engraving. Plate VI of William Hunter's 1774 book The Anatomy of the Human Gravid Uterus. Illustrated by Jan van Rymsdyk. © NIH Dream Anatomy / Wikimedia Commons / Public Domain

Page 123: Engravings of a foetus in the womb, from an English translation of Eucharius Rösslin's midwifery manual, The Byrth of Mankynde (1545). © Science History Images / Alamy Stock Photo

Page 128: One of the earliest American portraits showing Dr John Clarke trepanning a skull, 1664. © Beyond My Ken / Wikimedia Commons / Public Domain

Page 142: Painting by Robert C. Hinckley, depicting the first public demonstration of ether anaesthesia in surgical operations (1882–1893). © JonathanSmith18 / Wikimedia Commons / Public Domain

Page 150: Combined image of Beer Street and Gin Lane (1751), by William Hogarth. © Yomangani / Wikimedia Commons / Public Domain

Page 182: The great fear of the period that Uncle Sam may be swallowed, 1860. © Chronicle / Alamy Stock Photo

Page 193: New York: October 1916. Women and men sitting with baby carriages in front of the Sanger Clinic on Amber Street in Brooklyn. It was to eventually become the Planned Parenthood of America. © Underwood Archives, Inc / Alamy Stock Photo

Page 200: Wishbone stem pessary (Intracervical device), Europe, 1880–1940. © The Board of Trustees of the Science Museum / CC BY-SA 4.0

Page 203: Dr Stopes and her new baby son (17 April 1924). © Smith Archive / Alamy Stock Photo

Page 228: Trial of the Nagyrév poisoners, Nagyrév, Hungary, 18 December 1929. © Keystone-France / Contributor via Getty Images

Page 233: Chart from Nazi Germany explaining the Nuremberg Laws of 1935. © World History Archive / Alamy Stock Photo

Page 235: Awarding the Mother's Cross, 1943. © Sueddeutsche Zeitung Photo / Alamy Stock Photo

Page 250: Katherine Moore Dexter McCormick and other students in a chemistry laboratory class on MIT's Boston campus, circa 1890s. © MIT Museum / Wikimedia Commons / Public Domain

Page 261: Contraceptives are delivered to women via elephant in Ratangarh village, India, 20 January 1969, in a campaign called the 'Red Triangle'. Writing in Hindi reads: 'My job is to spread happiness among the people ... A small family is a happy family. Not more than two or three children.' © Associated Press / Alamy Stock Photo

Page 277: Elevated view of attendees at the March for Women's Lives rally, organized by NOW (the National Organization of Women), Washington DC, 5 April 1992. © Mark Reinstein / Contributor via Getty Images

Notes

INTRODUCTION

1 'Mamatoto' is a Swahili word meaning 'motherbaby', defining the mother and the child within her as one entity until the moment of birth.

CHAPTER ONE: THE REALM OF WOMEN

1 Sarah Bunney, 'Neanderthal baby was "buried"', *New Scientist* (June 1994).
2 Robert Sanders, University of Berkeley Press Release, 11 June 2003.
3 C. Clarkson, C. Harris, B. Li et al., 'Human occupation of northern India spans the Toba super-eruption ~74,000 years ago', *Nature Communications* 11, article 961 (2020).
4 C. Clarkson et al., 'Human occupation of northern Australia by 65,000 years ago', *Nature* 547 (2017), pp. 306–10.
5 Katerina Harvati (2012), 'What happened to the Neanderthals?', *Nature Education Knowledge*, vol. 3, no. 10, p. 13.
6 Anne Gibbons, 'Oldest Homo sapiens bones found in Europe', *SCIENCE*, vol. 368, issue 6492 (15 May 2020), p. 697.
7 Virginia Hughes, *National Geographic*, October 2013, on the work of Dr Dean Snow of the Department of Anthropology, Pennsylvania State University.
8 Kathleen McAucliffe, 'If modern humans are so smart, why are our brains shrinking?', *Discover Magazine* (January 2011).
9 Andrew Curry, 'The cave art debate', *Smithsonian Magazine* (March 2012).
10 Gillian Morriss-Kay, 'A new hypothesis on the creation of the Hohle Fels "Venus" Figurine', Pleistocene Art of the World, Actes de Congrès IFRAO, Tarascon-sur-Ariège, September 2010, symposium, p. 1.
11 Royal College of Obstetricians and Gynaecologists statistics for UK 2021, https://www.rcog.org.uk/
12 Juan-Sebastián Gómez-Jeria, 'Biology and philosophy, part I, the paleolithic', *World Journal of Research and Review (WJRR)*, vol. 4, no. 1 (January 2017), pp. 21–8.

13　Walpurga Antl-Weiser, 'The time of the Willendorf figurines and new results of Palaeolithic research in Lower Austria', *Anthropologie*, vol, 47, issues 1–2 (2009), pp. 131–41.
14　Lacy M. Johnson, *The Reckonings: Essays on Justice for the Twenty-First Century* (New York: Scribner, 2019), p. 237.
15　Emer O'Donnell, 'Birthing in prehistory', *Journal of Anthropological Archaeology*, vol. 23 (2004), p. 165.
16　Spencer P. M. Harrison, *Archaeology*, vol. 52, no. 5 (1999).
17　Maria Teschler-Nicola, Daniel Fernandes, Marc Händel et al., 'Ancient DNA reveals monozygotic newborn twins from the Upper Palaeolithic', *Communications Biology*, vol. 3, article no. 650 (2020).
18　Christiaan Monden, Gilles Pison and Jeroen Smits, 'Twin peaks: More twinning in humans than ever before', *Human Reproduction*, vol. 36, no. 6 (June 2021), pp. 1666–73.
19　Teschler-Nicola, Fernandes, Händel et al., 'Ancient DNA reveals monozygotic newborn twins from the Upper Palaeolithic'.
20　Randall Haas et al., 'Female hunters of the early Americas', *Science Advances*, vol. 6, issue 45 (4 November 2020).
21　Theya Molleson, 'The eloquent bones of Abu Hureyra', *Scientific American*, vol. 271, issue 2 (August 1994), pp. 70–75.
22　Molleson, 'The eloquent bones of Abu Hureyra'.
23　The term 'totem pole' is problematic even within archaeology. It is, however, the title most commonly given to this sculpture, and is not to be confused with what are termed 'Tree of Life' sculptures.
24　Çiğdem Köksal-Schmidt and Klaus Schmidt, 'The Göbekli Tepe "totem pole": A first discussion of an autumn 2010 discovery (PPN, Southeastern Turkey)', *Neo-Lithics*, 1/10 (January 2010).
25　To come
26　E. B. Banning, 'So fair a house: Göbekli Tepe and the identification of temples in the pre-pottery Neolithic of the Near East', *Current Anthropology*, vol. 52, no. 5 (2011), p. 627.
27　Kimberley C. Patton and Lori D. Hager, '"Motherbaby": A death in childbirth in Çatalhöyük', *Religion at Work in Neolithic Society: Vital Matters*, ed. Ian Hutton (Cambridge: Cambridge University Press, 2014), p. 251.
28　Patton and Hager, 'Motherbaby', pp. 228–9.
29　M. Chyleński, E. Ehler, M. Somel et al., 'Ancient mitochondrial genomes reveal the absence of maternal kinship in the burials of Çatalhöyük people and their genetic affinities', *Genes* [Basel], vol. 10, no. 3 (March 2019), doi: 10.3390/genes10030207
30　https://www.catalhoyuk.com/archive_reports/2005/ar05_01.html
31　'Neolithic Baby Burial [Archeology]', *Children and Youth in History*, item 213, https://cyh.rrchnm.org/items/show/213
32　J. Pearson, M. Grove, M. Ozbek and F. Hongo, 'Food and social complexity at Çayönü Tepesi, southeastern Anatolia: Stable isotope evidence of differentiation in diet according to burial practice and sex in the early Neolithic', *Journal of Anthropological Archaeology*, vol. 32, issue 2 (June 2013), pp. 180–89.

33 M. Özbek, 'Dental pathology of the prepottery Neolithic residents of Çayönü, Turkey', *Rivista di Anthropologia*, 73 (1995), pp. 99–122.
34 J. A. Pearson et al., 'Exploring the relationship between weaning and infant mortality: An isotope case study from Aşıklı Höyük and Çayönü Tepesi', *American Journal of Physical Anthropology*, vol. 143, issue 3 (November 2010), pp. 448–57. Deniz Erdem, 'Social Differentiation in Çayönü and Abu Hureyra through Burial Customs and Skeletal Biology', thesis submitted to the Graduate School of Social Sciences of Middle East Technical University, June 2006, p. 37.
35 Karina Croucher, *Death and Dying in the Neolithic Near East* (Oxford: Oxford University Press, 2012), p. 222. Pearson, Grove, Ozbek and Hongo, 'Food and social complexity at Çayönü Tepesi, southeastern Anatolia'. Carney D. Matheson and T. H. Loy, 'Genetic sex identification of 9400-year-old human skull samples from Çayönü Tepesi, Turkey', *Journal of Archaeological Science*, vol. 28 (2001), p. 572, doi:10.1006/jasc.1999.0615, available online at http://www.idealibrary.com.
36 A. Lieverse, V. Bazaliiskii and A. Weber, 'Death by twins: A remarkable case of dystocic childbirth in Early Neolithic Siberia', *Antiquity*, vol. 89, issue 343 (2015), pp. 23–38.
37 Nils-Gustaf Gejvall, 'The fisherman from Barum – mother of several children! Palaeo-anatomic finds in the skeleton from Bäckaskog', *Fornvännen* (1970), pp. 281–9. Sabine Sten, 'Barumkvinnan: nya forskningsrön', *Fornvännen*, vol. 95 (2000), pp. 73–87.
38 Mark Golitko and Lawrence H. Keeley, 'Beating back ploughshares into swords: Warfare in the Linearbandkeramik', *Antiquity*, 81 (2007), pp. 332–42.
39 David W. Anthony, Peter Bogucki, Eugen Comşa et al., 'The "Kurgan culture", Indo-European origins, and the domestication of the horse: A reconsideration [and comments and replies]', *Current Anthropology*, vol. 27, no. 4 (1986), pp. 291–313, http://www.jstor.org/stable/2743045
40 Hermann Parzinger, 'Burial mounds of Scythian elites in the Eurasian steppe: New discoveries', *Journal of the British Academy*, vol. 5 (2017), p. 332.
41 Parzinger, 'Burial mounds of Scythian elites in the Eurasian steppe', p. 332.
42 C. Batini, P. Hallast, D. Zadik et al., 'Large-scale recent expansion of European patrilineages shown by population resequencing', *Nature Communications*, vol. 6, article 7152 (2015), https://doi.org/10.1038/ncomms8152

CHAPTER TWO: THE REALM OF MEN

1 John W. Martens and Kristine Henriksen Garroway (eds), *Children and Methods: Listening to and Learning from Children in the Biblical World* (Leiden: Brill, 2020), p. 114.
2 Charles Halton and Saana Svärd (eds), *Women's Writing of Ancient Mesopotamia* (Cambridge: Cambridge University Press, 2016).
3 Quoted in, M. Stol, *Birth in Babylonia and Its Mediterranean Setting* (Groningen: Styx, 2000), p. 1.
4 Electronic Corpus of Sumerian Literature, UET 6/2 301, University of Oxford, etcsl.orinst.ox.ac.uk 2016.
5 Stol, *Birth in Babylonia and its Mediterranean Setting*, p. 5.

6 Stol, *Birth in Babylonia and its Mediterranean Setting*, pp. 39–40.
7 CAD E s.v, pp 325–6 and CAD A/1 s.v., pp. 287–294 quoted in M. Erica Couto-Ferreira, 'Being mothers or acting mothers? Constructing motherhood in ancient Mesopotamia', in *Women in Antiquity, Real Women from Across the Ancient World* (Abingdon: Routledge, 2016), p. 27.
8 Law A53, quoted in Stol, *Birth in Babylonia and its Mediterranean Setting*, pp. 39–48.
9 Jonathan Valk, '"They enjoy syrup and ghee at tables of silver and gold": Infant loss in ancient Mesopotamia', *Journal of the Economic and Social History of the Orient*, vol. 59 (Leiden: Brill, 2016), p. 697.
10 Quoted in M. Erica Couto-Ferreira, '"She will give birth easily": Therapeutic approaches to childbirth in 1st millennium BCE cuneiform sources', *Dynamis*, vol. 34, no. 2 (2014).
11 Christina M. Elson and Kenneth Mowbray, 'Burial practices at Teotihuacan in the early Postclassic period: The Vaillant and Linné excavations (1931–1932)', *Ancient Mesoamerica*, vol.16, no. 2 (2005), pp.195–211.
12 J. A. Scurlock, 'Baby snatching demons, restless souls and the dangers of childbirth: Magico-Medical means of dealing with some of the perils of motherhood in ancient Mesopotamia', *Incognita*, vol. 2 (1991), pp. 137–41
13 H. Avalos, S. J. Melcher and J. Schipper, *This Abled Body: Rethinking Disabilities in Biblical Studies* (Leiden: Brill, 2007), pp. 21–2.
14 Valk, 'They enjoy syrup and ghee at tables of silver and gold', p. 697.
15 Robert Jutte, *Contraception* (Oxford: John Wiley, 2008), p. 45.
16 Photini J. P. McGeorge, 'Morbidity and medical practice in Minoan Crete', in *From the Land of the Labyrinth: Minoan Crete, 3000–1100 B.C.*, ed. Maria Andreadaki-Vlazaki, Giorgos Rethemiotakis and Nota Dimopoulou-Rethemiotaki (New York and Athens: Alexander S. Onassis Public Benefit Foundation, 2008), pp. 118–27.
17 Simone Zimmerman Kuoni, 'The obstetric connection: Midwives and weasels within and beyond Minoan Crete', *Religions*, vol. 12, no. 12 (2021), p. 1056.
18 Lynne A. Shepartz, 'Differential health among the Mycenaeans of Messenia: Status, sex, and dental health at Pylos', *Hesperia Supplements*, vol. 43 (2009), p. 171.
19 Rita Roberts, 'Supersyllabograms in the agricultural sector of the Mycenaean economy', https://www.academia.edu/33542173.
20 Barbara A. Olsen, 'The worlds of Penelope: Women in the Mycenaean and Homeric economies', *Arethusa*, vol. 48, no. 2 (2015), p. 116.
21 Olsen, 'The worlds of Penelope', pp. 107–38.
22 P. J. P. McGeorge. 'Intramural infant burials in the Aegean Bronze age: Reflections on symbolism and eschatology with particular reference to Crete', *Deuxièmes Rencontres d'archéologie de l'IFEA: Le Mort dans la ville: Pratiques, contextes et impacts des inhumations intra-muros en Anatolie, du début de l'Age du Bronze à l'époque romaine*, Istanbul, Turkey, November 2011, pp. 1–20.
23 Olsen, 'The worlds of Penelope', p. 117.
24 For these translations I am indebted to Linear B scholars Richard Vallance Janke and Rita Roberts respectively, 2014.

25 Helen Askitopoulou, Ioanna A. Ramoutsaki and Eleni Konsolaki, 'Archaeological evidence on the use of opium in the Minoan world', *International Congress Series*, vol. 1242 (December 2002), p. 3.
26 Glenn Markoe, *Phoenicians* (Berkeley, CA: University of California Press, 2000), pp. 12–13.
27 Mark A. Christian, 'Phoenician maritime religion: Sailors, goddess worship, and the Grotta Regina', *Die Welt des Orients*, vol. 43, no. 2 (2013), p. 191.
28 Christian, 'Phoenician maritime religion', p. 194.
29 Quoted by Jeffrey H. Schwartz, *What the Bones Tell Us* (Tucson, AZ: University of Arizona Press, 1998), p. 31.
30 Susanne Töpfer, 'The physical activity of parturition in ancient Egypt: Textual and epigraphical sources' (2014), https://scielo.isciii.es/
31 Foy Scalf, 'Magical bricks in the Oriental Institute Museum of the University of Chicago', *Studien zur Altägyptischen Kultur*, vol. 38 (2009), pp. 275–95.
32 Josef Wegner, 'The magical birth brick', *Expedition Magazine*, vol. 48, no. 2 (2006), p. 35.
33 W. Benson Harer, 'New evidence for King Tutankhamen's death: His bizarre embalming', *Journal of Egyptian Archaeology*, vol. 97 (2011), pp. 228–33.
34 Zahi Hawass and Sahar N. Saleem, 'Mummified daughters of King Tutankhamun: Archaeological and CT studies', *American Journal of Roentgenology*, vol. 197, no. 5 (2011), W829–W836.
35 Wojciech Ejsmond et al., 'A pregnant ancient Egyptian mummy from the 1st century BC', *Journal of Archaeological Science*, vol. 132, no. 51 (August 2021), 105371.
36 https://www.cam.ac.uk/research/news/youngest-ancient-egyptian-human-foetus-discovered-in-miniature-coffin-at-the-fitzwilliam-museum
37 Joseph, J. Hobbs, 'Troubling fields: The opium poppy in Egypt', *Geographical Review*, vol. 88, no.1 (January 1998), pp. 64–85.
38 Anne Austin and Cedric Gobeil, 'Embodying the divine: A tattooed female mummy from Deir el-Medina', *Bulletin de l'Institut français d'archéologie orientale*, vol. 116 (2017), pp. 23–46.
39 W. B. Harer Jr and Z. el-Dawakhly, 'Peseshet – the first female physician?', *Obstetrics and Gynecology*, vol. 74, no. 6 (December 1989), pp. 960–61.
40 Courtesy University College Hospital: https://www.ucl.ac.uk/museums-static/digitalegypt//med/birthpapyrus.html, col. 1, lines 1–5)
41 Jacques Jouanna, 'Egyptian and Greek medicine', *Greek Medicine from Hippocrates to Galen* (Leiden: Brill, 2012), p. 5.
42 Paul John Frandsen, 'The menstrual "taboo" in ancient Egypt', *Journal of Near Eastern Studies*, vol. 66, no. 2 (2007), p. 90.
43 Berlin Papyrus, quoted in Glenn D Braunstein, 'The long gestation of the modern home pregnancy test', *Clinical Chemistry*, vol. 60, issue 1 (1 January 2014), pp. 18–21.
44 Kelsey Tyssowski and Olivia Foster, 'Pee is for pregnant: The history and science of urine-based pregnancy tests' (sitn.hms.harvard.edu, 2018).
45 A. Tzvi and D. Schwemer, *Corpus of Mesopotamian Anti-Witchcraft Rituals in Ancient Magic and Divination* (Leiden and Boston, MA: Brill, 2010), p. 51.
46 Maryam Navi, 'The naked Elamite figurine: A talisman to facilitate difficult labour', *Research on the History of Medicine*, vol. 10, no. 4 (November 2021), pp. 243–52.

47 Stephanie Lynn Budin, and Jean MacIntosh Turfa (eds), *Women in Antiquity: Real Women across the Ancient World* (Abingdon and New York: Routledge, 2016), pp. 319–28.
48 Yonatan Adler amd Omri Lernau, 'The Pentateuchal dietary proscription against finless and scaleless aquatic species in light of ancient fish remains', *Tel Aviv*, vol. 48, no. 1 (2021), pp. 5–26.
49 Exodus 15.26.
50 Samuel Kottek, Manfred Horstmanshoff, Gerard Baader, and Gary Ferngren (eds), 'An Akkadian vademecum in the Babylonian Talmud', in *From Athens to Jerusalem: Medicine in Hellenized Jewish Lore and in Early Christian Literature* (Rotterdam: Erasmus, 2000), p. 17.
51 Exodus 1.15–21.
52 Aristotle, *Politics*, 1.2.
53 Helen King, in *Women in Antiquity: New Assessments*, ed. Richard Hawley and Barbara Levick (London: Routledge, 1995), p. 114.
54 King, pp. 130–31.
55 J. Kremer, 'The haematogenous reproduction theory of Aristotle', *Nederlands Tijdschrift voor Geneeskunde*, vol. 147, no. 51 (December 2003), pp. 2529–35.
56 Aristotle, *Historia Animalium*, Book VII, Chapter 4.
57 James Longrigg, 'Anatomy in Alexandria in the third century B.C.', *British Journal for the History of Science,* vol. 21 no. 4 (1988), pp. 455–88.
58 Heinrich von Staden, 'The discovery of the body: Human dissection and its cultural context in ancient Greece', *Yale Journal of Biology and Medicine*, vol. 65, no. 3 (May–June 1992), p. 224.

CHAPTER THREE: DARKNESS FALLS

1 From Oxyrhynchus Papyrus 774, quoted in Eleanor Scott, *The Archaeology of Infancy and Infant Death*, BAR International Series 819 (Oxford: BAR Publishing, 1999), p. 71
2 Aristotle, *Historia Animalium*, Book VII, Chapter 4.
3 Marcus Cato, quoted in F. E. Adcock, 'Women in Roman life and letters', *Greece & Rome*, vol. 14, no. 40 (1945), p. 3.
4 Nicolas Siron and Ethan Rundell, 'Girl with a heron: Gender and the erotic in Greek iconography (sixth-fourth centuries BCE)', *Clio. Women, Gender, History*, no. 42 (2015), pp. 213–39.
5 John Scarborough, 'Theophrastus on herbals and herbal remedies', *Journal of the History of Biology*, vol. II, no. 2 (autumn 1978), pp. 370–71.
6 Theophrastus, 9,9,8, quoted in Charles Brewster Randolph, 'The mandragora of the ancients in folk-lore and medicine', *Proceedings of the American Academy of Arts and Sciences*, vol. 40, no. 12 (1905), p. 489.
7 John M. Riddle and J. Worth Estes, 'Oral contraceptives in ancient and medieval times', *American Scientist*, vol. 80, no. 3 (1992), pp. 232–3.
8 Holt N. Parker, 'Galen and the girls: Sources for women medical writers revisited', *Classical Quarterly,* vol. 62, no. 1 (2012), pp. 359–86.

9. Soranus, *Gynaecology*, trans. Owsei Temkin (London and Baltimore, MD: Johns Hopkins University Press, 1956), pp. 190–91.
10. Soranus, *Gynaecology*, pp. xxxi–xxxvii.
11. Soranus, *Gynaecology*, pp. 5–6.
12. Soranus, *Gynaecology*, pp. 21–9.
13. Soranus, *Gynaecology*, p. 49.
14. Soranus, *Gynaecology*, pp. 63–7.
15. Soranus, *Gynaecology*, pp. 198–204.
16. Soranus, *Gynaecology*, p. 180.
17. L. Totelin, 'Old recipes, new practice? The Latin adaptations of the Hippocratic Gynaecological Treatises', *Social History of Medicine*, vol. 24, issue 1 (April 2011), pp. 74–91.
18. Rebecca Flemming, 'Women, writing and medicine in the classical world', *The Classical Quarterly*, vol. 57, no. 1 (2007), p. 259.
19. Katie Campbell Hurd-Mead, 'And Introduction to the History of Women in Medicine II: The Medical Women of the Middle Ages', *Annals of Medical History*, September 1933 (5), pp. 490-495.
20. Scott, *The Archaeology of Infancy and Infant Death*, p. 57.
21. Pliny the Elder, quoted in Valerie Hansen, *The Silk Road: A New History* (Oxford: Oxford University Press, 2012), p. 20.
22. John 19.14–16; Luke 3.23.
23. Mark 6.3; Matthew 13.55.
24. Flavius Josephus, Book 18, ch. 3, v. 3.
25. *Protoevangelium*, 4.1.
26. *Protoevangelium*, 4.3.
27. *Protoevangelium*, 4.8.
28. *Protoevangelium*, 7.10.
29. *Protoevangelium*, 8.1.
30. *Protoevangelium*, 9.6–9.
31. *Protoevangelium*, 10.6–8.
32. *Protoevangelium*, 11.6–9.
33. *Protoevangelium*, 13.1.
34. *Protoevangelium*, 13.9.
35. *Protoevangelium*, 17.10.
36. *Protoevangelium*, 18.1.
37. Talmud (Shabbat 18.2).
38. *Protoevangelium*, 19.18–19.
39. *Protoevangelium*, 20.5–10.
40. Flavius Josephus, *Against Apion*, 2.25.
41. Aída Besançon Spencer, 'Leadership of women in Crete and Macedonia as a model for the church', *Priscilla Papers*, vol. 27, no. 4 (Autumn 2013), pp. 5–15.
42. Celsus, 3.44.
43. Tertullian, *To His Wife*.
44. He drew up the edict alongside Emperor Licinius, with whom Constantine shared the rule of a divided empire until he seized it all for himself.

45 Nicaea Council I, Canon XIX.
46 St Jerome, *Letter LXXVII, to Oceanus*.
47 St Jerome, *Letter LXXVII, to Oceanus*.
48 al-Bukhari, 3894; Muslim, 1422.
49 Female genital cutting prevalence among women aged 15–49 years. Sources: Demographic and Health Surveys and Multiple Indicator Cluster Surveys. Female Genital Mutilation/Cutting: A Statistical Exploration. New York: UNICEF; 2005:4.
50 Rufus of Ephesus, *On the Names of the Parts of the Human Body*, 109–12.
51 Lucia Corno, Eliana La Ferrara and Alessandra Voena, *Female Genital Cutting and the Slave Trade*, CEPR Discussion Paper No. DP15577 (Paris and London: CEPR Press, December 2020).
52 Anne-Frederique Minsart, Thai-Son N'guyen, Rachid Ali Hadji and Martin Caillet, 'Maternal infibulation and obstetrical outcome in Djibouti', *Journal of Maternal-Fetal & Neonatal Medicine*, vol. 28, no. 14 (2015), pp. 1741–6.
53 Quoted in Dariusch Atighetchi, *Islamic Bioethics: Problems and Perspectives* (Dordrecht: Springer, 2007), p. 306.
54 Ingrid Hehmeyer and Aliya Khan, 'Islam's forgotten contributions to medical science', *Canadian Medical Association Journal*, vol. 176, no. 10 (8 May 2007), pp. 1467–8.
55 Tacitus, *Germania*, on the Suebi, 31.
56 Scott, *The Archaeology of Infancy and Infant Death*, p. 110.
57 M. J. Elsakkers, 'Reading between the Lines: Old Germanic and Early Christian Views on Abortion', thesis, externally prepared, University of Amsterdam (2010), p. 332.
58 Carla Spivack, 'To bring down the flowers: The cultural context of abortion law in early modern England', *William & Mary Journal of Women and the Law*, vol. 14, no. 1 (2007). p. 107.
59 Nancy L. Wicker, 'Selective female infanticide as partial explanation for the dearth of women in Viking age Scandinavia', in *Violence and Society in the Early Medieval West*, ed. Guy Halsall (Woodbridge: Boydell, 1998), p. 205.

CHAPTER FOUR: THE RISE OF THE MACHINES

1 L. M. C. Weston, 'Women's medicine, women's magic: The Old English metrical childbirth charms', *Modern Philology*, vol. 92, no. 3 (1995), p. 280.
2 S. Crawford, 'Children, death and the afterlife in Anglo-Saxon England', in *Anglo-Saxon Studies in Archaeology and History*, vol. 6, ed. W. Filmer-Sankey (1993), pp. 83–91.
3 L. Whaley, *Women and the Practice of Medical Care in Early Modern Europe, 1400–1800* (London: Palgrave Macmillan, 2011), p. 15.
4 W. L. Minkowski, 'Women healers of the middle ages: Selected aspects of their history', *American Journal of Public Health*, vol. 82, no. 2 (1992), pp. 288–95.
5 *Niddah*, 41.
6 Renate Blumenfeld-Kosinski, *Not Born of Woman: Representations of Caesarean Birth in Medieval and Renaissance Culture* (Ithaca, NY, and London: Cornell University Press, 1990), p. 26.

7 Piero d'Argellata, *Chirurgia*, Book 5, Chapter 7, Treatise 19.
8 Katharine Park, 'The death of Isabella Della Volpe: Four eyewitness accounts of a postmortem Caesarean section in 1545', *Bulletin of the History of Medicine*, vol. 82, no. 1 (2008), p. 174.
9 Blumenfeld-Kosinski, *Not Born of Woman*, pp. 36–7.
10 Peter Dunn, 'Robert Felkin MD (1853–1926) and Caesarean delivery in Central Africa (1879)', *Archives of Disease in Childhood – Fetal and Neonatal Edition*, vol. 80, no. 3 (1999), F250–F251.
11 Blumenfeld-Kosinski, *Not Born of Woman*, p. 1.
12 Park, 'The death of Isabella Della Volpe', pp. 169–87.
13 J. M. Mishra, T. K. Behera, B. K. Panda and K. Sarangi, 'Twin lithopaedions: A rare entity', *Singapore Medical Journal*, vol. 48, no. 9 (2007), pp. 866–8.
14 N. Lachman, K. S. Satyapal, J. M. Kalideen and T. R. Moodley, 'Lithopedion: A case report', *Clinical Anatomy*, vol. 14 (2001), pp. 52–4.
15 P. M. Dunn, 'The Chamberlen family (1560–1728) and obstetric forceps', *Archives of Disease in Childhood – Foetal and Neonatal Edition*, vol. 81 (1999), F232–F234.
16 W. F. Bynum and Roy Porter, *William Hunter and the Eighteenth Century Medical World* (Cambridge: Cambridge University Press, 2002), p. 15.
17 Ludmilla Jordanova and Deanna Petherbridge, *The Quick and the Dead: Artists and Anatomy* (Berkeley and Los Angeles, CA, and London: University of California Press, 1997), p. 8.
18 J. L. Thornton, *Jan Van Rymsdyk: Medical Artist* of the *Eighteenth Century* (Cambridge: Oleander Press, 1982), p. 65.
19 Lisa Forman Cody, 'Living and dying in Georgian London's lying-in hospitals', *Bulletin of the History of Medicine*, vol. 78, no. 2 (2004), p. 318.
20 Cody, 'Living and dying in Georgian London's lying-in hospitals', p. 318.
21 Frank Nicholls, *The Petition of the Unborn Babes to the Censors of the Royal College of Physicians of London* (London, 1752), p. 5.
22 Elizabeth Nichell, *Treatise on Midwifery* (London, 1760), p. 50.
23 Nichell, *Treatise on Midwifery*, p. 76.
24 Nichell, *Treatise on Midwifery*, p. 4.
25 William Godwin, *Memoirs of the Author of a Vindication of the Rights of Woman* (gutenberg.org), (Joseph Johnson, London, 1798) p. 198.

CHAPTER FIVE: ANARCHA, BETSEY AND LUCY

1 Alan G. Waxman, 'Navajo childbirth in transition', *Medical Anthropology*, vol. 12, no.2 (1990), pp. 187–206.
2 Patton and Hager, 'Motherbaby'.
3 Giles Milton, *Big Chief Elizabeth – How England's Adventurers Gambled and Won the New World* (London: Hodder & Stoughton, 2000).
4 The Historical Marker Database, no. 33871.
5 W. C. Armstrong, *The Life and Adventures of Captain John Smith* (London: H. Dayton, 1859), p. 186.

6 George Percy, *A Trewe Relacyon of the precedeings and ocurrentes of Momente which have hapned in Virginia from the Tyme Sir Thomas Gates was Shippwrackte uppon the Bermudes Anno 1609 untill my departure owtt of the Cowntry which was in Anno Domini 1612*.
7 Paula Neely, 'Jamestown colonist resorted to cannibalism', *National Geographic* (May 2013).
8 William Bradford, *Of Plimouth Plantation* (1624), Chapter IX.
9 Eugene Aubrey Stratton, *Plymouth Colony: Its History and People, 1620–1691* (Salt Lake City: Ancestry Publishing, 1986), p. 79.
10 J. S. Marr and J. T. Cathey, 'New hypothesis for cause of epidemic among native Americans, New England, 1616–1619', *Emerging Infectious Diseases*, vol. 16, no. 2 (February 2010), pp. 281–6.
11 W. L. Grant and J. F. Jameson, *Voyages of Samuel de Champlain 1604–1618* (New York: Barnes & Noble, 1946) p. 4.
12 James C. Riley, 'Smallpox and American Indians revisited', *Journal of the History of Medicine and Allied Sciences*, vol. 65, no. 4 (2010), pp. 445–77.
13 John Demos, 'Notes of Plymouth Colony', *William & Mary Quarterly*, 3rd ser., vol. 22, no. 2 (April 1965), p. 274.
14 *A present for teeming women, or, Scripture-directions for women with child how to prepare for the houre of travel / written first for the private use of a gentlewoman of quality in the West, and now published for the common good by John Oliver* (London: 1663), Chapter IX.
15 Per Sörlin and Eszter Csonka-Takács, 'Child witches and the construction of the witches' sabbath: The Swedish blåkulla story', in *Witchcraft Mythologies and Persecutions*, ed. Gábor Klaniczay and Éva Pócs (Budapest: Central European University, 2008), pp. 99–126.
16 Eric H. Christiansen, *The Medical Practitioners of Massachusetts 1630-1800: Patterns of Change and Continuity* (Colonial Society of Massachusetts, 1978) p. 54.
17 Eric H. Christianson, 'The medical practitioners of Massachusetts, 1630–1800: Patterns of change and continuity', in *Medicine in Colonial Massachusetts, 1620–1820* (Boston, MA: Colonial Society of Massachusetts, 1980), pp. 48–67.
18 Josiah Henry Benton, *The Story of the Old Boston Town House, 1658–1711*, (Boston, 1908) p. 82.
19 Eugenia W. Herbert, 'Smallpox inoculation in Africa', *Journal of African History*, vol. 16, no. 4 (1975), p. 539.
20 Herbert, 'Smallpox inoculation in Africa', p. 541.
21 Zabdiel Boylston, *An historical account of the small-pox inoculated in New England ... : With some account of the nature of the infection in the natural and inoculated way, and their different effects on human bodies* (1726), p. 14.
22 P. S. Brown, 'Female pills and the reputation of iron as an abortifacient', *Medical History*, vol. 21, no. 3 (1977), pp. 291–304.
23 Zachary Dorner, '"No one here knows half so much of this matter as yourself": The deployment of expertise in Silvester Gardiner's surgical, druggist, and land speculation networks, 1734–83', *The William and Mary Quarterly*, vol. 72, no. 2 (2015), pp. 287–322.
24 Martha Ballard's diary online.

25 Laurel Thatcher Ulrich, *A Midwife's Tale* (New York: Vintage, 1991), p. 171.
26 R. Wertz and D. Wertz, *Lying-In: A History of Childbirth in America* (New Haven, CT: Yale University Press, 1989), p. 5.
27 Claire L. Jones, 'Instruments of medical information: The rise of the medical trade catalog in Britain, 1750–1914', *Technology and Culture*, vol. 54, no. 3 (2013), p. 570.
28 The Medical and Chirurgical Faculty of the State of Maryland, accession no. 302606.
29 J. Marion Sims, *Story of My Life* (New York: Appledore, 1884), p. 60.
30 Sims, *Story of My Life*, p. 227.
31 Sims, *Story of My Life*, p. 231.
32 Sims, *Story of My Life*, p. 228.
33 Sims, *Story of My Life*, pp. 229–30.
34 Sims, *Story of My Life*, p. 230.
35 Sims, *Story of My Life*, p. 234.
36 Sims, *Story of My Life*, p. 236.
37 Sims, *Story of My Life*, p. 237.
38 Sims, *Story of My Life*, p. 240.
39 Sims, *Story of My Life*, p. 242.
40 Sims, *Story of My Life*, p. 242.
41 Sims, *Story of My Life*, p. 246.

CHAPTER SIX: THE NUMBERS GAME

1 The Keep and Longfellow birth quoted in Jacqueline H. Wolf, *Deliver Me from Pain: Anesthesia and Birth in America* (Baltimore, MD: Johns Hopkins University Press, 2009), p. 13.
2 F. Cartwright, 'The early history of ether', *Anaesthesia*, vol. 15 (1960), pp. 67–9.
3 Cartwright, 'The early history of ether', pp. 67–9.
4 Nathan Payson Rice, *Trials of a Public Benefactor, as Illustrated in the Discovery of Etherization* (New York: Pudney & Russell, 1859), p. 137.
5 Almiro dos Reis Júnior, 'The first to use surgical anaesthesia was not a dentist, but the physician Crawford Williamson Long', *Revista Brasileira de Anestesiologia*, vol. 56, no. 3 (June 2006).
6 Reis Júnior, 'The first to use surgical anaesthesia was not a dentist, but the physician Crawford Williamson Long'.
7 J. Wawersik, 'Die Geschichte der Chloroformnarkose [History of chloroform anaesthesia]', *Anaesthesiologie und Reanimation*, vol. 22, no. 6 (1997), pp. 144–52. English translation courtesy National Library of Medicine, PMID: 9487785.
8 Recorded in the *Edinburgh Medical Journal* (1874), p. 774.
9 E. W. Lee, 'Ether versus chloroform', *Chicago Medical Journal* (1875), p. 137.
10 Lee, 'Ether versus chloroform', p. 137.
11 Later published in the *Boston Medical and Surgical Journal*, vol. 25 (1842), pp. 409–15.
12 As taken from Snow's diary by the editor of John Snow, *On Chloroform and Other Anaesthetics: Their Action and Administration, with a Memoir of the Author, by Benjamin W. Richardson* (London, 1858), p. xxxi.

13 W. Stanley Sykes, *The History of Anesthesiology*, vol.16 (Wood Library, NY), p. 79.
14 Science Museum Group, letter from Queen Victoria mentioning chloroform use in childbirth. 1992–295.
15 John H. Dye, in his book *Painless Childbirth or Healthy Mothers and Healthy Children* (Buffalo, NY: 1889), p. 79.
16 L. Betti and A. Manica, 'Human variation in the shape of the birth canal is significant and geographically structured', *Proceedings of the Royal Society B: Biological Sciences*, vol. 285, issue 1889 (24 October 2018). J. Gorman, C. A. Roberts, S. Newsham, G. R. Bentley, 'Squatting, pelvic morphology and a reconsideration of childbirth difficulties', *Evolution Medicine and Public Health*, vol. 10, no. 1 (April 2022), pp. 243–55, figure 2.
17 oldbaileyonline.org
18 oldbaileyonline.org
19 Gillian Wagner, *Thomas Coram, Gent., 1668–1741* (Woodbridge: Boydell Press, 2004), p. 147.
20 David Jones, *Disordered Personalities and Crime: A Historical Analysis of Moral Insanity* (Abingdon: Routledge, 2015).
21 Roderick Floud and Donald McCloskey (eds), *The Economic History of Britain since 1700*, vol 1, *1700–1860* (Cambridge: Cambridge University Press, 1981), p. 21.
22 Adam Smith, *Wealth of Nations* (London, 1776), I: V, p. 48.
23 Lynn MacKay, 'The mendicity society and its clients: A cautionary tale', *Left History*, vol. 5, no. 1 (1997), p. 49.
24 Francis Place, *The Autobiography of Francis Place* (Cambridge: Cambridge University Press, 1972), p. 52.
25 Hera Cook, *The Long Sexual Revolution* (Oxford: Oxford University Press, 2004), p. 71.
26 George R. Drysdale, *The Elements of Social Science, or, Physical, Sexual, and Natural Religion* (London: E. Truelove, 1867), p. 350.
27 Charles Knowlton, *The Fruits of Philosophy, or, The Private Companion for Young Married People* (London: James Watson, 1845), p. 13 (reprinted from the American edition).
28 S. Pooley 'Parenthood, child-rearing and fertility in England, 1850–1914', *The History of the Family*, vol. 18, no. 1 (March 2013), pp. 83–106.
29 Peter M. Dunn, 'Dr Thomas Radford (1793–1881) of Manchester and obstructed labour', *Archives of Disease in Childhood*, vol. 69, no. 3 (October 1993), p. 327.
30 Thomas Radford, *Observations on the Caesarean Section and Other Obstetric Observations* (Manchester, 1865), p. 1.
31 Radford, *Observations on the Caesarean Section and Other Obstetric Observations*, p. 2.
32 Radford, *Observations on the Caesarean Section and Other Obstetric Observations*, p. 7.
33 Radford, *Observations on the Caesarean Section and Other Obstetric Observations*, p. 47.
34 Radford, *Observations on the Caesarean Section and Other Obstetric Observations*, Table of recorded cases, back matter.

35 Gomes Eanes de Azurara, 'The discovery and conquest of Guinea (1453)', in Elizabeth Donnan (ed.), *Documents Illustrative of the History of the Slave Trade to America, 1441–1700,* vol. 1 (Washington, DC: Carnegie Institution, 1930), p. 40.
36 Alexander Falconbridge, *An Account of the Slave Trade on the Coast of Africa* (London, 1788), p. 24.
37 Charles Darwin, *The Descent of Man, and Selection in Relation to Sex* (London: John Murray, [2nd edn] 1874), pp. 28–9.
38 Richard B. Sheridan, 'The slave trade to Jamaica, 1702–1808', in *Trade, Government and Society: Caribbean History 1700–1920*, ed. B. W. Higman (Kingston: Heinemann Educational Books Caribbean, 1983), p. 3.
39 B. W. Higman, *Slave Populations of the British Caribbean, 1807–1834* (Baltimore, MD: Johns Hopkins University Press, 1984), pp. 74–5.
40 Edward Long, *A History of Jamaica* (1774), vol. II, p. 380.
41 Long, *A History of Jamaica*, vol. II, p. 436.
42 Quoted in Kenneth Morgan, 'Slave women and reproduction in Jamaica, c. 1776–1834', *History: The Journal of the Historical Association*, vol. 91, issue 302 (April 2006), pp. 231–53.
43 Morgan, 'Slave women and reproduction in Jamaica, c. 1776–1834'.
44 Morgan, 'Slave women and reproduction in Jamaica, c. 1776–1834'.
45 Long, *A History of Jamaica*, vol. II, p. 437.
46 Morgan, 'Slave women and reproduction in Jamaica, c. 1776–1834'.
47 Long, *A History of Jamaica*, vol. II, p. 375.
48 Charles White, *An Account of the Regular Gradation in Man, and in Different Animals and Vegetables* (London, 1799), p. 43.
49 White, *An Account of the Regular Gradation in Man, and in Different Animals and Vegetables*, pp. 48, 59.
50 Jodie G. Katon et al., 'Racial disparities in uterine fibroids and endometriosis: a systematic review and application of social, structural, and political context', *Fertility and Sterility*, vol. 119, issue 3 (2023), pp. 355–63.
51 Clarkson quoted in White, *An Account of the Regular Gradation in Man, and in Different Animals and Vegetables*, p. 104.
52 White, *An Account of the Regular Gradation in Man, and in Different Animals and Vegetables*, p. 105.
53 Darwin, *Descent of Man*, pp. 117–18.
54 C. R. Darwin, 1834.07. *Zoological diary: Chiloé.* CUL-DAR31.315. Edited by John van Wyhe.
55 Darwin, *Descent of Man* vol. I, pp. 219–20.
56 Darwin, C. R. 1921. [Letter to H. Denny, 1844 and G. Cupples, 1874]. Maggs Bros. *Autograph letters: historical documents…no. 401.* (Maggs: London)
57 Lewis M. Terman, 'The intelligence quotient of Francis Galton in childhood', *American Journal of Psychology*, vol. 28, no. 2 (1917), p. 210.
58 Francis Galton, *The Art of Travel* (London: John Murray, [5th edn], 1872), p. 209.
59 Francis Galton, *The Narrative of an Explorer in Tropical South Africa* (London: John Murray, 1853), p. 88.
60 Galton, *The Narrative of an Explorer in Tropical South Africa*, pp. 134, 1–2.

61 Francis Galton, 'Composite portraits made by combining those of many different persons into a single figure', *Journal of the Anthropological Institute of Great Britain and Ireland*, vol. 8 (1879), pp. 132–48.
62 Francis Galton, 'Hereditary talent and character', *Macmillan's Magazine*, vol. 12 (1865), pp. 157–66.
63 Galton, 'Hereditary talent and character', p. 157.
64 Galton, 'Hereditary talent and character', p. 157.
65 Galton, 'Hereditary talent and character', p. 161.
66 Galton, 'Hereditary talent and character', p. 161.
67 Francis Galton, 'The comparative worth of different races', in *Hereditary Genius: An Inquiry Into Its Laws and Consequences* (London: Macmillan, 1869); Galton, *Hereditary Genius*, p. 14.
68 Francis Galton, *Inquiries into the Human Faculty and Its Development* (London: J. M. Dent and Sons, 1883), p. 24.
69 Francis Galton, 'Hereditary Talent and Character', *MacMillan's Magazine*, vol. 12 (1865).
70 Dr J. Arthur Harris, 'Francis Galton', *Popular Science Monthly*, vol. 79 (August 1911), p. 179.

CHAPTER SEVEN: SOMETHING WICKED THIS WAY COMES

1 Sterilizations were halted in 1909 by Governor Thomas R. Marshall. In 1921 the Indiana Supreme Court ruled the 1907 law unconstitutional, citing denial of due process under the 14th Amendment. 1927 law reinstated sterilization, adding court appeals.
2 Paul Popenoe, 'The progress of eugenical sterilization', *Journal of Heredity*, vol. 25, no.1 (1934), p. 19.
3 *California Star* (28 August 1847) and Henry G. Langley, *The San Francisco Directory* (April 1871 and September 1862): San Francisco, California, and US Census 1860.
4 Paul Rodman, 'The origin of the Chinese issue in California', *Mississippi Valley Historical Review*, vol. 25 (September 1938), p. 182.
5 B. E. Lloyd, *The Lights and Shades of San Francisco* (San Francisco, CA, 1870), p. 245.
6 Ronald Takaki, *Strangers from a Different Shore* (Boston, MA: Little, Brown, 1998), p. 3.
7 Act for the Suppression of Trade in, and Circulation of, Obscene Literature and Articles of Immoral Use, 1873, Public Law 42–438.
8 Joseph Spillane, *Cocaine: From Medical Marvel to Modern Menace in the United States, 1884–1920* (Baltimore, MD: Johns Hopkins University Press, 2000), p. 75.
9 *Songs of the Temperance Movement and Prohibition*, 1874.
10 Nathaniel Deutsch, *Inventing America's Worst Family: Eugenics, Islam and the Fall and Rise of the Tribe of Ishmael* (Berkeley and Los Angeles, CA, and London: University of California Press, 2009), p. 27.
11 Deutsch, *Inventing America's Worst Family*, p. 34.
12 'The Jukes of New York', *The Wilson Quarterly (1976–)*, vol. 5, no. 1 (1981), p. 22.

13 Elsa F. Kramer, 'Recasting the tribe of Ishmael: The role of Indianapolis's nineteenth-century poor in twentieth-century eugenics', *Indiana Magazine of History*, vol. 104, no. 1 (2008), p. 52.
14 Oscar C. McCulloch, *The Tribe of Ishmael: A Study in Social Degradation* (Indianapolis, IN: Charity Organization Society, [5th edn] 1891), title page.
15 Margaret Sanger, *What Every Girl Should Know* (Reading, PA: Sentinel, 1916), title page.
16 Sanger, *What Every Girl Should Know*, p. 25.
17 Sanger, *What Every Girl Should Know*, p. 87.
18 Sanger, *What Every Girl Should Know*, p. 48.
19 Sanger, *What Every Girl Should Know*, p. 91.
20 measuringworth.com
21 Jill Lepore, *The Secret History of Wonder Woman* (New York: Knopf, 2014), p. 95.
22 *New York Times* (9 January 1917).
23 Ellen Chesler, *Women of Valor: Margaret Sanger and the Birth Control Movement* (NY: Simon & Schuster, 1992), p. 255.
24 CNN (22 July 2020).
25 Lepore, *The Secret History of Wonder Woman*, pp. 81–3.
26 Marie C. Stopes, *Married Love* (New York: Eugenics Publishing Co., [9th edn] 1927), p. xi.
27 Stopes, *Married Love*, pp. 34–5.
28 Stopes, *Married Love*, p. 38.
29 Stopes, *Married Love*, p. 110.
30 Stopes, *Married Love*, p. 31.
31 Stopes, *Married Love*, p. xi.
32 Marie C. Stopes, *Wise Parenthood: The Treatise on Birth Control for Married People* (London: Putnam, [8th edn] 1922), p. 1.
33 Stopes, *Wise Parenthood*, p. 17.
34 Stopes, *Wise Parenthood*, p. 37.
35 Stopes, *Wise Parenthood*, p. 37.
36 Stopes, *Wise Parenthood*, p. 10.
37 Stopes, *Wise Parenthood*, p. xi.
38 Sir James Barr to Marie C. Stopes, from Paris, 26 May 1921.
39 Bentley B. Gilbert, 'Health and politics: The British physical deterioration report of 1904', *Bulletin of the History of Medicine*, vol. 39, no. 2 (1965), pp. 143–53.
40 Marie C. Stopes, *Radiant Motherhood: A Book for Those Who Are Creating the Future* (London, New York: Putnam, 1920), p. 3.
41 Stopes, *Radiant Motherhood*, p. 236.
42 June Rose, *Marie Stopes and the Sexual Revolution* (London: Faber & Faber, 2010), p. 229.
43 Rose, *Marie Stopes and the Sexual Revolution*, p. 235.
44 Stopes, *Married Love*, p. 13.
45 Marie Stopes International Submission to the International Development Committee – Effectiveness of UK Aid and the work of the Department for International Development (DFID).

CHAPTER EIGHT: 'A VIOLENT AND MESSIANIC AGE'

1. Marguerite Tracy and Mary Boyd, *Painless Childbirth* (London: Heinemann, 1917), p. 13.
2. Tracy M, Leupp C. 'Painless Childbirth', *McClure's Magazine*, 1914, Issue 43, p. 38.
3. Tamar A. Lindenbaum, *Patient's Orders: Twilight Sleep and the Female Medical Consumer in the Turn-of-The-Century United States, 1880–1920* (Barnard, 2018), p. 47.
4. Tracy and Boyd, *Painless Childbirth*, p. 126.
5. BK Ng, et.al. 'Maternal and foetal outcomes of pregnant women with bacterial vaginosis', *Frontiers in Surgery.* 2023 Feb 13, 10, p. 2.
6. Mazhar Osman Uzman, *Konferanslarım (Medikal, Paramedikal)* (İstanbul: Kader Basımevi, 1940), pp. 120–21.
7. Willard A. Hanna, 'Indonesian Banda: Colonialism and its aftermath in the Nutmeg Islands', Philadelphia, PA, Institute for the Study of Human Issues, 1978, pp. 53–54.
8. Frederick W. MacCallum, letter, 1916, quoted in D. Hertzog (ed.), *Brutality and Desire: War and Sexuality in Europe's Twentieth Century* (London: Palgrave Macmillan, 2009), p. 41.
9. Hertzog (ed.), *Brutality and Desire*, p. 25.
10. Quoted in J. Bryce and A. Toynbee, *The Treatment of Armenians in the Ottoman Empire, 1915–1916*, uncensored edition, ed. A. Sarafian (Princeton, NJ, 2000 [1916]), pp. 68, 160.
11. Irving Fisher, 'Impending problems of eugenics', *Scientific Monthly*, vol. 13, no. 3 (1921), p. 67.
12. Fisher, 'Impending problems of eugenics', p. 216.
13. Fisher, 'Impending problems of eugenics', p. 216. The singularly unappealing phrase of 'germ plasm' (although beloved of the eugenicists) refers to the discovery of gametes by August Weisman and his book of 1892 *Keimplasma*. *Keimplasma* posited rightly that the characteristics we inherit from our parents come from the cells of the sexual organs, not from the body itself.
14. Fisher, 'Impending problems of eugenics', p. 227.
15. Corrado Gini to Leonard Darwin, 1 August 1919, Wellcome Institute, SA, EUG, c. 123.
16. Giovanni Battista Morgagni, *De sedibus et causis morborum per anatomen indagatis* (1761).
17. David Starr Jordan, *War and the Breed: The Relation of War to the Downfall of Nations* (Boston, MA: Beacon Press, 1915), p. 118.
18. Jordan, *War and the Breed*, p. 118.
19. Jordan, *War and the Breed*, p. 118.
20. Christabel Pankhurst, *The Great Scourge, and How to End It* (London, 1913), p. ix.
21. Christabel Pankhurst, *The Great Scourge, and How to End It*, p. vi.
22. Christabel Pankhurst, *The Great Scourge, and How to End It*, p. 16.
23. Christabel Pankhurst, *The Great Scourge, and How to End It*, p. 19.
24. Stephen Graham, *A Private in the Guards* (London: Heinemann, 1928), p. 244.

25 Mark Harrison, 'The British Army and the problem of venereal disease in France and Egypt during the First World War', *Medical History*, vol. 39 (1995), p. 142.
26 Fisher, 'Impending problems of eugenics', p. 223.
27 *Surveys in Mental Deviation in Prisons, Public Schools and Orphanages* (Sacramento, 1918), p. 74.
28 *Surveys in Mental Deviation in Prisons, Public Schools and Orphanages*, p. 74.
29 *Surveys in Mental Deviation in Prisons, Public Schools and Orphanages*, p. 38.
30 *Surveys in Mental Deviation in Prisons, Public Schools and Orphanages*, p. 62.
31 Chap. 394. - An ACT to provide for the sexual sterilization of inmates of State institutions in certain cases. [S B 281]
32 Laughlin, quoted in Michelle Goodwin and Erwin Chemerinsky, 'No immunity: Race, class, and civil liberties in times of health crisis', *Harvard Law Review*, vol. 129, issue 4 (February 2016).
33 Béla Bodó, 'Progress or national suicide: The single child family in Hungarian political thought, 1840–1945', *Hungarian Studies Review*, vol. 28, no. 1–2 (2001), pp. 185–208.
34 David Laszlo Tarnoki et al., 'The population-based Hungarian twin registry: An update', *Twin Research and Human Genetics* (Cambridge: Cambridge University Press, 2024), pp. 27, 115–19.
35 Marius Turda, 'In pursuit of Greater Hungary: Eugenic ideas of social and biological improvement, 1940–1941', *Journal of Modern History*, vol. 85, no. 3 (September 2013), pp. 558–91.
36 Henry Field to Major John McDonough, 3 December 1943, declassified CIA report, p. 8.
37 Field to McDonough, pp. 22–3.
38 Max Wallace, *The American Axis: Henry Ford, Charles Lindbergh, and The Rise of The Third Reich* (New York: St Martin's Press, 2003), p. 1.
39 Library of Congress.
40 Edwin Black, *War Against the Weak: Eugenics and America's Campaign to Create a Master Race* (New York, NY: Thunder's Mouth Press: 2003), p. 125. Between 1928 and his death in 1942, Gosney pursued his ideas of 'betterment', undeterred by the horrors unfolding on the other side of the Atlantic. On his death, the Foundation's assets were sold and in 1943 his daughter donated the papers of the HBF and the remaining assets to the California Institute of Technology (Caltech) to establish the Gosney fund for biological research.
41 Peter Campbell, 'The "Black Horror on the Rhine": Idealism, pacifism, and racism in feminism and the left in the aftermath of the First World War', *Social History*, vol. 47 (June 2014), pp. 471–96.
42 Cecil Gosling to the Earl Curzon, quoted in R. C. Reinders, 'Racialism on the left: E. D. Morel and the "Black Horror on the Rhine"', *International Review of Social History*, vol. 13, no. 1 (1968), pp. 1–28.
43 Reinders, 'Racialism on the Left'.
44 From the Gestapo Office, Cologne, 3 March 1938, quoted in C. P. Blacker, '"Eugenic" experiments conducted by the Nazis on human subjects', *Eugenics Review* (1952), p. 11.
45 C.P. Blacker, '"Eugenic" experiments', p. 13.

46 Y. Arad, Y. Gutman and A. Margaliot (eds), *Documents on the Holocaust* (New York, NY: Ktav Publishing House in Association with Yad-Vashem, 1981), p. 272.
47 Jewish Virtual Library/Ravensbruck.
48 Wanda Półtawska, 'Experimental operations at Ravensbrück concentration camp', trans T. Bałuk-Ulewiczowa, *Medical Review – Auschwitz* (6 September 2018).
49 Kate Docking, 'Gender, recruitment and medicine at Ravensbrück concentration camp, 1939–1942', *German History*, vol. 39, issue 3 (September 2021), pp. 419–41.
50 Taken from the Belsen trial, *Law-Reports of Trials of War Criminals, The United Nations War Crimes Commission*, vol. II (London: HMSO, 1947).
51 Barbara Möller, 'Hitler's helpers: The murderers of opportunity', *Die Welt* (30 August 2014).
52 Gisella Perl, *I was a Doctor in Auschwitz*.
53 Docking, 'Gender, recruitment and medicine at Ravensbrück concentration camp'.
54 Arnold Sorsby, Felix S. Besser, A. Meyer et al., 'Medical war crimes', *British Medical Journal*, vol. 2, issue. 5090 (1958), pp. 246–8.
55 M. M. Weber, 'Ernst Rüdin, 1874–1952: A German psychiatrist and geneticist', *American Journal of Medical Genetics*, vol. 67, no. 4 (July 1996), pp. 323–31.
56 William E. Seidelman, 'Mengele medicus: Medicine's Nazi heritage', *Milbank Quarterly*, vol. 66, no. 2 (1988), p. 226.
57 E. Fusco, F. Padula, E. Mancini et al., 'History of colposcopy: A brief biography of Hinselmann', *Journal of Prenatal Medicine*, vol. 2, no. 2 (April 2008), pp. 19–23.
58 C. Castelo-Branco and J. Lejárcegui, 'Obstetrics and gynecology in Third Reich concentration camps: A never-ending nightmare', *GREM Gynecological and Reproductive Endocrinology & Metabolism*, vol. 4, no. 2/2023 (2024), pp. 55–61.
59 Seidelman, 'Mengele medicus: Medicine's Nazi heritage', p. 229.
60 Beverley Chalmers, *Birth, Sex and Abuse: Women's Voices under Nazi Rule* (Surbiton: Grosvenor House, 2015) p.??
61 Robert Jay Lifton, *New York Times* (21 July 1985), Sunday, Late City Final Edition, section 6, p. 16, col. 1, Magazine Desk.
62 M. Turda, 'The ambiguous victim: Miklós Nyiszli's narrative of medical experimentation in Auschwitz-Birkenau', *Historein*, vol. 14, no. 1 (2014), pp. 43–58.
63 Półtawska, 'Experimental operations at Ravensbrück concentration camp'.
64 *New York Times* (30 October 2023).

CHAPTER NINE: LIVING MEMORY

1 Irene Harris, personal correspondence between mother and daughters, January 2025.
2 Irene Harris, personal correspondence.
3 Grantly Dick-Read, *Natural Childbirth* (London: Heinemann, 1933), pp. ix, vii.
4 Dick-Read, *Natural Childbirth*, p. 14.
5 John Nichol and Tony Rennell, *Medic: Saving Lives* (London: Penguin, 2010), p. 220.
6 'Obituary: Prunella Briance (1926–2017)', *The Independent* (4 August 2017).
7 Institute of Medicine (US) Committee on Nutritional Status during Pregnancy and Lactation, Nutrition during Pregnancy: Part I, Weight Gain: Part II, Nutrient Supplements. Washington (DC): National Academies Press (US); 1990.

8 Gregory A. Chinn, Andrew T. Gray and Merlin Larson, 'Overcoming obstacles: The legacy of Fidel Pagés, founder of the epidural, 100 years after his passing', *Anesthesia & Analgesia*, vol. 138, no. 2 (February 2024), pp. 475–9.
9 D. M. Potts, 'Termination of pregnancy', *British Medical Bulletin*, vol. 26, issue 1 (January 1970), pp. 65–71.
10 www.bletchleyparkresearch.co.uk
11 C. Lyons, 'Penicillin therapy of surgical infections in the U.S. Army: A report', *JAMA (Journal of the American Medical Association)*, vol. 123, no. 16 (1943), pp. 1007–18.
12 A. Richards, 'Production of penicillin in the United States (1941–1946)', *Nature*, vol. 201 (February 1964), pp. 441–5.
13 Brennan, closing remarks, 405 U.S. 438 (1972), p. 453.
14 Joshua Prager, 'The Accidental Activist', *Vanity Fair*, 18 January 2013
15 Joshua Prager, 'The Accidental Activist', *Vanity Fair*, 18 January 2013
16 Alvin L. Buchanan v. Charles Batchelor.
17 Revealed by Joshua Prager as the subject of his book, *The Family Roe: An American Story* (New York: W.W. Norton, 2021).
18 *Roe v. Wade*, 314 F. Supp 1217, N.D. Texas, 1970.
19 www.nixonlibrary.gov
20 Joshua Prager, 'The Accidental Activist', *Vanity Fair*, 18 January 2013
21 Leonard A. Gordon, 'Wealth equals wisdom? The Rockefeller and Ford Foundations in India', *The Annals of the American Academy of Political and Social Science*, vol. 554 (1997), pp. 104–16.
22 Gordon, 'Wealth Equals Wisdom?', p. 109.
23 Gordon, 'Wealth Equals Wisdom?', p. 111.
24 Gyan Prakash, 'Emergency Chronicles: Indira Gandhi and Democracy's Turning Point' (Princeton University Press, 2019), p. 266.
25 Gyan Prakash, 'Emergency Chronicles: Indira Gandhi and Democracy's Turning Point' (Princeton University Press, 2019), p. 266.
26 Gyan Prakash, 'Emergency Chronicles: Indira Gandhi and Democracy's Turning Point' (Princeton University Press, 2019) p. 266.
27 Matthew Connelly, *Fatal Misconception: The Struggle to Control World Population* (Harvard University Press, 2088), p. 420.
28 M. H. Johnson, S. B. Franklin, M Cottingham and N. Hopwood, 'Why the Medical Research Council refused Robert Edwards and Patrick Steptoe support for research on human conception in 1971', *Human Reproduction*, vol. 25, no. 9 (July 2010), pp. 2157–74.
29 Kat Brown, *No One Talks about This Stuff: Twenty-Two Stories of Almost Parenthood* (London: Unbound, 2024), p. 39.
30 Recounted to author, 19 May 2020.
31 M. G. Rosenstein, Y. W. Cheng, J. M. Snowden et al., 'Risk of stillbirth and infant death stratified by gestational age', *Obstetrics and Gynecology*, vol. 120, no. 1 (July 2012): pp. 76–82.
32 Office of National Statistics, ons.gov.uk
33 Lucia Hug et al., 'Global, regional, and national estimates and trends in stillbirths from 2000 to 2019: A systematic assessment', *The Lancet*, vol. 398, issue 10302 (2021), pp. 772–85.

34. These figures rose during the Covid-19 pandemic but thorough data is not yet available.
35. Jody Day speaking to Kat Brown, *No One Talks about This Stuff*, p. 17.
36. Kavitha Surana, 'Abortion bans have delayed emergency medical care. In Georgia, experts say this mother's death was preventable', *ProPublica* (16 September 2024).
37. D. Granberg, 'The abortion issue in the 1984 elections', *Family Planning Perspective*, vol. 19, no. 2 (March–April 1987), pp. 59–62.
38. Brian Pendleton, 'The California Therapeutic Abortion Act: An Analysis', 19 Hastings L.J. 242 (1967).
39. Ronald Reagan, quoted in Blake Scott Ball, *Charlie Brown's America* (Oxford: Oxford University Press, 2021), p. 168.
40. Reagan to Schultz, 30 July 1970.
41. https://www.reaganlibrary.gov/archives/
42. https://www.reaganlibrary.gov/archives/
43. 505 U.S. 833.
44. *New York Times* (14 March 1993).
45. *New York* Times (5 March 1994).
46. *Washington Post* (3 September 2003).
47. Guttmacher Institute, State Laws and Policies, *Medication Abortion*, 23 April 2025.
48. *Washington Post on Sunday* (25 July 1999), p. 1.
49. Drouot sale catalogue, 2013.
50. 18 USC 1531.
51. NBC, 8 April 2024; NBC, October 1999.
52. Trump on banning abortions: 'There'd Be "Some Form of Punishment"', YouTube, March 2016.
53. MSNBC interview with Chris Matthews, 26 July 2016.
54. *The Independent* (26 February 2016).
55. Kitty Kelley, 'Death and the all American boy', *Washingtonian* (1 June 1974).
56. NBC, 20 April 2024.
57. A. M. Branum and K. A. Ahrens, 'Trends in timing of pregnancy awareness among US women', *Maternal and Child Health Journal*, vol. 21, no. 4 (April 2017), pp. 715–26.
58. Branum and Ahrens, 'Trends in timing of pregnancy awareness among US women'.
59. Mississippi Department of Health, *Annual Report 2023*, p. 43.
60. Melania Trump, *Melania* (New York: Skyhorse, 2024), p. 60, and as reported by the BBC, 3 October 2024.
61. 'How U.S. religious composition has changed in recent decades', Pew Research Center, 13 September 2022; *National Geographic*.
62. Alan G. Waxman, 'Navajo childbirth in transitin', *Medical Anthropology*, vol. 12, no. 2 (1990), pp. 187–206.
63. 'Statewide survey on maternal mortality in Georgia', Research!America with Emory University, October 2023.
64. *Today*, September 7, 2022.

Selected Further Reading

1. Marija Gimbutas, *The Civilization of the Goddess: The World of Old Europe* (San Francisco, Harper, 1991).
2. eds., Richard Hawley and Barbara Levick, *Women in Antiquity: New Assessments* (London: Routledge, 1995).
3. Eleanor Scott, *The Archaeology of Infancy and Infant Death* (Oxford: BAR publishing, 1999).
4. L. Whaley, *Women and the Practice of Medical Care in Early Modern Europe, 1400-1800* (London: Palgrave Macmillan, 2011).
5. J. Marion Sims, *Story of My Life* (New York: Appledore, 1884).
6. Jacqueline H. Wolf, *Deliver Me From Pain: Anesthesia and Birth In America* (Baltimore MD: John Hopkins University, 2009).
7. Margaret Sanger, *What Every Girl Should Know* (Reading, PA: Sentinel, 1916), Marie C. Stopes, Married Love (London, 1918).
8. Max Wallace, *The American Axis: Henry Ford, Charles Lindbergh, and The Rise of The Third Reich* (New York: St Martin's Press, 2003).
9. Kat Brown, *No One Talks About This Stuff: Twenty-Two Stories of Almost Parenthood* (London: Unbound, 2024).

Index

Page numbers for illustrations are in *italic*.

A, B, C and D classifications 201
Abolition of the Slave Trade Act (1807) 164
Aboriginal people 191
Aboriginal rock art (Namondjok), Nourlangie, Kakadu National Park, Australia 5, *5*
abortion
    abortifacients 65, 131, 154, 192, 200
    illegal 30, 75, 228, 263
    The Pirates and 243
    in US 272–85, 286
    'violent' 84
    See also US states
Aburel, Eugen 248
'active birth' 269
adoption 61, 255–6
Affordable Care Act (2010) 282
Africa 3, 10, 50, 173–4, 217
    sub-Saharan 74, 270, 288
'Air Tractor' (vacuum) 144
Aisha (Muhammad's third wife) 79–80
Akkadian, *The Cow of Sîn* 31
Alaska 253–4
Alfred the Great 84
Alis 59, 75
Allerton, Mary Norris 118, 119
alloparenting (communal childcare) 157
Alphonso II 216
American Birth Control League (ABCL) 194, 195
Amish people 106
amniotic fluid 269
Amnisos cave 'temple', Crete 34
anæsthesia 140–4
Anarcha (slave girl) 135–9
Angel Makers, Nagyrév 228, *228*
Anglicanism 120

Anglo-Saxons 84, 87–8, 219
animalistic carvings 5, 14
animism 42–3, 58
Ankhesenamun 45
anti-fertility drugs 65
anti-immigrant cartoon (1800) *182*
Anti-Saloon League (ASL) 184
antibodies 121
Antinori, Severino 267
Antona, Annetta 230
Anzio Effect 246
Argellata, Pietro d', *Chirurgia* 93–4
Aristotle 55, 57, 59–60
Armenian genocide (1915–16) 212–14
Army of God (terrorist group) 275, 279, 280
artwork 14
Aryanism 219, 234, 235
Asexualization Act, Californian (1909) 223
Asherah 39
Ashtart 39
Asia 10, 50, 80, 120, 259, 270
Asiya 78
atlatl (spear-thrower) 11
Aurora borealis *3*
Auschwitz camp 238, 241
Austria 99–100
autopsies 91, 108–9
Aztec peoples 116

Ba'al Hamon 39, 40
Baba Yaga (folk tale) 126
Baby Loss Certificate 270
Babylonian empire 27
Bachofen, Johann Jakob, *Das Mutterrecht* 227
bacterial vaginosis 210
Baird, William 254

INDEX

Balaskas, Janet 269
Ballard, Martha 132–3
Banks, Sir Maurice Alfred Lister 263
Barbados 165–6
barbarians 83
barber–surgeons 92, 98
Barr, Sir James 199, 201
Barrett, Lt Col James and June 279
Barry, James 159
Bauhin, Gaspar 95
Bayt al-Hikma (House of Wisdom) 82
Beagle, HMS 162, 170, 171
bearing down 9
Beecher, Henry Knowles 246
begging 151–2
Bentham, Jeremy 152
Bergen-Belsen camp 238
Beringia 20, 23
Berlin Papyrus 49
Bernard of Gordon 93
Bertheim, Alfred 218
Betsey (slave girl) 135, 136, 138, 139
Better Baby contest, US 209–11
Biden, Joe 283, 287
Bigelow, Jacob 142
Billington, Elinor 122
birth control *see* contraception
Birth of Antichrist, Germany 96, *96*
birthing brick 43–4
birthing positions 67
birthing stools 35, 52
Black women
    Dunlop and 264
    enslaved 164
    menstruation 169
    midwives 166
    'painless birth' 146
    Sanger and 194
    treatment in labour 287
Blackfoot people 114
bleeding, vaginal 29
'blue baby' 267–8
Boaistuau, Pierre, *Histoires prodigieuses* 100
body-snatching 108
Boer War (1899–1902) 201
Bolce, Harold and Mrs Evadne 177
Bologna, Italy 89, 90, 91
Boston 128–31, 142
Boston Revolt (1687) 125
Bouhler, Philipp 240
Bouri Formation, Ethiopia 2
Boylston, Zabdiel 129–30
Brack, Viktor Hermann 235–6
Brandt, Karl 240
breastfeeding 13, 113, 163–4
breech position 20, 21, 99, 115, 268

Brennan, William J. Jr 254
Brewster, Mary 122
Briance, Prunella 246–7
Bridget of Kildare 83
British Medical Association 158, 239
British Medical Journal (BMJ) 199, 239
British Slavery Compensation Act
    (1837) 171–2
Britton, Dr John 279
Brockhoeft, John 276
brothels 218, 219–20
Brown, Lesley and John 265–6
Brownsville Clinic, New York 192–3, *193*
Brunhilda of Austrasia 83
Bryant, Lane 207–8
Buck, Carrie 224–5
Buck v. *Bell* (US, 1927) 224–5
Buddhism 50
al-Bukhari 79–80
Bulgarian Balkans 4
Bureau of Social Hygiene (Rockefeller
    Foundation) 220
burial sites 10, 12–19, 84, 86, 88, 118
Burnley, Lancashire 157
Burt, John 275–6, 278, 279, 280
Bush, George H. W. 275, 277
Bush, George W. 280
Bush, Jeb 280
Bush, Prescott 277
Buxton, Dr C. Lee 253
Byrne, Ethel 192–3
Byrne, Olive 192, 196

C-section 20, 92–8, 158–61, 246, 286
Calenza, Constance 89
California 178–9, 222–3, 230
caliphs 81–2
cannibalism 24, 118
cap, contraceptive 194–5, 199, 250
Cape Town prison 174
'cargo slaves' 163
Caribbean, the 163, 165–6, 166, 171
Carnegie, Andrew 184
Carr, Judith and Elizabeth Jordan 266
Çatalhöyük, Turkey 16–19, *18*
Catholicism 74, 120, 126, 215, 239, 251–2,
    272, 283
Cato, Marcus, *De agri cultura* 62
cave dwellings 3–11
cave paintings 2, 4–6, *5*, 10, 39
Çayönü Tepesi, Turkey 19
Celsus 76
cerebral palsy 240
cervical cancer 287
Chain, Ernst 249
Chamberlen, Guillaume 102–3

Chamberlen, Hugh the Younger 106
Chamberlens (male midwives) 102–6
'Changing Birth' (British parliamentary report, 1993) 287
Charles VIII 216
Charley app 287
Charter Street Ragged School, Manchester (CSRS) 158
Chauvet Cave, Vallon, France 10
Chesterton, G. K., *Eugenics and Other Evils* 177
childbed fever 112
Chiloé Island 170
China 69
Chinese Exclusion Act (1882) 182
Chinese population, US 180–2, 222–3
chloroform 143–5, 161, 242
cholera 144
Christian Arabs 215
Christianity 70–8, 83, 91, 259, 279
Churchill, Winston 176–7
circumcision, female 80–1
City of Peace (*now* Baghdad) 82
Clarke, Dr John 127, *128*
Clarkson, Thomas 169
Clauberg, Carl 241
Clay, Dr Charles 159
climate change 3, 20, 50
Clinical Research Bureau, US 195
Clinton, Bill and Hillary 278, 280
cloning 267
Coca-Cola 183
cocaine 183, 232
codebreakers, Bletchley Park 248–9
Coffee, Linda 254, 256
coitus interruptus (pulling out) 154, 155
colposcopy techniques 241
Colson, Charles 257–8
Columbus, Christopher 116
Comstock Act (1873) 183, 191, 195
Comstock, Anthony 183, 192
concentration camps 236
condoms 155, 194, 219–20, 254
Congo Free State 212
consent, age of 185
Constantine I, Emperor 76
consumption 131
contraception 154–7, 192–6, 198–204
   breastfeeding as 13
   cap 194–5, 199, 250
   Catholic eugenicists 215
   diaphragm 194–5, 199, 250
   goat's bladder 34
   Indian 261, *261*
   morning after pill 280, 286
   'morning-after' plant medicine 65

   the Pill 195, 251–3, 254
   spermicides 199
Coram, Thomas 148–9
Correns, Carl Erich 189–90
Council of Nicaea, First (325 CE) 76
Cova Dels Cavalls, Valltorta, Spain 5
Crane, Frederick 194
Crete 33–5, 36, 38
Cro Magnon people 6–11
Croatan people 117
Cross of the German Mother 234–5, *235*
Crow people 114
Crusades, The 89–90, 92, 217
Cyrene (Greek city-state) 65

Dabitum (slave girl) 27, 33
Dachau camp 241
Damara people 173
Darwin, Charles 162–3, 165, 170, 174
Davis, Wendy 286
de Crollis of Cossato, Battista 98
De Vries, Hugo Marie 189–90
deformity 33, 104, 105
   pelvis 105, 158, 159
Deir el-Medina mummies 46–7
della Volpe, Isabella 98
Delos, Greece 55
Denny, Henry 171
dental health 35, 37
Desai, Moraji 259–60
Dhaba, Sonr River Valley 2
diabetes 91
diamorphine 205
diaphragms 194–5, 199, 250
Dick-Read, Grantly 245–7, 268
diets 52, 122, 207, 247, 263
   poor 37, 153, 158, 167, 237
difficult births 62, 107, 111, 133, 144, 161, 246
'dilation and curettage (D&C)' 271–2
'dirt-eating' 167
disability 115, 149, 239–40
disease 3, 112–13, 120–1, 131, 153–4, 219
divorce 62, 77, 152, 194, 196, 197
DNA analysis 3, 10, 19, 25–6, 243
Dobbs v. Jackson Women's Health Organization (US, 2022) 271–89
doctors, female Roman 68, *69*
doctors, qualified 127–8, 134–9
Dogliotti, Achille Mario 248
'doll', pregnancy (phantom) 107, 111
domus (household unit) 60–5
Donnally, Mary 161
'Double Goddess Figures' 6
douching, vagina 156, 199
Douglas, James 108

'The Douglas Adams Event' 3–4
Down's syndrome 240, 287
Dr John Hooper's Female Pills 131
drug importation 130–1
Dubya, Gee 280, 281
Dugdale, Richard L., *The Jukes: ...* 186–7
Dunlop, Joan 263–4
dwarfism 105, 158
Dye, John H., *Painless Childbirth ...* 146

ectopic pregnancies 100, 265, 266
Edwards, Robert 265–7
Egyptians, ancient 42–9, 80
Ehrlich, Paul, *The Population Bomb* 218, 258–9
Eileithyia 38
Eisenhower, Dwight D. 252
Elamite people 50–1
Elena (midwife) 98
Eleuthia 34
Elvira of Castile 90
embryology 54, 221, 251, 265–7
Emmett, Mrs C. Temple 206, 207
endometriosis 265
Engel, J. L. 22
Enlightenment, the 106
Enovid (contraceptive pill) 195, 252, 253
Ensminger, Douglas 260, 261–2
epidurals 248, 286
Erasistratus of Ceos 57–8
ergotism (St Anthony's Fire) 126–7
Eritha 37, 38
ether ('fifth element') 140, *142*, 237
Ethiopia 2, 46, 48, 215
eugenics 178–204, 209–11, 240–3
    American 229–30
    Galton and 176–7
    inter-war 214–15, 226–7
    post-Second World War 254, 258
    Progressive Era 221–2
    'Race suicide' 218–19
Eugenics Record Office (ERO) 188, 225
euthanasia programme, Aktion T4 239–40
Evans, Arthur 34
Evipan (hexobarbitone) 237, 242
exercise 56
extramarital sex 55, 234

Fabian Society 196
Fabiola 77
factory work 147, 153, 157
Falconbridge, Alexander 164
fallopian tubes, blocked 265
farmers, first 11–20
Farrington, James 133
Fatima 78

Fawcett, Millicent Garrett 217
'feeble-minded' population 179, 199, 201–2
female genital mutilation (FGM) 80–1
Fertile Crescent, Middle East 11–20
fertility treatments 10, 198, 265–7
fibroids 169
figurines 6–11, 14, 35, 38, 50–1
Fildes, Mary 154–5
Finland 270
First Nation peoples 3, 20, 114–16, 121, 287
first pregnancies 13
First World War 212–14, 218, 219–20, 246
Fisher, Irving 214, 220–1
'The Fisher of Barum', Sweden 21–2, *23*
fishing industry 120
fistulas 92, 135–9
'five-year pregnancy' 99–102
Fleming, Alexander 249
Florey, Howard 249
foetuses 32–3, 100–1, 280–2
    aborted 275
    deformed 33
    immunity 121
    miscarried 54, 269–70
    mummified 45–6
    mutilated 213
food shortages 11, 36
forceps 82–3, 103, 135, 144, 206–7
Ford Foundation 259–63
Ford, Henry 184–5, 220, 230
Foundling Hospital, London 148–9
France 6, 216, 231
Francis, Pope 283
Frauenklinik, Freiburg 205–9
Fuller, Brigit Lee 119

Gabriel, angel 73, 79
Galen 65
Galileo 102
Galton, Francis 172–7
Galton Laboratory, UCL 176
Gandhi, Indira 262, 263
Gandhi, Mahatma 260
Gardiner, Silvester 130–1
Gaskin, Ina May 268
Gauss, Karl 205, 206, 208–9
Gebhardt, Karl 237–8
Gemina 68
gender selection 266
genocide 172, 212–14, 240
Georgia 272
germ theory 211
German Girls, League of 234, 238
Germanic peoples 83, 84
Germany 6–11, 24, 94, 95–6, 206, 229–43
Gestational Age Act (2018) 284

Gibson Girl adverts 207
Giffard, William, *Cases in Midwifry* 105
Gilgameš and Enkidu 33
Gillard, Lynette 267
Gin Craze 149–51, *150*
Gini, Corrado 215
Girsu (*now* Tello), Iraq 28
Göbekli Tepe site 14–16, *15*
Godwin, William 113
Goethe, C. M. 230–1
'gold pin' (coil precursor) 199–200, *200*
Gold Rush, Californian 179
Goldsby, Matt 275
Gondishapur, Academy of 77, 78, 82
gonorrhoea 53, 215–16, 218, 249
good luck charms 31–2, *32*, 51
Gordon, Alexander, *Treatise on the Epidemic Puerperal Fever of Aberdeen* 112
Gosney, Ezra Seymour (E. S.) 230–1
graffiti 14
grave goods 21, 24, 25, 86
'Great Chain of Being' theory 168
Greece, Classical 40, 42, 54–8
Grese, Irma 'The Hyena' 238
Griffin, Michael Frederick 278
Griswold, Estelle 253
Griswold v. *Connecticut* (1965) 253
Grotto Regina, Palermo 39
Guillemeau, Jacques 101
Gunn, Dr David 278
Gunnlaugs Saga (Norse poem) 84
gynaeceum (female Roman chamber) 62–3
Gynaikeia (Soranus) 66–8
Gypsy people 169–70, 187, 242

hadiths 79–81
haemorrhoids 92
handprints, cave 6
Harris, Sister Muriel 267
Hathor 47
Hauptmann, Gerhart, *Die Insel der großen Mutter* 227
Hawaii 253–4
health, cornerstones of 63
heat source 9
Hebrew traditions 40
Herodotus 80
Herophilus of Chalcedon 57–8
Herto Man 2
hieroglyph, childbirth 43, *43*
Hilarion 59, 60, 75
Hilda of Whitby 83
Hill, Paul 278–80
Himmler, Heinrich 234, 235, 237, 241
Hinduism 50
Hinselmann, Hans 241

Hippocratic Corpus 56–7, 65
HitchHiker's Guide to the Galaxy, The (Adams) 3–4
Hitler, Adolf, *Mein Kampf* 202, 229–43
Hitler Youth movement 234
Hittite people 51–2
Hody, Edward, *Cases in Midwifry* 105
Hogarth, William 108, 149, 150, *150*, 155
Hölbling, Miksa 225
Holmes, Oliver Wendell Sr 142, 225
Holocaust, the 235, 236–43
Homer 54–5
homo sapiens 2–4, 20
homosexuality 185
Hopkins, Elizabeth 118, 122
Hopkins, Ellice 185
Hormone Replacement Therapy (HRT) 198
hormones 100, 198, 251, 270
horses 24–5
hospitals 77–8, 110–12, 131, 158, 168
Hottentot people 173
Human Betterment Foundation (HBF), California 230
human papillomavirus (HPV) vaccine 287–8
Hungary 225–8, 229
hunter–gatherers ix, 4, 11, 13, 20, 23, 114, 157
Hunter, John 108
Hunter, William, *Anatomy of the Gravid Uterus, Exhibited in Figures* 106, 108–9, *110*
Huxley, Aldous, *Brave New World* 250–1
Hyde Amendment (1976) 272, 273
hygiene 92, 119, 158, 210, 211

iatromaeae (physician/midwife) 68
Ice Age 1–3, 11
Iceland 84, 120–1, 270, 287
identical twins 10–11
immaculate birth, Biblical 70–8
Immigration Act, US (1924) 224
immunity 121
in vitro fertilization (IVF) 198, 265–7
incest 284
indentured servitude 166, 180–2
India 2, 50, 65, 77, 101, 217, 259–63
Indiana State Reformatory 178
Industrial Revolution 147, 151, 157
infanticide 75, 77, 84–5, 148
infection 91
infertility 30, 89
Initial Upper Paleolithic go-bags ('IUP toolkits') 4
innoculation 130
innovation, cost of 127–39
intercourse, sexual 29, 52–3, 156, 164, 198, 219, 233

INDEX

'interlocking twins' 21
International Women's Health Coalition (IWHC) 164
IQs 223
Iran 50–1, 77
Iraq 82
Irish population, US 181
irritations, common 210
Ishmaelites 186–7
Isis 43
Islam 78–83
Italy 88–91, 98, 215, 216
Izbū (deformed child) 33

Jackson Women's Health Organization 271–89
Jacqueline Felice de Almania 91–2
Jahn, Walter 238
Jainism 50
Jamaica 164, 165, 166, 168
James VI of Scotland 124
Jamestown Colony, Virginia 117–18
Japan 50, 195, 217
Japanese population, US 222–3
jar burials 31
Jerome, St 77
Jerusalem 70
Jewish populations 169, 176, 185, 229, 232–3, 241, 242
Joachim and Anna 71–2
John of Arderne 92
Jones, Dr Rush 138
Joseph (*Protoevangelium*) 72, 73–4
Josephus, Flavius 71, 75
Judaism 50, 52–4, 75, 185
'Jukes' family 186–7

Kahun Medical Papyrus 48
Kaninchen of Ravensbruck 237, 238, 239, 243
Karve, Prof Raghunath Dhondo and Malati 260
Khadīj (Muhammad's first wife) 78–9
Kitzinger, Sheila 268
Klebelsberg, Kunó 226
Kleitarchos 40
Kneeland, Abner 157
Knights Hospitaller of Jerusalem 89–90
knots 51, 115
Knowlton, Charles, *The Fruits of Philosophy*... 156, 157
Koch, Robert 210–11
Kom Obo Temple, Egypt 43
Krems, Austria 10
Krönig, Bernhardt 205, 208–9
Kūbu (foetus) 32–3

!Kung people 13
Kurgans, the 24–6

labiaplasties, cosmetic 106
labour, death during 16
Lacnunga (medical text) 87
Ladies Center abortion clinic, Pensacola 278, 279
Lamaštu (goddess-demon) 31, 32
Lancet, The 145
Laschamps Excursion 3
laudanum 141, 161
Laughlin, Harry 225
Laydon family 117–18
Lebensborn ('Fount of Life') programme 234
Leechbook (medical text) 87
legal texts, early 30
Leonardo da Vinci 102
Leopold, Prince 145
Lewis, Matthew 166
libraries 128–9
lice 170–1
ligation of arteries 99
linea nigra 51
Linearbandkeramik people 24
literature, Sumerian 29–31
London 148–52
Long, Dr Crawford W. 143, 145
Long, Edward 166, 168, 170
Longfellow, Fanny Appleton 140
Lontor, Banda Islands 212
Löwenmensch of Hohlenstein-Stadel, Swabian Jura, Germany 6, 7
Lucy (slave girl) 135–9
Lunardi, Vincent 106
lying-in hospitals 110–12, 158
lying-in period 133, 153

McCluskey, Henry 256, 258
McCormack, Katherine 195
McCormick, Katharine 249–53, *250*
McCorvey, Melissa 255
McCorvey, Norma 254–7, 258
McCulloch, Oscar Carleton, *Tribe of Ishmael: A Study in Social Degradation* 186–8
Madjedbebe cave complex, Australia 2
Maidment, Jo 267
Maitland, Charles 130
malnutrition 11, 20, 121, 237
Mal'ta people 20
Malthus, Thomas 152
mamatoto viii–x
mammoth 10, 11
Manchester 157–8
Manchester Lying-In Hospital 158, 168

marijuan 222
marriage 79–80, 196–204
　colonists 122
　Egyptian 44–5
　Greek 55
　interracial 157, 166
　mixed-race 215, 233
　Roman 61–2
Marshall, James W. 179
Marston family 196
Martin, Bruce 279
Martin, Matthew 151–2
Mary, mother of Jesus 70–8, 80
Massachusetts Bay Colony, Royal Charter of the (1686) 125
Massachusetts General Hospital, Boston 142
maternity clothing 207–8
Mather, Increase and Cotton 125, 129–30
Matthews, Chris 282
Mauriceau, François 105
Maximilian I 217
Mayan peoples 116
Mayflower Compact (1620) 120
Mayflower ship 118–19, 121
Medical Act (1858) 158
medical schools 89–92, 127, 134, 195
medical texts 29–30, 49, 87, 93, 95, 106, 260
medicinal plants 29–30, 35, 56–7, 63–4, 131
　See also opium poppy
medicines 130–1, 146, 218
Mendel, Gregor 189–90
mendicity (begging without cause) 151–2
Mengele, Joseph 240–3
Menkin, Miriam 250
menstruation
　absent 131
　Black women 169
　breastfeeding and 13
　cycle 47, 241, 284
　disorders 252
　hsmn 48
　mikveh bath 52–3
　studies 66, 67
Mesopotamian people 28–33, *32*
Mexico 31, 116, 222, 230, 252, 256, 260
Mexico City Rule, US (1985) 276
Michael, George 267
'The Middle Passage' (African slaves) 163–4
midwives
　abortionists 192, 228
　Black African 166
　C-sections 93, 94, 161
　colonial 122, 124, 127
　court testimonies 148
　Hebrew 53, 73–4
　Hungarian 228
　male 102–6, 107, 111, 133, 134, 210
　manuals for 95
　Minoan recipes 35
　Nagyrév 228
　named 287
　natural childbirth 247, 268
　nineteenth century 147, 161
　plantation 166
　reputation of 141
　Roman 62, 68
　rural 132
　at sea 119
　Soranus on 66
Mindell, Fania Esiah 192–3
Minoan people 33–5, 36, 38, 42, 49
Minos, King 34
miscarriage 29, 30, 32–3, 45, 124, 130, 167, 269–71
Mishnah (rabbinic literature) 92
Mitchella Compound Tablets 146
mixed-race children 232–3
Molech 41
Montagu, Lady Mary Wortley 130
Montpellier, France 90, 91, 92
morality 120, 149–51, 183, 185–6, 199, 208, 212
Morgagni, Giovanni Battista 216
morning after pill 280, 286
'morning-after' plant medicine 65
'morons' 223–4
morphine 183, 208, 248
mortality, infant 13, 17, 19, 30, 45, 98, 101, 105, 133, 160, 167, 225
mortality, maternal 13, 16, 17, 45, 98, 101, 105, 112, 133, 160
Morton, William Thomas 142
MSI Reproductive Choices 203–4
Muhammad 78–9, 81
mulieres saleritanae (medical females in Salerno) 88–92
multiple births 10
Mumsnet 286–7
Mycenaean people 33, 36–8, 42, 49

Nagyrév, Hungary 228, *228*
nameless children 40–1
Namibia 173
National Childbirth Trust (NCT) 246, 268
National Right to Life Committee (NRLC) 272, 278
Native American nations 114–16, 146
Natufian people 12–13
natural childbirth 167, 245–8, 286
Natural Childbirth Association (NCA) 246–7

INDEX

Navajo people 114–16
Neanderthals 1–4, 11
needs, Palaeolithic basic 9
Németh, László 226
Neolithic people 13, 22
Nepal 266
New York 186–7, 253–4
Nicholls, Frank 111
Niddah (rabbinic literature) 92
Nietzsche, Friedrich 190
Nihell, Elizabeth 111, 112
Nile Valley 43, 44
Nisibis, Mesopotamia 77
Nixon, Richard 257
Norway 84
Nubia 46, 48–9
Nufer, Jakob and Elisabeth 94–5
Nuremberg Laws (1935) 233–4, *233*

Obama, Barack 281–2
Oberheuser, Gerta 237–8, 239
'Obstetrical Dilemma' 2
obstetrical tools 134
obstetrix/maia (professional midwife) 68
Odon de Sully 93
oestrogen regulation 146
offerings 1, 32–3, 35, 39–41, 51
okytokia (clay animals) 35
'old Europe', decline of 20–4
Oliver, John 124
O'Neil, Alice 161
Onesimus (slave) 129
opium poppy 12, 24, 35, 47, 57, 64, 131, 141, 161, 222
orgasm, female 198
osteomalacia (*mollities ossium*) 158
osteoporosis 35–6, 37
Ostia Antica, Rome 64
Ottoman empire 211–14
Ovampo people 173
over-the-counter medications 280, 284, 286

pagans 75, 78, 83–4
Pagés, Fidel 248
pain, experience of 74
pain relief 35, 47, 64, 140–6, 161, 205–9, 248
  See also opium poppy
pain theory 245–6
Palestine 12
Pankhurst, Christabel, *The Great Scourge, and How to End It* 218–19
Paré, Ambroise 99, 101, 102
Paris, France 90–1, 105
Partial-Birth Abortion Act (2003) 281
'partial-birth abortion' ban 280–2

Pasiphaë 34
paterfamilias (household's most senior man) 60–1
pea plant reproduction 189
Pearson, Karl 176
Pendle witch trial (1612–34) 124–5
penicillin 249
Pennsylvania Abortion Control Act (1982) 273, 277
People v. Sanger (US, 1918) 194
Perl, Dr Gisella 238
Peru 11
Peseshet 47
Peterkin, Dr 244
Petsophas, Crete, (Minoan peak sanctuary) 35
phallus 8, 14
phantom limb syndrome 99
pharaohs 43–6
Phillips, Henry 129
Phillips, Teresia Constantia 155
Phoebe of Cenchrea 75
Phoenician people 33, 38–42, 49–50
Phoenician Tophet of Carthage 40
pica 66–7
Pill, the 251–3, 254
Pincus, Gregory Goodwin, *The Eggs of Mammals* 195, 250–3
Pirates, The (internment prisoners) 243
Place, Francis 153–4
placenta 44, 67, 74, 100, 113, 115, 269
planned parenthood 188–204
Planned Parenthood clinics 253, 277
Planned Parenthood Federation of America 195–6, 281, 283, 285–6
Planned Parenthood v. Casey (1992) 277, *277*, 284
Pliny the Elder 70
Plötzensee camp 241
Plymouth settlers 119–22
Pneumatic Institution, Bristol 141
Pockorny, Adolf 235
poetry, Anglo-Saxon 87
Półtawska, Wanda 236, 243
Pontic steppe 24–5
Poor Law Amendment Act (1834) 152
poor relief, medieval 147
population growth 25, 60, 151, 157, 161, 179, 258–64, 274
positions, sexual 60
post-natal care 9
Potnia 37
Potsdam Giants regiment 165
Powhatan people 117–18
pre-natal care 9
pregnancy, early 51

pregnancy tests 49
Priscilla of Macedonia 75
pro-choicers 258, 273, 276, 277, 278, 282, 283, 285
Pro-Life Act, US (1988) 276
pro-lifers 258, 273, 278, 282–3, 286
pro-natalists 274
Prochownik, Abraham 247
prohibition 183–4
prolapses 48, 67, 136
prostitution 148, 155, 216, 217–18, 219–20
Protestantism 124, 126, 127, 183, 184, 185, 239
Proto-Indo-European (PIE) languages 24, 51
Protoevangelium (Infancy Gospel) 71–4
pubic symphysis gap 22
Pueblo peoples 18
puerperal fever 112–13, 142
Purdy, Jean 265–7
Puritans 118–26
Pylos Tablets 36–7

'rabbit births' 106
'Race suicide' 218–19
racial hygiene 211, 214, 240
Radford, Dr Thomas, *Observations ...* 158–61
'ragged schools' 158
rape 66, 133, 213, 258, 284
rape, marital 198
Rascher, Sigmund and Karoline 'Nini' 241
Ravensbrück concentration camp 236–9, 241, 243
Reagan, Ronald 273, 274–7
Reeves, Carlton W. 284
religion 37–41, 50, 70–83, 106, 163, 186–7, 285
Renaissance, the 97–112
repatriation, body 91
Restell, Madame (Ann Lohman) 192
resting poses 9
Rhazes, *Liber Continens* 82
Richards, Ann 286
Richards, Cecile 281, 285–6, 287
Richmond, Duke of 149
rickets 105, 154, 158, 160
ringworm 154
ritual cord-cutting tools 9
rituals 9, 14, 30–1, 40, 47, 93, 114–16
Roanoke, US 'Lost Colony' 117
Roberts, Justine 286
Rock, John 250–3
Rockefeller Foundation 220, 226–7, 240, 259–61, 262
Rockefeller III, John D. 263–4
Rockefeller, J. D. and Laura 184, 195

Rockefeller, William Avery 184
Roe, Humphrey Verdon 197, 202
Roe v. Wade (1973) 277, 280, 281, 283
overturned 272, 284
presidents on on 257, 276
*rofe*s, Jewish 53
Roma people 169–70, 187, 234
Rome, ancient 59–65, 68–70, 75–8
Roosevelt, Theodore 219
root-diggers (*rhizotomoi*) 56–7, 63–4
Rorer & Sons 134
Rose, Nurse 244–5
Ross, Edward A. 218–19
Rösslin, Eucharius, *The Birth of Mankind* 95, 123, *123*
Rothwell, Mary 124
Rousay, Orkney 86
Rousset, François, *Traité nouveau de L'hystérotomotokie, ou enfantement césarien* 101–2
Rüdin, Prof Ernst 240
Ruggles Gates, Reginald 197
Ruhr, Germany 231–2, 233
Rusk, Dean 260
Russia 229, 269
Rwanda 95

sacrifice, children as 40–1, 42
St Mary's Hospital, Manchester 158, 160, 161
Salem witch trials (1692–3) 126–7
Salerno, Italy 88–92
Salome (*Protoevangelium*) 74
Salvarsan 218, 258
same-sex relationships 55
Samuel Laundy of London 134
San Francisco 179–81, 222
Sanger, Margaret 188–96, 210, 250, 251
Sanitation Reform Bureau (Hungary) 226–7
sarcophagi, mummies and 45–6
Scandinavia 21, 84, 215, 217
Scholtz, Kornél 227
Schultz, Charles, *Peanuts* 274–5
Schumann, Horst 241
scopolamine (henbane) 205, 208, 209
Scotland 287
sea, superstitions of the 33–42
Second World War 236–43, 246, 248–9
security 10
sedation 140
selective breeding 165
semen 57, 221
settlers, British US 116–23
Sewell, Hannah 133
sex education 107
sex shops 155

INDEX

sex workers 90, 148
Sexual Revolution 252
sexually transmitted diseases 53, 168, 185, 194, 215–20, 287
Sharp, Dr Harry 178
Shaw, George Bernard, *Man and Superman* 191
Shelley, Mary 113
Shintoism 50
Siberian people 20–1
Siegel method 208–9
silphion plant 65
Simmons, Jimmy 275
Simpson, James Young 143–4, 145–6
Sims, (James) Marion 134–9
Sims, Marion 281
Skull Building 19
skulls 16, 24, *128*
slavery 27, 30, 33, 81, 129, 135–9, 143, 162–72
Slee, Noah 194, 196
Sloane, Hans 109
smallpox 120–1, 129–30
Smellie, William, *Treatise of the Theory and Practice of Midwifery* 106–8, 109, 111
Smith, Adam 151
Smith, Eliza, *The Compleat Housewife* 132
snake symbolism 36, 38, 39, 46, 116, 227
Snow, John 143–4, 145
Soranus of Ephesus 65–8
Spain 6
Sparta, Greece 56
speculum, vaginal 82, 83, 136
sperm 221, 266
spermicides 199
Sphagianes (cult site) 37
squatting 13, 21, 146
Sredni Stog tribe 25
Starling, Ernest 198
Starr Jordan, David 217
Stefano de Fango 98
Steptoe, Patrick 265–7
Steptoe, Prof Andrew 267
sterility 51, 168, 218
sterilization 176–9, 222–5, 240–1
　compulsory 202, 229, 230, 232, 263, 287
　Ensminger's programmes 260, 262
　interned Bolsheviks 235–6
　Kaninchen 239
　McCulloch on 186, 188
Sterilization Act (1924) 224
'sterilization law', German (1934) 235–6
Stevens, Nettie 221
Stieve, Hermann 241
stillbirths 33, 37, 133, 201, 270
'stone baby' (*lithopaedion*) 100–1

Stopes, Marie 196–204, *203*, 210
Stopes-Roe, Harry and Mary 202, *203*
Storey, Giles 126
stretch marks 7, 66
Strother, Edward, *Criticon febrium* 112
Sudan 46, 48, 80
suffrage movement 217–18
Suffragette Movement 204
Sulawesi, Indonesia 2
Sumerian people 28–30, 33
superstitions 33–42, 48–9, 62, 115
supine position 9, 67, 201
surgery, early 91
surgical instruments 134
surrogacy 266
Swan the jeweller 136, 138
Sweden 287
Switzerland 94–5
symptoms, pregnancy 29
syphilis 215–19, 232, 238, 258

al-Tabari 80
Talmud (Rabbinic Judaism central text) 52–3
Tarbell, Ida 184
tattoos 7, 46–7
Tell Abu Hureyra, Syria 12
temperance movements 183–4, 211
Teotihuacán, Mexico 31
Tertullian of Carthage 76
tetanus 166
Texas 254–7
textile industry 37, 157
Therapeutic Abortion Act (1967) 274
Thornton, Shelley 256, 258
Thorstein and Jofrid 84–5
Thoth 47
Thurman, Amber Nicole 271–2
Tiberius, Audrey Flake 289
Tinnīt 39–40
Tlaltecuhtli ('sin/filth-eater') 116
Tlazolteotl ('sin/filth-eater') 116
Toft, Mary 106
tooth formation 11
tophets 40–1
Torsåker, Sweden 125
'totem poles', Göbekli Tepe 14, *15*
trade routes 23–4, 55, 69–70, 130
trauma, birth 102, 206, 246, 287, 288
Traveller people 169–70
trepanning *128*
Trianon, Treaty of (1920) 226
triplets 289
Trota de Salerno, *Trotula* 88–9
Trump, Donald 282–3, 284–5
Trump, Melania 285
Tschermak, Erich 189–90

Turkey 211–14
Tutankhamun 45
Twelve Tables of Rome 61
'Twilight Sleep' (*Dämmerschlaf*) 205–9, 286
twins 20–1
    conjoined 104
    Galton and 176
    Hungarian 226
    identical 10–11
    'interlocking twins' 21
    IVF 266
    Mengele and 242–3
    'stone baby' (*lithopaedion*) 101
typhus 120, 131

Uganda 95
Ukraine 24–5
umbilical cord 44, 116, 166
UNICEF 80, 270
US states
    abortion 253–8, 272, 282–5, 287
    premarital testing 215
    prohibition 183–4
    sterilization 222
    See also individual states

vagina, treating complaints of the 48
Valley of the Workers, Deir el-Medina 46–9
Van Hoosen, Bertha 209
Van Rymsdyk, Jan 106, 107, 108–10, *110*
variolation 129
vasectomies 178, 262
vases, Greek 63
Veblen, Thorstein, *The Theory of the Leisure Class: ...* 208
venereal diseases 53, 168, 185, 194, 215–20
ventouse 144
Venuses 8, 17, *18*
'The Venus of Hohle Fels', Swabian Jura, Germany 6–11
Vesalius, Andreas, *The Human Body in Seven Books* 97, *97*, 102
Vestal Virgins, House of the 61–2

Victoria, Queen 144–5
Vinson, Hon Clyde Roger 275
Virginia settlers 116–18
Von Verschuer, Prof Dr Otmar Freiherr 240–1, 242

Wade, Henry 256
Walezer, Marguerite and George 99–100
'wandering womb' theory 48, 56, 65, 90, 102
Ware, David 278
Washington 178, 253–4
Washington, Booker T. 210
water birth 269
waters breaking 107, 267–8
weaning 19
weasels 35–6
weaving 62–3, 116, 147, 154, 157
Weddington, Sarah 254, 256
Wells, H. G. 191, 194
West Indies 164
wet-nursing 32, 96, 146, 149
White, Charles, *An Account of the Regular Gradation in Man ...* 130, 168–70, 171
White, Susanna 118–19, 122
Wilhelm I 165
Wirths, Eduard 241
witch trials 124–6
Witchcraft Acts (1542–1604) 103–4
wolf-dogs, domesticated 10
Wollstonecraft, Mary 112–13
womb, treating complaints of the 48
women, in the Christian church 75–6
Women's Christian Temperance Union 184
Woolf, Virginia 113
workhouses 152–3
working conditions 153

Yamnaya Kurgans 25

al-Zahrawi, Abu al-Qasim 82
Zimmerman, Tom 135
Zoroastrianism 50